Ideas for the Future of the International Monetary System

Ideas for the Future of the International Monetary System

edited by

Michele Fratianni
Indiana University

Dominick Salvatore
Fordham University

Paolo Savona
University of Rome "Tor Vergata"

Reprinted from
Open Economies Review
Volume 9, Supplement 1

KLUWER ACADEMIC PUBLISHERS
Boston / Dordrecht / London

Distributors for North, Central and South America:
Kluwer Academic Publishers
101 Philip Drive
Assinippi Park
Norwell, Massachusetts 02061 USA
Telephone (781) 871-6600
Fax (781) 871-6528
E-Mail <kluwer@wkap.com>

Distributors for all other countries:
Kluwer Academic Publishers Group
Distribution Centre
Post Office Box 322
3300 AH Dordrecht, THE NETHERLANDS
Telephone 31 78 6392 392
Fax 31 78 6546 474
E-Mail <orderdept@wkap.nl>

Electronic Services <http://www.wkap.nl>

Library of Congress Cataloging-in-Publication Data

Ideas for the future of the international monetary system / edited by Michele Fratianni, Dominick Salvatore, Paolo Savona.
p. cm.
"Reprinted from Open economies review, volume 9, supplement 1."
Presented at a conference in Florence, Italy on June 19, 1998.
Includes bibliographical references.
ISBN 0-7923-8435-0
1. International finance—Congresses. I. Fratianni, Michele. II. Salvatore, Dominick. III. Savona, Paolo, 1936– .
HG205.I33 1999
332'.042—dc21 98-54142
CIP

Printed on acid-free paper.

Printed in the United States of America.

OPEN ECONOMIES REVIEW

Contents Volume 9 Special Supplemental Issue 1998
Edited by: Michele Fratianni, Dominick Salvatore and Paolo Savona

This volume has been made possible by the financial support of Cesifin Foundation, a foundation sponsored by Cassa di Risparmio di Firenze s.p.a.

Open economies review **9:S1** 371 (1998)

Editors' Preface

Approximately two years ago the Guido Carli Association charged a group of distinguished economists to study various aspects of the international monetary system and propose ways to improve it. The studies were presented at a conference in Florence (Italy) on June 19, 1998 and their edited versions are published herewith. The volume consists of two parts: Part I contains the studies commissioned by the Carli Association—those by Dominick Salvatore; Koichi Hamada; Forrest Capie; Michele Fratianni, Andreas Hauskrecht and Aurelio Maccario; Jürgen von Hagen and Ingo Fender; Michael Artis, Marion Kohler and Jacques Mélitz; Barry Eichengreen; Michele Fratianni and Andreas Hauskrecht; Paolo Savona and Aurelio Maccario; and Elvio Dal Bosco—the comments by Paul de Grauwe and William Branson, and the editors' conclusions. Part II contains three papers presented at the Florence conference, by Antonio Fazio, Carlo Scognamiglio, and Alberto Predieri.

This volume has been made possible by the financial support of Cesifin Foundation, a foundation sponsored by Cassa di Risparmio di Firenze s.p.a.

Michele Fratianni
Dominick Salvatore
Paolo Savona

Open economies review 9:S1 373 (1998)

In Memory of Guido Carli

PAOLO SAVONA

This volume is dedicated to the memory of Guido Carli who, from 1945 to 1992, played a leading role in the international monetary scene. In his memoirs, Carli (*Cinquant'anni di vita italiana*, Rome, Laterza, 1993, p. 40) recalls: "What we inherited in 1945 was a shattered, incoherent system of bilateral relations. A decisive step forward on the road to 'multilateralism' was the creation of the 'payment agreements.' I worked hard in my Via dell'Umiltà office, writing what was later ratified by governments."

Carli had a rich and illustrious career: Director of the European Payments Union, Executive Director of the International Monetary Fund, Minister of the Italian Office of Foreign Trade, Governor of the Bank of Italy, President of the Italian Industrial Confederation, President of the European Industrial Confederation, and Minister of the Treasury. As a Governor, he foretold (L'eurodollaro: una piramide di carta?, *Moneta e Credito*, March 1971) the collapse of the Bretton Woods agreement five months before it happened. As a Treasury Minister he negotiated and signed the Maastricht Treaty for Italy.

I am not revealing a secret by saying that Carli "charged" Treasury Minister Ciampi with the task of bringing Italy into the European Monetary Union. He has been proved right, in the choice of both the person and the objectives. Nonetheless, Carli had doubts on the effectiveness of the European Monetary Union because he thought that the Union was only a piece within the unstructured mosaic of the present international monetary system. After signing the Maastricht Treaty he encouraged me to continue the research on the existing system with the goal of finding solutions to the sources of systemic instability.

This publication, which has been made possible through the generous initiative of Antonio Fazio, Governor of the Bank of Italy and President of the Carli Association, and Carlo Scognamiglio, former President of the Italian Senate and Vice President of the Carli Association, is a modest response to that challenge.

Open economies review 9:S1 375–415 (1998)

International Monetary and Financial Arrangements: Present and Future

DOMINICK SALVATORE Salvatore@Murray.Fordham.edu.
Department of Economics, Fordham University, New York 10458, USA

Key words: central bank independence, early-warning system, euro, European Central Bank, European Monetary System, European Monetary Union, exchange rate arrangements, exchange rate mechanism, global financial integration, International Monetary Fund, international monetary system, international policy coordination, optimum currency area, target zones

JEL Classification Number: F3

Abstract

The paper deals with a broad range of topics under the rubric of the international monetary system: exchange rate agreements, International Monetary Fund structure, history and functioning of the European Monetary Union, monetary and fiscal policies adopted in recent years by different countries, with a special emphasis on central bank independence and inflation control, capital flows and cross-border assets growth and their influence on financial stability, and policy proposals to enhance financial stability. With more than four-fifths of world trade conducted under managed or full flexibility the present system can be regarded more as a flexible than a fixed exchange rate regime. EMU is a major institutional innovation; while its economic benefits have been amply discussed and perhaps exaggerated, the economic costs seem to have been underestimated. Financial liberalization has resulted in huge benefits to savers and borrowers as capital has tended to flow to its most productive uses around the world, but it has also led to fears that this has sharply reduced the effectiveness of monetary policy. This liberalization imposes a constraint on monetary policy in the sense that it forces a much higher degree of economic convergence than was true before.

Introduction

This paper examines present and future international monetary and financial arrangements and was prepared in response to the request for a background paper for the Final Report of the Guido Carli Foundation. Section 1 of the paper presents an overview of the functioning of the present international monetary system and its shortcomings, as well as proposals for reforming it. Section 2 examines the functioning of the European Monetary System (EMS) and the move toward full European Monetary Union (EMU). Section 3 of the paper deals with national economic policies, while Section 4 analyzes the relationship between international capital flows and international financial stability.

1. The present international monetary system: Operation, shortcomings, and reforms

This part of the paper examines the operation of the present international monetary system, current IMF operation and international reserves, potential international financial fragility, and calls for reform.

1.1. Current exchange rate arrangements

The present international monetary system has four main characteristics. (1) There is a wide variety of exchange rate arrangements. Of the 181 members of the International Monetary Fund (IMF, 1998b) in 1998, 66 (mostly developing countries) have pegged or quasi-pegged exchange arrangements, with the remaining 115 countries having managed or full flexibility. With more than four-fifths of world trade conducted under managed or full flexibility (see IMF, 1998c), however, the present system can be regarded more as a flexible than a fixed exchange rate regime. (2) Countries have almost complete freedom of choice of exchange rate regimes. All that is required by the l978 Jamaica Accords (which formally recognized prevailing exchange rate arrangements) is that a nation's exchange rate actions should not be disruptive to trade partners and the world economy. (3) Exchange rate variability has been substantial. This is true for nominal and real, bilateral and effective, and short-run and long-run exchange rates. The IMF estimated that exchange rate variability has been about five times larger during the period of flexibility (i.e., since l971) than under the preceding fixed exchange rate or Bretton Woods System. Exchange rate variability of 2 to 3% per day and 20–30% per year has been common under the present system. Exchange rate variability has been larger than originally anticipated, does not seem to be declining over time, and is for the most part unexpected. (4) Contrary to earlier expectations, official intervention in foreign exchange markets (and therefore the need for international reserves) has not diminished significantly under the present flexible exchange rate system as compared with the previous fixed exchange rate system. Nations have intervened in foreign exchange markets not only to smooth out day-to-day movements, but also to resist trends.

The period of the flexible exchange rate system since l971 has been characterized by far greater macroeconomic instability in the leading industrial countries than during the previous fixed exchange rate or Bretton Woods period (see Fratianni and Hauskrecht, 1998). The system was jolted by two rounds of large petroleum price increases (l973–74 and l979–80) which resulted in double-digit inflation and led to recessions (as industrial nations sought to break the inflationary spiral with tight monetary policies). The period also saw the rapid growth of the Eurodollar market and the liberalization of capital controls. The resulting sharp increase in international capital flows, as well as the institutional changes and adjustments following the collapse of the Bretton Woods System in l97l, rather than the prevailing flexible exchange rates, as such, were the primary cause of the large macroeconomic instability suffered by the leading industrial countries, however. Indeed, it is now widely agreed that no fixed exchange rate system could have survived the combination of oil shocks, portfolio shifts, and structural and institutional changes that the world faced during the 1970s and 1980s (see Kenen, 1994). It must also be remembered that the present managed exchange rate system was not established deliberately as the result of an international agreement, but was instead forced upon the world by default as the result of the collapse of the Bretton Woods System because of lack of an adequate adjustment mechanism and dollar overvaluation.

1.2. Operation of current exchange rate arrangements

The present international monetary system does, however, face some important shortcomings. These are the large volatility of exchange rates, the wide and persistent misalignments of exchange rates, the failure to promote greater coordination of economic policies among the leading industrial nations, and the inability to prevent international financial crises or to adequately deal with them when they do arise. Let us briefly examine these shortcomings.

There is little disagreement that exchange rates have exhibited large volatility since the establishment of the present managed exchange rate system. There is also no question that large exchange rate volatility, by adding to transaction costs, has affected the volume and pattern of international trade. These costs, however, are not very large and are not greater than those faced by firms in many other markets, as in the metal and agricultural sectors. Firms engaged in international trade also seem to have learned how to deal with volatility by pursuing hedging and diversification strategies quickly and at little cost. The IMF (1984) concluded that exchange rate volatility did not seem to have had a significantly adverse effect on international trade. Measures could, of course, be devised to reduce exchange rate volatility, but the costs of these measures would in all likelihood not justify the benefits resulting from them.

Potentially more damaging to the flow of international trade and investments than excessive exchange rate volatility are the wide and persistent exchange rate misalignments (see Williamson, 1986). Misalignment refers to the departure of exchange rates from their long-run, competitive equilibrium levels. An overvalued currency has the effect of an export tax and an import subsidy on the nation and, as such, it reduces the international competitiveness of the nation and distorts the pattern of specialization, trade, and payments. A significant exchange rate misalignment that persists for years cannot possibly be hedged away and can impose significant real costs on the economy in the form of unemployment, idle capacity, bankruptcy, and protectionist legislation.

The most notorious example of exchange rate misalignment is the overvaluation of the US dollar during the l980s. According to the Board of Governors of the US Federal Reserve System, from 1980 to its peak in February 1985, the dollar appreciated by about 40% on a trade-weighted basis against the currency of the ten largest industrial countries. This resulted in the huge trade deficit of the United States and equally large combined trade surplus of Japan and Germany. It also resulted in increasing calls for and actual trade protectionism in the United States. It has been estimated (see Council of Economic Advisors, 1986, 1987) that the 1985 US trade deficit was $60 to $70 billion greater (about twice as large) than it would have been had the dollar remained at its 1980 level, and that this deficit cost about two million jobs in the United States. Despite the fact that by the end of 1988 the international value of the dollar was slightly below its 1980–1981 level, so that all of its overvaluation had been eliminated, large global trade imbalances remained and did not show signs of declining rapidly. Economists have borrowed the term "hysteresis" from the field of physics to characterize the failure of trade balances to return to their original equilibrium once exchange rate misalignments have been corrected. The other bout of major misalignment of the dollar was during the past three years. In June 1995, the dollar was worth 85 yen, while in July 1998 it was 140 yen.

While misaligned exchange rates can be regarded as the immediate cause of prevailing global trade imbalances, however, they were themselves the result of internal structural disequilibria in the leading nations. It is these structural disequilibria and not exchange rate misalignments that were and are the fundamental cause of the global imbalances facing the leading industrial countries today. What can be blamed on the current international financial system is its failure to provide smoother and more timely adjustment to such large and persistent global imbalances as the trade deficit of the United States, the trade surplus of Japan, and the large and persistent unemployment in Europe. It seems that trade flows now respond with longer than usual lags (ranging up to two years) to exchange rate changes (see Salvatore, 1998a, chap. 16) and exchange rates changes respond primarily to international financial flows rather than to trade flows.

More serious is the charge that the present international monetary system failed to promote greater coordination of macroeconomic policies among the leading industrial countries. To a large extent this is due to their very different inflation-unemployment tradeoffs. Policy coordination under the present system has taken place only occasionally and has been very limited in scope. One such episode was in 1978 when Germany agreed to serve as a "locomotive" to stimulate growth in the world economy. Another episode of limited policy coordination was the Plaza Agreement of September 1985, under which the G-5 countries (United States, Japan, Germany, United Kingdom, and France) intervened in foreign exchange markets to induce a gradual depreciation or soft landing of the dollar in eliminating its large overvaluation. Successful international policy coordination can also be credited for greatly limiting the damage from the 1987 world stock market crash and for preventing the 1994–1995 Mexican crisis from spreading to or having a lasting damaging effect on other emerging markets. These instances of international macroeconomic policy coordination, however, were sporadic and rather limited in scope.

Finally, the present international monetary system seems unable to prevent international financial crises such as the one that hit Mexico in 1994–1995 and many East Asian emerging economies in 1997–1998. Perhaps, in a world of highly integrated financial markets and huge international financial flows, it may be impossible to avoid some financial crises. But an international financial system that is prone to frequent and deep international financial crises that require immediate and massive financial resources to prevent their spreading to other nations is certainly not a very good system. The challenge is how to prevent or minimize the number and depth of financial crises and how to resolve the crises that do occur without falling into the moral hazard trap. Be that as it may, there is today a great deal of dissatisfaction with the operation of the present international monetary system and widespread calls for reforms. These are discussed in the last part of this section of the paper.

1.3. Current IMF operation

The present international monetary system has been greatly affected by several recent changes in the operation of the IMF. The quotas of IMF member nations have been increased across the board several times, so that in July 1998 the Fund's resources totaled $202 billion (up from $8.8 billion in 1947) and may increase by another 45% if the new IMF request is met. Members are generally required to pay 25% of any increase in its quota in SDRs or in currencies of other members selected by the Fund, with their approval, and the rest in their own currency. New members pay in their quota in the same way. The old gold tranche is now called the first credit tranche.

The IMF has also renewed and expanded the General Arrangements to Borrow (GAB) several times since setting them up in 1962, and in 1998 these were $24 billion. Another $2 billion could be borrowed under the associated arrangement with the Saudi Arabian Monetary Agency (SAMA). At the beginning of 1997, the IMF negotiated a New Arrangement to Borrow (NAB) under which 25 participant countries and institutions agreed to lend up to SDR34 billion (about $47 billion) to supplement the GAB for a period of five years (subject to renewal). Central bankers also expanded their swap arrangements to over $54 billion and their standby arrangements to $32 billion. Borrowing rules at the Fund were also relaxed, and new credit facilities were added that greatly expanded the overall maximum amount of credit available to a member nation. However, this total amount of credit consists of several different credit lines subject to various conditions. IMF loans are now specified in terms of SDRs rather than dollars. There is an initial fee, and the interest charged is based on the length of the loan, the facility used, and prevailing interest rates. Besides the usual surveillance responsibilities over the exchange rate policies of its members, the

Fund has recently broadened its responsibilities to include help for members to overcome their structural problems.

The new credit facilities set up by the IMF include (1) the Extended Fund Facility (EFF)—this was set up in 1974 and allows members to draw up to 140% of their quotas, phased over a period of 3 or 4 years to overcome serious structural imbalances; (2) the Structural Adjustment Facility (SAF)—set up in 1986, it provides resources on concessionary terms to low-income developing member countries facing protracted balance-of-payments problems in support of medium-term macroeconomic and structural adjustment programs; (3) the Enhanced Structural Adjustment Facility (ESAF)—established in 1988 to supplement the SAF; (4) the Compensatory and Contingency Financing Facility (CCFF)—this was originally set up in 1963 to enable a member to draw up to 100% of its quota to make up for a shortfall in export earnings or for an increase in the cost of imported cereals due to an unanticipated adverse external shock beyond the member's control; (5) the Buffer Stock Financing Facility (BSFF)—established in 1969, allowed a member to draw up to 50% of its quota to help finance an approved international buffer stock scheme (no drawings have been made under this facility since 1984, however, and no credits under the facility are currently outstanding); (6) the Oil Facility (OF)—under this, the IMF borrowed funds from petroleum-exporting nations to lend to deficit nations at competitive rates. This facility was set up in 1974 after petroleum prices shot up and was extended in 1975, but by 1976 it had already been fully utilized for a total of 6.9 billion SDRs (about $9.9 billion at the SDR rate of $1.4304 at the end of 1991) and was phased out at the end of 1991 (since real petroleum prices were then lower than they were in 1973); (7) Systemic Transformation Facility (STF)—this was created in April 1993 to extend financial assistance to Russia, the other former Soviet Republics, and other economies in transition in Eastern Europe and elsewhere experiencing balance-of-payments difficulties due to severe disruptions in their traditional trade and payments arrangements.

Member-country overall access to Fund resources is now up to 300% of its quota in any single year or three times the old limit of 100%. The recipients of the loans as well as the type of loans made by the Fund also changed significantly over time. During the first 20 years of its existence, industrial countries accounted for over half of the use of Fund resources, and loans were made primarily to overcome short-term balance-of-payments problems. Since the early 1980s, most loans were made to developing countries and an increasing share of these loans was made for the medium term in order to overcome structural problems (see Milner, 1997).

Total Fund credit outstanding was about $14 billion in 1980, $41 billion in 1986, and $61 billion at the beginning of 1997. Of the total of $61 billion of Fund loans outstanding at the beginning of 1997, $29 billion were provided under the standby and credit tranches, $13 billion under the extended Fund facility (EFF), $5 billion under the compensatory scheme, $8 billion under the structural adjustment facility (SAF) and enhanced structural adjustment facility (ESAF), and $6 billion under the systemic transformation facility (STF).

In the face of the huge international debt problems of many developing countries since 1982, particularly the large countries of Latin America, the IMF has engaged in a number of debt rescheduling and rescue operations. As a condition for the additional loans and special help, the IMF usually requires a reduction in government spending, in the growth of the money supply, and in wage increases in order to reduce imports, stimulate exports, and make the country more nearly self-sustaining. Such IMF conditionality, however, was very painful and led to riots and even the toppling of governments during the late 1980s, and to accusations that the IMF did not take into account the social needs of debtor nations and the political consequences of its demands (i.e., that its policies were "all head and no heart") (see Sachs, 1989). Partly in response to this, the IMF has become more flexible in its lending activities in recent years and has begun to grant medium-term loans to overcome structural problems (something that was traditionally done only by the World Bank). Since 1993, most of the republics of the former Soviet Union have become members of the IMF. During the 1997–98 financial crisis in East Asia, the IMF lent more than $100 billion to South Korea, Indonesia, Thailand and the Philippines, and is putting together a large loan, in excess of $20 billion, at the time this article was revised.

1.4. Gold, SDRs, and international reserves

Under the present managed float, nations still need international reserves in order to intervene in foreign exchange markets to smooth out short-run fluctuations in exchange rates and to cover balance of payments deficits not immediately corrected by equilibrating exchange rate changes. At present such interventions are still made mostly in dollars. In January 1975, US citizens were allowed for the first time since 1933 to own gold, and the United States sold a small portion of its gold holdings on the free market. The price of gold on the London market temporarily rose above $800 an ounce in January 1980, but it soon fell and stabilized at about half of its peak price (and it was $290 an ounce in July 1998).

As part of the Jamaica Accords, the IMF sold one-sixth of its gold holdings on the free market between 1976 and 1980 (and used the proceeds to aid the poorest developing nations) to demonstrate its commitment to eliminate gold (the "barbarous relic"—to use Keynes' words) as an international reserve asset. The official price of gold was abolished, and it was agreed that there would be no future gold transactions between the IMF and member nations. The IMF also continued to value its gold holdings at the pre-1971 official price of $35 or 35 SDRs an ounce. It may be some time, however, before gold completely "seeps out" of international reserves—if it ever will. In fall 1996, the IMF agreed to sell about $2 billion of its gold holdings and use the proceeds to reduce the foreign debt of the poorest developing countries. In July 1997, Australia sold

Table 1. International reserves, 1997 (billions of US dollars and SDRs, at year end).

	US dollars	SDRs
Foreign exchange	1,601	1,186
SDRs	27	20
Reserve position in the IMF	63	47
Total minus gold	1,692	1,253
Gold at official price	42	31
Total with gold at official price	1,773	1,284

Source: IMF, International Financial Statistics (July 1998).

two-thirds of its gold reserves for $1.8 billion and caused the price of gold to fall to $325 per ounce.

Up to 1971, one SDR was valued at $1.00. After the devaluation of the dollar in December 1971, one SDR was valued at $1.0857, and after the February 1973 devaluation of the dollar, one SDR was valued at $1.2064. In 1974 the value of one SDR was made equal to the weighted average of a "basket" of 16 leading currencies. This was done to stabilize the value of SDRs. In 1981, the number of currencies included in the basket was reduced to the following five (with their relative 1996 weights given in parentheses): US dollar (39%); German mark or Deutschmark (21%); Japanese yen (18%); French franc and British pound (11% each). At the end of 1997, one SDR was valued at about $1.35. Since 1974, the IMF has measured all reserves and other official transactions in terms of SDRs instead of US dollars. Table 1 shows the composition of international reserves in US dollars and in SDRs (valued at $1.35) at the end of 1997 (see also Dal Bosco, 1998; Fratianni, Hauskrecht and Maccario, 1998).

1.5. Proposals for reforming the present system

Several proposals have been advanced to reduce exchange rate volatility, and avoid large exchange rate misalignments and deal with increased international financial instability. One proposal first advanced by Williamson (1986) is based on the establishment of *target zones*. Under such a system, the leading industrial nations estimate the equilibrium exchange rate and agree on the range of allowed fluctuation. Williamson suggests a band of allowed fluctuation of 10% above and below the equilibrium exchange rate. The exchange rate is determined by the forces of demand and supply within the allowed band of fluctuation and prevented from moving outside the target zones by official intervention in foreign exchange markets. The target zones would be soft, however, and would be changed when the underlying equilibrium exchange rate moves outside of or near the boundaries of the target zone. Although not made explicit, the leading industrial nations agreed upon some such "soft" target or "reference zones" for the exchange rate between the dollar and the yen and between the dollar and the German mark at Louvre in February 1987 (but with the allowed band of fluctuation much smaller than the 10% above and below the par value advocated by Williamson). During the early 1990s, however, this tacit agreement was abandoned in the face of strong market pressure which saw the dollar depreciate very heavily with respect to the mark and the yen.

Critics of target zones believe that target zones embody the worst characteristics of fixed and flexible exchange rate systems. As in the case of flexible rates, target zones allow substantial fluctuation and volatility in exchange rates and can be inflationary. As in the case of fixed exchange rates, target zones can only be defended by official interventions in foreign exchange markets and thus reduce the monetary autonomy of the nation. In response to this criticism, Miller and Williamson (1987) have extended their blueprint to require substantial policy coordination on the part of the leading industrial nations so as to reduce the need for intervention in foreign exchange markets to keep exchange rates within the target zones.

Other proposals for reforming the present international monetary system are based exclusively on extensive *policy coordination among the leading countries* (see Bryant, 1995; Hamada and Kawai, 1997; Milner, 1997). The best and most articulated of these proposals is the one advanced by McKinnon (1984, 1988, 1996). Under this system, the United States, Japan, and Germany would fix the exchange rate among their currencies at their equilibrium level (determined by purchasing-power parity) and then closely coordinate their monetary policies to keep exchange rates fixed. A tendency for the dollar to appreciate vis-a-vis the yen would signal that the United States should increase the growth rate of its money supply, while Japan should reduce it. The net overall increase in the money supply of these three countries would then be expanded at a rate consistent with the noninflationary expansion of the world economy.

Another proposal advocated by the IMF Interim Committee (1986) is based on the development of objective indicators of economic performance to signal the type of coordinated macropolicies for nations to follow, under the supervision of the Fund, in order to keep the world economy growing along a sustainable noninflationary path. These objective indicators are the growth of GNP, inflation, unemployment, trade balance, growth of the money supply, fiscal balance, exchange rates, interest rates, and international reserves. A rise or fall in these objective indicators in a nation would signal, respectively, the need for restrictive or expansionary policies for the nation. Stability of the index for the world as a whole would be the anchor for noninflationary world expansion.

As long as nations have very different inflation-unemployment tradeoffs, however, effective and substantial macroeconomic policy coordination is practically impossible. During the late 1980s, it was often asserted that the EMS provided evidence that significant macroeconomic policy coordination was possible. However, the EMS currency crises of September 1992 and August 1993 caused by Germany's refusal to lower interest rates in the face of widespread recession in the rest of Europe and the United States proved otherwise (see Salvatore, 1996, 1997a, 1998b). Empirical research has also shown that although nations seem to gain from international policy coordination about three-quarters of the time, the welfare gains from coordination, when it occurs, are not very large (see Frankel and Rockett, 1988; McKibbin, 1997).

Another class of proposals for reforming the present international monetary system is based on the premise that huge international capital flows in today's highly integrated international capital markets are the primary cause of exchange rate instability and global imbalances. These proposals are, therefore, based on *restricting international speculative capital flows*. Tobin (1978, 1996) would do this with a small flat transaction tax (which, therefore, becomes progressively higher the shorter the duration of the transaction) in order "to put some sand in the wheels of international finance." Dornbusch and Frankel (1987) would instead reduce international financial capital flows with dual exchange rates—a less flexible one for trade transactions and a more flexible one for purely financial transactions not related to international trade and investments. By restricting international "hot" money flows through capital market segmentation or the decoupling of asset markets, Tobin, Dornbusch and Frankel believe that the international financial system can be made to operate much more smoothly and without any need for close policy coordination by the leading industrial countries—which they regard as neither feasible nor useful. Critics of these proposals, however, point out that it is next to impossible to separate "nonproductive" or speculative capital flows from "productive" or nonspeculative ones related to international trade and investments. Finally, Cooper (1984) pointed out that in a world of large and growing interdependence, only through international cooperation and policy coordination can sovereignty be wisely and usefully exercised.

It remains to be seen if the leading nations are prepared to give up some of their autonomy in the coming years in order to have greater success in achieving their economic objectives. In the end, reform of the present international monetary system is likely to involve improving the functioning of the present system rather than replacing the present system with a brand new one (Fratianni and Salvatore, 1993; Bretton Woods Commission, 1994; Kenen, 1994; Salvatore, 1994; Eichengreen, 1994; Goldstein, 1995; Baldassarri et al., 1996; Fratianni et al., 1997; Salvatore, 1998c, 1998d).

One reform drafted by the IMF in 1996 (see IMF, 1996a, 1996b; Kaminsky et al., 1998) to improve the functioning of the present international monetary system is an *early-warning system* to avoid the type of monetary and exchange crisis that hit Mexico at the end of 1994 and shook global financial markets. The plan recommends that nations, particularly those that borrow heavily in international capital markets (such as China, Argentina, Brazil, Chile, South Korea, Malaysia, Mexico, Peru, and Thailand), provide accurate and timely data on such variables as inflation, the growth of the money supply, and foreign-currency reserves, so that investors can anticipate problems before they become crises. Although these data disclosures are voluntary, the IMF believes that global markets would very likely punish (with reduced capital flows) those countries that do not co-operate.

As pointed out by Calvo and Mendoza (1996) and Flood and Marion (1997), however, in today's highly integrated international capital markets, where capital flows can take place at the speed of PC computer blimp and foreign investors have a great deal of choice of where to invest their liquid funds, investors are likely to immediately shift their funds to what they consider more secure financial markets at the first sign of financial difficulties in a nation. Under such conditions (and as the 1997–1998 speculative attack against East Asian currencies shows), Mexican-style financial crises probably cannot be avoided even with the early-warning system (Eichengreen and Portes, 1996). What this plan does is to expose an unsustainable financial situation sooner so that markets and the nation can take quicker action to avoid the crisis or actually precipitate the crisis sooner when it would be less serious.

It is here that economic and financial indicators are useful. That is, a nation would be more likely to avoid a financial crisis, or face a smaller one if the crisis did come, if the nation had a smaller current account deficit, a smaller total foreign debt, a smaller short-term foreign debt, a smaller reliance on financing its debt service by hot money inflows, a smaller short-term debt in relation to its international reserves, a smaller ratio of debt service to export earnings, and a greater import cover from its international reserves. The 1994 Mexican crisis provides a set of economic and financial indicators that show the very serious financial crisis that can happen when a nation does not manage its finances conservatively (see Frankel and Rose, 1996; Mishkin, 1997; Salvatore, 1997b).

In order to make it possible to deal with a Mexican-style financial crisis, if one does arise, the IMF also negotiated the doubling (to $47 billion) of the amount that it could borrow under the (New) General Agreement to Borrow. This was accomplished by increasing the commitment of the 11 original participating industrial countries by 50% (the US share thus became $9.25 billion) and by bringing 15 more countries into the agreement, including the smaller industrial countries (such as Austria) and the fast-growing Southeast Asian countries (such as Singapore and Malaysia). Most economists, however, believe that providing more financial help to nations hit by a financial crisis leads to the problem of moral hazard because international investors may undertake unnecessarily risky investments believing that in case of crisis the IMF will step in to bail the nation out. Thus, a balance must be struck between trying to avoid a moral hazard problem and the need to provide financial resources to prevent a financial crisis in one nation from spreading to the entire international financial system.

2. The European Monetary System and European Monetary Union

This part examines the 1992–93 crisis of the EMS and the move toward full European Monetary Union (EMU) with a single currency (the euro) and an EU-wide central bank.

2.1. The 1992 EMS crisis

Until September 1992, the EMS was regarded as a great success by most economists on both sides of the Atlantic (see, for example, Frankel and Phillips, 1991; Giavazzi and Giovannini, 1989; MacDonald and Taylor, 1991). They pointed out that the economies of the large EU countries had converged toward lower rates of inflation and that no currency realignments had taken place since 1987 (except for the technical depreciation of the lira by 3.7% on January 8, 1990). These accomplishments were taken as evidence of success and of the feasibility of moving toward a single currency and full economic union in Europe. In fact, suggestions were made on how the EMS experience could be used as a blueprint for reforming the entire world monetary system.

A minority of economists (including the present author) were skeptical and refused to be swayed by the EMS euphoria (see, for example, Eichengreen, 1991; Feldstein, 1991; and Salvatore, 1989). We regarded the EMS as a system untried under stress and suggested that it might, therefore, be a sort of "fair weather system"—working reasonably well only because of the absence of a major crisis, but that in a major crisis the system would probably unravel and fall. The reason is that we cannot have simultaneously fixed exchange rates, unrestricted international financial capital flows, and even a semiautonomous monetary policy. In the face of a large asymmetric demand shock affecting only some EU countries, something had to give, and this is exactly what happened in September 1992.

In September 1992, the United Kingdom and Italy abandoned the Exchange Rate Mechanism (ERM) and this was followed by the devaluation of the Spanish peseta later in September 1992, of the peseta and the Portuguese escudo in November 1992, of the Irish pound in January 1993, and of the peseta and the escudo again in May 1993 (see Capie, 1998; Hamada, 1998). High interest rates in Germany to contain inflationary pressures (in the face of the high cost of financing the restructure of East Germany) made the German mark strong against other currencies and have been widely blamed for the EMS crisis. In the face of deepening recession and high and rising unemployment, the United Kingdom and Italy felt that the cost of keeping exchange rates within the ERM had become unbearable and so they left the ERM. This allowed the United Kingdom to reduce interest rates from 10 to 6%, thus stimulating investments, which, together with the increase in exports resulting from the depreciation of the pound, provided a much-needed stimulus to growth. Because of serious political problems, dropping out of the ERM and regaining greater monetary independence only prevented a deeper recession in Italy. In fact, one could say that the depreciation of the lira in September 1992 and the stimulus that this provided for exports was the only stimulus to growth in Italy during 1993. The devaluations of the peseta, the escudo and the Irish pound, on the other hand, were the result of overwhelming speculative attacks.

The dropping out of the ERM by the United Kingdom and Italy in September of 1992 and their ability to lower interest rates and thereby stimulate growth was not lost on France, which continued to keep high interest rates in order to remain in the ERM. Indeed, France was able to remain in the ERM after September 1992 only as the result of massive intervention in currency markets by the Bank of France and the Bundesbank to repel heavy speculative attacks on the franc. France and other countries that remained in the EMR only received partial relief from the three smaller reductions in German interest rates during the spring of 1993. At that time, the fate of the French franc had become synonymous with the very survival of the ERM and continued movement toward further economic and political unification in Europe. In short, it was felt that if the franc fell the entire EMS would unravel. There was also a fear that this could lead to competitive devaluations and unstable international relations reminiscent of the interwar period in the 1930s. The hope was that, faced with deep recession in spring 1993, Germany would cut interest rates substantially and that this would bring a much-needed stimulus not only to France but also to other EU countries and the rest of the world.

Some top EU officials at this time were so fearful of a French devaluation and the complete collapse of the entire ERM that they advocated a swift move toward a French-German currency union. Instead of a single currency for every EU country, there would be a two-track monetary union. Under such a system France, Germany, Belgium, Luxembourg, and the Netherlands (which had the economic will and the political strength to do so) would proceed at a faster speed toward monetary union than the other countries (the United Kingdom, Italy, Spain, Portugal, Ireland, and Greece) that did not. As expected, there was not much enthusiasm by the B team for such a two-speed European monetary union. In the background, there were also widespread fears (that now seem confirmed) that the recession in Europe in the early 1990s was not similar to other postwar recessions, with only temporary high unemployment, but was in fact part of an ominous long-run trend of loss of European competitiveness to newly industrializing countries, the United States, and Japan in a world where capital moves freely and investment and technology flow to wherever labor is skilled and cheaper.

2.2. The 1993 EMS crisis

On Monday, August 2, 1993, a new EMS crisis erupted, this time involving the French franc. This new currency crisis was touched off when the Bundesbank, the German central bank, refused to lower the discount rate on the previous

Thursday, as many financial analysts and currency traders had expected. Speculators responded by unloading the currencies of France, Denmark, Spain, Portugal, and Belgium with a vengeance. After massive interventions in foreign exchange markets, especially by the Bank of France, in concert with the Bundesbank, failed to put an end to the massive speculative attack, EU finance ministers agreed on August 2 to abandon the narrow band of 2.25% on either side of their "central rates" of allowed fluctuation for their currencies in favor of the much wider band of 15% on either side of parity. Only the Dutch guilder retained the narrow band vis-a-vis the German currency. (The United Kingdom and Italy had already left the ERM in September of 1992 and were not directly involved in the latest currency crisis, while the Spanish peseta and the Portuguese escudo already had a 6% band of allowed fluctuation above and below parity before the latest crisis.)

During the crisis, the Bundesbank sold more than $35 billion worth of marks in support of the franc and other currencies, and the total spent on market intervention by all the central banks involved exceeded $100 billion. But with over $1 trillion moving each day through foreign exchange markets, even such massive intervention could not reverse market forces in the face of a massive speculative attack. The crisis also sent the price of gold soaring to a three-year high of $409 per ounce.

Greatly widening the band of fluctuation allowed the ERM currencies to depreciate further vis-a-vis the mark and ended the speculative attack. It also allowed these countries to lower interest rates to combat recession. The Bundesbank had not heeded the pleas of France, Denmark, Spain, Portugal, and Belgium to lower its discount rate in order to fight a domestic inflation rate of 4.2% per year (double its medium-term target) and restrain its rapidly growing money supply, both of which resulted from spiraling costs associated with the economic restructuring of East Germany. Germany, it was clear, was not going to compromise domestic goals to sustain the ERM. But with German interest rates high, other countries could not lower theirs to combat recession. Any attempt on their part to lower interest rates unilaterally would only have led to capital outflows to Germany (see Salvatore, 1996).

The collapse of the ERM was a big blow to France, which had staked its honor on maintaining the parity of its currency with the mark, and badly bruised the Franco-German alliance, which had been regarded as the bedrock of the ERM and EMS. Only a month before, Edouard Balladur, France's new Prime Minister, had said that he would rather resign than allow a devaluation of the franc. Yet the crisis was inevitable because speculators had clearly understood that with an inflation rate of only 2% per year, three-months interest rates of 8.8%, and unemployment running at a postwar high of 11.6%, the pressure to abandon the ERM by France had become irresistible. Now France could lower its interest rates without fearing a massive capital outflow by simply allowing the franc to depreciate vis-a-vis the mark.

Establishing a band of fluctuation of 30% (15% on either side of parity) in the EU on August 2, 1993, however, was tantamount to a de facto free float or flexible exchange rate system. After all, the free-floating US dollar fluctuated by less than 30% during its roller coaster ride against the German mark in the three years after German unification. The choice of a band of fluctuation of 15% on either side of parity was even larger than the 10% one usually advocated by the target zone proposals for reforming the entire international monetary system and was in line with the size of the depreciation of the British pound immediately after it abandoned the ERM during the September 1992 crisis (Williamson and Miller, 1987).

2.3. The aftermath of the 1993 ERM crisis

Right after the August 1993 ERM crisis, the expectation was that the ERM currencies, especially the French franc, would soon depreciate by 10 to 15% and that interest rates would be lowered quickly to stimulate the economy—exactly as it occurred in the United Kingdom soon after it abandoned the ERM in September 1992. In fact, anticipating interest rate cuts, stock prices rose in Europe in the days immediately following the crisis. France and most other ERM countries, however, made little use of their newly found freedom to cut interest rates and allow their currencies to depreciate in the six months following the ERM crisis. They still seemed to operate as if their interest rates were constrained by Germany's within the narrow-band ERM. During August 1993, the French finance minister even vowed to keep the franc close to its old parity and interest rates at their recession-perpetuating levels. Only when the Bundesbank finally lowered its discount rate on September 9, 1993, did France and the other ERM countries involved in the crisis lower theirs also. While the reduction of the discount rate by the Bundesbank came as a great relief in Europe and the United States, its decline by one-half of a percentage point was too small to give much stimulus to recession-hit European economies facing a 12% average unemployment rate.

Why did ERM countries not lower interest rates or allow their currencies to depreciate soon after the ERM crisis (as Britain had done in September 1992) but only lowered their interest rates after the Bundesbank moved and even then reduced interest rates by relatively small amounts? One reason was the fear of reducing the value of their currencies too quickly, thus making the reestablishment of the narrow-band ERM that much more difficult. A related reason might have been that national monetary authorities feared competitive and chaotic depreciations, which were precisely what the narrow-band ERM sought to avoid. In the September 1992 crisis, only the United Kingdom and Italy left the ERM, and so the danger of competitive devaluations was much less (even though the depreciation of the pound by as much as 9% within three days of the crisis angered the UK's European trade partners). Indeed, there are those, particularly Jacques Mélitz, who commented to me that widening the band of allowed fluctuation of exchange rates from 2.25 to 15% around the old parities was a fortuitous and extremely successful move that calmed foreign exchange markets and allowed member nations to actually keep exchange rates fluctuating within the narrower band, while continuing to pursue the Maastricht criteria and moving ahead toward EMU. The fact remains, however, that markets had forced a large widening of the band of fluctuation, which at the time was viewed in the EU as a major crisis and a step backward from EMU.

2.4. Is the EU an optimum currency area?

It is clear from the above discussion that belonging to the EMS and the ERM confers costs and benefits to its members. The costs arise from the member's loss of the ability to change the value of its currency and conduct an independent monetary policy, such as devaluing its currency and lowering its interest rates in the face of an asymmetric shock that lowers the demand for the nation's products. With wages and prices sticky and adjusting only slowly downward, output and employment in the nation would suffer by the nation remaining in the EMS and ERM. Deflation rather than currency depreciation would be the only method of adjustment. The benefit of belonging to the EMS and ERM arises because of the monetary discipline forced on a nation, such as Italy, that might be unable or unwilling to have discipline without being a member of the EMS and ERM. Through the formation of a community-wide central bank, each member would also have a voice in the formulation of community-wide monetary policy. As it was, EU policy was virtually decided by the Bundesbank alone and reflected its strong preference toward fighting inflation over promoting economic growth. A community-wide central bank with representation by all members, on the other hand, could take more into account the economic condition in other member countries and be more growth oriented than otherwise (Fratianni and Von Hagen, 1992). With a single currency (the euro), EU members obtain the additional benefits of not having to exchange the currencies of EU members, avoiding excessive exchange rate volatility among EU currencies, and experiencing more rapid economic and financial integration.

The question then becomes "Is the EMS an optimum currency area?" An optimum currency area is one for which the net benefits of belonging to the area exceed the costs (see Mundell, 1961; McKinnon, 1963; Tavlas, 1993, 1994; Artis et al., 1998). The formation of an optimum currency area is more likely to be beneficial the greater is the mobility of resources among the various member nations and the greater are their structural similarities. Then specific regional problems, such as excessive regional unemployment resulting, for example, from an asymmetric reduction in aggregate demand in the region, would be overcome by labor migration and fiscal redistribution.

For example, if the Northeast of the United States were in a recession, labor would migrate to other parts of the nation. The Northeast would also receive a great deal of fiscal redistribution from other parts of the nation not affected by the recession. Bayoumi and Masson (1994) found that the cyclical change in the tax revenues of the US federal government offsets about 28% of the fall in regional revenues. Thus, the harmful impact of the recession in the Northeast would be greatly dampened despite the fact that the Northeast, being, as it is, part of the United States, cannot have an independent expansionary regional monetary policy. These benefits would not flow anywhere near the same extent to a EU nation facing recession because of the much lower labor mobility and fiscal redistribution in the EU than in the United States. As a result, a EU member nation that finds itself in a recession, asymmetrically from other EU members, has practically no escape valve other than passively waiting for the recession to end or to leave the Union or its exchange rate mechanism (see Salvatore, 1997a).

To be sure, despite much greater labor mobility and fiscal redistribution in the United States than in the EU, the United States may not be an optimum currency area either. The reason is that the United States comprises at least four major regions, each specializing in a different sector or sectors—the Northeast in financial services, the Midwest in mining and manufacturing, the West in high technology, and the Southeast in tourism and agriculture. Since it is unlikely for these four major regions to move in step cyclically with one another, there would be a need and a benefit for region-specific monetary policies and perhaps even for having regional currencies. However, while the United States, very likely, is not an optimum currency area, it gets much closer to being one than the EU.

In fact, the OECD (1986) and the European Commission (1990) found significantly (from two to three times) lower labor mobility among the EU members than in the United States. This led Eichengreen (1991) to conclude that (1) the EU is less of an optimum currency area than its North American counterpart (NAFTA), (2) the establishment of a single currency in the EU will be associated with non-negligible regional problems, and (3) even with the implementation of the single market, it is unlikely that labor mobility in Europe will reach the North American levels very soon, if ever, in view of the large differences in language, customs, and national temperament among EU countries. Sala-i-Martin and Sachs (1991) and Eichengreen (1993) also point out that the EU budget is only a little more than 1% of its GDP and most of it is devoted to the Common Agricultural Policy, and thus not available for fiscal redistribution. Thus, it is clear that the EMS is not an optimal currency area. Canzoneri and Rogers (1990) reached the same conclusion from a public finance point of view.

Furthermore, the future likely enlargement of the 15-member EU to include Central and Eastern European countries would make the EU even less of an optimal currency area. Such a 25-plus-member currency area would resemble the old Bretton Woods System—which collapsed precisely because nations (in particular, the United States) were unwilling to give up control over their money supply and direct monetary policy to achieve external rather internal balance.

A recent study by Bini-Smaghi and Vori (1993) compared the United States to the European Union and came to the conclusion that the 50 states of the United States were much less alike than the countries of the EU. This does not make sense, however, because we cannot compare the 12 (at the time the authors wrote) countries of the EU (or even the 15 of today) with the fifty states of the United States. If the three natural regions (north, center, and south) of Italy were considered separately instead of the nation as a whole and if the same was done for the other EU nations (so as to have forty or fifty regions of the EU), we would surely find the regions of the EU to be less alike than the states of the United States. But even that completely misses the point. The point is how much flexibility and how much labor mobility and fiscal redistribution are there in the United States as compared to the EU? As pointed out above, we know that there is much more labor mobility and fiscal redistribution in the United States than in the EU. Therefore, although the United States is not an optimum currency area, it is much closer to being one than the EU. In fact, if pushed hard enough, most European statesmen would probably admit that the major benefit of the EMS is more political than economic (Feldstein, 1991; Dornbusch, 1996; Bayoumi et al., 1997). Thus, what we have here is that political benefits might justify economic costs, rather than the other way around.

The establishment of a European Central Bank (ECB) and a single European currency (the euro) leaves the serious problem of how an EU member will respond to an asymmetric shock unresolved. This is important because it is practically inevitable that a large and diverse single currency area such as the European Union will face periodic asymmetric shocks that will affect various member nations differently and drive their economies out of alignment. In such a case, there is practically nothing that a member nation so adversely affected can do aside from deflation. The nation cannot change the exchange rate or use monetary policy because of the existence of a single currency, and fiscal discipline will also prevent it from using fiscal policy to deal with the problem. And, as we have seen, the EU cannot rely (as the United States can) on adequate labor mobility to overcome the problem.

Some economists (e.g., Mélitz, 1997), however, reply that geographical labor mobility is an extremely costly and slow-working method of dealing with asymmetric shocks and that highly integrated EU capital markets can make up for low labor mobility in the EU. But this has not occurred adequately even within individual EU nations and large regional inequalities remain and so it is entirely unrealistic to expect it to take place on a sufficient scale among EU nations. Indeed, capital flows may even be perverse and move out of an EU nation facing a negative asymmetric shock. Furthermore, while there may be a great deal of regional fiscal redistribution within each EU member nation, fiscal federalism is grossly inadequate among EU member nations in view of the very meager EU-wide budget. Thus the serious problem of adjusting to asymmetric shocks in the EU remains (Dornbusch, 1996; Bayoumi et al., 1997; Salvatore, 1998d).

2.5. *The move to the EMU*

At the time of the August 1993 ERM crisis, many economists and policy makers believed that the move toward monetary union and a single currency in Europe had been permanently derailed. Soon after the crisis, however, this belief was revised and replaced by the widespread view that the crisis had only delayed the process toward monetary union and that the 1999 date was still possible for the start of the European Monetary Union (EMU) with at least some of the nations. This is, indeed, what happened. Here, we examine the process by which the single currency (the Euro) and the European Central Bank (ECB) were created in May 1998.

The 1991 Maastricht Treaty established five criteria that member nations had to meet in order to join the single currency and be part of the EMU. These were that a EU member nation's (1) average exchange rate was to deviate by no more than 2.25% on either side of its central or parity rate for the two years before joining the EMU; (2) inflation rate must not exceed by more than 1.5 percentage points the average rate of inflation of the three community nations with the lowest inflation rate; (3) long-term interest rate was not to exceed by more than two percentage points the average interest rate of the three countries with the lowest inflation rates; (4) budget deficit was not to exceed 3% of its GDP; and (5) overall government debt must not exceed 60% of its GDP.

At the time of the Maastricht Treaty only a few EU members met all five criteria and it seemed all but impossible that all would do so by 1998 when a decision was to be reached as to which member nations were to participate in the Euro from the beginning. Some economists, such as Paul de Grauwe (1994) and Richard Portes (1993), pointed out that there was nothing scientific about the Maastricht criteria and favored relaxing them because they believed that it was much easier for nations to meet the criteria if they were part of the EMU than if they were not. For example, if Italy were in the EMU, its real interest rate would not include a credibility penalty and this would reduce its budget deficit. It must also be pointed out that, contrary to the inflation and interest criteria, the 3% deficit/GDP and the 60% debt/GDP criteria were only reference values and that the Maastricht Treaty allowed a nation to join the EMU if it was close to meeting those criteria and/or had made significant progress toward meeting them. For example, Ireland would qualify for excemption from the 60% debt/GDP criterion because that ratio fell from 116.6% in 1987 to 66.3% in 1997 and the ratio deficit/GDP fell from 8.5% in 1987 to 2.7% in 1995 and −0.9 (a surplus) in 1997.

As it was, as a result of falling interest rates (and thus reduced burdens from servicing national debts) as well as tightened budgets, a decision was reached on May 2, 1998 by the European Commission to allow all members of the European Union, except Greece, to participate in the Euro from the beginning in 1999. Italy and Belgium still had national debts in excess of their GDP but were judged to have made sufficient progress in putting their fiscal houses in order to admit them. The United Kingdom, Denmark and Sweden, however, decided not to join the single currency move from the beginning but reserved the right to do so later. Thus, 11 of the 15 EU members (Austria, Belgium, Germany, Finland, France, Ireland, Italy, Luxembourg, Spain, Portugal and the Netherlands) are now part of the single currency and the new European Central Bank.

The ECB was inaugurated on June 30, 1998 in Frankfurt with the Win Duisenberg, the former head of the Dutch Central Bank, as its first governor until 2002 to be followed by the head of the French Central Bank, Jean-Claude Trichet for the following 4 years. According to the schedule, member countries' exchange rates are to be irrevocably fixed with respect to the euro on January 1, 1999, euro notes and coins are to be issued on January 1, 2002, and on July 1 of the same year old currencies are to be withdrawn and the euro established as the sole legal tender.

One question left unanswered is the relationship between the euro, the common currency of the EMU members, and the currencies of those nations that either cannot (Greece) or will not participate (the United Kingdom, Denmark, and Sweden) in the EMU from the beginning. One possibility is the establishment of an ERM between the currencies of the 4 "outs" and the euro. The problem with this arrangement, of course, is the possibility of currency crises similar to those of September 1992 and August 1993, and that the outs will use competitive devaluations to confer unfair advantages to their industries vis-a-vis the industries of the ins (Begg et al., 1997).

At this point we must go back to the question "Is a single currency necessary for EU members to get the full benefits of economic union?" Judging from the effort put to achieve a single currency by the EU, the answer seems obviously, yes. But not everyone agrees with this evaluation. Feldstein (1991), for example, feels that free trading areas do not require a single currency or even an ERM with a narrow band of allowed fluctuation. He points out that econometric studies have failed to show that exchange rate volatility has adversely affected international trade and investments and, in any event, traders and investors can hedge the foreign exchange risk. On the other hand, the inability of members of a monetary union with a single currency or of a currency zone with fixed exchange rates to change the exchange rate when in fundamental disequilibrium and to conduct a monetary and fiscal policies tailored to their specific needs is likely to be very costly.

Feldstein concludes that the reason that the European Community has moved toward a currency zone and aimed at a single currency is more political than economic. Laidler (1991) and Emerson (1991) took an intermediate position: a currency zone may be beneficial to Europe if we consider its political aims, but not for North America where a free trade zone has not been accompanied by closer political ties. The same is potentially true for Asia. The question, however, is posed incorrectly. The question is not whether to have a single currency in the EU or three currencies as in NAFTA, but whether to have a single currency and 14 different currencies (Luxembourg shares the same currency with Belgium) in the EU (and more if more nations join the EMU). Posed that way, a single currency becomes much more attractive and necessary.

From all that has been said, it is clear that the formation of the EMU is likely to confer major benefits but also to impose major costs to its members. While the economic benefits from the EMU have been amply discussed and perhaps exaggerated, the economic costs seem to have been underestimated. In particular, in a large and growing monetary union such as the EMU, formed as it is by a large number of very diverse countries, it is inevitable that over the years unpredictable shocks will affect the various members differently and drive their economies out of alignment. In the face of limited labor mobility and little federal fiscal redistribution, a member nation facing a deep recession or other shock asymmetrically will have few if any policies at its disposal to overcome its economic difficulty (Salvatore, 1997b). At that point, the nation may wish to leave the union, but this seems to be precluded by the Maastricht Treaty.

Be that as it may, the next few years may prove to be difficult for Europe because of the immediate increase in EU-wide competition resulting from the Euro and the need for rapid deregulation of the economies made necessary by the rapid globalization in the face of very large structural unemployment (Salvatore, 1998b). Improving economic conditions throughout Europe, however, may reduce the pain somewhat.

2.6. The euro and the dollar

One important question often asked these days is "will the euro be a strong currency?" It is very likely that the euro will be a strong currency from the beginning. The reasons are (1) the GDP of the 15-nation EU is larger than that of the United States and the EU is the largest trading block in the world. As the currency of such an important economic unit, the euro will inevitably be an important international currency. (2) The euro must be strong to be acceptable to Germans who gave up their venerable Deutschmark for the euro. (3) The European Central Bank (ECB) must create a reputation and, as the saying goes, the first impression can only be made once. While the euro is likely to be a strong currency from the beginning, however, it cannot be so strong as to discourage exports and growth in the EU. Some rough estimates put the substitution of dollars for euros at about $500 billion to $1 trillion. But since this is likely to take place gradually over time, it may not put undue pressure on the dollar (Fratianni et al., 1998).

Will the euro displace the dollar as the most important international currency? It probably won't because (1) most primary commodities are priced in dollars and this is likely to remain the case for some time to come, (2) non-EU countries are likely to continue to use the dollar for most of their international transactions and (3) of sheer inertia that favors the incumbent (the dollar). Again rough estimates seem to indicate that about 50% of international transactions may be conducted in dollars in the future (down from about 65% now), 40% in euro, and the remaining 10% in yens and other smaller currencies. There are of course, some European economists, such as Portes and Rey (1998), who believe that the euro will replace the dollar as the most important international currency. This is not likely to occur, especially in the near future. The gradual partial move from dollars to the euro is not likely, by and of itself, to create problems for the working of the international monetary system.

What may create problems is the fact that with most trade conducted within rather than between the three major trading blocks (the EU, NAFTA, and Asia), there will inevitably be less concern about the exchange rate between the dollar, the euro and the yen and so the exchange rates among these currencies are likely to be much more volatile than they are today. Much more serious, however, would be possible large misalignments between the euro and the dollar and the euro and the yen and this, as pointed out in Section 1.1, may create a great deal of friction between Europe, the United States and Japan in the future. The competition that the euro will provide for the dollar, however, will impose more discipline in the conduct of economic policies in the United States than has been the case since the collapse of the Bretton Woods System and, as such, will be beneficial, not harmful, to the United States over time.

3. National economic policies under the present international monetary system

In this part, we examine central bank independence and monetary and fiscal policies under the present international monetary system. We also examine global financial integration and the effectiveness of monetary policy.

3.1. Central bank independence

In recent years, many nations have passed laws removing government control on their central bank (i.e., making their central bank more independent) in order to overcome the inflationary bias that was otherwise believed to exist in the conduct of monetary policy. The central banks of some nations, such as Switzerland and Germany, have enjoyed a high degree of independence during most of the postwar period. Recently, Canada, Chile, and New Zealand enacted legislation to make their central banks more independent. In May 1997, England also did so. A common ingredient of economic reforms in Latin America and in the ex-communist nations of Central and Eastern Europe has been the creation of independent central banks—at least legally—if not yet in their actual day-to-day operation. The Maastricht Treaty prohibits central banks from taking instructions from the government, as one of the requirements for monetary union in Europe. To ensure central bank independence, the Treaty also requires that central bank governors be appointed for a term of at least five years. More importantly, the Treaty forbids central banks from purchasing debt instruments directly from the government and from providing credit facilities to the government. This is done in the belief that a central bank that is free from political pressure would achieve a lower inflation rate.

But what is meant by central bank independence? Fisher (1995) introduced the distinction between goal independence and instrument independence. A central bank has goal independence if it can set its own goals, such as the rate of inflation that the nation should aim for. Instrument independence means that the central bank has control over the levers of monetary policy. That is, it has no obligation to finance government deficits, directly or indirectly, and that it has the power to set interest rates. Of course, a central bank that has goal and instrument independence can set its own monetary goals and is free to use the instruments at its disposal to achieve those goals. Even in nations with the most independent central banks, however, the government rather than the central bank usually has a final say on the type of exchange rate arrangement for the nation to have, and on changing the exchange rates in a fixed exchange rate system, or on foreign exchange market interventions to affect the level of exchange rates if the nation chooses to have a flexible exchange rate system (Capie, 1998).

Theoretically, there are two different approaches to central bank independence. One is the conservative-banker approach of Rogoff (1985) and the other is the principal-agent approach of Walsh (1995). In the conservative-banker approach, the central bank has both goal and instrument independence. Presumably, the conservative banker will weigh deviations of both inflation and output from target levels in setting monetary policy, but with a bias in favor of lower inflation, even if this comes at the expense of lower growth. In the principal-agent approach, on the other hand, the central banker has instrument independence, but not goal independence. That is, the government sets the monetary goal, such as the rate of inflation for the nation, and then the central bank is free to employ whatever monetary instruments it has at its disposal in trying to meet the monetary goal. The principal-agent goal is most explicit in the case of New Zealand, where the governor of the central bank formally agrees to meet the inflation target set by the government, with his job on the line if he fails to meet the target. In Canada and England, it is the reputation of the central bank that is on the line if the inflation target is exceeded.

Today, there is general agreement that a central bank should have instrument, but not goal independence. There are two reasons for this. The first is that the monetary goal of the nation should reflect the social welfare function of the nation and not just the preferences of the central bank governor. The second is that there is the need to coordinate monetary and fiscal policies to avoid their operating at cross purposes of each other. Central bank accountability, however, is needed to ensure that the monetary goals of the nation are, in fact, pursued by the nation's central bank. In the case of New Zealand the governor of the central bank is accountable to the finance minister. In the United States, the Federal Reserve Bank or the Fed (the US central bank) is generally accountable to Congress, which must ratify the choice of the chairman of the Fed and can summon him to explain his policies. In Germany, the Bundesbank is accountable to the public at large for its policies in defense of the currency.

In recent years, a growing number of countries are following the lead of New Zealand in setting explicit inflation targets for the central bank. This provides transparency and accountability, which are very important in establishing credibility for the government's monetary policy. The more credible a central bank is, the more it will be able to cut interest rates in a slowdown without triggering higher inflationary expectations and hence higher long-term interest rates, or raising interest rates to curb emerging inflationary pressures without the fear of triggering a recession. It is to increase transparency and accountability, and hence its credibility and effectiveness, that the central bank of several countries, including the United States, have recently started to explain their decision-making process (including the lagged publication of the minutes of their meetings by the US Fed) and operating procedure in their conduct of monetary policy. The fact, however, that the US Fed, as opposed to most other central banks, is constitutionally required to pursue both price stability and full employment, reduces its effectiveness as an inflation fighter when a conflict arises between its two goals (Salvatore, 1998d).

3.2. Central bank independence and inflation

As expected, a number of empirical studies have shown an inverse relationship between central bank independence and the rate of inflation in industrial countries. That is, the more independent the central bank of an industrial country is, the lower the rate of inflation in the nation. One of the most comprehensive of these studies is the one by Alesina and Summers (1993). The authors included the following 16 industrial countries in the study: Australia, Belgium, Canada, Denmark, France, Germany, Italy, Japan, the Netherlands, New Zealand, Norway, Spain, Sweden, Switzerland, the United Kingdom, and the United States. The sample period was from 1955 to 1988. As in previous studies, the authors found a negative correlation between the level of central bank independence and the rate of inflation. They also found that the more independent a central bank was, the smaller was the variability of the inflation rate (because of the positive correlation between the level and variability of inflation).

As it is well known, however, correlation does not establish causality. That is, the negative correlation between central bank independence and inflation found in empirical studies does not imply that the former causes the latter. It may very well be that countries with a stronger aversion to inflation are more likely to give more independence to their central banks. Thus, it is the inflation aversion in the nation that gives rise both to lower inflation and to a more independent central bank in the nation, rather than a more independent central bank being responsible (i.e., causing) lower inflation. Unless, however, we believe that laws and institutions are entirely irrelevant and have no effect whatsoever on economic performance (here the rate of inflation) we must conclude that a more independent central bank is more likely, other things equal, to lead to lower inflation than a less independent central bank.

As support for central bank independence has increased around the world, so has the tendency to entrust to central banks the sole function of achieving a given inflation target or range. This, however, raises the question of whether it would be more appropriate to entrust the central bank with a target that is more directly controllable by the central bank, such as the growth of a narrow money aggregate, rather than a specific inflation target. Setting an inflation target, however, seems more appropriate today in view of the collapse of the relationship between money growth and inflation in one country after another. As a result, it is better to assign an explicit inflation target to the central bank and provide it with instrument independence to pursue the inflation target.

As to why the central bank should be given a specific inflation target rather than a growth-of-real-GDP or rate-of-unemployment target, the answer is that inflation is a monetary phenomenon while the rate of growth of real GDP and the rate of unemployment are real phenomena. Real phenomena are, of course, affected by monetary phenomena, but here the chain of causality depends on policies and institutions that are not under the direct control of the central bank. In giving a specific inflation target to the central bank, it is important to point out that fixed exchange rates are less inflationary than flexible exchange rates. Thus, a country that is trying to move from a high to a low inflation environment would do well to adopt a fixed rather than a variable exchange rate system as a means of anchoring monetary policy and market expectations. Many developing countries, however, have been moving toward greater exchange-rate flexibility in order to cope better with big swings in foreign capital flows.

Although many empirical studies have found a negative correlation between central bank independence and inflation in industrial countries, this is not the case for developing countries. Cukierman (1992) found a positive, not a negative, relationship between central bank independence and inflation for a group of 70 developing countries that he studied over the 1950–1989 period. This, however, may be due to the fact that the central banks of many developing countries are independent legally but not in reality, as evidenced by the fact that they continue to finance government deficits. This has certainly been the case for Mexico and Venezuela. For example, when Venezuela suffered a wave of bank failures in 1994, it decided that the best way to address the problem was to print billions of bolivars and impose capital controls. The same happened in Mexico following the deep financial crisis that started at the end of 1994.

3.3. Central bank independence, the real economy, and fiscal deficits

Does the lower inflation rate with an independent central bank come at the expense of growth of output for the nation? Alesina and Summers (1993) found no negative correlation between central bank independence and average growth of real GDP or the variability of growth of real GDP for the same 16 industrial countries that they used to examine the relationship between central bank independence and inflation over the 1955–1988 period. Barro (1995) and Sarel (1996) confirm this for inflation rates below 8%. Thus, it does not seem that central banks in industrial nations trade a lower growth rate of output for the sake of a lower rate of inflation.

The same conclusion was reached for industrial nations in another study by Cukierman, Kalaitzidakis, Summers, and Webb (1992) by regressing the nation's growth rate of real GDP on the degree of central bank independence, the initial level of real GDP in the nation, the initial level of primary and secondary education in the nation, and the nation's terms of trade. For developing nations, however, Cukierman, Kalaitzidakis, Summers, and Webb found that central bank independence did have a significantly positive effect on growth. When inflation is high, as in most developing countries, and to the extent that a more independent central bank is associated with a higher inflation rate (which encourages growth), a more independent central bank is then also associated with more rapid growth. Since industrial nations do not generally face high inflation, this vehicle to higher growth is not available to them.

Empirical studies were also conducted to examine the relationship between central bank independence and fiscal deficits as a percentage of GDP in the nation. The expectation was that a more independent central bank would be able to resist better government efforts to monetize fiscal deficits and thus lead to lower long-run average fiscal deficits as a percentage of GDP in the nation. Such a negative relationship was in fact found by Parkin (1987) and Grilli et al. (1991) for industrial countries. Thus, the overall conclusion that can be reached from empirical studies to date is that an independent central bank is associated with lower inflation rates and lower fiscal deficits as a percentage of GDP but is unrelated to growth in industrial nations.

Although empirical studies have found no relationship between central bank independence and the rate of economic growth in industrial nations, there is a theoretical reason for expecting that a central bank that can set its own inflation target and operate independently of the fiscal authority of the nation can lead to a lower rate of growth in the nation. This can result when there is a conflict between the goals of the monetary and the fiscal authority of the nation. Then monetary and fiscal policies can move at cross purposes from each other and result in suboptimal economic performance for the nation. Thus, a central bank can be too independent. For example, a central bank that is excessively inflation averse, such as the Bundesbank, may excessively restrain the growth of the nation. Better economic performance for the nation would result with the coordination of fiscal and monetary policies. This can be accomplished by giving the central bank instrument but not goal independence.

Thus, the general tendency for economists today of endorsing the separation of power in the conduct of monetary and fiscal policies may not be the best policy to maximize non-inflationary growth in the nation (see Nordhaus,

1994). Better results can be obtained by the coordination of monetary and fiscal policies. It is not just that in the absence of such a coordination, fiscal and monetary authorities might pursue contradictory goals. Suboptimal results may arise simply because of the different time horizon for monetary and fiscal policies. Monetary authorities usually have a longer time horizon than fiscal authorities and often respond only slowly and cautiously to changed economic conditions. Because of this, fiscal authorities might not be willing to adopt deficit-reduction policies and risk an economic slowdown (which may cost them re-election) if they cannot be sure that their contractionary fiscal policies will be offset by sufficiently strong and timely expansionary monetary policies.

3.4. Global financial integration and central bank performance

The past decade has seen a revolution in financial markets around the world. This has been the result of deregulation of domestic financial markets, the liberalization of international capital flows, rapid financial innovation in the form of fancy new instruments such as derivatives, and the arrival of powerful computers and telecommunications that have dramatically lowered the cost of information gathering, processing, and transmission. World financial markets have experienced explosive growth. Since 1980, the total stock of financial assets has increased two-and-a-half times faster than the growth of real GDP of industrial countries and the volume of daily trading in foreign-exchange, bonds and equities has increased more than 10 times faster than GDP. At the same time, the relative importance of commercial banks has been sharply reduced, as both depositors and borrower have sought alternative sources for investment and financing.

Financial liberalization has resulted in huge benefits to savers and borrowers as capital has tended to flow to its most productive uses around the world, but it has also led to fears that this has sharply reduced the effectiveness of monetary policy. Specifically, fears have been expressed that in a world of deregulated capital markets and huge international capital flows, central banks may have lost the power to set interest rates and that changes in interest rates may have much less effect on the economy than they did one or two decades ago. Let us examine each of these considerations separately.

Have central banks lost their power to set interest rates in today's world of highly integrated financial markets? Thirty years ago, commercial banks in the United States provided three-quarters of short-term and medium-term credit and together with savings and loans associations held more than two-thirds of residential mortgages. Furthermore, legal ceilings on interest rates offered by commercial banks provided the Fed an immediate and quick lever for the conduct of monetary policy. Today, however, commercial banks provide less than half of short-term and medium-term credit and commercial banks and savings and loans associations hold less than one quarter of residential mortgages. Furthermore, legal ceilings on interest rates that commercial banks can pay have been abolished. As a result, it is argued that central banks have lost their power to set interest rates and thus their ability to conduct monetary policy. Bluntly, how can the Fed through its open market operations (i.e., purchases and sales of securities) amounting to only a few billions dollars per year affect the $7 trillion dollar US economy with some $25 trillion of financial claims outstanding?

The answer is that the Fed controls the nation's money supply and the reserves that the banks must hold. Since bank reserves amounted to only $65 billion in 1996, open market operations of even a few billions dollars per year can have a significant effect on the price of those reserves (i.e., on short-term interest rates). While this effect may now be more indirect, take longer to arise, and require a larger movement in short-term interest rates to have a given effect on output in today's world of highly integrated financial markets, the Fed can still set interest rates and is still able to conduct monetary policy. The job, however, has become much more difficult because it is no longer possible for the Fed to implement monetary policy by simply following an intermediate monetary target such as M1 (the narrow measure of the money supply) or M2 (the broad measure of the money supply) since they can provide very different and contradictory signals. In any event, financial deregulation and innovation has delinked the traditional relationship between the money supply (under any definition) and inflation in today's world. Thus, the Fed must now look at a wider range of economic and financial indicators and exercise more judgement in its conduct of monetary policy. It should also exploit more effectively its ability to affect expectations.

The situation is somewhat different for most other central banks, which retain somewhat more direct control over monetary policy by relying on an auction market where they quote a price for central-bank credit to commercial banks (vaguely resembling the setting of the rediscount rate in the United States) rather than on open market operations. The same is envisaged for the ECB.

3.5. Global financial markets and the effectiveness of monetary policy

The relationship between the globalization of financial markets and the effectiveness of monetary policy and the future of central banking are hotly debated issues (Capie et al., 1994; Capie and Wood, 1996; Von Hagen and Fender, 1998). Today, it is widely believed that the effectiveness of monetary policy has been sharply reduced by the use of derivatives (futures, swaps, and options) which multinational corporations increasingly use to insulate themselves against domestic interest rate and exchange rate swings. The Bank for International Settlements or BIS (1994) in Basle, however, concluded that while derivatives can make monetary policy more difficult and delay its effect, they do not prevent it from working.

The effectiveness of monetary policy also depends in a crucial way on the type of exchange rate arrangements that the nation chooses to have. We know from international financial theory that with perfect international capital mobility, monetary policy would be completely ineffective under a fixed exchange rate system. Under such a system, the nation must passively allow its money supply to change in such a way as to ensure external equilibrium in defense of the par value of the currency. Thus, the nation loses complete control over the money supply and cannot use monetary policy to correct a domestic imbalance such as inflation and/or recession. On the other hand, a flexible exchange rate system allows the central bank to have an independent monetary policy even with highly mobile financial capital internationally (but gives up control over its exchange rate).

Have financial markets become too powerful to the point that they must be restrained? The answer is probably no. Although financial markets do not always get it right and often respond with excessive delay, and then tend to overreact, in general they impose a strong discipline on governments and central banks to adopt better economic policies. For example, by making interest rates higher in a nation such as Italy when it had very high budget deficits as a percentage of GDP, international financial markets induced the nation to reduce its budget deficit. Most recent big swings in asset prices, such as the collapse of the Mexican peso at the end of 1994 and in early 1995 can be traced to large imbalances in the nations. In the Mexican crisis, financial markets were too late in recognizing the problem, and when they did, they overreacted and caused the collapse of the currency and a huge capital outflow that resulted in a deep recession of the Mexican economy.

There is now evidence, however, that the delay of financial markets in anticipating the crisis in Mexico was due to lack of information about the worsening financial situation of the country. The same was generally true in the East Asian countries affected by the financial crisis in 1997–98. Had more complete and timely information been provided, financial markets would have reacted earlier, thus making the correction smaller and less painful. Therefore, rather than restraining international financial markets by a transaction tax a-la-Tobin, international capital controls, or greater international macroeconomic policy coordination on the part of industrial nations, financial markets can be made to operate more smoothly and induce better national economic policies by the provision of better and more timely information on economic conditions in the nation. This is the reason the IMF has put in place its "early-warning system" in 1997. Financial markets take power from governments that borrow recklessly, run inflationary policies, and try to defend unsustainable exchange rates. Rather than restraining financial markets, governments should put their houses in order and pursue better economic policies, and if financial markets force them to do so sooner, that much the better.

Under the present increasingly integrated international capital market and interdependent world economic system, international macroeconomic policy coordination can also be useful. For example, if all or most industrial nations face a recession, each nation may hesitate to stimulate its economy to avoid a deterioration in its trade balance. Through a coordinated simultaneous expansion of all nations, however, output and employment can increase in all nations without any of them suffering a deterioration in its trade balance.

There are several obstacles to successful and effective international macroeconomic policy coordination, however. One is the lack of consensus about the functioning of the international monetary system. For example, the United States may believe that a monetary expansion would lead to an expansion of output and employment, while Germany may believe that it will result in inflation. Another obstacle arises from the lack of agreement on the precise policy mix required. For example, different macroeconometric models give widely different results as to the effect of a given fiscal expansion. There is then the problem of how to distribute the gains from successful policy coordination among the participants and how to spread the cost of negotiating and policing agreements. Empirical research reported in Frenkel et al. (1991) indicates that nations gain from international policy coordination about three-quarters of the time but that the welfare gains from coordination, when they occur, are not very large. The empirical studies undertaken so far, however, may not have captured the full benefits from successful international policy coordination.

4. International financial capital flows and international financial instability

We now examine the reasons for increased international financial capital flows and financial instability.

4.1. Reasons for increased international financial capital flows

The past two decades have witnessed a massive increase in the volume of international financial capital flows among industrialized countries, and during the past decade international financial capital flows between developed and emerging markets have also increased dramatically.

The sharp increase in international financial flows among industrial countries during the past two decades is due to many factors. First, during the 1970s and 1980s, industrialized countries removed almost all exchange controls. This trend was facilitated by the Code of Liberalization of Capital Movements of the Organization for Economic Cooperation and Development and the European Union's Second Directive on Liberalization of Capital Movements. As a result, domestic and offshore markets became increasingly integrated. Just as important was the liberalization and deregulation of domestic markets. As recently as 1980, most industrial countries still imposed significant restrictions on the location of financial firms, on the types of financial businesses open to them, the interest that they could pay to depositors, and the types of lending that they could make.

By the early 1990s, most industrial countries had eliminated or greatly reduced the scope of these controls. They eliminated ceilings on lending and interest rates, and reduced bank reserve and portfolio investments requirements. This greatly increased the spectrum of financial instruments available and the types of hedging and position taking possible. The introduction of high-speed computers and the revolution in telecommunications, which lowered very significantly the costs of processing information and executing transactions, also greatly stimulated the flow of international financial capital. Furthermore, securitization greatly increased the share of financial claims and liabilities that are readily tradeable and the increasing institutionalization of investment activity sharply increased crossborder securities trade. All these developments led to massive increases in crossborder financial instruments and flows among industrial countries.

During the past decade, international financial flows between industrial and emerging countries have also increased sharply. This has been made possible by the partial liberalization of financial markets and crossborder financial transactions, as well as the gradual modernization and internationalization of the domestic banking system in many emerging markets in Asia and Latin America, and in Europe's transition economies. Capital markets in many developing countries are, as a result, becoming more closely integrated with capital markets in the rest of the world. To be sure, developing countries still retain many controls but every day new countries and currencies are added to the list of markets available for portfolio diversification.

For their part, investors from industrial countries have flocked to emerging markets in search of much higher returns (based on much higher growth rates in emerging markets) and for international portfolio diversification. In recent years, portfolio flows have assumed growing importance in Asia's emerging markets and have dominated Latin American inflows. The pull forces of higher returns were relatively more important in attracting financial capital to Asia, while the push forces of escaping low interest rates in industrial countries were relatively more important in portfolio inflows to Latin American emerging markets (Salvatore, 1998d).

4.2. International financial capital flows and international instability

The massive increase in international financial capital flows among industrial countries and between industrial and emerging market economies during the past two decades is generally acknowledged to have led to a more efficient allocation of world savings and investments and thus to greater global economic welfare. But along with this benefit came the risk of greater international financial instability from the quick and massive shifts of financial capital that often takes place among monetary centers in response to even small changes in underlying economic variables and "news". A financial crisis in one market can then quickly spread to other markets and could possibly lead to a global financial collapse.

This danger has become all the more realistic in view of the rapid growth of derivatives and the revolution in telecommunications. A major global economic crisis as a result of the 1987 worldwide stock market crash was prevented only by the immediate, appropriate, and concerted response of the world's major central banks. But the fact that the international financial system continued to function well in the face of a number of shocks such as the Mexican crisis, the failure of Barings, the trading losses of Daiwa and Sumitomo, the 1987 stock market crash, as well as the present financial crisis in East Asia does not justify complacency, especially in today's world, where the interdependence among international financial sectors and markets has become so complex as to defy the ability of regulators and the markets themselves to effectively discipline participants. For example, hedge funds and unregulated derivative subsidiaries of major investment houses often take huge speculative positions but fall outside the purview of both securities and bank regulators.

Increased global financial market integration can also lead to large exchange rate misalignments and overshooting. One of the most notorious examples of this was the gross overvaluation of the dollar during the 1981–1985 period and its subsequent large undervaluation in the early 1990s. Exchange rate misalignments and overshooting can then lead to massive international financial capital flows and magnified international financial instability. When it comes to emerging markets, increased global financial integration can lead to even greater instability, especially if inflows are of a short-term nature. The reason is that the pool of funds managed by major financial firms dwarfs the capitalization of most emerging stock markets, with the result that even small changes in investors sentiments can have dramatic effects on the stock market and the entire economies of emerging markets, as the 1994–95 Mexican crisis and the 1997–98 financial crisis in East Asia clearly demonstrated.

Global financial integration can also reduce the effectiveness of monetary policy. For example, by being able to borrow abroad, major corporations can easily circumvent a rise in interest rates engineered by the nation's monetary authorities as part of a restrictive monetary policy. This means that a bigger change in interest rates may now be required to provide a given effect on domestic spending. Global international financial integration also makes it more difficult to operate a fixed exchange rate system, as the European Community found out the hard way in 1992 and 1993. The increase in interest rates by Germany in 1991 and 1992 in order to fight inflationary pressures resulting from unification imposed unbearable pressure on other Community members such as Italy and England that were in deep recession, and led to a serious crisis of the European exchange rate mechanism.

In short, the present international financial system permits much less deviations (i.e., it requires a much higher degree of economic convergence) in underlying conditions, such as interest and inflation rates, among nations operating under a fixed exchange rate system (as the European Union did until the fall of 1992) than in the 1950s and 1960s. The exchange rate crisis in Europe also showed how futile even coordinated central bank intervention and capital controls become in the face of a massive speculative attack. On the other hand, flexible exchange rates in today's world of highly integrated capital markets can lead to large exchange rate overshooting and great financial market instability.

4.3. Dealing with international financial instability

There are several things that industrial and developing countries can do to reduce the international financial instability that results from the massive crossborder financial flows which have come to characterize today's international financial markets. One such policy to reduce the systemic risks arising from the use of derivatives is to follow the recommendations of the IMF to channel more of (the now mostly unregulated) over-the-counter (OTC) derivatives business to organized exchanges, where margin requirements and loss-sharing arrangements have gone a long way toward eliminating the danger that a large derivative loss by a major dealer might spill to other dealers in a domino effect that could result in the collapse of the entire derivatives and financial markets. The US Financial Accounting Standards Board (FASB) recommends that most of a company's derivatives transactions be recorded into its balance sheet. The Basle Committee recommends incorporating market risks from the use of derivatives into a risk-based capital standards for banks, while the Group of Thirty calls on financial firms to improve their market and credit risk management functions. All of these policies can be of some use in reducing international financial instability.

Another policy often advocated to reduce the financial instability that results from massive crossborder financial flows is to increase the scope and depth of international policy coordination among the leading industrial economic powers. It is true that countries should focus on getting their own economies in order and getting their macroeconomic policies right. There remains, however, an important role for international policy coordination to prevent the occurrence of massive crossborder financial flows that do not reflect economic fundamentals or grossly misaligned exchange rates or, if they do occur, to minimize their destabilizing impact on the economic and financial sectors of the nations involved.

Successful international policy coordination can be credited for greatly limiting the damage that resulted from the 1987 world stock market crash and for preventing the 1994-95 Mexican crisis from spreading to or having a lasting effect on other emerging markets. The IMF proposal to become the lender of last resort and to require nations, especially emerging markets, to provide better and more timely economic data on their economies in the aftermath of the Mexican crisis may be a useful first step in reducing international financial markets instability and encouraging more formal and lasting international macroeconomic policy coordination.

There are also policies that would clearly be wrong and should not be undertaken. One such a policy would be to encourage the perception that the government would bail out a firm in trouble or that the IMF would bail out a nation lacking economic discipline. Such a policy would only encourage the very undisciplined behavior that got the firm or country in trouble in the first place. Another policy that also seems inappropriate would be to restrict crossborder financial flows or "throwing sand in the wheels of international finance" to avoid or reduce international financial instability. First of all, such a policy can hardly be successful since money is fungible and financial operators can easily find ways to overcome the restrictions. Second, restricting financial markets often allows governments to pursue wrong or inconsistent economic policies much longer, thus imposing much greater adjustment costs on society when the adjustment finally and inevitably comes.

For example, when speculators attack a currency (such as the pound sterling in September 1992) they usually tend to have a good reason. They detect an inconsistency and they try to profit from it. If they are wrong they lose their bet. If they are right they can gain handsomely and in the process force a needed adjustment more quickly. Sometimes speculators are late in recognizing a problem (as in the case of the Mexican crisis). But we can expect governments to make even bigger mistakes—speculators after all are betting their own (and investors') money and have a much bigger incentive to get it right. In short, while speculators can be wrong, they are less likely to be so than governments and represent the best way that society has to evaluate a nation's economic conditions and policies. Restricting speculators and crossborder financial flows can only make matters worse later.

Thus, aside from directing more of the OTC derivatives business to organized markets, recording most of a company's derivatives transactions in its balance sheet, incorporating market risks from the use of derivatives into risk-based capital standards for banks, improving financial firms' market and credit risk management functions, and increasing international macroeconomic policy coordination—there is little else that can usefully be done to reduce the increased international financial instability that accompanies the massive increase in crossborder financial flows taking place in the world today. Restricting international financial capital flows is likely to be ineffective and counterproductive. In the final analysis, it can be said that some increase in financial instability may be the inevitable result of increased international financial integration and can be regarded as the cost to be paid for the much larger benefits that result from the growing integration of world financial markets (Eichengreen and Portes, 1996; Eichengreen, 1998; Salvatore, 1997b, 1998d).

Acknowledgment

I would like to thank the members of the Associazione Guido Carli for very helpful comments on an earlier draft and especially Michele Fratianni, Jacques Mélitz, and Paolo Savona.

References

Abdullah, F.A. and B.J. Shah (1995) "Emerging Patterns of Future Global Banking Competitiveness." *Multinational Business Review*, Fall.

Alesina, A. and L.H. Summers (1993) "Central Bank Independence and Macroeconomic Performance: Some Comparative Evidence." *Journal of Money, Credit, and Banking* 2.

Artis, M., M. Kohler, and J. Mélitz (1998) "Trade and the Number of the OCAs in the World." in this volume.

Baldassarri, M., C. Imbriani, and D. Salvatore (eds.) (1996) *The International System Between Integration and Neo-Protectionism*. London: Macmillan.

Banca D'Italia (1998) *Relazione Annuale*. Rome: Banca D'Italia.

Banca Nazionale del Lavoro (1996) "The European Monetary Union: The Problems of a Transition to a Single Currency." *BNL Quarterly Review*. special issue, March.

Barro, R. (1995) "Inflation and Economic Growth." *Bank of England Quarterly Bulletin*, May.

Bayoumi, T., B. Eichengreen, and J. Von Hagen (1997) "European Monetary Unification: Implications of Research for Policy, Implications of Policy for Research." *Open Economies Review*, Jan.

Bayoumi, T. and P. Masson (1994) "Fiscal Flows in the United States and Canada: Lessons for Monetary Union in Europe." CEPR Discussion Paper No. 1057.

Begg, D., F. Giavazzi, J. Von Hagen, and C. Wyplosz (1997) *EMU: Getting the End-Game Right*. London: Center for Economic Policy Research.

Berger, A.N., A.K. Kashyap, and J.M. Scalise (1995) "The Transformation of the US Banking Industry." *Brookings Papers on Economic Activity* 2.

Biasco, S. (1987) "Currency Cycles and the International Economy." *BNL Quarterly Review* 1.

Biasco, S. (1996) "L'Economia Internazionale negli Anni Ottanta: Rottura e Continuita." *Storia della Repubblica Italiana*, Volume Terzo, Giulio Einaudi Editore.

BIS (1993, 1996, 1997a, 1998) *Annual Report*. Basle, BIS.

BIS (1997b) *International Banking and Financial Market Developments*. Basle, BIS.

BIS (1994) *Macroeconomic and Monetary Policy Issues Raised by the Growth of Derivatives Markets*. Basle, BIS.

Buiter, W.H., G.M. Corsetti, and P. Pesenti (1998) "Interpreting the ERM Crisis: Country Specific and Systemic Issues." *Princeton Studies in International Finance*, vol. 84, March.

Bini-Smaghi, L. and S. Vori (1993) *Rating the EC as an Optimal Currency Area*. Temi di Discussione No. 187, Roma: Banca d'Italia.

Blinder, A.S. (1996) "The Role of the Dollar as an International Currency." *Eastern Economic Journal*, Spring.

Bloomfield, A.I. (1959) *Monetary Policy under the International Gold Standard: 1880–1914*. New York: Federal Reserve Bank.

Bordo, M.D. and B. Eichengreen (eds.) (1993) *A Retrospective on the Bretton Woods System.* Chicago: University of Chicago Press.

Bretton Woods Commission (1994) *Bretton Woods: Looking to the Future*. Washington, D.C.: Bretton Woods Commission.

Bryant, R.C. (1995) *International Coordination of National Stabilization Policies*. Washington, D.C.: The Brooking Institution.

Calvo, G. and E.G. Mendoza (1996) "Mexico's Balance of Payments Crisis: A Chronicle of a Death Foretold." *Journal of International Economics*, Nov.

Canzoneri, M.B. and C.A. Rogers (1980) "Is the European Community an Optimal Currency Area? Optimal Taxation Versus the Costs of Multiple Currencies." *American Economic Review*, March.

Capie, F. and G. Wood (eds.) (1996) *Monetary Economics in the 1990s*.

Capie, F., C. Goodhart, and S. Fisher (1994) *The Future of Central Banking*. Cambridge: Cambridge University Press.

Capie, F. (1998) "Monetary Unions in Historical Perspective: What Future for the Euro in the International Financial System." this volume.

Carli, G. et al. (1972) *A Debate on the Eurodollar Market*. Luigi Einaudi, Quaderni di Ricerche 11.

Ciampi, C.A. (1996) "Enhancing European Competitiveness." *Banca Nazionale del Lavoro Quarterly Review* 197.
Ciocca, P. (1997) "Memoria sull'Attuazione del Trattato di Maastricht da Parte delle Banche Centrali." Roma: Banca d'Italia, June.
Ciocca, P. (1987) *Money and the Economy: Central Bankers' View.* New York: St. Martin.
Ciocca, P. and G. Nardozzi (1996) *The High Price of Money*. New York: St. Martin.
Cohen, B. (1996) "The Political Economy of Currency Regions." In E. Mansfield and H. Milner (eds.), *The Political Economy of Economic Regionalism*. New York: Columbia University Press.
Cooper, R.N. (1984) "A Monetary System for the Future." *Foreign Affairs*, Fall.
Corden, M. (1994) *Economic Policy, Exchange Rates, and the International System.* Chicago: University of Chicago Press.
Cukierman, A. (1992) *Central Bank Strategy, Credibility, and Independence.* Cambridge, MA: MIT Press.
Cukierman, A. et al. (1992) "Central Bank Independence, Growth, Investment, and Real Rate." *Carnegie Rochester Conference Series on Public Policy* 3.
Dal Bosco, E. (1993) *L'Economia Mondiale in Transformazione*. Bologna: Il Mulino.
Dal Bosco, E. (1997) "L'FMI: Da Manager Globale a Poliziotto Finanziario." *Giano*, No. 25.
Dal Bosco, E. (1998) "Central Banks' Management of Foreign Exchange Reserves." in this volume.
Davidson, P. (1982) *International Money and the Real World*. New York: Wiley.
De Cecco, M. (1971) *Economia e Finanza Internazionale dal 1890 and 1914*. Bari: Laterza.
De Grauwe, P. (1994) "Towards European Monetary Union Without the EMS." *Economic Policy* 1.
DeVries, M.G. (1996) "The International Monetary Fund and the International Monetary System." In M. Fratianni, D. Salvatore, and J. Von Hagen (eds.), *Handbook of Macroeconomic Policy in Open Economies*. Westport, CT: Greenwood Press.
Dornbusch, R. (1996) "Euro Phantasies." *Foreign Affairs*, Sept.–Oct.
Dornbusch, R., C. Favero, and G. Giavazzi (1998) "Immediate Challenges for the European Central Bank." *Economic Policy*, April.
Dornbusch, R. and J. Frankel (1987) "The Flexible Exchange Rate System: Experience and Alternatives." Working Paper No. 2464, Cambridge, MA: National Bureau of Economic Research.
Eichengreen, B. (1991) "Is Europe an Optimum Currency Area?" NBER Working Paper No. 3579, Cambridge, MA: National Bureau of Economic Research.
Eichengreen, B. (1992) *Gold Fetters: The Gold Standard and the Great Depression: 1919–1939.* New York: Oxford University Press.
Eichengreen, B. (1993) "European Monetary Unification." *Journal of Economic Literature*, June.
Eichengreen, B. (1994) *International Monetary Arrangements for the 21st Century.* Washington, D.C.: Brookings.
Eichengreen, B. (1996a) *A More Perfect Union? The Logic of Economic Integration*. Essays in International Finance, vol. 198, Princeton, NJ: Princeton University.
Eichengreen, B. (1996b) *Globalizing Capital.* Essays in International Finance, vol. 200, Princeton, NJ: Princeton University.
Eichengreen, B. and R. Portes (1996) "Managing the Next Mexico." In P.B. Kenen et al. (eds.), *From Halifax to Lyons: What Has Been Done About Crisis Management*? Essays in International Finance, vol. 200, Princeton, NJ: Princeton University.
Eichengreen, B. (1998) "Exchange Rate Stability and Financial Stability." in this volume.
Emerson, M. (1991) "The Transformation of Trade and Monetary Regimes in Europe." In *Symposium on Policy Implications of Trade and Currency Zones*, Kansas City: Federal Reserve Bank of Kansas City.
European Commission (1990) "One Market, One Money." *European Economy*.
European Monetary Institute (1997) *The Single Monetary Policy in Stage Three*. Frankfurt: Kern & Birner GnbH Co.
Fatemi, K. and D. Salvatore (1993) *Foreign Exchange Issues, Capital Markets, and International Banking in the 1990s.* Washington, D.C.: Francis & Taylor.
Fazio, A. (1996) *In Praise of Monetary Stability*. Rome: Banca d'Italia.

Fazio, A. (1997) *Sviluppo Economico e Mercato Globale*. Rome; Banca d'Italia.

Feldstein, M. (1991) "Does One Market Require One Money?" In *Symposium on Policy Implications of Trade and Currency Zones*, Kansas City: Federal Reserve Bank.

Fisher, S. (1994) "Modern Central Banking." In F. Capie et al. (eds.), *The Future of Central Banking*, Cambridge: Cambridge University Press.

Flood, R. and N. Marion (1997) "Speculative Attacks: Fundamentals and Self-Fulfilling Prophesies." Working Paper No. 5789, Cambridge, MA: National Bureau of Economic Research.

Frankel, J. (1995) "Still the Lingua Franca: The Exaggerated Death of the Dollar." *Foreign Affairs*.

Frankel, A.B. and J.D. Montgomery (1991) "Financial Structure: An International Perspective." *Brookings Papers on Economic Activity* 1.

Frankel, J. and S. Phillips (1991) "The European Monetary System: Credible at Last?" Working Paper No. 3819. Cambridge, MA: National Bureau of Economic Research.

Frankel, J. and K. Rockett (1988) "International Macroeconomic Policy Coordination When Policy Makers Do Not Agree on the Model." *American Economic Review*, Jan.

Frankel, J. and A.K. Rose (1996) "Currency Crashes in Emerging Markets: An Empirical Treatment." *Journal of International Economics*, Nov.

Fratianni, M. (1992) "Dominant and Dependent Currencies." In P. Newman, M. Milgate, and J. Eatwell (eds.), *The New Palgrave Dictionary of Money and Finance*, vol. I, New York: Macmillan Press.

Fratianni, M. (1998) "Maxi vs. Mini EMU: The Political Economy of Stage II." *The Columbia Journal of European Law*, Spring.

Fratianni, M. and A. Hauskrecht (1998) "From the Gold Standard to a Bipolar Monetary System." this volume.

Fratianni, M., A. Hauskrecht, and A. Maccario (1998) "Dominant Currencies and the Future of the Euro." this volume.

Fratianni, M. and D. Salvatore (eds.) (1993) *Handbook of Monetary Policies in Developed Countries*. Amsterdam: North-Holland.

Fratianni, M., D. Salvatore, and J. Von Hagen (eds.) (1997) *Handbook of Macroeconomic Policies in Open Economies.* Westport CT.: Greenwood Press.

Fratianni, M. and P. Savona (1972) *La Liquidita' Internazionale—Proposta per la Redifinizione del Problema*. Bologna: Il Mulino.

Fratianni, M. and F. Spinelli (1997) *A Monetary History of Italy.* New York: Cambridge University Press.

Fratianni, M. and J. Von Hagen (1992) *The European Monetary System and European Monetary Union.* Boulder, CO: Westview Press.

Frenkel, J., M. Golstein, and P.R. Masson (1991) *Characteristics of a Successful Exchange Rate System.* IMF Occasional Paper 82, Washington, D.C.: IMF.

Giavazzi, F. and A. Giovannini (eds.) (1989) *Limiting Exchange Rate Flexibility: The European Monetary System.* Cambridge, MA: MIT Press.

Goldstein, M. (1995) *The Exchange Rate System and the IMF: A Modest Agenda.* Washington, D.C.: Institute for International Economics.

Goldstein, M. and C. Reinhart (1997) *Forecasting Financial Crises: Early Warning Signals for Emerging Markets.* Washington, D.C.: Institute for International Economics.

Goodhart, C. and F. Capie (1995) "Central Banks, Macro Policy and the Financial System: The Nineteenth and Twentieth Century." *Financial History Review*, Oct.

Gray, P.H. (1996) "The Ongoing Weakening of the International Financial System." *BNL Quarterly Review* 197.

Grilli, V., D. Masciandaro, and G. Tabellini (1991) "Political and Monetary Institutions and Public Financial Policies in Industrial Countries." *Economic Policy* 3.

Group of Thirty (1993) *Derivatives: Practices and Principles.* Washington, D.C.: Group of Thirty.

Hamada, K. and M. Kawai (1997) "Strategic Approaches to International Policy Coordination: Theoretical Developments." In M. Fratianni., D. Salvatore., and J. Von Hagen (eds.), *Handbook of Macroeconomic Policies in Open Economies*, chap. 4, Westport, CT: Greenwood Press.

Hamada, K. (1998) "The Choice of International Monetary Regimes in a Context of Repeated Games." in this volume.

Hausler, G. (1996) *Derivatives and Monetary Policy.* Washington, D.C.: Group of Thirty.

Henning, C.R. (1997) *Cooperating with Europe's Monetary Union.* Washington, D.C.: Institute for International Economics.

Hume, D. (1898), "Of the Balance of Trade." *Essays, Moral, Political and Literary*, vol. 1, London: Longmans Green.

IMF (1984) *Exchange Rate Volatility and World Trade.* Washington, D.C.: IMF.

IMF (1986) *Interim Committee Report.* Washington, D.C.: IMF.

IMF (1995) *International Capital Markets: Developments, Prospects, and Policy Issues*. Washington, D.C.: IMF.

IMF (1996a) *International Capital Markets: Developments, Prospects, and Policy Issues*. Washington, D.C.: IMF.

IMF (1996b) "Standards for the Dissemination by Countries of Economic and Financial Statistics." Discussion Draft prepared by a staff team, Washington, D.C.: IMF.

IMF (1996c) *International Financial Statistics*. Washington, D.C.: IMF.

IMF (1997a) *International Capital Markets: Developments, Prospects, and Key Policy Issues*. Washington, D.C.: IMF.

IMF (1998a) *Annual Report*. Washington, D.C.: IMF.

IMF (1998b) *International Financial Statistics*. Washington, D.C.: IMF.

IMF (1998c) *World Economic Outlook*. Washington, D.C.: IMF.

Kaminsky, G., S. Lizondo, and C.M. Reinhart (1998) *Leading Indicators of Currency Crisis*. IMF Staff Papers, Spring.

Kenen, P.B. (ed.) (1994) *Managing the World Economy: Fifty Years After Bretton Woods*. Washington, D.C.: Institute for International Economics.

Kenen, P.B. (1995) *Economic and Monetary Union in Europe*. New York: Cambridge University Press.

Kenen, P.B. (ed.) (1996) *Making EMU Happen—Problems and Proposals: A Symposium*. Essays in International Finance, vol. 199, Princeton, NJ: Princeton University.

Kenen, P.B. et al. (eds.) *From Halifax to Lyons: What Has Been Done About Crisis Management?* Essays in International Finance, vol. 200, Princeton, NJ: Princeton University.

Kindleberger, C.P. (1986) "International Public Goods Without International Government." *American Economic Review*, Jan.

Krugman, P.R. (1989) *Exchange Rate Instability.* Cambridge, MA: The MIT Press.

Krugman, P.R. (1984) "The International Role of the Dollar: Theory and Prospect." In J. Bilson and R. Marston (eds.), *Exchange Rate Theory and Practice*. Chicago: University of Chicago Press.

Laidler, D.E.W. (1991) "One Market, One Money? Well, Maybe...Sometimes..." In *Symposium on Policy Implications of Trade and Currency Zones.* Kansas City: Federal Reserve Bank of Kansas City.

MacDonald, R. and M.P. Taylor (1991) "Exchange Rates, Policy Convergence, and the European Monetary System." *Review of Economics and Statistics*, Aug.

Marcuzzo, M.C. and A. Rosselli (1991) *Ricardo and the Gold Standard.* London: Macmillan.

Marston, R.C. (1996) *International Financial Integration*. New York: Cambridge University Press.

Masera, F and P. Savona (1972) "Outlines of a Common Policy for Intervention on the Eurocurrency Market." Debate on the Eurodollar Market, Quaderni di Ricerca No. 11, Roma: Ente Einaudi.

Masson, P. and B.G. Turbelbum (1997) "Characteristics of the Euro, the Demand for Reserves, and Policy Coordination under EMU." Working Paper 97/58, Washington, D.C.: IMF.

Masson, P.R. (1995) "Gaining and Losing EMR Credibility: The Case of the United Kingdom." *Economic Journal*, May.

McKibbin, W. (1997) "Empirical Evidence on International Economic Policy Coordination." Fratianni M., D. Salvatore, and J. Von Hagen (eds.), *Handbook of Macroeconomic Policies in Open Economies*, chap. 5, Westport, CT.: Greenwood Press.

McKinnon, R.I. (1963) "Optimum Currency Areas." *American Economic Review*, Sept.

McKinnon, R.I. (1984) *An International Standard for Monetary Stabilization.* Washington, D.C.: Institute for International Economics.

McKinnon, R.I. (1988) "Monetary and Exchange Rate Policies for International Financial Stability: A Proposal." *Journal of Economic Perspectives*, Winter.

McKinnon, R.I. (1993) "International Money in Historical Perspective." *Journal of Economic Literature*, March.

McKinnon, R.I. (1996) *The Rules of the Game: International Money and Exchange Rates.* Cambridge, MA: MIT Press.

Melitz, J. (1995) "The Current Impasse in Research in Optimum Currency Areas." *European Economic Review*, April.

Melitz, J. (1996) "The Theory of Optimum Currency Areas, Trade Adjustment and Trade." *Open Economies Review*, April.

Melitz, J. (1997) "The Evidence About the Costs and Benefits of EMU." Background Report for the Swedish Government Commission on EMU. Forthcoming in *Swedish Economic Policy Review.*

Melitz, J. and S. Vori (1993) "National Insurance Against Unevenly Distributed Shocks in a European Monetary Union." *Richerches Economiques de Louvain*, 59.

Melitz, J. and A. Weber (1996) "The Benefits/Costs of a Common Monetary Policy in France and Germany and Possible Lessons for Monetary Union." CEPR Discussion Paper No. 1374, April.

Michaely, M. (1968) *Balance-of-Payments Adjustment Policies*. New York: National Bureau of Economic Research.

Miller, M.H. and J. Williamson (1987) *Targets and Indicators: A Blueprint for the International Coordination of Economic Policy.* Washington, D.C: Institute for International Economics.

Milner, H.V. (1997) "The Political Economy of International Policy Coordination." In M. Fratianni, D. Salvatore, and J. Von Hagen (eds.), *Handbook of Macroeconomic Policies in Open Economies*, Westport, CT.: Greenwood Press.

Mishkin, F.S. (1997) "Understanding Financial Crises: A Developing Country Perspective." In *Annual World Conference on Development Economics*, Washington, D.C.: World Bank.

Minsky, H. (1982) *Can It Happen Again?* Armonk, New York: Sharpe.

Mundell, R. (1961) "The Theory of Optimum Currency Areas." *American Economic Review*, Sept.

Mundell, R. (1983) "International Monetary Options." *The Cato Journal*, Spring.

Nurkse, R. (1944) *International Currency Experience*. Princeton, NJ: League of Nations.

Obstfeld, M. (1998) "The Global Capital Market: Benefactor or Menace?" NBER Working Paper No. 6559.

OECD (1986) *Flexibility in the Labor Market*. Paris, OECD.

OECD (1997) *Financial Market Trends.* Paris, OECD, June.

Pappadia, F. and C. Santini (1998) *La Banca Centrale Europea*, Bologna: Il Mulino.

Park, K.H. and W.V. Agtmael (1993) *The World's Emerging Stock Markets*. Chicago: Probus Publishing Company.

Portes, R. (1993) "The EMS and EMU After the Fall." *The World Economy*, No. 1.

Portes, R. and H. Rey (1998) "The Emergence of the Euro as an International Currency." In D. Beggs, J. von Hagen, C. Wyploz, and K.F. Zimmermann (eds.), *EMU: Prospects and Challenges for the Euro*. Oxford: Blackwell.

Rogoff, K. (1985) "The Optimal Degree of Commitment to an Intermediate Monetary Target." *Quarterly Journal of Economics*, Nov.

Roselli, A. (1995) *La Finanza Americana tra gli Anni Ottanta e Novanta: Instabilita' e Riforme*. Bari: Laterza.

Sala-i-Martin, X. and J. Sachs (1991) "Fiscal Federalism and Optimal Currency Areas: Evidence for Europe from the United States." NBER Working Paper No. 3855, National Bureau of Economic Research.

Sachs, J. (ed.) (1989) *Developing Country Debt and Economic Performance*. Cambridge, MA.: MIT Press.

Salvatore, D. (1989) "Concepts for a New International Trade and Financial Order." In G. Fink (ed.), *The World Economy and the East*. Vienna and New York: Springer-Verlag.
Salvatore, D. (ed.) (1993) *The New Protectionist Threat to World Welfare.* Cambridge: Cambridge University Press.
Salvatore, D. (1994) "The International Monetary System: Past, Present, and Future." *Fordham Law Review*, May.
Salvatore, D. (1996) "The European Monetary System: Crisis and Future." *Open Economies Review*, Dec.
Salvatore, D. (1997a) "The Common Unresolved Problem with the EMS and EMU." *American Economic Review*, May.
Salvatore, D. (1997b) "Capital Flows, Current Account Deficits, and Financial crises in Emerging Market Economies." *International Trade Journal*, March.
Salvatore, D. (1998a) *International Economics*, 6th edition, Upper Saddle River, NJ: Prentice-Hall.
Salvatore, D. (1998b) "Europe's Structural and Competitiveness Problems and the Euro." *The World Economy*, March.
Salvatore, D. (1998c) "How Can Exchange Rate Arrangements Be Made To Work Better." In S. Rehman (ed.), *The Quest for Exchange Rate Stability in the Next Millenium*. Greenwich, Connecticut: JAI Press.
Salvatore D. (1998d) *La Finanza Internazionale sul Finire del Secolo*. Arezzo: Banca dell'Etruria e Lazio.
Sarel, M. (1996) "Non-linear Effects of Inflation on Economic Growth." Staff Papers, International Monetary Fund, vol. 43, March.
Savona, P. (1995) *Il Nuovo Contratto Sociale per gli Italiani e la Grande Svolta dello Sviluppo*, Documento dei Trenta, Milano, Libri Scheiwiller.
Savona, P. (1996) *Gli Enigmi dell'Economia*, Milano, Arnaldo Mondadori.
Savona, P. and A. Maccario (1998) "On the Relation between Money and Derivatives and its Application to the International Monetary Market." in this volume.
Secchi, C. (1998) *Verso L'Euro*, Venezia, Marsilio Editori. Milano: Etas Libri.
Spinelli, F. and M. Vassalli (1996) "Il Costituzionalismo Monetario e Fiscale nel Mondo." *Studi e Note di Economia* 1.
Taussig, F.W. (1927) *International Trade*. New York: Macmillan.
Tavlas, G.S. (1991) *On the International Use of Currencies: The Case of Deutsche Mark.* Essays in International Finance, vol. 181, Princeton, NJ: International Finance Section, Princeton University.
Tavlas, G.S. (1993) "The 'New' Theory of Optimum Currency Areas." *The World Economy* 2.
Tavlas, G.S. (1994) "The Theory of Monetary Integration." *Open Economies Review*, Jan.
Tavlas, G.S. (1997) "The International Use of the U.S. Dollar: An Optimum Currency Area Perspective." *The World Economy*, Forthcoming.
Tavlas, G.S. and Y. Oseki (1992) *The Internationalization of Currencies: An Appraisal of the Japanese Yen*, Occasional Paper 90, Washington, D.C.: IMF, January.
The Economist (1996) "International Banking." *The Economist*, April, 1–38.
Tobin, J. (1978) "A Proposal for International Monetary Reform." *Eastern Economic Journal*, July/Oct.
Tobin, J. (1996) "A Currency Transaction Tax, Why and How." *Open Economy Review*, Dec.
Triffin, R. (1961) *Gold and the Dollar Crisis*. New Haven: Yale University Press.
Von Hagen, J. (1997) "Monetary Policy and Institutions in the EMU." *Swedish Economic Policy Review*, vol. 4.
Von Hagen, J. and I. Fender (1998) "Central Bank Policy in a More Perfect Financial System." in this volume.
Walsh, C. (1995) "Optimal Contracts for Central Bankers." *American Economic Review*, March.
Williamson, J. (1986) "Target Zones and the Management of the Dollar." *Brookings Papers on Economic Activity* 1.
World Bank (1996a) *Financial Flows and the Developing Countries*. Washington, D.C.: World Bank.

World Bank (1996b) *Global Economic Prospects and the Developing Countries*. Washington, D.C.: World Bank.
World Bank (1996c) *World Development Report.* Washington, D.C.: World Bank.
World Bank (1997, 1998) *World Development Report*. Washington, D.C.: World Bank.
Zimmerman, G.C. (1995) "Implementing the Single Banking Market in Europe." *Federal Reserve Bank of San Francisco Economic Review* 3.

Open economies review **9:S1** 417–445 (1998)

The Choice of International Monetary Regimes in a Context of Repeated Games

KOICHI HAMADA
Economic Growth Center, Yale University, P.O. Box 208269, New Haven, CT 06520-8269

Key words: international monetary regime, system, game theory, and collective action

JEL Classification Numbers: C70, E42

Abstract

A game theoretic and incentive approach is used to explain an international monetary regime. Decisions concerning a fixed exchange rate regime are difficult because they involve cooperation among participants, but decisions concerning defections from a fixed exchange rate regime are relatively easy because they are taken unilaterally. This may explain the difficulties for the completion of Economic and Monetary Union (EMU) in Europe well as the instability recently observed in the quasi-fixed exchange regimes of the Asian countries. EMU is now in full force. The perception of political benefits by national leaders has been the driving force of currency unification in Europe. The cost of a monetary union is the loss of monetary control by each participating nation. If countries cannot contain their desire to deviate from the common monetary expansion, then the currency could potentially be under speculative attack. After January 1, 1999, theoretically each EMU country can no longer deviate from the common norm; but the question remains how to implement this mode of conduct. Even the country in the center, Germany, may find a cost associated with the loss of its leadership role.

Introduction

When one discusses the topic of the choice of international monetary regimes, the question usually arises as to what kind of international monetary regime is desirable for the participating countries and for the system as a whole. This question is an economic one in the sense that it is concerned with the economic mechanism of a regime. It is also a question of a normative nature, or mechanism design, in the sense that it asks which monetary system should be adopted for the world. By the same token, on a regional scale, one asks what should be the ideal size and operation of a currency union?

One seldom asks, however, under what conditions a monetary union is established as a result of a political-economic choice of participating nations. Further, under what conditions a reform of an international regime is achieved through incentives of national governments is another consideration which is often ignored. These are political-economic rather than purely economic questions, and they are positive rather than normative. They are not concerned with what monetary regimes or currency arrangements are desirable or optimal but with what regimes or monetary unions are likely to be realized if we consider the political incentives of (potentially) participating nations. This study focuses on political-economic and positive aspects of monetary integration and regime choices.

Instead of studying what the benefits will be when a monetary union is achieved, we ask under what circumstances economic agents are motivated to join such a union. We also ask under what circumstances other countries in the rest of the world are affected by the formation of a new monetary union. The study thus covers the incentive structures for European countries, countries that will be left behind and non-European countries. It examines the question of motivation for the countries in the world to strive for a more basic monetary reform like a single currency, the gold standard or independent flexible exchange rates.

Methodologically, most of the approaches to international monetary regime have been of a "mechanism design" type that study how to construct a system that works best for all participants. Here we follow the calculus of participation approach and ask if there are sufficient incentives for nations or governments to participate in the arrangement. Unless there are incentives for participating in a joint action, the plan is "pie in the sky" (or a "painted rice cake" as Japanese say). In the Aesop fable of the cat and mice, the mice think that the best solution is to put a bell around the cat's neck, but the real problem is who dares to do the job! One can conceive of the ideal reform plans for an international monetary arrangement, but unless nations are motivated to agree on the system, the arrangement will never materialize. Indeed, the process of European monetary integration is a good illustration of how these political and economic factors interact in the process of planning for and realizing monetary integration.

Each nation has a minimum reservation utility below which it does not wish to participate in a joint action. In the language of game theory, each nation has to satisfy the individual "national" rationality. In an uncertain world, the incentive compatibility has to be analyzed, but in this paper we abstract from the element of strategic uncertainty.

In reality, a national government consists of various groups that have differences of opinions and conflicting interests and stays in power by the balance of conflicting opinions. Thus, negotiators and governments conduct negotiations subject to domestic political constraints. The two-level game theory emphasizes that negotiators can use only limited options in the presence of domestic conflicts. The fact that they are bound, however, may not always be disadvantageous: the precommitment to certain actions may be advantageous, as it was for tightly bound Ulysses when he heard the Sirens.

The process of agreeing on a regime and playing by the rules of that agreement was conceived as a two-stage game (Hamada, 1985). The first stage is a (sub)game of choosing an international regime and the second stage is a (sub)game of policy interplays. Here one can apply the principle of backward induction. If there is a reasonable policy outcome for each policy game under a given regime, then one can solve, by backward induction, the game of choosing an international regime. Only when the outcomes of the policy game are credible, would the game of choosing a regime be equivalent to the choice among these outcomes. If one restricts the equilibria to Nash equilibria, the requirement will be essentially that of subgame perfectness.

Similar reasoning has already been used in international economics and in the history of institution building. Matsuyama et al. (1993) utilize the biological game theory to analyze the emerging process of an international currency or currencies. A crucial role is played by the frequency or the density of trade. Greif (1991) and Greif et al. (1994) developed persuasive accounts of historical events where trade opportunities create incentive compatible trade patterns by guilds or coordinating institutions in repeated game settings. This approach does not rely on the infinite horizon cherished by biological game theory; rather, it is closely related to the concept of a regime for which common knowledge and expectations by players are essential ingredients. Bagwell and Staiger (1990, 1997) analyze the time pattern of the benefit-cost structure of a collective action and institution building like the World Trade Organization and the willingness to commit to or to defect from a cooperative action. This paper differs from Matsuyama et al. in that it focuses on the incentive for a political rather than individual decision process. In contrast to Greif and Bagwell and Staiger, the paper is concerned with international monetary regimes rather than trade related institutions.

The plan of this paper is as follows: In Section 1, we review the meaning of a "regime" defined by economists and political scientists. Then we describe the characteristics of the fixed exchange rate regime, the flexible exchange rate regime and many exchange regimes that lie in between. The process of European Monetary Unification (EMU) can be regarded as a process going from the flexible to the fixed type of regime and eventually to a single currency regime. We discuss the benefits and costs that those regimes provide to participating nations and the time profile of these benefits and costs.

In Section 2, we develop a pure theory of regime choice in a dynamic game framework. We stress the "once and for all" nature of the regime choice, the repetitive nature of policy interactions that may lead to cooperation, and the role of the end-game or escape from a regime. In the theoretical sense, choosing a monetary regime is like entering into an incomplete contract. In Section 3, we discuss the role of international political leadership and its effectiveness in coordinating a perception of the regime as well as in facilitating side payments.

In Section 4 we apply our tools to understand why some attempts at monetary integration have succeeded and others have failed in the past, and why an international regime was agreed to by participants and later collapsed. This is a brief sketch of historical events; Capie (1998) provides a more detailed account of these events. We show a striking contrast between the incentives for participants for agreeing on a relatively fixed exchange rate regime and the incentives for participants to defect from the fixed exchange rate regime to floating rates.

In the concluding section we ask if our analysis can add anything to our prediction on the future of EMU and the future of the international monetary system.

1. Benefits and costs of adopting alternative monetary regimes

Let us start with the meaning of "regime." Cooper (1975) defines a monetary regime as a particular set of rules and conventions governing monetary and financial relations between countries. The meaning of regime is broader than the meaning of system, the latter implying consistent rules and conventions. In fact, the existing regime of floating exchange rates can be properly named as "nonsystem" (Corden, 1983). Rules or conventions in an international regime may allow considerable freedom of action by participating agents or countries. On the other hand, "regime" is distinguished from "agreement," because one does not regard a once-and-for-all ad hoc international agreement as a regime. The words "regime" and "rules" or "conventions" suggest a situation where agents themselves interact repeatedly following some specific patterns of behavior. Therefore, the analysis of a regime possesses a strong bearing on the discussion of repeated plays, commitment to rules and reputation building that are popular in recent game-theoretic literature.

Some political scientists define regime in a slightly different fashion. Many authors in Krasner (1982) take a consensus view: A regime is "a set of implicit or explicit principles, names, rules, and decision-making procedures around which actors' expectations converge in a given area of international relations." Here principles are defined as "beliefs of fact, causations, and rectitude." Norms are "specific prescriptions or proscriptions for action." Decision-making procedures are "prevailing practices for making and implementing collective choice" (Krasner, 1982, p. 2).

The latter half of the above definition by Krasner suggests the importance of expectations held by actors involved in a particular regime. In a sense, a regime describes a situation where expectations are more or less self-fulfilling. I find Cooper's definition to be comprehensive enough and useful for most analytical purposes. It is worth noting, however, that credible expectations held by actors and the creation of common knowledge can be important ingredients of a stable regime.[1]

In order to address the question of regime choices within a simple game theory framework, one has to specify the rules of the game, the set of players, feasible strategies, and pay-offs to players. Often, it is difficult to distinguish the game of choice of rules from policy interactions under a set of given rules. But the following are the basic features of various international monetary regimes. Most regimes can be roughly, if not linearly, ordered as combinations of the two port-type pure regimes, the fixed exchange rate regime and the flexible exchange rate regime.

1.1. Single money

1.1.1. A unified money with a single government. A single currency circulates in a region. Since the government is also unified, differences in fiscal policy can be neglected. More importantly, people believe that this currency area will never be divided again. For example, after German monetary unification, Germans trusted in the irrevocable "exchange rate" between the D-Mark and the O-Mark again. In this regime, in general, the fixed parity has high credibility, and the exit option is out of the question as long as the political unity persists.

1.1.2. A unified money with multiple governments. This is the situation that best describes EMU. Each participating nation retains the right to exit the union, and the exit option is conceptually possible. But, in practice, to leave a currency union where a single money circulates is extremely difficult. This adds to the credibility of the continuation of the currency union.

1.2. Fixed exchange rates

1.2.1. Metallic and commodity standards. Here a metal or commodities are used as an anchor for keeping the fixed exchange parities among currencies. Because of the species flow mechanism, coordination of monetary policy is supposed to function automatically. In this regime, however, the credibility of the constancy of parities is not absolute. History abounds with examples where credibility for the parities eroded, and where governments betrayed the expectation of the public on the fixed parity.

1.2.2. Fixed exchange rates by political commitment. Governments can announce the fixity of exchange rates. Whether the public believes in the endurance of the fixed exchange rates depends on many economic and political factors. Europe, in 1998, can be said to be in this situation.

1.2.3. The adjustable peg (Bretton Woods) regime. This is a variant of Section 1.2.2. The major features of this system were as follows: Its participants agree on the regime in the form of an IMF Charter. The IMF was created as an institution to oversee the rules of the game. Gold played the role of anchor for the fixed parity initially but later lost its importance. Most notably, there was an escape clause in the system. Participants could change the parity if they could demonstrate "fundamental disequilibrium," a phrase that caused lots of policy controversies and academic discussions but was never defined clearly by the IMF.

There are several regimes between the pure regimes of fixed and flexible exchange rates.

1.3. Eclectic regimes

The following regimes fall in the spectrum between the fixed and the flexible exchange rate regime, though the degree of rate "flexibility" may not be exactly ordered as shown below.

1.3.1. The wider band system. Under this regime, the government intervenes soon after the exchange rate deviates from the central parity. The wider the band in which exchange rates can fluctuate, the more the system behaves like a flexible rate system.

1.3.2. The crawling-peg system and snakes. Under this regime monetary authorities intervene in the exchange market to smooth exchange rate movement. Fixed parities do not persist and exchange rates adjust but not necessarily to equate the supply and the demand in the exchange market. Recent Asian financial crises took place in countries that adopted the crawling peg system vis-à-vis the U.S. dollar.

1.3.3. Target zones. In this regime there is an explicit or implicit target zone, within which monetary authorities attempt to contain the exchange rate. It is documented (Funabashi, 1988) that key industrial countries made an effort to stabilize exchange rates without announcing the exact ranges of the zones in several occasions after the Plaza Accord.

1.3.4. Exchange rates coordination. Under the floating regime, monetary authorities can cooperate to keep exchange rates in a certain range, or a zone. Naturally, joint interventions are more effective than unilateral interventions. As shown in Hamada (1985), the fixed exchange rate necessitates, at least partially, exchange rate coordination by the nature of its rule. The need for, as well as the benefit from, coordination is limited. The benefits come only when there is a short-term interdependence due to beggar-thy-neighbor effects, as analyzed by Mundell (1968) and Dornbusch (1976). Often, exchange rate coordination under flexible rates results in denying the very merit of the flexible exchange rate regime.

1.3.5. Managed float. Monetary authorities tend to exercise more discretion under this regime than under target zones. The comments on the system of coordinated exchange rates apply to this system as well.

1.4. *Pure flexible rates*

Here monetary authorities do not intervene in the exchange market in principle. We may note that the shift from any variants of fixed exchange rates, with the possible exception of the single money, to this system is not difficult. The exit option to flexible rates is always available. On the other hand, the exit from flexible rates, a nonsystem, to the fixed rates system or its variants always requires a concerted collective action.

It seems appropriate here to consider the nature of monetary union in terms of the above clarification of regimes (Hamada and Porteous, 1992). The term "monetary integration" or "monetary unification" encompasses varying degrees of integration; it is usually used for a group of countries and not for all countries of the world. In the weakest sense, monetary integration implies the linking of national currencies to fixed parities accompanied by a narrowing or vanishing band of exchange without common reserves or a common central bank. This is what Corden (1972) called the pseudo-exchange rate union. The coordination of economic policies, particularly monetary policies, is needed to prevent disequilibria in the balance of payments. The degree of monetary integration is enhanced by the establishment of public confidence in the irrevocable nature of the fixed exchange parities, accompanied by full convertibility between currencies for capital and current account transactions. This confidence normally emerges only after a substantial transition period during which de facto fixed exchange parities are successfully maintained, or after some kind of political unification. However, full monetary integration or unification is only realized when a common currency issued by a single central bank circulates in the area of the monetary union. Now we turn to the basic benefits and costs of attempting monetary integration.

The benefits from monetary integration are microeconomic benefits: users of a common currency economize on information costs and transaction costs. A member of a monetary union enjoys the benefits of increased trade as a result of the reduction or even disappearance of uncertainty in exchange rate movements. This benefit is partially delivered by a pseudo-exchange union, but fully realized only after the emergence of public confidence in the fixity of exchange rates. Only after full monetary unification is achieved, are the transactions costs arising from currency conversion eliminated, and the consequent benefits of increased trade and tourism enjoyed.

These microeconomic benefits are closely associated with the function of money as a medium of exchange. Money economizes on the information costs required for transactions and allows for the procurement of a stable bundle of goods at a lower cost than under barter. The use of a common currency carries an intrinsic externality as a result of its informational properties. These benefits from information spillover are nonrival in consumption: enjoyment by one member does not reduce the enjoyment of other members. This jointness in consumption is one characteristic of a public good. Benefits from monetary integration accrue also to the fixed exchange rate regime, because this regime is tantamount to creating a monetary union for the world.

A secondary benefit from monetary integration is macroeconomic. Mundell's theory of policy assignment indicates that the effect of regionally specific real shocks may be best absorbed by flexible exchange rates. However, recent studies on regime choice show that country, foreign, and specific monetary shocks can be better managed under fixed exchange rates or under highly managed exchange rates (e.g., Boyer, 1978; Fukuda and Hamada, 1987; Eichengreen, 1998).

Whereas the primary benefits of joining a monetary union are microeconomic, the costs are mainly macroeconomic. By joining a monetary union, or by adopting a fixed exchange rate, a country has to give up its monetary independence. This is particularly true when international capital mobility is high and when wages and prices are rigid. Therefore, a nation must sacrifice the attainment of locally desired levels of unemployment and prices. The floating exchange rate system gives national economies the opportunity to secure the minimum state of affairs that can be obtained independently, that is, the opportunity to follow a max-min strategy in the interplay of monetary policies. By joining a monetary union, a country gives up this max-min position and must adhere to the mutual consensus that results from policy coordination. Since countries differ in their rates of productivity growth, and in their preferences concerning the choice between unemployment and inflation, a fixed exchange rate or a single currency often means that the participating countries or regions have to abandon their individual policy objectives.

Loss of segniorage revenues is another cost of monetary union. This was explicitly recognized in the 19th century and was somewhat neglected later; recently it has been reemphasized. When countries allowed foreign coins to circulate within their borders as legal tender they gave up the coinage charge, which they would have earned by reminting the foreign coins into their own. Today, seigniorage is earned through currency and required bank reserves. Differences in the degree of dependence on seigniorage revenues among potential member countries in a currency union mean that the opportunity costs of foregoing this revenue are unevenly distributed. Large differences have the potential to destabilize a union (Grilli, 1989). Although individual nations may forfeit seigniorage on their own currencies as the result of creating a unified currency, seigniorage revenue may be earned on the common currency in a monetary union. Whether a member would, on balance, lose from foregoing seigniorage at the national level would depend on the mechanisms stipulated for distribution of common revenues amongst members.

The benefits and costs of monetary integration thus have several characteristics. The following description is in terms of monetary integration, but applies also to a fixed exchange rate regime. First, in contrast to benefits, which are international and have a public-good nature, the costs are not public, but mostly national. This contrast between the benefits and costs of monetary integration is a crucial element when we apply the calculus of participation to the problem of monetary integration.

Second, the benefit-cost payoff to participating countries changes over time. Initially, the costs of sacrificing domestic economic objectives and an independent monetary policy are large. As capital market integration proceeds, so the financing of fiscal deficits becomes easier and hence these adjustment costs become smaller. However, the common benefits of monetary integration are enjoyed only at a later stage. For example, the cost saving of currency conversion occurs only after a complete exchange rate union has been attained; the benefits arising from the stability of exchange rates are reaped only after confidence in the fixity of parities has been established. Therefore, the benefits may be attained only in the long run, and uncertainty remains as to whether they will actually be realized. On the other hand, the costs of sacrificing an independent monetary policy are incurred with certainty at an early stage. If currency markets detect any time inconsistency as a result of an unsustainable temporal distribution of costs and benefits, they will require a premium to hold a national currency during the progression towards full integration.

Third, the openness to trade and factor flows has an important influence on the magnitude of the benefits and costs derived from monetary integration. If an economy is relatively open, with large import and export flows relative to domestic transactions, the costs of adjusting its output or employment level for balance of payments reasons are small (McKinnon, 1963). The savings in currency conversion costs are also proportionately larger in a more open economy. If the economy is closed, however, these savings are less significant, while the costs of adjustment are relatively large. Prior integration of the markets for goods and services and factors of production among member countries may increase the desirability of monetary integration by raising average levels of openness.[2]

Finally, we have to note the asymmetry of incentives between those countries forming or participating in a monetary union, and those leaving it. A nation can unilaterally leave a monetary union or a fixed exchange rate regime (except for the single money system), but to form or to join a monetary union or a fixed exchange rate system collective action is required.

2. A pure theory of regime choices

According to the theory of rational participation (Riker and Ordeshook, 1973, chap. 3), an individual decision unit decides to participate in a collective action if the expected benefit is larger than the expected cost. When the benefits of collective action exhibit a public-good character, however, the amount of collective action may be less than Pareto optimal. Olson showed this by applying the theory of public goods to collective action (Olson, 1965; Olson and Zeckhauser, 1966). Following the Samuelson principles of public goods provision, a rational individual decides on the level of public good provision by equating the marginal private benefit from the public good with the marginal cost of supplying a unit of the good. Thus, the supply of the public good may be less than optimal because an individual decision unit does not take into account the external effect on other decision units. Therefore, even when a consensus exists concerning the objective of a collective action, the amount produced may be too small.

Let us proceed to examine the process of regime choice and policy interactions under a regime. If we observe the rule-making process of international monetary unification or a regime choice followed by the subgame of policy interactions, we find that it can be formulated as a two-stage game (Hamada, 1985, 1991). Nations as players of the total dynamic game choose international regimes with expectations of a particular exchange rate regime that is chosen or agreed upon. The choice can be decomposed into the choice of a regime and the subgame of policy interactions under the rule chosen in the first stage. The subgame of the first stage has a pay-off structure of the "Battle of the Sexes," because the present status quo continues unless a new regime is agreed upon. The backward induction, or more precisely the subgame perfectness, reduces the choice of regimes to the choice among the outcomes of policy games under alternative regimes.

In this paper we are more careful about the time process of regime choices and policy interactions. At any instant, when we play the game of choosing a regime, we are at a turning point within some regime. Here by "regime" we mean the system where the payoff to a set of actions by actors is specified and where the players have reasonable expectations of what other players are doing, in the spirit of Krasner's definition of regime as a system where expectations of actors converge. This is quite close to the situation where game theorists would say that the rules of the game are known to the players. The actors' preferences and payoffs are common knowledge to the players. At the time the new regime has to be chosen, players are still playing according to the ongoing rules. Today, in the world, flexible rates are prevalent among advanced non-European countries. New regimes emerge, if they do, when policy interactions occur according to the rule of flexible rates.[3]

Players in the game can either be individual persons or governments. An important requirement in the game is individual rationality: an actor agrees to a contract or to a regime as long as it guarantees him an improvement over the existing situation.[4] In the international sphere, usually national governments are the players. Therefore, the individual rationality constraint implies that each nation agrees on a regime so long as it improves its situation. However, in the real world, active players are not limited to nations. Interest groups within a country are affected by the same regime in a different manner. Some of them are opposed to the new regime and some welcome it. Therefore, in order to make everybody happy, the reservation utility level of each group has to be satisfied.

In reality politicians need not satisfy all interest groups. A government can agree with other nations as long as it does not endanger its political power, that is, as long as it does not jeopardize re-election. This idea was formalized by Putnam (1988) as a "two-level" game, where groups impose restrictions on the government concerning feasible choices in international negotiations. If the government adheres to the restrictions, it will be re-elected. In this two-game approach, the win-set is defined as the set of actions (or outcomes) in the international strategy space that would allow the re-election of the incumbent government. If the government is able to handle domestic opposition, the so-called "win-set" is enlarged and more opportunities exist for an international agreement.

Once the role of the game is agreed upon, participating nations share common knowledge or expectations about how the playing of policy interaction will proceed. However, there are ample occasions for changing rules even when a regime is agreed upon. The first joint action of building the Bretton-Woods system was rule setting. The shift to floating exchange rates in 1973 was not a jointly intended action. Countries were compelled to abandon the fixed exchange system and shift to other rules. The shift to another game can be analyzed as an escape from the existing regime. This aspect has an interesting connection with modern literature. Obstfeld (1997) analyzed a specific rule of intervention where the rule of the ongoing regime is disrupted by shifts to another regime. A fixed exchange rate regime cannot be sustained if large shocks occur; government can escape from the fixed rate regime to another regime, for example, flexible exchange rates. The exit possibility becomes part of the regime structure.

Agreeing on a monetary regime is equivalent to writing an incomplete contract. This aspect is common in many legal situations. It would be ideal to write a contract covering every possible contingency. However, it is not always economical to do so. One cannot write a complete contract in a world filled with uncertainty. Accordingly, a contract is more or less incomplete. Incompleteness gives room to uncertainty and creates incentive problems as well (Hart, 1995).

Under a given rule, nations engage in repeated policy games. In many cases the policy interaction game has the nature of a prisoner's dilemma, creating incentives for noncooperation (Hamada, 1985). Usually, the game is played repeatedly. Thus, if players play again and again, they are likely to reach some cooperative activities (Canzoneri and Henderson, 1991). In other words, cooperation is likely to emerge as a result of repeated games and the application of trigger strategies (Folk theorem). That is, the logic of "we retaliate against you if you do not cooperate" will achieve outcomes close to the Pareto efficient frontier.

The problem of cooperation is more easily achieved and sustained when players consider that the game will continue for a long time. Emergence of cooperation is conditioned by a long time horizon and a low discount rate (Matsushima and Yanagara, 1993; Abreu, 1986). Whenever participants realize that the game will be over soon, the logic for sustaining cooperation ceases to work. As soon as participants realize that the game reaches an end, the mechanism of trigger strategies disappears. The game will then become an outright prisoner's dilemma and cut-throat competition will ensue. Financial collapses illustrate these situations. If a financial institution faces its end, it has no incentive to behave gentlemanly. Similarly, in international financial crises, nations no longer wish to play cooperative monetary policy "games." By the same token, in order to agree on a certain regime, participants should have trust in the longevity of the system. Otherwise, the regime will fall into a prisoner's dilemma situation.

When large disturbances occur, cooperation is disrupted. To accommodate large disturbances one tends to resort to a nonsystem like flexible exchange rates, where nobody takes the blame. Even under flexible exchange rates, there are positive and negative monetary policy spillovers. The degree of monetary interdependence is, however, much less direct than under the fixed exchange regime. Under the fixed exchange regime, spillovers of monetary policy are strong through the balance of payments, and incentives for speculative attack are high. Flexible exchange rates guarantee independence of monetary policy. In the short run, negative monetary policy spillovers may exert beggar-thy-neighbor effects (Mundell, 1968; Dornbusch, 1976). But the chain of interdependence is weaker than under the fixed rate and disappears in the long run when prices are flexible.[5]

Let us illustrate the strategic structure of the game of regime choices and policy interactions. Forget all the realistic complications like conflicts of group interests within a nation and assume that there are two nation players, A and B, each behaving according to its national interest. Policy instruments are restricted to monetary policies. Timing of regime choices, policy interactions and defection from the regime are shown in figure 1. Under flexible rates, monetary policy gains autonomy. In particular, in the long run, if the two economics are in the classical world where money is neutral, there is no interdependence in monetary policy. The policy reaction curves intersect as in figure 2. If country A desires a higher monetary expansion rate than B for some reason, the pay-off

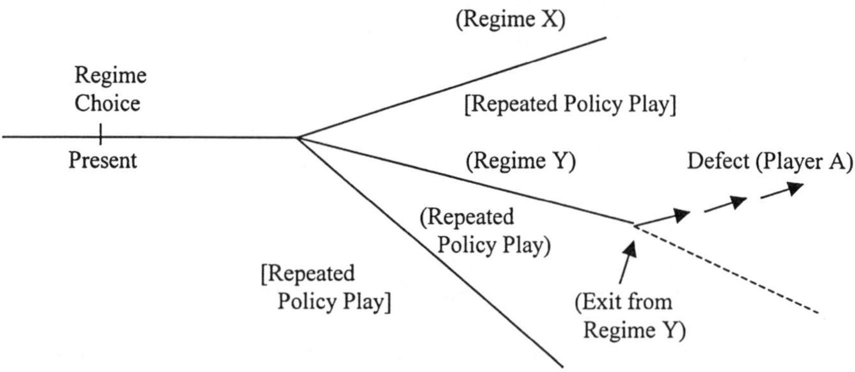

Figure 1.

Table 1. Flexible exchange rates: classical world.

A \ B	Expansion	Contraction
(Monetary) Expansion	(1, 0)	(1, 1)*
Contraction	(0, 0)	(0, 1)

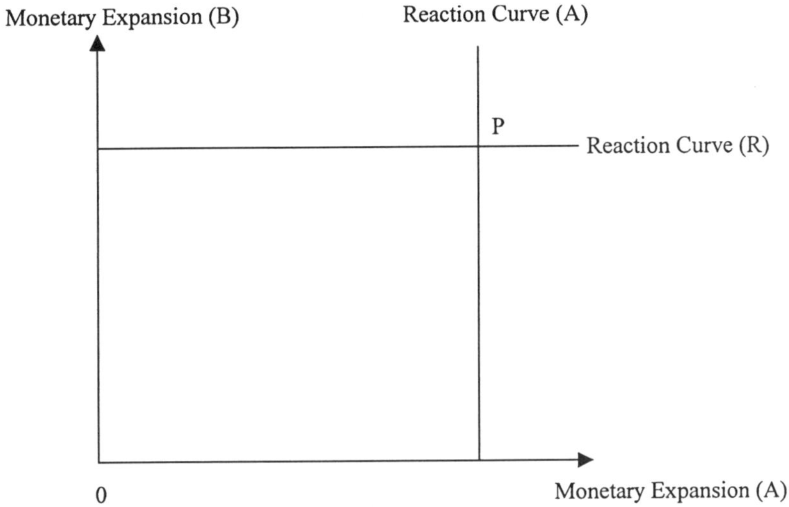

Figure 2. Flexible exchange rates: classical world.

matrix appears as in Table 1; the situation leaves no conflict of interest or strategic interaction between countries.

In the short run, in particular when inertia exists in prices and wages, there is independence in monetary policies and room for conflicts of interest. When the beggar-thy-neighbor effect is strong as in Mundell (1968) and in Dornbusch (1976), the strategic situation is depicted by the upward sloping reaction curves shown in figure 3 (Cooper, 1975). This is the case called the "strategic complements" in the Nash equilibrium literature. Usually, the Nash equilibrium is more inflationary than the Pareto efficient combination of monetary policies because the monetary expansion of a single country invokes the monetary expansion of the other. The pay-off matrix is, for example, as in Table 2, where ε is a small magnitude and signifies that the degree of interdependence is limited in the flexible rates even in the short run.

Under the fixed rate the price level becomes a kind of public good. Each country behaves by neglecting the spill-over of its monetary policy to the other. Because of the saving in transactions and information costs, the system enjoys an advantage over the flexible rates, denoted by α. The reaction curves become as in figure 3 and depict the property of "strategic substitutes." The

Table 2. Flexible exchange rates: inertia in price.

A \ B	Expansion	Contraction
Expansion	$(-\varepsilon, -\varepsilon)$	$(2\varepsilon, -3\varepsilon)$
Contraction	$(-3\varepsilon, 2\varepsilon)$	$(0, 0)$

ε: A small number.

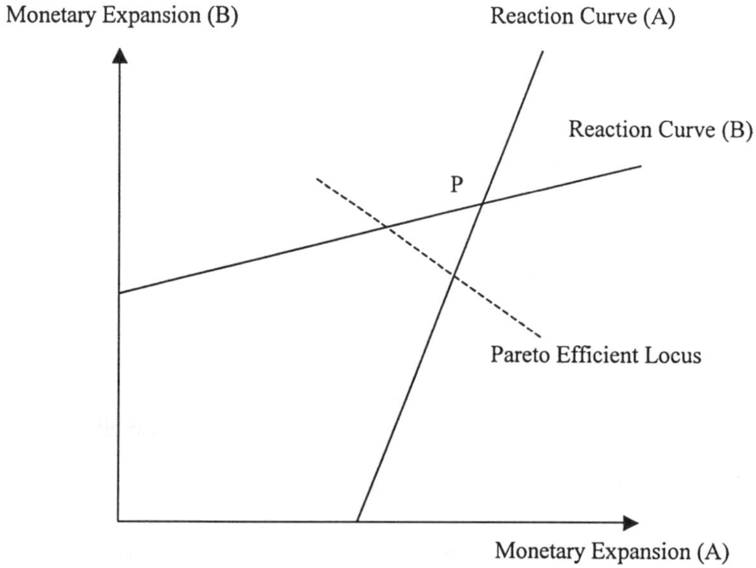

Figure 3. Flexible exchange rates: inertia in price.

pay-off matrix is illustrated in figure 4. Whether the Nash equilibrium lies on the inflationary or deflationary side of the Pareto frontier depends on the supply of outside money to the world (Hamada, 1985).

Under the flexible rate with price-wage inertia as well as under the fixed rates, the strategic structure has the nature of the prisoner's dilemma. Canzoneri and Henderson (1991) point out, however, that cooperation can emerge in this policy interaction game because the game is usually repeated. By considering the trigger strategy to retaliate against a noncooperating opponent, one can find certain cooperative solutions that can be sustained under certain conditions. Among the important conditions are such factors as the low discount rate of the future net benefit and the high degree of certainty that the game of policy interactions will be played for a long time. Instability in real as well as financial factors makes it difficult to implement a cooperative solution.

Table 3. Flexible exchange rates: excess supply of world reserves.

A \ B	Expansion	Contraction
	$(-1+\alpha, -1+\alpha)$	$(2+\alpha, -5+\alpha)$
	$(-5+\alpha, 2+\alpha)$	(α, α)

α: The gain from the economy of transactions cost and information cost.

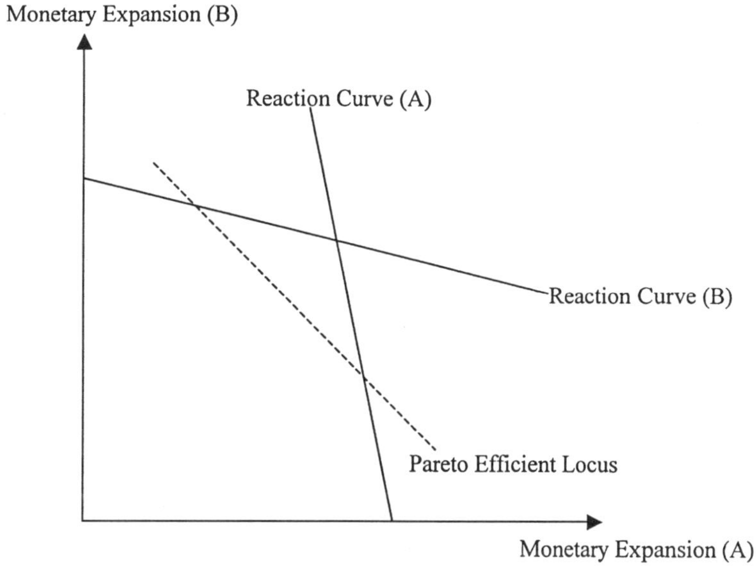

Figure 4. Flexible exchange rate: excess supply of world reserves.

The game of the regime choice anticipates the probable outcomes of the policy interaction game of the second stage. When exogenous shocks are stable and nations are patient, the probable outcomes are cooperative solutions brought about by trigger strategies. The flexible exchange rate gives the cooperative equilibrium of $(0, 0)$ and the fixed exchange rate gives the cooperative equilibrium of (α, α). Therefore, one can state that *under stable macroeconomic conditions the choice of international monetary regimes tends to favor the fixed exchange rate*. By the same token, monetary unification among nations is likely to proceed under a stable environment (see Table 3).

If nations are myopic, however, they are less likely to cooperate. Or, if macroeconomic disturbances are prevalent, the fixed exchange rate regime is likely to terminate or shift back to the flexible exchange rate. Then at the end of the game, or when the end of the game is seen, the players will play the strategies that correspond to the prisoner's dilemma Nash equilibrium. Then the choice is between the prisoner's dilemma pay-off of the flexible rate $(-\varepsilon, -\varepsilon)$ and the prisoner's dilemma pay-off of the fixed rate $(-1 + \alpha, -1 + \alpha)$. *In sum, under volatile conditions, nations favor flexible exchange rates.*

The view that each country needs individual national rationality or win-set rationality seems to be the corner stone of the "liberal" view of international political economy. So far we have considered the world where perceptions and preferences of people are fixed and side payments among various groups within a nation are not feasible. The concept of the win-set illustrates the difficulty for national governments to agree to or improve on the rules of the game and engage in fruitful policy coordination. Here enters political leadership or entrepreneurship.[6] As Frolich et al. (1971) developed years ago, politicians exert influence by spending money and effort in order to gain more rewards in terms of political power, votes and influence. According to these authors, politicians employ resources as long as the marginal gain from political efforts is more than their marginal costs. Since they equate the marginal gain of leadership to the marginal cost, they obtain leadership surplus just like consumers obtain consumers' surplus. Consider a two-level game where an international agreement makes a nation better off in terms of national income, but the outcome is not in the win-set because it hurts a group of important voters. There will be politicians who will exploit this situation for their political advantage.

There are two ways for a politician to manage this situation. One is to change the perception of the benefit-cost structure. A politician may tell voters that the new regime is good for those who are perceived to be losing from the agreement. Changes in perception are often very effective. The alternative is for the politician to devise a subsidy scheme to change the benefit-cost structure of groups. By effecting side-payments among groups the politician can expand the win-set.

This possibility also applies to the policy game of repeated policy interactions. According to Frankel and Rockett (1988) there is no coordination if countries disagree on the way the economy works. If, instead, countries share common knowledge and common perceptions of the working of the economy, policy coordination is feasible. Haas (1992) says that if countries have common perceptions, they can achieve better cooperation in international relations. Haas emphasizes the need for epistemological convergence of policy makers and the public to render international agreement effective. Thus, political leadership in the world can certainly change the payoff structure by persuasion, deception, or side-payments.

In this context, the role of a hegemon is important. A hegemon is interested, of course, in enhancing its own welfare. A hegemon has the power to change the perceptions of other nations and create side-payments necessary for agreement. Olson (1965), on the other hand, emphasizes that a hegemon behaves as if the world's interests were approximately its own.

A hegemon is also well-qualified to be a political entrepreneur. Though many nations do not enjoy being dictated to, the hegemon can sometimes be effective in exercising persuasive skills and leadership to achieve desirable changes from the status quo.

In sum, a monetary regime can be thought of in terms of a two-stage game, the first stage consisting of the group choice and the second stage of policy interactions. The following propositions summarize our discussion.

(i) A country decides to join a monetary union or to agree on a new monetary regime if the new regime improves the national well-being or the well-being of the incumbent's constituency.

(ii) The deterioration of the status quo facilitates the adoption of a new regime. A crisis liquidates the ongoing rule and, usually by way of discretion, a new regime is created.

(iii) A transition from a variant of flexible exchange rates to a variant of fixed exchange rates requires time, effort, and participants' cooperation. A transition in the other direction is easier. Even a single country can defect from a system of fixed exchange rates to flexible exchange rates (with the possible exception of a single money system).

(iv) The time profile of benefits and costs is important. The costs of coordinated action come immediately; the benefits much later. Therefore, unless the government can exert strong leadership and act on a very long-run view of the economy, a currency union may not be realized.

(v) Exit possibilities from a regime affect the choice of regimes (Folk theorem). In the presence of ample opportunities to defect, players are not motivated to employ the trigger strategy to realize cooperative outcomes.

(vi) Metallic money works as the anchor of the regime credibility. It is not a perfect anchor because a nation can devalue in principle against the metal.

(vii) Economic knowledge, belief, political or economic policy ideology, persuasion and coercion help nations change perceptions of reality, economic models and the future outcomes of cooperation. These factors may even change the pay-off structure itself. Hence, the role of international leadership is significant.

(viii) Positive externalities from a monetary union extend beyond the union's border. American tourists or businessmen, for example, benefit from the reduction of exchange and computational costs due to a common money in Europe. The Wall Street Journal no longer will have to print the dollar equivalent of European currencies.[7] It follows that the size of a currency union is likely to be smaller than the optimal size for the world (Cassella, 1992; Hamada, 1985).

(ix) There is asymmetry between agreeing on a regime that requires a lot of action to maintain the fixed rate and exiting from that regime. The former requires a joint action, the latter a simple unilateral action.

3. Interpretations of historical examples of monetary unions and regime choices

Given the framework of regime choices sketched above, let us review and interpret historical examples of monetary unions, the concerted choice of new regimes, and the shifts from one regime to another. Some of these examples are within a nation, some are among a group of nations in a region, and others are among most nations of the world.

We can trace back to the 19th century for many examples of monetary unification. The German Monetary Union among Zollverein members from 1857 to 1967, the Latin Monetary Union established in 1865 under the leadership of France, Italian monetary unification, and the unification of currency by redeeming paper notes (han satsu) in Japan are all examples of monetary unification (see also Capie, 1998).

3.1. Scandinavian Monetary Union

A monetary union was formed between the neighboring Scandinavian countries of Sweden and Denmark in 1873. Norway joined this union in 1875. A common currency unit, the krone, was based on gold and circulated as legal tender in member countries. In Sweden, note issue was in the hands of the Bank of Sweden and private banks, while in Norway and Denmark note issue was restricted to the Bank of Norway and the National Bank of Denmark, respectively. The union was extended to cover note circulation when in 1894 note issuing banks in Norway and Sweden agreed to accept each other's notes at par. Denmark joined this agreement in 1900. From 1905, the conditions of circulation of note issue were amended to allow for a commission to be charged on foreign notes. Despite this added cost, joint circulation of notes continued until the outbreak of World War I, when redemption of bank notes was suspended and the union in effect ended (Nielsen, 1933).

The history of the Scandinavian Monetary Union illustrates many factors that contributed to the success of a monetary union without unified government. In substantial conformity to the theory described above, one sees the similarity of economic shocks, the trust in not only one's own government but also in others', the anchor provided by gold, gold's credibility during the emerging era of the gold standard, and Swedish leadership. The outbreak of World War I, was the principal factor that led to the breakup of the union.

3.2. National monetary disintegration: Austro-Hungary

This is an interesting case study of the effect on money of a political break-up. While the converse process of monetary union formation is commonly studied, dissolution of a currency area is not. This case does fit, however, some of the patterns and propositions of the earlier section. Dornbusch (1992) and Garber and Spencer (1992) chronicle the breakup of the Austro-Hungarian empire into the separate nations of Austria, Hungary, Czechoslovakia, Rumania, Poland and Yugoslavia following World War I. Prior to the breakup, the Austrian crown, issued by the Austro-Hungarian Bank located in Vienna, was the currency of the Empire. During the war, the Bank had increasingly become involved in financing the fiscal deficit of the imperial government. After the breakup of the empire, the new states continued to use the crown and constituted a de facto monetary union. However, the Austrian government used its privileged access to the Bank to secure continued inflationary financing of its spending. The negative spillovers from sharing a common currency over which they had no control soon became more apparent to the other new states as hyperinflation set in. Attempts to shore up the currency union through formal representation of other states on the board of the Bank failed. In 1920, Yugoslavia and Czechoslovakia were the first of the new states to require that crown notes circulating in their territories had to be stamped with their own mark in order to be legal tender. The macrostabilization of these economies in the wake of hyperinflation required further drastic measures. The consequences were particularly severe for the states which were slow to leave the crown monetary area. Thus, without the overarching political system of control and decision making under the old empire, there was no framework for credible coordination of monetary policy. The Austro-Hungarian crown currency area did not survive long due to the end of the Austro-Hungarian empire.

This example shows the difficulty of having a single money with different governments. The trust for the single currency regime eroded. The temptation for conducting easy fiscal policy and the public's recognition of this temptation were primary catalysts for destroying the single money regime.

Incidences of lasting monetary union among states not politically unified have been relatively rare. We will discuss here three historical examples: the German Monetary Union with Austria, which was short lived, the Latin Monetary Union and the Scandinavian Monetary Union, both of which lasted several decades. Then we will describe two present day examples, the West African Monetary Union and the European Monetary System (and the move to European Monetary Union).

3.3. Gold standard

The movement to the gold standard was a transition from the de facto flexible system of national currencies, subnational currencies in various parts of Europe, and the bimetallic regime of the Latin Monetary Union. England was a leader and London functioned as the coordinating market. No explicit joint actions were taken but countries other than England were motivated to join. Academic belief in the gold standard was strong due to the influence of economists' like Hume. This shift to the gold standard was one of few cases where market forces rather than concerted actions sufficed to create a fixed exchange rate regime. The credibility of in the gold standard was high and succumbed only because of World War I.

3.4. Interwar period of flexible rates

After the war, many countries returned to the gold standard, some to the old parity and others with new parities. Here one could see the arbitrariness of the fixity of the gold standard. For example, in Japan, the attempt to return to the gold standard with the old parity created speculation and economic panic. The instability of the world economy in this period was attributed to the flexible exchange rate (Nurkse, 1944). This period showed the difficulty of returning to a fixed exchange rate regime where parities to gold were not predetermined.

3.5. Bretton Woods system

The Bretton Woods Regime can be characterized as an "adjustable peg" system because of the escape clause that was implicitly written in the Bretton Woods Charter to the effect that a country with "a fundamental equilibrium" could devalue its currency by more than 10%. The United States and the United Kingdom assumed the leadership of this regime. Partly because of Nurkse's persuasion, everybody aimed at a regime with a fixed exchange rate system. The rivalry between White and Keynes was not on the fixity of exchange rates but concerned the lending capacity of the central bank (Clearing Union) of the world. Thus, except for Canada, major countries in the world adopted fixed exchange rates.

3.6. Flexible exchange rates since 1973

Since the late 1960s, major industrial countries were subject to significant economic shocks that were difficult to absorb with fixed exchange rates. Since 1968, European currencies were appreciating vis-à-vis the U.S. dollar. Japan appreciated the yen in 1971, and after a short interlude of the wider band rates of the Smithsonian period, exchange rate flexibility started in 1973. This period shows the end with which a shift from a fixed rate regime to a flexible regime can occur. However, one could not deny the impression that exchange rates fluctuated probably much more than a smooth resource allocation would require.

3.7. After the Plaza accord

Most policy makers agreed that the U.S. dollar appreciated too much in 1985. Perhaps partly influenced by the academic work of policy coordination, but mostly by the urgency to correct the U.S. external deficit by depreciating the U.S. dollar, countries engaged in exchange rate coordination. This coordination was aimed at managing the flexible rate regime as if it were a quasi fixed exchange rate regime.[8]

3.8. West African Monetary Union

The longest surviving present day monetary union is probably the West African Monetary Union (WAMU) among seven countries of francophone West Africa (Hamada and Porteous, 1992). This union was created around the Central Bank of West African States (BCEAO) in 1962 and has continued since then, with a major revision in its operating arrangements in 1974. WAMU is one region in the wider CFA Franc zone in francophone Africa, originally established in 1948. In the other region, six central African states have a common central bank, the Bank of Central African States (BEAC), which issues in each state a separate currency that is legal tender in all six. Our focus here, however, is on the former region, WAMU, which constitutes a more tightly defined monetary union. In WAMU, the BCEAO issues a common currency, the CFA franc, which was tied to the French franc at a rate of 50 : 1, and now at a rate of 100 : 1 with the "support" of the French government. This support now takes the form of an overdraft facility at the French Treasury with which the bulk of foreign exchange reserves of the union are deposited. In return, France exercises direct influence—i.e., leadership—over the affairs of the union through appointees on the Board of the Bank. France also exercises considerable indirect influence on individual members through concessional assistance and commercial links.

Within WAMU, Côte d'Ivoire, accounting for almost a third of the total GDP, is the dominant state. Monetary policy within the union operates in a fairly decentralized fashion in that the National Monetary Committees in each member country decides on the issue of currency within the overall credit allocation guidelines decided by the BCEAO Board. The Bank itself sets rediscount ceilings for each member, reserve ratios and the rediscount rate. Total bank lending to a member government may not exceed 20% of total revenues from the previous year. The Union was under considerable strain until its drastic devaluation in 1994 of 100% as a result of the overvaluation of the CFA franc relative to other currencies. This occurred due to its peg to the relatively strong French franc.

However, without the maintenance of the convertibility of the CFA franc, which is supported by France, one of the main "raisons d'être" of the union would be removed. The union has low levels of intraunion trade (only 7.5% of total international trade) and factor market integration; hence, the external link to larger trade markets is all the more important (Robson, 1983; Bhatia, 1985). Broughton (1991) suggested that WAMU did not meet conventional criteria for an optimal currency union. Its survival should be linked to the French franc and France's political leadership rather than to an appropriate monetary union.

Consequently, WAMU could be interpreted more as a monetary standard than a currency union, in which the external anchor has brought discipline and credibility to the economic policy regime of member countries.

3.9. EMS and EMU

The development of the EMS since its inception in 1979 has offered a striking contemporary example of the process of monetary integration. The EMS was founded as a "flexible, symmetric version of the Bretton-Woods system" (Kenen, 1992), following long-standing plans of monetary union in Europe. The Werner Report of 1970 envisaged the development of a monetary union by 1980, although the turbulent environment of the 1970s was not conducive to economic harmonization. Harmonization implies that differences in key national economic indicators such as the inflation rate, interest rates and levels of government deficits and accumulated debt gradually narrowed. By contrast with the 1970s, remarkable harmonization of intent at least, if not always harmonization of actual economic conditions, took place in the 1980s amongst the original eight EMS members. Spain joined in 1989, the UK in 1990, and Portugal in 1992. After frequent realignments in the early period, there were no major realignments from 1987 until September 1992. This period of calmness contributed to a sense of inevitability in the progression towards a fixed parity system, but proved to be the lull before the storm of suspensions and devaluations of member currencies in September 1992.

Increasingly, the Deutsche Bundesbank served as the monetary anchor of the EMS by virtue of the size of the German economy and strength of the Deutschmark. This strength was jealously guarded by the Bundesbank with its reputation for high inflation aversion. In a decade when anti-inflationary political commitment ran high, the credibility offered to the EMS by Germany came to be valued by politicians in other European countries. Late EMS entrants such as Britain sought a mechanism for disciplining domestic wages and prices. By joining the currency system, participating nations signaled an anti-inflationary stance to the market and bought into the credibility of the Bundesbank, with benefits in terms of lower interest rates. By claiming that their economic policy options were limited through the constraints of EMS membership, politicians could avoid some of the blame for higher unemployment and lower income in noncompetitive industries, which failed without the protection of a depreciating exchange rate.

However, the monetary discipline provided by the Bundesbank became punitive as Germany suffered the real fiscal shock of monetary unification. The costs to other countries of enjoying Bundesbank credibility soared, as high German real interest rates were transmitted throughout the fixity of the exchange rate. Members with less than full employment felt the effects of the squeeze on interest-sensitive sectors like housing and construction. The growing divergence between the costs and benefits of maintaining the fixed parity created uncertainty about the future unified money. It opened the door for speculators. Despite repeated public pronouncements to preserve fixed currency links and despite defensive purchases of weaker currencies by central banks, the speculative attacks of September 1992 succeeded in forcing several devaluations. Confidence in the EMS was substantially undermined. The succeeding events will be discussed in the final section.

3.10. German Economic Monetary and Social Union (GEMSU)

The most recent example of monetary union following political unification is the German Economic Monetary and Social Union (GEMSU) Treaty between West Germany and the German Democratic Republic (East Germany), which came into force on July 1, 1990. Driven by the political necessity of symbolic unity, but also by fears of economic instability in the GDR, the treaty called for a two-tier system of conversion of Ostmarks (OM) into Deutschmark (DM). Salaries and wages, pensions, debt contracts and personal savings up to OM 2000 were converted at a rate of 1 for 1. This rate was well in excess of both the black market exchange rate prior to the union and measures of purchasing power parity. Other balances were converted at the rate of 2 OM to 1 DM, resulting in an average conversion rate of 1.8 to 1 for all exchanges.

Alerlof et al. (1991) have studied the effects of monetary unification. The conversion of labor costs at the preferential exchange rate level caused a cost-price squeeze for eastern German firms that were unable to raise prices. This was because demand for their goods had declined dramatically, as Germans in the East took advantage of their newly gained purchasing power to obtain western products of higher quality. However, a large fiscal burden followed unification as a result of the costs of harmonizing physical and social infrastructure and selling off or closing bankrupt firms caught in the cost-price squeeze. In the absence of politically unpopular tax increases, the German budget deficit ballooned. As a result, the German inflation rate moved above that of other northern European nations for the first time in years. Monetary policy was left to bear the brunt of the battle against inflation, resulting in high interest rates, which caused unsustainable strains to many EMS partners.

In terms of our basic framework, this unification represents a shift to a single money with a single government. People expected the irrevocability of the single money; therefore, the credibility of the reform was perfect. West Germany as the dominant partner in the union undertook the role of monetary entrepreneur in initiating the union and in underwriting the fiscal consequences. The stated conversion rates caused large distributional consequence to both economies.

3.11. The monetary disintegration in the CIS countries

In the Commonwealth of Independent States (CIS), after the disintegration of political unity, many countries started adopting their own currencies rather than the ruble. Before political dissolution, there was an incentive to use the ruble because the satellite countries depended heavily on Russia for trade. Countries near Europe, such as Estonia, Latvia and Lithuania introduced—after a transition period—new currencies whose values were fixed to European currencies. Belarus and Ukraine pegged their currencies to the dollar. Moldova, Kazakhastan, Uzbekistan and Azerbaijan adopted, after creating a new currency, flexible rates. Space considerations do not permit a discussion of the political economy of monetary disintegration in CIS countries (Greene and Isard, 1991; IMF, 1994, 1995). These examples offer a warning to Europe as well. Even after the state of a single currency is achieved in Europe, European countries need to make continuous efforts to enhance political cooperation in order to sustain monetary union.

4. Insights from historical experiences

These historical experiences provide several insights, some of which coincide with the theoretical predictions of Section 2. First, political integration usually preceded complete monetary integration, while other (non-currency) aspects of economic integration sometimes preceded and sometimes followed political integration (Capie, 1998). Monetary unions across national borders often did not last long because the political integration needed to consolidate them did not occur. This observation was true in the reverse process, as in the case of the break-up of the Austrian-Hungarian empire as well as in the CIS countries. Monetary unification was eroded by political disintegration in the empire. This outcome is predicted by the theoretical property that trust in the irrevocable fixity is important for the use of a common currency. Even with a single currency political disintegration can easily result in monetary disintegration.

Second, a monetary union was generally effective if the political leadership of a dominant country was strong, if there were few participating nations, and if there was extensive economic integration. France has provided the leadership for the existing West African Monetary Union; Sweden started the Scandinavian Monetary Union with only three member countries which had been closely integrated both geographically and culturally. The Scandinavian Union proved remarkably stable over time. These tendencies are consistent with the calculus of participation and can be regarded as direct implications for the theory of collective action (Olson, 1965).

Third, the existence of metal money was helpful in anchoring an exchange rate union. This is because the cost of coordination is substantially reduced when there is a common commitment to a standard that constrains economic policy options. In unions without a metallic base, the issue of irredeemable paper money by some members caused severe tensions. Adherence to the gold standard undoubtedly strengthened the Scandinavian Monetary Union. Indeed, the gold standard system itself may be seen as a form of a giant pseudo-currency union. The simplicity of the rules of the system made it possible for widespread participation with minimum policy coordination, or, more precisely, forced rules of coordination according to the specie-flow mechanism. In more recent times, when currencies no longer have a metallic base, a commitment to maintain a firm peg has also served as the basis for ongoing monetary union. This is the case both for WAMU, with its peg to the French franc, and for the EMS in its earlier period, when currencies were de facto pegged to the Deutschmark.

Fourth, the benefits of monetary unification can be enjoyed only when strong confidence is attained in the fixed parities or when only one single currency circulates. Therefore, the metallic content of currencies was important in creating confidence in the exchange rate union. Some effective political integration was still necessary to sustain that confidence over prolonged periods of time.

Fifth, the cost of participation in a monetary union involves the sacrifice of seigniorage as well as the cost of policy adjustments. The costs associated with the underutilization of resources incurred in order to correct a disequilibrium in the balance of payments were hardly perceived before the Great Depression (Guggenheim, 1973). Recent studies of the EMS have revived interest in the seigniorage issue. Emerson et al. (1992) simulated the effect of EMU on those member countries most dependent on seigniorage revenue. According to their estimates, only two (Greece and Portugal) of the four countries currently earning more than 1% of their GDP in seigniorage would forfeit more than 1% of GDP in revenues under the envisaged EMU. Consequently, Emerson et al. argue that the micro welfare benefits from fixity in exchange exceed the opportunity costs of this nature even for these nations. Therefore, segniorage gains may constitute an important component of the benefit-cost calculations.

5. Concluding remarks

We have applied the game theoretic and incentive approach to explain an international monetary regime. We have found that decisions concerning the formation of a fixed exchange rate regime and sustaining it are difficult, but that decisions concerning defections from a fixed exchange rate regime are relatively easy. This may explain the difficulties for the completion of EMU as well as the instability recently observed in the quasi-fixed exchange regimes of the Asian countries.

Despite criticism by economists (Feldstein, 1992, 1997) and severe speculative attacks in 1992, the momentum for EMU is now in full force. The economic benefit of unification is clear: the saving in transaction and information costs. The perception of political benefits by national leaders has been the driving force of currency unification in Europe. This benefit is enhanced if one single money circulates. (Recall that the process may *not* be irrevocable even after the realization of a single currency.) The cost of a monetary union is the loss of monetary control by each participating nation. If countries cannot contain their desire to deviate from the common monetary expansion, then the currency could potentially be under speculative attack. After January 1, 1999, theoretically each

EMU country can no longer deviate from the common norm; but the question remains of how to implement this mode of conduct. Even the country in the center, Germany, may find a cost associated with the loss of its leadership role.

The *Economist*'s Survey of April 11, 1998 cites that opposition to the euro is rather weak in most of participating countries. However, since unemployment and inflation affect different groups in a nation differently, there is still room for potential domestic conflicts (Fratianni et al., 1998).

From now until January 1, 1999, room exists for speculative attacks in the proposed EMU. How to establish the par value is a crucial concern for each currency. After January 1, 1999, possibilities for speculative attacks will be much reduced. However, the joint circulation of currencies is somewhat similar to the situation where SDRs and the dollar jointly circulate. Might there be a chance for speculation to occur between the euro and the German mark or Italian lira? This possibility may be more realistic if unexpected shocks were to motivate a country to defect from the monetary union. After the euro notes and coins start circulating (January 1, 2002) and become the only medium of exchange (July 1, 2002), the benefits from currency unification will rise. Still, without political unification, any nation can defect in theory, however difficult it may be in practice. The benefit of a single currency will finally be enjoyed in full only after the system survives severe shocks and speculative turbulence and only after the participating nations develop confidence in the system.

Acknowledgments

I thank David Porteous for allowing me to use the materials from our joint study (Hamada and Porteous, 1992) and Carolyn M. Beaudin for her editorial contributions. I also thank Paul de Grauwe, Michele Fratianni, Masahiro Okuno, Akihisa Shimmi, Robert Staiger, and Noriyuki Yanagawa for their comments.

Notes

1. Krasner claims that principles and norms provide the basic defining characteristics of a regime and that changes in rules and decision making procedures are changes within regimes while changes in principles and norms are changes of the regime itself. Most economists consider, however, that a basic change in rules of interventions in exchange markets, say from fixed exchange rates to floating exchange rates, represents a change in regimes. Thus, even though one has to distinguish regime changes from "one shot" arrangements, basic changes in rules of the game should be regarded as regime changes (For a similar view see Kehoane, 1984, p. 59).
2. Feldstein (1992) makes the case that monetary integration is not a necessary condition for the benefits of other forms of economic integration to be enjoyed. De Grauwe et al. (1992) object to this argument.
3. Corden (1972) once characterized the flexible exchange rate as a nonsystem: a country is not restricted against the use of any policy instruments. It can do almost anything; it does not need to defend the exchange rate; it does not need to keep foreign reserves; it is simply required to follow the rule of the market. But even a nonsystem it is a regime in the sense that specific policies generate specific outcomes.

4. In a world with uncertainty, another important requirement is the incentive compatibility constraint that players are motivated to tell the truth. People should have incentives not to lie, otherwise the incentive to cheat will harm incentive mechanisms of the whole system. In this paper, we abstract from this incentive compatibility constraints to consider other aspects of the joint action.
5. Incidentally, in the current Asian experiences many Asian currencies were fixed mainly to the U.S. dollar. Japan depreciated the yen relative to the U.S. dollar. There was a need for these Asian countries to devalue according to the negative spillover scenario. The U.S. did not need or want to depreciate, counteracting the depreciation of the yen because of the strength of the U.S. economy. For Thailand or Indonesia, however, this meant the loss of export opportunities to Japan and other Asian countries. They started expanding the money supply so that it could not support its fixed exchange rate with respect to the dollar. The yen/dollar flexibility combined with, say, the ruble/dollar peg thus created a heavy burden for these countries.
6. In economics, the Stackelberg solution is well known and often called the "leadership solution." By "leadership" I mean political entrepreneurship. Charles Kindleberger once told me that he would call the Stackelberg solution the exploitation solution and entrepreneurship the leadership solution.
7. Often one neglects the welfare of outsiders or nations who are left behind. In the case of a trade agreement, such as a Free Trade Agreement or more for a custom union, the spillover to the rest of world of a joint action is almost always negative (Goto and Hamada, 1996) because of the trade diversion effect. However, the spillover effect is usually positive in the case of monetary integration because of the reduction in transaction and information costs to the rest of the world.
8. Feldstein (1992) is critical of policy coordination and of the exchange rate mechanism in the European Union.

References

Abreu, D. (1986) "External Equilibria of Oligopolistic Supergames." *Journal of Economics Theory* 39, 191–225.

Abreu, D., D. Pearce, and E. Stacchetti (1990) "Toward a Theory of Discounted Repeated Games with Imperfect Monitoring." *Econometrica* 58, 1041–1064.

Alerlof, G. et al. (1991) "East Germany in from the Cold: The Economic Aftermath, of Currency Union." *Brookings Papers on Economic Activity* 22, 1–87.

Bagwell, K. (1997) "Multilateral Tariff Cooperation During the Formation of Customs Unions." *Journal of International Economics* 42(1/2), 91–133.

Bagwell, K. and R. Staiger (1990) "A Theory of Managed Trade." *American Economic Review 80*, 779–795.

Bhatia, R. (1985) "The West African Monetary Union," IMF Occasional Paper 35.

Boyer, R.S. (1978) "Optimal Foreign Exchange Market Intervention." *Journal of Political Economy* 86, 1045–1055.

Broughton, J.M. (1991) "The CFA Franc Zone: Currency Union and Monetary Standard," IMF Staff Working Paper 91/133.

Buiter, W.H., C. Corsetti, and N. Roubini (1993) "Excess Deficits: Sense and Nonsense in the Treaty of Maastricht." *Economic Policy* 16.

Canzoneri, M.B. and D.W. Henderson (1991) *Monetary Policy in Interdependent Economies: A Game-Theoretic Approach.* MA: MIT Press.

Caple, F. (1998) "Monetary Unions in Historical Perspective: What Future for the Euro in the International Financial System." in this volume.

Cassella, A. (1992) "Participation in a Currency Union." *American Economic Review* 84, 847–888.

Cooper, R.N. (1975) "Prolegomena to the Choice of an International Monetary System." In C.F. Bergsten and L.B. Krause (eds.), *World Politics and International Economics*.

Corden, W.M. (1972) "Monetary Integration." *Essays in International Finance*, vol. 93, Princeton: Princeton University Press.

Corden, W.M. (1983) "The Logic of the International Monetary Non-System." In F. Machlup (ed.), *Reflection of a Troubled World Economy*. London: Macmillan.

de Grauwe, P. et al. (1992) "In Reply to Feldstein." *Economist* 4, 67.

Dornbusch, R. (1976) "Expectations and Exchange Rate Dynamics." *Journal of Political Economy.*

Dornbusch, R. (1992) "Monetary Problems of Post-Communist States: Lessons from the End of the Austro-Hungarian Empire," IMF Research Department Seminar Paper, August.

Eichengreen, B. (1991) "Is Europe an Optimum Currency Area?" University of California, Berkeley Working Paper 91-150.

Eichengreen, B. (1992) "Should the Maastricht Treaty be Saved?" Working Paper 1-10, Center for German and European Studies, University of California, Berkeley.

Eichengreen (1998) "Exchange Rate Stability and Financial Stability." in this volume.

Emerson, M. et al. (1992) *One Market, One Money*. Oxford: Oxford University Press.

Feldstein, M. (1992) "The Case against EMU." *Economist* 13, 19–22.

Feldstein, M. (1997) "EMU and International Conflict." (European Monetary Union) *Foreign Affairs* 76(6), 60–74.

Frankel, J.A. and K.E. Rockett (1988) "International Macroeconomic Policy Coordination when Policymakers do not Agree on the True Model." *The American Economic Review*, 78(3), 318–340.

Fratianni, M., A. Hauskrecht, and A. Maccario (1998) "Dominant Currencies and the Future of the Euro." in this volume.

Frolich, N., J.A. Oppenheimer, and O.R. Young (1971) *Political Leadership and Collective Goods*. Princeton: Princeton University Press.

Fukuda, S. and K. Hamada (1987) "Towards Implementation of Desirable Rules of International Coordination and Intervention." In Y. Suzuki and M. Okabe (eds.), *Towards a World of Economic Stability*. Tokyo: University of Tokyo Pres, chap. 11.

Funabashi, Y. (1988) *Managing the Dollar: From the Plaza to the Louvre*. Institute for International Economics.

Garber, P.M. and M.G. Spencer (1992) "The Dissolution of the Austro-Hungarian Empire: Lessons for Currency Reform," IMF Working Paper, July.

Goto, J. and K. Hamada (1996) "Regional Economic Integration and Article XXIV of the GATT," Yale University Economic Growth Center Discussion Paper No. 754.

Greene, J. and P. Isard (1991) "Currency Convertibility and Transformation of Centrally Planned Economies," IMF Occasional Paper, 81, June.

Greif, A. (1991) "The Organization of Long-Distance Trade: Reputation and Coalitions in the Geniza Documents and Genoa During the Eleventh Centuries." *Journal of Economic History* 51(2), pp. 459–463.

Greif, A., P. Milgrom, and B.R. Weingast (1994) "Coordination, Commitment, and Enforcement: The Case of the Merchant Guild." *Journal of Political Economy*, 102(4), 745–776.

Grilli, V. (1989) "Seigniorage in Europe." In M. de Cecco and U. Giovannini (eds.), *A European Central Bank.* Cambridge: Cambridge University Press.

Guggenheim, T. (1973) "Some Early Views on Monetary Integration." In the *Economies of Common Currencies*. London: Allen and Unwin.

Haas, P. (1992) "Introduction: Epistemic Communities and International Policy Coordination." *International Organization* 46(1), 1–35.

Hamada, K. (1985) *The Political Economy of Economic Integration*. Cambridge MIT Press.

Hamada, K. (1991) "On the Political Economy of Regime Choice," Osaka Economic Papers (New Series), vol. 40, March 1991. Reprinted in Ali M. El-Agraa (ed.), *Public and International Economics*. St. Martin's Press, 1993.

Hamada, K. and D. Porteous (1992) "L'integration Monetaire en Perspective Historique," (Monetary Integration in Historical Perspective) in *Revue d'economie financiere*, No. 22, Automne.

Hart, O.D. (1995) *Firms, Contracts, and Financial Structure*. Oxford: Oxford University Press.

International Monetary Fund (IMF) (1994, 1995) "World Economic Outlook," May.

Kehoane, R.O. (1984) *After Hegemony: Cooperation and Discord in the World Political Economy*. Princeton University Press.

Kenen, P. (1992) *EMU after Maastricht*. Washington: Group of Thirty.

Kramer, H.R. (1971) "Experience with Historical Monetary Unions." In H. Giersch (ed.), *Integration durch Wahrungsunion*. Mohr, Tubingen: Institut fur Weltwirtschaft an der Universitat Kiel.

Krasner, S.D. (1982) "Structural Causes and Regime Consequences: Regimes as Intervening Variables." In Krasner (ed.), *International Regimes*. Ithaca: Corness University Press.

Matsushima, H. (1989). "Efficiency in Repeated Games with Imperfect Monitoring." *Journal of Economic Theory* 48, 428–442.

Matsushima, H. and N. Yanagawa (1993) "Implicit Collusion, Limit Pricing and Price Fluctuation with Multiple Incumbents, mimeo.

Matsuyama, K., N. Kiyotaki, and A. Matsui (1993) "Toward a Theory of International Currency." *Review of Economic Studies* 60(2), 283–325.

Mayer, T. and G. Thumann (1990) "Paving the Way for German Unification." *Finance and Development*, Dec., 9–11.

McKinnon, R. (1963) "Optimum Currency Areas." *American Economic Review* 53, 712–724.

Muhleman, M. (1985) *Monetary Systems of the World*. New York: Charles Nicholl.

Mundell, R.A. (1968) *International Economics*. New York: Macmillan.

Nielsen, A. (1933) "Monetary Union." *Encyclopedia of Social Science*, vol. 10, New York: MacMillan.

Nurkse, R. (1944) *International Currency Experience: Lessons of the Interwar Period*. Princeton: League of Nations.

Obstfeld, M. (1997) "Destabilizing Effects of Exchange-Rate Escape Clauses." *Journal of International Economics* 42(1/2), 61(17).

Olson, M. (1965) "The Logic of Collective Action: Public Goods and the Theory of Groups." *Harvard Economic Studies*. Cambridge: Harvard University Press, vol. 124.

Olson, M. and R. Zeckhauser (1966) "An Economic Theory of Alliances." *Review of Economics and Statistics* 48, 266–279.

Putnam, R. (1988). "Diplomacy and Domestic Politics: The Logic of Two-Level Games." *International Organization* 42(3), 427–460.

Riker, W.H. and P.C. Ordeshook (1973) *An Introduction to Positive Political Theory*. Englewood Cliffs, NJ: Prentice Hall.

Robson, P. (1983) *Integration, Development and Equity*. London: George Allen and Unwin.

Sala-i-Martin, X. and J. Sachs (1991) "Fiscal Federalism and Optimum Currency Areas: Evidence from the US," NBER Working Paper No. 3855.

Stolper, G. (1967) *The German Economy: 1870 to the Present*. New York: Harcourt Brace and World.

Ungerer, H. et al. (1990) "The European Monetary System: Developments and Perspectives," IMF Occasional Paper 73.

Wagner, R.E. (1966) "Pressure Groups and Political Entrepreneurs: A Review Article," Papers on Non-Market Decision Making 1.

Open economies review **9:S1** 447–465 (1998)

Monetary Unions in Historical Perspective: What Future for the Euro in the International Financial System

FORREST CAPIE F.H.Capie@city.ac.uk
City University Business School, Frobisher Crescent Barbican Centre, London EC2Y 8HB

Key words: European Central Bank, central bank credibility, monetary union, political accountability

JEL Classification Numbers: E42, E58, F33

Abstract

This paper discusses the introduction of the euro in the present international monetary context. European Monetary Union is not only an economic concept but also primarily a political one. Based on past experience, two aspects of monetary union seem essential: the nature of the future European Central Bank and the necessity that monetary union is implemented with a fiscal union. The euro's success on world markets, as a dollar substitute, depends on monetary authorities' credibility in targeting low-inflation, and on fiscal authorities' reputation. A central bank that does not respond to a political authority can cause social difficulties, especially if social policies are left in the hands of single countries and fiscal transfers, to support these policies, are not allowed.

Introduction

The proposed monetary union in Europe is largely a political issue. Clearly, not everyone accepts that political union is the basic objective of European Monetary Union (EMU). But even if that explicit political goal is left aside, it remains that the process itself of monetary unification is driven by political considerations; that is what informs the direction of this paper.

Economic forecasting is hazardous; yet, there are some things that can be said, with differing degrees of confidence, about the future of the international monetary system.[1] This paper seeks to contribute to that discussion by offering some speculation about the euro, not based entirely on historical experience, but certainly with an historical perspective.

Over the last three years there has been an outpouring of literature speculating on whether the euro would come about, and in what form. In the belief that sometime soon the euro would come into being, a rather hasty assumption has been that the world will then have three key currencies: the dollar, the yen, and the euro. We know a lot about the other two, their strength and likely continuing position, but where will the euro feature?

Some speculation is based on sounder footing than others. But the task in this particular case is not made easier by the fact that events are unfolding at a rapid pace. Each event or announcement affects our view, and more importantly the market's view, of what is likely to happen. Indeed each event of significance has more than one interpretation.[2]

The euro is about to be born, but clearly there is a range of possibilities on its prospective size and strength. Working on the assumption that it will survive the intermediate three-year stage, this essay concentrates on its prospects in the medium to longer term. Section 1 sets out the path to the proposed monetary union and Section 2 provides a basic reminder of the entry qualifications. Section 3 then gives an outline of some historical experience of monetary unions, to define the relationship between political union and monetary union. We then consider two important dimensions. The first, which is the subject of Section 4, is to examine the possible need for fiscal union to support monetary union. The second is the nature of the European Central Bank (ECB) and what its strategy might mean. Might this latter produce strain that would require support of a fiscal union (Section 5)? Finally, Section 6 provides some conclusions.

1. EMU: Beginnings and timetable

The proposed EMU has been considered and discussed since the nineteenth century, when the beginnings of European nation states and unions got under way. It became much more specific after the Second World War, as a variety of schemes for cooperation in Europe were adopted. According to Duisenberg (Governor of the Nederlandsche Bank, and first President of the ECB), the first president of the Nederlandsche Bank was told, when taking office in 1946, to provide a sound silver guilder, "...which will in time become part of a single European currency" (Vanthoor, 1996). Almost 30 years ago the Commission of the European Union (Commission) published a proposal for EMU to occur in three stages. At the Hague Summit in 1969, a committee was set up, under the chairmanship of the Prime Minister of Luxembourg, Pierre Werner. In March 1970 the Council of Ministers set up a working group to report on political cooperation in Europe.

Towards the end of 1970, the Werner report appeared and set out the proposed three-stage plan to achieve union by 1980. In 1971, France and Germany agreed on this plan, to create a monetary union with the other four members. The first stage, the exchange rate alignment called the 'snake,' got under way in 1972 but ran into problems almost immediately with the differential impact of the oil shock of 1973. The European Monetary System followed in 1979, the core of which being the Exchange Rate Mechanism (ERM). Countries could realign their currencies under this system; the next several years saw the progress of such realignments.

The next initiative came in the form of the Delors Report (1989). Again, three stages were proposed and, again, the ambition was to achieve union within 10 years. The dramatic political events of 1989 may have had some impact on the process. German unification in September of that year may have led to more serious consideration of pursuing a united Europe that would have the effect of containing a bigger and more confident Germany. But it may simply be coincidence that sterling entered the ERM one month later.

Stage 1 of the Delors plan was to run from July 1, 1990, while prospective dates for Stages 2 and 3 were agreed to later at Maastricht and by the European Council in Madrid in December 1995. In fact, Stage 1 lasted from July 1990 to the end of 1993, and involved liberalizing capital movements and enhancing policy coordination. Stage 2 began on January 1, 1994 as a period of transition ensuring readiness for Stage 3, with the emphasis being on convergence. Maastricht stipulated that Stage 3 should begin not later than December 12, 1996 but, if no date had been set by the end of 1997, Stage 3 would begin automatically on January 1, 1999.[3]

The Maastricht Treaty was signed by twelve member states in February 1992 and outlined the plan for monetary union. No sooner was the plan in place than the process was plunged into crisis in the Autumn of 1992, when sterling and the lira left the ERM and some devaluations took place (Eichengreen, 1998). Nevertheless, the scheme moved forward and in January 1994 Stage 2 of the plan came into effect and, as part of that, the European Monetary Institute (EMI) was established. Delors reappeared in October 1994 (in a private capacity) to remind member states that a common monetary policy carried out by the ECB would have to be accompanied by a common fiscal policy and other macro policy.[4] At the same time, Chancellor Kohl expressed the view that political union should accompany monetary union. This, as we can see from a current perspective, is a theme that has run through the whole process, even if it has not always received much attention. This occurred in May 1998.

Towards the end of 1995, it was agreed that the new currency would be called the euro and a new intergovernmental conference was scheduled to begin in March 1996. The decision was also made that in January 1998 (or as soon as possible in 1998 in some interpretations), a decision would be made on which countries would participate; and this would be based on hard figures for 1997.

The Maastricht treaty had Stage 3 of EMU starting as early as on January 1, 1997. That date passed and implementation was postponed for two years. From January 1, 1999, qualifying countries (or countries otherwise accepted) will lock their currencies irrevocably together at the prevailing exchange rate. No deviation will be permitted. On December 31, 1996 the EMI was scheduled to set out the framework for the conversion rates between national currencies and the European Currency Unit (ECU). The Council of Ministers (Council) was also supposed to decide which countries were meeting the criteria.

At a meeting of finance ministers and central bank governors in Spain in October 1995, it was agreed that the new currency would be brought into circulation in 2002 at the latest, and should replace the domestic currency within six months. That is, both the domestic currency and the euro will exist side by side for a limited period of transition. Thus within Stage 3 there are three further stages. The ECB was established in 1998. During the second period, participating countries irrevocably fix their exchange rates, EMI will be liquidated and ECB begin operations. The European System of Central Banks (ESCB) will begin to conduct a single monetary policy. The final period will begin on January 1, 2002 with the introduction of euro notes and coin.

2. Entry qualifications

It is appropriate to address the qualifying criteria in this paper, albeit briefly, since any deviation from a strict interpretation will inevitably affect the nature of the euro. There are four monetary and fiscal criteria. The best known and most frequently quoted are the two fiscal criteria: a country should not have a budget deficit in excess of 3% of its GDP and, furthermore, the outstanding debt should not be more than 60% of GDP. Secondly, a country must have an inflation rate "that does not exceed by more than 1.5 percentage points, that of the three best performing member states." An associated criterion, relating to long-term interest rates, states that such a rate should average over the period of one year a rate "that does not exceed by 2 percentage points that of, at most, the three best performing member states in terms of stability." Finally, to qualify, a country must have demonstrated that for at least two years it has held to "normal" fluctuation margins, and has not devalued its central rate against any other member country's rate. (Since 1993 these bands have been widened to 15%. So what is to be regarded as normal is now questionable.)

Adjusting the qualifications

Ever since these criteria were spelled out there has been discussion on their precise meaning. Even where precision was agreed upon, various possibilities for bending interpretations have been explored. This is an important issue for, once again, the financial markets will take a view on whether qualifying criteria are being dispensed with. At one extreme the whole future of monetary union and the euro are at stake.

The monetary criteria are not problematic. In a world where inflation has been the devil and has been attacked remorselessly almost to the point of temporary defeat there is less to worry about. Most countries in and outside of Europe have low inflation rates. It is the fiscal criteria that pose, and are likely to continue to pose, problems.

There have been far too many suggestions on rule interpretation to recite even a fraction of them here. The Maastricht Treaty (Treaty on European Union, Art. 104C) says that if *in the opinion of the Commission* a country is moving in the right direction, or indeed is simply planning to get to the destination, then all may be well and such a country could be waved through. Thus, in September 1994 the Commission opined that Ireland, with a debt ratio of 100% but a deficit ratio of 2.3%, could qualify since the debt ratio was falling at a satisfactory rate. This approach has been taken up with enthusiasm to encourage potential EMU participants who otherwise seemed doomed. An example will suffice. In June 1996 the Belgian Minister of Finance and Deputy Prime Minister made a speech in which he argued the case for Belgium. In 1993 Belgium's debt ratio was 138%. By 1995 it had fallen to 134% and estimated to fall to 132% in 1996. This was said to be good evidence of the fiscal consolidation strategy.

3. Monetary unions in history

While it is true that there is no strict historical precedent for the proposed EMU, there are instructive similarities with previous experience. Two important points should be made at the outset and held in view throughout. The first is that significant monetary unions occurred in the nineteenth century, at a time when metallic monetary standards were almost universally used (Tables 1 and 2). This makes for considerable differences with any union, which would take place now in a world of fiat money. The second point is that the nineteenth century was the century of the nation state when there was widespread desire for political union among smaller states.

This survey covers attempts to form monetary unions in Switzerland, Germany, Italy, the Latin Monetary Union, and the Scandinavian Currency Union (see also Hamada, 1998).

Switzerland

Although a territory recognized as Switzerland has been around for many hundreds of years, serious political union did not take place until 1848. There were 22 cantons in the union and many different currencies. There was discussion about how to rationalize such a system and the preference was for the French franc-based system, which came into being in 1850. The Swiss silver franc happened to coincide with the French franc and by the early 1850s 80% of Swiss coins originated in France. An Act of 1860 allowed for the reduction of

Table 1. Chronology of monetary unions.

Germany	1834–1871
Switzerland	1848
Austro German	1857
Italy	1861
Latin monetary union	1865–1926
Scandinavian monetary union	1872/4–1914

Table 2. Metallic standards.

	On	Off	On	Off
UK	1816	1914	1925	1931
US	1879	1916	1919	1933
Germany	1871	1914		
Netherlands	1873	1914	1926	1931
Norway	1874	1914		
Denmark	1874	1914		
Sweden	1875	1914		
Belgium	1875	1914		
Switzerland	1878			
Italy	1866	1899	1914	
Argentina	1881(B)		1929	
Russia				
Japan				
France			1926	1936

the metal content in coins and that led to some problems with Switzerland's monetary partners in the Latin Monetary Union, to which we will return. In the 1880s and 1890s the Swiss franc depreciated against the French franc and Swiss banks began losing silver.

Paper money was in limited use in Switzerland; bank notes were not legal tender and their regulation was left to individual cantons. In 1876 a Konkordat was made agreeing to a rationalization of the bank notes and in 1907 the Swiss National Bank was founded following discussion and legislation of 1905. The Bank was given a monopoly on the issue of bank notes.

In sum, the Swiss experience suggests that the organization of the currency was simply a rationalization that came after political union had been achieved.

Germany

The German case is more interesting and at least at some levels would appear to have some striking parallels with EMU: substantial moves toward *economic* union clearly preceded political union, although political union was the objective. There were hundreds of German states in the early nineteenth century and some attempts were made at removing obstacles to trade; first of all in the formation of the Zollverein in 1834. After the Congress of Vienna in 1815, 35 principalities and four free cities had full sovereignty and particularly the authority to regulate their own money systems. They had independent fiscal systems too, though in most cases the power to tax had been heavily circumscribed and customs duties remained an important source of revenue. In most of the territories a silver standard was in use. There was some government paper, but it was not a significant proportion of total money. Fiscal needs were invariably the source of such paper.

The Munich Coinage Treaty of 1837 represented a step toward monetary union. Some states renounced their rights of monetary sovereignty. In 1838 following the Dresden Coinage Convention each state was obliged to adopt either the Thaler or the Gulden. Additionally, to promote the idea of a unified system a common coin was minted (the Vereinsmunz—meaning "union coin"). It was equal in value to two Thaler and 3.5 Gulden.[5] In fact, the Prussian Thaler was beginning to penetrate all over Germany.

An important aspect of the Dresden Convention was that it established permanently fixed exchange rates between the two currency areas of the Zollvorein. However, some states within the Zollverein had opt-out clauses and did not participate in these arrangements (e.g., Luxembourg), while other important German states were outside the Zollverein.

The political turmoil of 1848 brought changes in Europe but failed to unify Germany. The Vienna Coinage Treaty of 1857 was the next important step towards monetary union. It standardized the silver coinage system, laid down strict rules on the circulation and minting of gold coins, and prohibited the conversion of gold to silver at a fixed exchange rate and thus prevented the emergence of a bimetallic system. The Treaty also tackled the issue of paper money, aimed at Austria whose paper money was inconvertible. The Treaty insisted on convertibility and coinage became standardized after 1857.

The German Reich was founded in 1871. At that time there were still different coinage systems in place and paper money was highly variant. The acts of 1871 and 1873 unified the coinage across the Reich. The set of rules meant that in fact something close to a common currency existed; paper money remained a small proportion of total money in circulation.

There is some disagreement over whether monetary union led or followed political union in Germany. There can be no doubt that political union was a desired objective, as it was for other states. And it does seem that steps taken in that direction were frequently of an economic kind so that it could be argued that the path to monetary union was well advanced by 1871.

As to how this union performed over the next 30 years, it has recently been argued that because the central authority had limited taxing powers and limited income from the individual states, strains developed leading directly to World War I (WWI) and on to the ensuing hyperinflation. Ill-designed fiscal federalism (which happens to look surprisingly like that proposed for the EU) proved fatal (Hefeker, 1997).

Italy

The story of Italy can be treated at lesser length. The drive for political union was a romantic vision of the nation state that drove the separate kingdoms and territories to forge unification in 1861 under the King of Sardinia. When that union was completed it became necessary to remove many of the obstacles to trade, including the many different currencies in existence. Steps therefore followed to convert the country to a monetary union as well. In 1862 a unified system was introduced based on the Sardinian lira. Sardinia was French oriented which accounts in part for the adoption of a system closely related to the French. A bimetallic standard was adopted in common with Italy's main trading partners and also to allow for the fact that silver coins were prevalent in the south of Italy. We will have more to say about Italy in connection with the Latin Monetary Union of which this country was a founding member.

Latin monetary union

In 1865 Belgium, France, Italy, and Switzerland agreed to coordinate their monetary systems under the Latin Monetary Union. Some scholars have seen it as an attempt at establishing bimetallism but Redish (1993) has argued convincingly otherwise. These four countries had strong monetary links and were on a de facto gold standard. The union stated the type of token and the quantity that would be issued, and the conditions of convertibility. It is not without significance that the union was formed soon after the rapid fall in the price of gold that was consequent upon the Californian and Australian gold discoveries. This drove silver out of circulation.

When the price of gold started to rise in the 1870s one would have expected that the de jure bimetallic standard would turn into a de facto silver standard. In fact, union members abandoned bimetallism. Again the important fact was the nineteenth century climate of economic integration. Some background may be helpful. In 1798 the French had invaded the Netherlands on which they imposed the new French monetary system. When the Belgian provinces revolted and went their own way they kept the French monetary system. In 1798 the French had also invaded Switzerland and instituted a system based on the franc. By 1852 the silver coins of France, Belgium, and some Italian states were made legal tender. We noted above that, upon political unification, Italy adopted the French system with which large parts of the country were already familiar.[6] It was thus the case that the coins of Belgium, Switzerland, and France had legal tender status. So by 1852 these countries all used the same unit of account and gave legal tender status to each other's coins. It must be regarded as no great leap forward to form what they called a union—a currency union was in effect already in place.

Scandinavia

Much the same might be said for Denmark, Norway, and Sweden, countries with a long history of integration, similar units of account—principally the riksdaler—and exchange of coins. These countries were on a silver standard. After long discussion and with a view to joining the increasingly prosperous club, these countries joined the gold standard—Norway and Denmark in 1874 and Sweden in 1875. In 1873 they formed a currency union, and at that point the krona replaced the riksdaler. Gold and other coins circulated freely.

In the 1870s these countries had considered various proposals, such as joining the Latin Monetary Union, or the German Union, or the Sterling area. In the end they opted for the less adventurous case of forming their own union, a sort of natural evolution, given that they use each other's coins. The main step taken to enlarge the union was in 1885 when the "central banks" established intercountry drawing rights. This clearing arrangement cleared notes at par.

In 1901 the union was completed when bank notes freely circulated. However, no sooner had these levels been reached than political problems between Norway and Sweden erupted in 1905. The system was doomed in 1914, as the gold standard was starting to unravel.

The main lessons one can learn from these unions are as follows. First, they were principally driven by a desire for political union. Those that led to political union were successful and those that did not failed. Secondly, they were essentially currency unions in countries using the same metallic standard. As such, it can hardly be regarded as a great advance to make the formal announcement that all their notes and coins were acceptable to one another. Thirdly, they did not have fully developed central banks, or at least they did not have an explicitly unified monetary policy.

These findings make it natural to raise the question: Is it necessary for a monetary union to be supported by a fiscal union?

4. A fiscal union

What is the relationship between monetary and fiscal unions? As noted, a thread running through the post-WWII plans for European monetary union is the concern with political union, sometimes explicitly coupling monetary union with political union. On occasion that has been expressed as the need for fiscal harmonization. At one extreme there is the suspicion that monetary union is simply a means of promoting political union. The question we raise here is does currency union in any way lead to fiscal convergence and ultimately to political union? And/or does it in some way depend upon such union.[7]

The term fiscal union is taken to mean the presence of a central authority for the area, one gathering taxes across the whole area and deciding what revenue to spend. Further, there is in theory a connection between monetary policy and fiscal policy. Monetary policy is related to fiscal policy by an intertemporal budget constraint: the present value of future primary surpluses has to be able to pay off the current government debt. Furthermore, there does seem to be some historical support that monetary and fiscal unions go together.

In broad terms, the historical experience we have reviewed suggests two principal kinds of union. One was defined by a collection of states unifying

Table 3. Government spending as a percentage of national income.

	1900	1910
UK	9.4	7.0
US		
Germany	6.7	6.7
Spain	10.0	14.5
Norway	6.9	
Denmark	5.8	
Sweden	6.6	

politically as a country. Monetary union served either as smoothing the path to such a union or solidifying it. The second type of union involved independent countries that wanted to explore the possible advantages of standardizing their monies. Although such examples were based on a specie standard each country retained its own monetary authority. These unions broke up because of conflicts in monetary policy.

We have also noted that member states were more prepared to give up monetary sovereignty than fiscal sovereignty. Indeed states retained some fiscal independence in all unions whether they were independent states of the Scandinavian type or states such as the United States, Germany, or Italy—i.e., full political unions.

In the nineteenth century there was little concept of fiscal union and no notion at all of fiscal policy (Table 3). Furthermore, in so far as there were any allocation branches of the budget these were on a very modest scale. Consequently, linking currencies implied that members of the union were sacrificing less freedom than in today's environment. Indeed, fiscal matters were left entirely to individual countries. It is true that international trade was relatively free and reliance on customs duties was declining. But this should not be overdone, for a return to protection starts around 1880, which is when the gold standard began to spread in earnest. Nevertheless, as can be seen from Table 4 import duties as a percentage of trade were still relatively low and of a similar size across most countries (Capie, 1983).

How much, if any, fiscal convergence was there among the countries or unions we have looked at? It is clear from a casual knowledge of the data that this is not an easy question. Common external tariffs, common income or sales taxes may provide a partial answer. It may be that an index of transport costs is available. Sales taxes can differ by transport costs without instigating arbitrage activity; thus, if we found tax differences too small we would have supporting evidence for fiscal harmonization. Unfortunately, this kind of information is extremely limited.

The share of public spending in a country's total output was generally small—certainly by today's standards.[8] The First World War was something of a turning

Table 4. Import duties at percentage of GNP.

	France	Germany	Italy	UK	Russia
1870	2.9	—	8.3	6.6	12.8
1875	5.1	—	8.6	5.3	12.1
1880	5.2	5.8	10.6	4.6	15.4
1885	7.2	7.4	14.0	5.4	21.8
1890	8.0	8.8	17.5	4.8	34.9
1895	10.4	9.3	16.4	5.0	34.0
1900	8.8	8.1	11.9	5.2	32.6
1905	8.6	8.8	8.4	6.2	33.5
1910	8.2	7.4	7.7	4.9	27.8
1915	9.2	6.3	7.4	4.3	29.7

Source: (Capie, 1983).

point. Unfortunately, data required to allow the production of a table on the key variables, which could indicate fiscal convergence, are very hard to gather. Although government spending is a well-recorded figure in many countries before 1900, there are only scattered data on output and hence we are unable to show trends of the share of government spending in the economy for many countries. However, where some rough indication is present, it shows that the share before 1914 was around 6%. That was true for Britain: 7% in 1870 and, again, in 1913. The data for the Scandinavian countries and for Germany are very similar. Most countries were concerned with ease of collection and relied in roughly equal measure on customs duties, consumption taxes, and direct taxes (though the last were beginning to grow in importance).

Taxes and ideas on taxes are exceedingly old and while there had been discussion on the subject for many centuries, the principal concerns had been with being able to raise funds for war. But the nineteenth century was essentially a century of peace and revenues were not under great pressure. There was no clear notion of fiscal policy as a tool of economic management. It was essentially for these reasons that there was a common fiscal stance. It would be difficult, and probably misguided, to talk about fiscal convergence.[9]

The similarity of taxes and of government spending, as a share of GNP, existed outside of unions and was unaffected by it. The one tax consequence of monetary union—one that finds a close parallel with EMU—is the agreement to share seigniorage in the German monetary union (Chown, 1994). Seigniorage was an important form of taxation right up to the nineteenth century; by giving up monetary sovereignty countries could lose substantial tax revenue, unless there was a sharing agreement.

The United States in the 1930s provides some useful insights (Hartland, 1949). There was of course a fiscal union in the United States, but a monetary break-up could not be ruled out as a consequence of the loss of gold reserves by individual states, resulting from bank failures. In fact, no state banking system collapsed completely because of transfers from federal resources to alleviate poverty. Hartland concludes that these transfers were essential to the system's survival. While she did not ask if fiscal transfers could offset asymmetric shocks, her study bears directly on this issue. By the interwar years the United States had a common currency, a central fiscal authority, a central bank, and crucial for the study, no nationwide banking system other than the Federal Reserve itself. All other banks could do business (at most) across one state; and some states, such as Illinois, prohibited even intrastate banking.

How did the United States, effectively on a gold standard, hold onto its monetary system when the international gold standard broke apart? One answer is that there was complete confidence that it would. But there was nevertheless a good analogy to monetary break-up as a consequence of the loss of gold reserves. This was the collapse of a state's banking system consequent upon a loss of gold reserves. Although many problems were experienced, no state's system collapsed entirely. Hartland examined the flows of reserves through the Federal Reserve accounts (the only means of monetary movement apart from shipments of cash). A net loss of reserves on private sector accounts experienced by an individual state was offset by inflows from the central government's account, arising not as a financial stabilization measure but as a result of transfers from federal resources directed at alleviating poverty and depression.

The conclusion was that these transfers were essential to the system's survival. It must be admitted that the counterfactual question was not explicitly posed—what would have happened had there not been such transfers? Would confidence in the continued integrity of the United States as a currency area have been such that private sector funds would have responded? It seems unlikely given the economic difficulties of the time. The risk would have been too great.

This all points strongly to the conclusion that while monetary union may not lead automatically to fiscal union, without such a fiscal union a monetary union may well not last. This conclusion would appear to be particularly robust in that it does not depend on asymmetric shocks. In the 1930s the problem was quite plainly asymmetric responses to a common shock.

In sum, a close connection exists between monetary union and fiscal union. The US experience suggests that a monetary union might only be viable if it is associated with a fiscal union. This connection may be the natural consequence of political union. Whether monetary and fiscal union need to go together when the desire to assert political will is absent is another question. But the historical evidence looks highly suggestive. In some cases there seem to have been agreements over the sharing of seigniorage—paralleled in EMU.

5. European Central Bank

Might the new central bank produce the kinds of strains that require a fiscal union? There seems to be little doubt that the ECB will produce a sound monetary policy. A great deal of the discussion has concentrated on the need to establish a new central bank patterned on the Bundesbank model to ensure a strong currency. The issue we want to raise here is different and concerns the nature of the monetary system being designed.

Theory

According to theory, independent central banks deliver better price performance than dependent central banks. This is principally because of the time inconsistency problem. Where governments may be tempted to gain some short-term advantage (such as re-election) by surprising the electorate with some inflation, an independent central bank is in a position to prevent that. Of course, how it would prevent it depends on the particular model. If there is no long-run Phillips curve, no trade off between output and inflation over the long run, then the single purpose of monetary policy reduces to producing price stability. There may be a short-run trade-off and that matters when considering the nature of independence. But if the purpose is price stability it is better left in the hands of an independent central bank. There seems to be abundant historical evidence to support the theory. We next provide a brief survey of that history.

Brief historical survey

Central banks generally came into being in the late nineteenth century, and since then there have been alternating phases of independence and dependence. During the nineteenth century there was considerable, but not universal, freedom of interference from government. The First World War changed that as governments took control of resources and printed money. Then there was a dramatic swing back after WWI. Indeed the real origins of explicit central bank independence go back to the 1920s. But it was not long before the pendulum swung again. The period from the 1930s to the 1970s was, in contrast to the nineteenth century, the age of the state and of economic management, and so of more dependent central banks. That era has passed now and we are at the beginning of another period of relative economic freedom, and a desire to reduce the influence of the state (Capie and Goodhart, 1995).

Before WWI the legal status of central banks made little difference because many industrial countries were on the gold standard. Furthermore, the political economy was such that internal balance could readily be sacrificed to external balance. Workers were less aware of economic developments and certainly less well organized. Nevertheless, there were some differences among the few central banks that did exist. By 1913, however, a standard role for central banks had been adopted by the main industrial countries. The central bank's main functions and operational techniques were generally accepted, with little political controversy. The main objective was to maintain convertibility of the currency into gold. The main control instrument was to vary interest rates to that end; the interest rate was made effective by discounting bills and, increasingly, by open-market operations. The true central bank operated independently from government. But the decision to join the gold standard was a political one, taken by governments. In other words in today's terminology central banks did not have goal independence, only instrument independence.

The early period of central banking through to the First World War was relatively laissez-faire. The state tended to keep its distance, particularly in monetary matters. The belief that the gold standard, the prevailing international monetary system, provided a largely automatic means of adjustment was important to this philosophy. A considerable degree of independence was therefore obtained, particularly in so far as it related to the central bank assisting in the smooth working of the gold standard. Yet even for nineteenth-century England the precise nature of the relationship between the Bank and governments continues to be debated. The Bank of England was a joint stock company, with shareholders to satisfy but with a growing awareness of a public responsibility. In the financial crises of 1847, 1857, and 1866 there was a need either for the government to intervene or for the bank to consult the government. In the former case the 1844 Act was suspended and in the latter crises suspension actually took place. We may not go all the way with Fetter who maintained that the Bank of England's independence was a fiction, but it certainly was not total. And it would be misleading to suggest that independence prevailed elsewhere, even when it was seen as desirable. The Banque de France had been subjected to considerable control from its birth in 1800 until the mid nineteenth century. Plessis (1982) has argued that the Banque de France was subject to almost constant control throughout the period. However, there was surely a good measure of autonomy, or freedom of action in the operation of monetary policy, in many of the major countries by the late nineteenth century.

When the gold standard was abandoned at the outbreak of the First World War and governments sought greater control over resources, price levels soared almost everywhere. The nature of the relationship between the state and the central banks changed abruptly. Irrespective of the degree of independence, either statutory or in practice, the state enforces its authority in times of crisis. Central bank independence everywhere was severely diminished if not abandoned.

At the end of the First World War there was a widespread desire to return to the pre-1914 world of stability. The Bank of England, among other central banks, returned to its independent status after the First World War. Furthermore, at the Brussels and Genoa conferences the sentiment was to restore budgetary equilibrium, restore the gold standard, and establish independent central banks. The older established banks reverted to relative independence; and newly established central banks in the 1920s enjoyed greater freedom than was to be the case a decade later.

The great depression of 1929–1933 was regarded in many countries as a consequence of central and commercial bank failings. Reform was seen as urgently required; an aspect of this was the removal of independence as confidence in liberal capitalism had weakened. The factors primarily responsible for these changes were: the rise of Keynesian economics; the emergence of the managed economy; and more or less coincident with the second, the Second World War and its aftermath. There was also a generally improved price performance in the years 1939–1951, certainly compared with 1914–1923. Governments, therefore, felt encouraged to return to interventionist policies. Nationalization of central banks was prevalent as governments everywhere took a closer interest in monetary policy.

Also in the decades after the Second World War there was a great extension of national political independence. The birth of new states and acquisition of sovereignty by former colonies resulted in the emergence of governments that sought control over their own affairs. Governments either established central banks or took over or converted existing institutions.

The inflationary experience of the two decades that followed—roughly the late 1960s to the late 1980s—when the world for the first time ever, in a generally peaceful period, adopted fiat money, brought home again the relationship between expansionary monetary policy and inflation. Central banks that were less susceptible to government pressure delivered lower inflation. The pendulum swung, once more, this time for more central bank independence.

But what kind of central bank independence are we referring to? Many indicators of degrees of independence have been devised though none is easy to apply. In some of the most recent writing a distinction has been made between goal independence and instrument independence. An Anglo-Saxon consensus has perhaps emerged that goals should be set by governments, whereas central banks should be given the job of achieving these goals—since goal independence produces the "democratic deficit".

The issue of central bank independence was set out with typical clarity by Friedman (1968, p. 174) a long time ago:

> The problem is to establish institutional arrangements that will enable government to exercise responsibility for money yet will at the same time limit the power given to government and prevent the power from being used in ways that will tend to weaken rather than strengthen a free society.

Friedman went on to suggest (p. 179) that the central bank should be "...an independent branch of government co-ordinate with the legislative, executive, and judicial branches." In other words, it would have a mandate to carry out a law or laws passed by government, and would only be interfered with by government if the law—its mandate—were changed.

However, this is not what is contained in the Maastricht Treaty. The treaty gives the ECB complete freedom, that is goal independence. It is exceedingly doubtful if there is any historical precedent for this. Much is sometimes made of having goal independence and some have ranked central banks on this basis. But even the Bundesbank, which comes closest to the ECB, can be called to account by the Bundestag. And as we have seen in relatively recent times when it comes to the crunch the Bundesbank can be told what to do. In the ECB case there is no one to tell it what to do. As Volcker (1997, p. 104) put it recently:

> Independent countries would be ceding monetary sovereignty to a jointly sponsored entity without a parallel government body with which the central bank would interact. ...It would be the extreme of central bank independence.

In case some readers are tempted to think that some early private institutions enjoyed a position similar to the ECB, it may be worthwhile to consider what makes a central bank. Upon its establishment in 1694 the Bank of England was not a central bank. Something close to a modern conception of central bank emerged perhaps by the end of the eighteenth century. But some scholars would prefer to date the Bank of England's role as central banker from 1844, or at least see the 1844 Act as an important landmark, since that bolstered the bank's monopoly privileges. For others still one would have to wait until the 1870s when the bank accepted its function as a lender of last resort and effectively withdrew from any rivalry with the commercial banks. The inclination of this paper is to the last mentioned.

Lamfalussy, 1997, of the ECB's forerunner, the EMI, has recently set out with frankness the nature of the ECB's independence, but some will feel with an overly optimistic bias:

> The Treaty (in article 107) and the Statute of the ESCB (in article 7) both contain very clear provisions regarding the relationships with third parties, which leave no room whatsoever for misinterpretation. To quote a key sentence: "neither the ECB nor a national central bank, nor any member of their decision-making bodies shall seek or take instruction from Community institutions or bodies, from any government of a member state or from any other body: Moreover, the aforementioned authorities shall also—and I quote again—undertake to respect this principle and not to seek to influence the members of the decision-making bodies of the ECB or of the national central banks in the performance of their tasks". To put it simply: the door to the single monetary policy is locked from both sides, and neither the ESCB nor third parties can open the door for political instructions. Even attempts to do so would be in conflict with the provisions of the Treaty and the Statute of the ESCB.

In other words, the ECB will be uncontrolled and uncontrollable. This looks like a flawed institution. Democratic accountability is lost completely. And there is no obvious solution. The ECB will not be accountable to anyone. It will report to the Commission on what it is doing but be unable to take instruction. Even if it could take instruction, would democracy in any way be enhanced in the absence of an elected president? There is also the further point that the new central bank lacks transparency in its decision making. It has sometimes been argued that transparency can be a partial substitute for the lack of reputation from which a new institution inevitably suffers.

However, it might be argued that so long as the ECB's goal is a sensible one—and currently it is price stability (without that being defined too closely)—things may turn alright. But serious stresses are likely to develop. We leave aside here the question of how a satisfactory price index can be constructed. But with such a price index in place and the ECB set to let it rise by $x\%$ per annum it surely will not be long before one part of the union will experience some difficulty. And politicians of whatever hue will not be long in exploiting suspicions that the hardship is all the fault of unelected bankers in Frankfurt who are not accountable to anyone and cannot be removed. It is surely not being excitable to predict problems for the euro at that point.

6. Conclusions

We have reviewed the 19th century experience of monetary unions, in particular, the link with fiscal union. We have also reviewed the nature and development of central bank independence. What conclusions can we draw from these experiences concerning the possible strength of the euro in the medium to longer term? What gives currency strength after the fundamentals are in place are the credibility of the monetary authorities, acceptance of the monetary stance, and reputation of the monetary and fiscal institutions. The fact that EMU has no historical precedence is bound to affect the reputation of its central monetary institution (Fratianni et al., 1998). The problem is further aggravated by the inability of the union to make fiscal transfers and by the tight constraints that have been placed on member countries' fiscal policy. Finally, the granting of goal independence to a central bank that is not accountable to any government carries serious dangers. Again there is no historical precedent and all the more worrying for that. And we have noted the additional deficiency of lack of transparency. Thus, the uncertainty surrounding what will happen to the euro must of necessity weaken it. And then the question is, can it be sustained in the face of the pressures that seem to be inevitable?

There is an entire range of solutions, delimited by no political union at one end and a supranational government at the other end. For example, the German union of 1871 lay at the weaker end of the spectrum and in some sense was less successful as a result. The argument implicit in this paper is that something much closer to the strong version would be required for monetary union to work.

Notes

1. For a considered summary of the prospects based on an examination of the system over the last 130 years, see Eichengreen (1996).
2. For example, in late 1996 after a long blockade by French lorry drivers the French government gave into demands; and threats then followed by oil workers. Speculation followed on what this

meant for French Government spending, budget deficits, and euro-entry criteria. In one view it could damage French chances but in another more cynical view it could improve the prospects of the French entering at a preferred (i.e., beneficial) exchange-rate. French experience was soon followed by a Greek farmers' blockade. More recently, the French elections and German proposals for creative accounting with gold reserves have raised more serious questions.

3. Although the Rome Treaty of 1957 had set out to create a common market, in 1990 there was still no such market but the ambition in the Single Market Act was to bring that about by 1992. This was used as an economic argument to promote the scheme for monetary union by suggesting that such a market was either not possible or at least less efficient without monetary union.
4. See Vanthoor (1993). It should also be noted that both the Werner and Delors reports stressed the need for fiscal harmonization.
5. It proved to be too big in value for common use and was nicknamed the Champagne Thaler since it equaled in value the price of a bottle of Champagne, a considerable luxury.
6. Napoleon had already introduced the French system to Italy in 1793.
7. This section draws on some work being done with my colleague Geoffrey Wood.
8. A very severe caution has to be issued at this stage. Existing data are frequently in conflict and need to be treated very carefully. A major research effort needs to be made to try to bring together the most reliable estimates of the appropriate variables across European countries.
9. Some work is being done on compiling a database on some of the necessary variables for many European countries. Interestingly, an early finding from this work is that there was only a very limited amount of fiscal convergence (see Flandreau and Cacheux, 1997).

References

Bordo, M. and L. Jonung (1996) "Monetary Unions in History." Mimeo.

Cairncross, A. (1988) "The Bank of England." In Toniolo (ed.), *Central Bank Independence in Historical Perspective*. New York: W. de Gruyer.

Canzoneri, M.B., V. Grilli, and P.R. Masson (Eds.) (1992) *Establishing a Central Bank: Issues in Europe and Lessons from the US*. New York: Cambridge University Press.

Capie, F. (1983) "Tariff Protection and Economic Performance in the Nineteenth Century." In J. Black and A. Winters (eds.), *Policy Performance in International Trade*. London: MacMillan.

Capie, F. and C. Goodhart (1995) "Central Banks, Macro Policy and the Financial System; the Nineteenth and Twentieth Centuries." *Financial History Review* 2, 145–161.

Chown, J. (1994) *A History of Money: From AD 800*. New York: Routledge.

Cukierman, A. (1992) *Central Bank Strategy, Credibility and Independence*. Cambridge, MA: MIT Press.

Delors Report (1989) Committee for the Study of Economic and Monetary Union, *Report on Economic and Monetary Union in the European Community*. Luxembourg: Office for Official Publications of the EC.

Eichengreen, B. (1990) *Globalizing Capital*. Princeton: Princeton Univ. Press.

Eichengreen, B. (1993) "European Monetary Unification." *Journal of Economic Literature* 31, 1321–1357.

Eichengreen, B. (1998) "Exchange Rate Stability and Financial Stability." in this volume.

Eijffinger, S. and Schaling (1993) "Central Bank Independence in Twelve Industrial Countries." *Banca Nazionale del Lavoro Quarterly Review* 184, 1–41.

Fetter, F.W. (1978) *Development of British Monetary Orthodoxy*, 1797–1875. Fairfield: Augustus M. Kelly.

Fforde, J. (1992) *The Bank of England and Public Policy* 1941–1958. Cambridge: Cambridge University Press.

Flandreau, M. and J. le Cacheux (1997) "Central Bank Independence and Market Discipline under the European Gold Standard, 1880–1914." Mimeo.

Fratianni, M. and J. von Hagen (1990) "Public Choice Aspects of European Monetary Unification." *Cato Journal*, 389–441.
Fratianni, M., A. Hauskrecht, and A. Maccario (1998) "Dominant Currency and the Future of the Euro." this volume.
Friedman, M. (1968) "The Role of Monetary Policy." *American Economic Review* 58, 1–17.
Friedman, M. and A.J. Schwartz (1963) *A Monetary History of the United States:* 1867–1960. Princeton: Princeton University Press.
Hamada, K. (1977) "On the Political Economy of Integration. A Public Economics Approach." In Aliber (ed.), *The Political Economy of Monetary Reform*. Montclair, NJ: Allanheld, Osmun, pp. 13–31.
Hamada, K. (1998) "The Choice of International Monetary Regimes in a Context of Repeated Games." in this volume.
Hartland, P. (1949) "Interregional Payments Compared with International Payments." *Quarterly Journal & Economics* 63, 392–407.
Hefeker, C. (1997) "The Agony of Central Power: Fiscal Federalism in the German Reich." Mimeo.
Holtfrerich, C.L. (1989) "The Monetary Unification Process in Nineteenth Century in Germany: Relevance and Lessons for Europe Today." In de Cecco and Gioranníni (eds.), *A European Central Bank? Perspectives on Monetary Unification after Ten Years of the EMS*. Cambridge: Cambridge University Press.
Kramer, H.R. (1971) "Experience with Historical Monetary Unions." In H. Giersch (ed.), *Integration* durch Wahrungsumon Institute fur Weltwirtsidoft Kiel.
Lamfalussy, A. (1997) "The European Central Bank: Independent and Accountable." *Austrian National Bank.*
Nielsen, A. (1933) "Monetary Union." *Encyclopedia of Sciences.*
Plessis, A. (1982) "La Banque de France et Deux Cents Actionnaires Sous le Second Empire."
Plumtre, A.F.W. (1940) *Central Banking in the British Dominions*. Toronto: University of Toronto Press.
Redish, A. (1993) "The Latin Monetary Union and the Emergence of the International Gold Standard." In Bordo and Capie (eds.), *Monetary Regimes in Transition.* Cambridge: Cambridge University Press.
Sala-i-Martin, X. and J. Sachs (1992) "Fiscal Federalism and Optimum Currency Areas: Evidence for Europe from the United States." In Canzonieri et al. (eds.), pp. 195–219.
Salvatore, D. (1998) "Present International Monetary and Financial Arrangements." in this volume.
Sannucci, V. (1989) "The Establishment of a Central Bank: Italy in the Nineteenth Century." In De Cecco and Giovannini (eds.), *A European Central Bank? Perspectives on Monetary Unification after Ten Years of the EMS*. Cambridge: Cambridge University Press.
Sayers, R.S. (1976) *The Bank of England* 1891–1944. New York: Cambridge University Press.
Sylla, R. (1992) *The Federal Reserve* in Palgrave Dictionary of Finance.
Timberlake, R.H. (1993) *The Organs of Central Banking in the United States*. Cambridge: Harvard Univ. Press.
Treaty on European Union (1992).
Vanthoor, W.F.V. (1993) *European Monetary Union since 1848. A Political and Historical Analysis.* Brookfield, VT: Edward Elgar.
Vanthoor, W.F.V. (1996) "The Age of (Western) European Integretation." De Economist 144(2), 137–164.
Volcker, P. (1997) *International Monetary Survey* 26(7), 97–112.

Open economies review **9:S1** 467–491 (1998)

Dominant Currencies and the Future of the Euro

MICHELE FRATIANNI fratiann@indiana.edu
Department of Business Economics and Public Policy, Indiana University, Kelley School of Business, Bloomington, Indiana 47405

ANDREAS HAUSKRECHT Hauskrecht@aol.com
Deutsche Bundesbank Foundation, Free University of Berlin, Department of Economics, 14195 Berlin, Germany

AURELIO MACCARIO asscarli@luiss.it
Guido Carli Association, Rome, LUISS University, Department of Economics, 00198 Rome, Italy

Key words: vehicle currencies, transaction costs, financial markets, central bank reputation, portfolio shifts, exchange-rate fundamentals

JEL Classification Numbers: E42, E58, F31, F36

Abstract

The paper's thesis is that the US dollar, despite the inevitable erosion of market share that it will suffer at the hands of the euro, will remain the most important international currency. The transaction domain of an international currency depends on its ability to lower transaction costs relative to alternative currencies. The EMU financial markets will not be as integrated, and thus as liquid, as the US financial markets for quite some time, thus favoring the use of the dollar as a medium of exchange. Inertia and reputational considerations further favor the dollar. The future value of the exchange rate dollar-euro will depend on economic fundamentals more than on portfolio shifts. Portfolio shifts argue for an appreciation of the euro; but fundamentals can swamp the effects of portfolio shifts. Should the EMU fundamentals reflect the spirit of the Maastricht Treaty and the Growth and Stability Pact, the chances for a euro appreciation will increase. Some caution, however, is in order because the ECB is a new and untested central bank where consensus for a conservative policy may be harder to achieve than can be gleaned from a literal reading of the Maastricht Treaty.

Introduction and summary of conclusions

Money is held because it provides services as a medium of exchange and as a standard of value. Since modern (paper) money has no intrinsic value, people prefer a given medium of exchange over others if they expect other individuals to accept that medium in exchange for goods, services and assets. This implies that the larger the transaction domain of a money, the more desirable it is for individuals to use it; call this the network value of money. Monies, which are not widely used, have a low network value and face the difficult task of competing against widely used or high-network-value monies.

Money producers must establish and maintain brand name in the market place (Klein, 1974). A money bearing a rapid and variable inflation tends to discourage its use for the benefit of more stable monies. In practice, this substitution process tends to be slow. Inflation must reach high rates before individuals switch out of the inflated money. There are institutional reasons for this. Legal tender laws and the practice of governments to disburse funds and receive tax collections in the local currency raise the cost of using nonlocal currencies as alternative means of payment in the domestic market. These costs become virtually infinite when there is an outright prohibition to write contracts specifying foreign currencies as means of payment among residents.

Money competition occurs at the international level. The historical evidence indicates that one currency tends to dominate others both as an international medium of exchange and as a store of value. According to Cipolla (1956), the Byzantine *nomisma* was the unchallenged coin from the fifth to the seventh century, to be displaced later by the Islamic *dinar* in the Low Middle Ages. The *dinar*, in turn, was displaced by the Florentine *fiorino*, first, and the Venetian *ducato*, later, in the higher Middle Ages. These coins shared three attributes: large weight (high unitary value), high intrinsic (purchasing power) stability and a leading position in international commerce of the issuer. In more recent time, 1870–1914, the British pound rose to the status of dominant currency, reflecting the British attachment to the gold standard and the British supremacy in trade and banking. The interwar period left a vacuum in both currency and trade (Kindleberger, 1973). The US dollar emerged as the dominant international currency after World War II but lost some ground after the end of Bretton Woods to the Deutsche mark and the Japanese yen.

Historically, there is a positive correlation between relative size and dominant-currency status. The decline in the dollar share of world reserves after World War II occurred as the US share of world output was falling (Eichengreen and Frankel, 1996). Relative economic size may proxy for the relative transaction domain of the currency; as this shrinks so does the network value of that currency. On this score the formation of EMU-11 will give the euro a big push in competing against the dollar for the position of dominant currency. On the other hand, the euro will be issued by a new central bank representing a group of countries that have yet not achieved political unification. Thus, the benefits from a large economic area are partly offset by relatively untested institutions.

This paper is oraganized as follows. Section 1 reviews the evidence on internationally dominant monies. The key result is that the US dollar, despite the loss of market share in the last two decades, remains the undisputed dominant currency in the world. The German mark and the Japanese yen have made gains, especially in private portfolios; yet, they remain far distant cousins of the dollar.

Section 2 deals with the challenge of the euro to the supremacy of the dollar. There, we consider the merit of the hypothesis that lower transaction costs in the EMU financial markets will be the engine driving the euro to compete with the dollar as the dominant international currency. Our conclusion is that the EMU will exert a strong centripetal force on domestic financial markets, endowing them with depth, breath, and liquidity close to those in the United States. But financial integration will fall short of the degree of integration prevailing in the United States. For example, in the market for government securities, the absence of a Federal government in the EU puts a ceiling on the integration process. Transaction costs may remain lower in the US financial markets than in the EMU financial markets for quite some time. The euro will rise in importance but not enough to displace the dollar as primus inter pares, at least not for a few years. This conclusion is reinforced by the fact that the ECB is a new and untested central bank, serving eleven sovereign states. The "Excessive Deficit Procedure" and the "Stability and Growth Pact" are a poor substitute for the missing political integration. The latter places a second ceiling on the anti-inflation credibility of the new ECB. National interests will weigh in heavily in monetary policy decisions. The differentiated effects of monetary policy across Euro land and the likelihood of asymmetric shocks and asynchronous cyclical movements raise the potential for conflicts in the Governing Council of the ECB and raise the odds that the long-run inflation performance of the ECB will not match the Bundesbank's. Our "best" prediction is one where the euro will be a big international currency, but not big enough to dislodge the dollar from pole position.

In the final section we take up the issue of portfolio shifts and the prospective exchange rate between the euro and the dollar. The United States and the European Union are comparable in economic size, but the dollar is much more important than the sum of the EU currencies in the international money and capital markets. Should the euro get a share of the international money and capital markets that reflects the economic weight of EMU in the world, private and public portfolios will have to be reweighted in favor of the euro and against the dollar. Studies that address the portfolio issue fall into either of two categories: a group that makes back-of-the-envelope predictions based on broad relationships, such as relative economic size of the areas; and another that estimates demand functions for assets in the pre-EMU period and makes predictions for the EMU period, assuming that the underlying stochastic structure will not change. This assumption is hard to swallow because there is consensus that EMU will be a big innovation in the world economy, and consequently established relationships will be altered. According to the econometric exercise by Frenkel and Sondergaard (1997), EMU-11 would produce a shift of approximately 14% (of pre-EMU assets) out of dollar-denominated assets and 10% out of yen-denominated assets. The variable that does most of the work in the prediction is the relative size of the EMU. Strict portfolio diversification motives are ignored. That is, German investors will have fewer reasons to hold Italian assets as a result of the fact that the covariance between German assets and Italian assets will rise following currency unification. On the other hand, the German investor will have more reason to increase his or her holdings of dollar-denominated assets and yen-denominated assets so long as the ECB pursues an independent monetary policy relative to the Fed and the Bank of Japan.

Finally, we express caution on the merit of the hypothesis that said portfolio shift may automatically cause an appreciation of the euro relative to the dollar. Our caution stems from two reasons. The first is that prediction of the euro appreciation is predicated on assets supplies being rigid. There is no reason to assume that countries and firms will fail to exploit the opportunity of larger and more liquid markets to issue euro-denominated debt. Under these circumstances the simple portfolio model of the exchange rate can no longer predict unambiguously an appreciation of the euro. But more importantly, the relative strength of the euro in the exchange markets will be determined much more by fundamentals such as expectations of prospective monetary and fiscal policies, reputation of the respective central banks, and business cycles than portfolio shifts. EMU fiscal policy will be constrained by the excessive-deficit procedure. EMU monetary policy is likely to be less conservative than a strict reading of the Maastricht treaty suggests. The ECB will be a young and untested institution compared to the Federal Reserve System. Thus, it would seem premature at this point to state that, on the strength of the under representation of the EU currencies in the international money and financial markets, the euro is bound to appreciate relative to the dollar. The effects of the expected portfolio shift in favor of euro-denominated assets will occur against the background of fiscal and monetary policies in the United States and the EU. Even assuming comparable fundamentals, the appreciation of the euro relative to the dollar will take place over several years. Domestic and foreign investors are not likely to replace all of DM, pound, and lira assets in euro-denominated assets. A wait-and-see attitude is the appropriate strategy when one faces a new and untested player. Over the long run, the outcomes are wide open and are critically dependent on the relative fundamentals. Should those fundamentals be virtually the same, the success of the euro as a dominant money will rise over time.

1. Recent evidence on internationally dominant monies

Since money has several functions and is used by both the private and the public sector, it is useful to organize the discussion around the well-known 3×2 classification scheme adopted from Kenen (1983):

Functions	Private sector	Public sector
Means of payments	Vehicle	Interventions
Unit of account	Denomination	Anchor
Store of value	Portfolio allocation	Official reserves

When country A carries out transactions with country B, both currencies can be used. If A's currency is used in preference to B's currency, A's currency is an international currency for country B. Country A and B may use country C's currency, a third currency. In this case currency C is an international currency or a vehicle currency for both countries.

1.1. Unit of account and private means of payment

The dollar's dominance as a standard of value and as an international means of payment was overestimated for a long time until Grassman's study (1973) revealed that the bulk of world exports was invoiced in the exporter's currency. A study carried out by the European Commission (ECU Institute, 1995) on trade invoicing covering the period 1980–1992 reveals that the dollar, despite the decline, retained a market share in 1992 of 47% (Table 1). The evidence confirms that industrial countries increasingly invoice imports in local currency. The dollar, however, remains by far the most important vehicle currency.[1]

The US dollar also remains the largest currency traded in foreign exchange markets, according to a survey carried out in 1996 by the Bank for International Settlements (BIS, 1996, Table 2). Furthermore, the same survey notes that for seven of the ten most traded currency pairs the dollar appeared on the other side of the transaction: 97% for the Canadian dollar, 95% for the Australian dollar, 88% for the yen, and 57 to 73% for the main European currencies such as the Swiss franc, the French franc, the Deutsche mark and the UK pound. In markets where domestic currency business accounts for about 70% of total turnover, the pair US dollar/domestic currency accounts for at least half of total turnover compared with an average of 24% for all other currencies. Finally, the dollar continues to have more transactions than national currencies in all exchange markets except for Frankfurt. The Deutsche mark and Japanese yen are, respectively, number two and number three in the ranking of dominant monies in terms of the function of means of payment.

Table 1. Trade invoicing (% of trade invoiced in each currency).

	Main exporting countries		
	1980	1987	1992
US dollar	55	46	47
DM, Dutch guilder	16	19	17
Yen	4	7	8
FF, pound, Lira	15	15	15
Other currencies	10	13	13

Source: ECU Institute (1995).

Table 2. Currency breakdown of foreign exchange transactions*.

Currency	April 1989	April 1992	April 1995
US dollar	90	82	83
Deutsche mark	27	40	37
Japanese yen	27	23	24
Pound sterling	15	14	10
French franc	2	4	8
Swiss franc	10	9	7
Canadian dollar	1	3	3
Australian dollar	2	2	3
ECU	1	3	2
Other EMS currencies	3	9	13
Currencies of other reporting countries	3	3	2
Other currencies	19	8	8
All currencies	**200**	**200**	**200**

Source: BIS, Central Bank Survey of Foreign Exchange Market Activity (May 1996).
*Daily averages. Given that each transaction concerns two currencies, the percentages add up to twice the total amount of transactions (200%).

1.2. Official reserves

Central banks, like private agents, accumulate and use assets denominated in currencies that have a high frequency of exchange. Stabilizing exchange rate movements is the motive for holdings these assets. The dollar, again, is the dominant currency although its position has declined. In fact, between 1975 and 1995, the share of this currency in global official reserves has fallen from 78.2 to 62.5% (Table 3; Dal Bosco, 1998). Part of this drop reflects the dollar's depreciation relative to other key currencies; but part reflects a long-term shift in favor of Deutsche mark and yen assets. The long-term decline of the dollar's share encompasses the reversal of the 1990s when the Bank of Japan and European central banks accumulated dollar-denominated assets to "lean" against the depreciation of the US currency (Eichengreen and Frankel, 1996, p. 350).

Central banks are careful not to reveal the composition of their foreign reserves, thus preventing a detailed analysis of what changes may have taken place across countries. The best one can do is to differentiate the developing countries from the world as a whole (Table 4). There, too, the dollar's share declines, but the timing pattern is different from the world as a whole. The decline between 1976 and 1980 is very similar for the two groups and is in part explained by the dollar depreciation; after 1980 the dollar share remained virtually the same for the developing countries, but declined for the world as a whole.

Table 3. Share of major currencies in total foreign exchange reserves (in %).

End of period	US $	DM	Yen	Pound Ster.	Balances in private ECU	French franc	Swiss franc	Dutch guil.	Other[a]	Memo: Total res.[b]
1975	78.2	8.8	1.8	2.8	—	1.8	2.2	0.9	3.5	162.3
1976	77.6	9.3	2.2	1.7	—	1.5	2.1	0.8	4.8	187.7
1977	77.9	9.0	2.1	1.6	—	1.2	2.0	0.7	5.4	247.3
1978	76.2	10.7	3.1	1.5	—	1.2	2.0	0.8	4.5	291.8
1979	73.7	11.8	3.5	1.8	—	1.2	2.4	1.0	4.6	302.2
1980	69.7	14.7	4.2	2.9	—	1.7	3.2	1.3	2.4	324.6
1981	71.9	12.7	4.1	2.1	—	1.3	2.7	1.1	4.2	301.8
1982	71.2	12.0	4.6	2.4	—	1.2	2.7	1.1	4.9	282.3
1983	72.4	11.2	4.7	2.5	—	1.0	2.3	0.8	5.1	289.3
1984	70.7	11.8	5.4	2.9	0.2	1.0	2.0	0.7	5.4	315.9
1985	66.0	14.1	7.4	2.9	0.5	1.2	2.2	0.9	4.9	352.7
1986	69.1	13.5	6.9	2.5	0.8	1.1	1.7	1.0	3.5	411.3
1987	67.8	14.6	7.7	2.2	0.9	0.7	1.8	1.1	3.3	592.8
1988	64.6	15.7	7.9	2.5	2.1	0.9	1.9	0.9	3.4	624.4
1989	60.4	18.7	7.9	2.5	3.0	1.3	1.7	1.0	3.6	677.0
1990	56.4	19.1	9.0	3.1	4.6	2.1	1.7	1.0	2.9	806.4
1991	57.3	17.0	9.5	3.3	4.5	2.5	1.6	1.0	3.4	855.3
1992	62.0	14.7	8.6	3.1	2.7	2.3	1.3	0.6	4.7	852.1
1993	61.5	15.1	8.5	2.9	2.6	2.0	1.5	0.6	5.4	954.4
1994	61.0	15.4	8.8	3.2	2.7	2.0	1.3	0.4	5.2	1098.7
1995	60.8	14.7	7.4	3.1	2.3	1.9	1.1	0.4	8.3	1292.8
1996	63.7	14.0	7.0	3.5	1.8	1.6	0.8	0.4	7.2	1430.4

Source: IMF, Annual Report, and various issues.
[a]The residual is equal to the difference between total identified reserves and the sum of the reserves held in the seven currencies listed in the table.
[b]In billions of US $; including dollar holdings contributed to the EMI and balances in private ECU.

The inference is that the industrial countries, not the developing countries, effected the reserve diversification at the expense of the dollar. Not only the Deutsche mark and the Japanese yen gained in the process of diversification, but also the two artificial currencies, the SDR and especially the ECU (Eichengreen and Frankel, 1996, Table 2).[2] The developing countries, and in particular the Asian group, remained anchored to the dollar. This attachment to the US currency may be explained by the preference of developing countries to peg to the dollar and to issue debt denominated in dollars.

Table 4. Currency breakdown of developing countries' official reserves (% of identified official reserves in developing countries).

	US $	DM	Yen	Pound ster.	French franc	Swiss franc	Dutch guil.	Other[a]
1975	70.8	8.8	0.9	6.8	2.4	2.3	0.9	7.1
1976	72.7	10.1	1.1	3.2	1.7	1.9	0.7	8.6
1977	70.9	13.3	3.2	2.8	2.3	3.9	1.2	2.5
1978	66.6	15.9	4.9	3.2	2.3	3.6	1.5	1.9
1979	66.3	16.2	4.8	3.4	2.2	3.8	1.6	1.7
1980	60.1	16.7	5.6	5.4	3.1	4.9	2.0	2.2
1981	67.1	13.9	5.0	3.8	2.5	3.9	1.6	2.2
1982	66.5	13.3	5.1	4.4	2.4	3.9	1.7	2.8
1983	68.0	11.1	4.9	4.8	2.0	3.6	1.3	4.2
1984	69.2	10.6	5.3	4.8	1.9	3.0	1.0	4.1
1985	67.5	10.9	6.5	4.7	2.1	3.1	1.1	4.0
1986	63.2	11.1	7.1	4.6	2.0	2.5	1.1	8.4
1987	59.9	10.8	8.5	5.1	1.8	2.7	1.1	10.2
1988	57.4	11.4	9.2	5.5	1.7	2.5	0.9	11.3
1989	61.3	10.9	6.8	5.5	1.8	2.2	0.8	10.6
1990	60.7	11.6	7.3	6.4	2.0	2.2	0.7	9.1
1991	62.7	10.8	7.6	6.0	2.1	2.2	0.8	7.8
1992	63.8	10.8	9.1	4.5	1.8	2.4	0.9	6.8
1993	65.5	11.3	8.5	4.4	1.6	2.4	0.8	5.5
1994	64.3	12.3	8.6	5.0	1.6	2.1	0.7	5.3
1995	60.5	11.4	7.3	4.9	1.5	1.8	0.8	11.8
1996	62.5	10.6	6.2	4.9	1.5	1.4	0.5	12.3

Source: IMF, Annual Report, various issues.
[a]This residual is equal to the difference between the total identified reserves and the sum of the reserves held in the seven currencies listed in the table.

1.3. *International anchors*

After the breakdown of the Bretton Woods system, many countries abandoned fixed parities against the US dollar in favor of crawling-pegs, managed floating and pure floating regimes. At the end of 1994 this group of nonpeggers accounted for 97% of the world GNP (Table 5). Yet, this figure grossly understates the yearning for exchange rate stability, as it is amply demonstrated by the momentous decision of the European Union (EU) to create EMU. Furthermore, many of the countries classified as crawling-pegs and managed floating indirectly target their currencies to the US dollar. This is especially true for the so-called Asian tigers.

Table 5. The exchange rate regimes of IMF members in the end of years 1978, 1988 and 1994 (number of currencies under each regime).

Exchange rate regimes	1978	1994	1994[e] % of world GNP	1997 (June)
Pegged to a currency:				
US dollar	43	25	1.53	21
French franc	14	14	0.19	15
Pound sterling	4	0	0.00	0
Ruble	—	1	0.01	—
Deutsche mark	0	1	0.02	1
Other currencies[a]	3	6	0.02	8
Pegged to a basket of currencies:				
SDR	15	3	0.00	2
ECU[b]	—	1	0.03	1
Other baskets	21	20	1.40	17
Limited flexibility:				
European snake, European ERM	4	9	19.81	10
Other pegs with narrow fluct. Bands	cf. Pegging	4	0.78	2
Crawling-pegs and managed floats:	7[c]	36	10.48	53
Independently floating:	27[d]	61	65.73	51
Total	138	181	100.00	181

Source: International Monetary Fund, *Exchange Arrangements and Exchange Restrictions*, various issues.
[a]South-African Rand, Indian rupee, Spanish peseta, Italian lira, Portuguese escudo and Australian dollar.
[b]Austria (1984, 1988).
[c]Crawling-pegs only.
[d]Including managed floats.
[e]1995 GNP at market rates, Source: World Data Bank.

Peggers tend to be small open economies. For these countries changes in the exchange rate are reflected, to a large extent, in changes in the consumer price level. Since small open economies tend to be price takers, exchange rate fluctuations raise uncertainty without affecting the terms of trade. Pegging is also used to enhance the country's credibility with respect to its rate of inflation, provided the country pegs to a currency with a lower and more predictable rate of inflation that its own.

More countries peg to an individual currency than to a basket of currencies (Table 5). The advantages of pegging to an individual currency are transparency and the explicit commitment to mimic the rate of inflation of the reference currency. But there are also disadvantages in currency pegging. One disadvantage is that a currency peg does not ensure stability of the country's effective exchange rate. Say a small country trades with the United States, Germany, and Japan, but pegs its currency only to the US dollar. During periods when the dollar appreciates (depreciates) relative to the mark and the yen, the country experiences an effective appreciation (depreciation) of its currency, despite the fixity of the exchange rate with respect to the dollar. Another disadvantage is that trade and debt may be dominated by two or more different currencies. For example, for the Asian countries the United States and the dollar are the export center of gravity, but the yen is the currency of denomination of choice for foreign debt (IMF, 1997, p. 86). In addition to the credibility issue, basket pegging is marred by the practice of some countries of keeping the weights of the currencies entering the basket secret, changing these weights unpredictably, and also changing the parity unpredictably (Eichengreen and Frankel, 1996, p. 352). Finally, both currency and basket peggers are exposed to currency crises.

1.4. Asset and debt denomination

Generalizations of dominant monies in their role of store-of-value function are limited by incomplete statistical knowledge; in fact, there are no systematic data on foreign assets of individuals and of institutions. What we have are the Bank for International Settlements (BIS) data on international money market instruments, international bonds and notes, international loans, and banks' cross-border positions. The market for money market instruments—euro-commercial paper and other short-term paper—is valued at $180 billion as of June, 1997 and the US dollar has a commanding share of 59% (BIS, August 1997, Table 11A). The next money in the ranking is the Hong Kong dollar with one tenth of the US dollar's share.

The international market for international bonds and notes is valued at $3,225 billion, a much bigger market than the international money market instruments. There the US dollar accounts for 39% of the dollar (BIS, August 1997, Table 11B). The next currency in the ranking is the yen with 17%. More details are presented in Table 6 which distinguishes between Eurobonds, i.e., those bonds denominated in a currency not native to the country where the bonds are issued, and foreign bonds, i.e., bonds issued by a foreign entity in the currency of the country where the issue takes place. The share of dollar-denominated bonds has declined by half since the 1950s. In the foreign bond markets the Swiss franc has been the main rival of the dollar, gaining market share all the way through the 1980s and then declining afterwards. EU currency foreign bonds gained market share up to the 1960s, thanks to the attraction of Deutsche mark. This attraction diminished gradually all the way to peter out in the 1990s. In the Eurobond market, the most significant segment of the international bond market, the rivalry is between the dollar and the European currencies which have a slight edge over the dollar. The decline of the dollar's share is also evident in cross-border foreign currency assets (Table 7). Additional evidence on the relative strength of national monies comes from a comparison of currency of

Table 6. Funds raised on International Bond Market by currency of issue (in %).

Currency	1950–59	1960–69	1970–79	1980–89	1990–96
Total bonds					
US dollar	78.2	69.9	49.2	50.7	36.6
Japanese yen	0	0	5.2	8.9	14.8
Swiss franc	7.1	5.4	17.5	11.4	6.0
Deutsche mark	2.0	16.3	17.9	8.0	10.3
Total EU	11.9	23.4	24.8	22.6	36.5
Foreign bonds					
US dollar	78.2	65.1	42.2	19.7	32.9
Japanese yen	0	0	9.5	14.6	19.3
Swiss franc	7.1	8.5	33.4	50.1	30.9
Deutsche mark	2.0	16.4	8.3	4.7	0
Total EU	11.9	25.3	13.2	15.3	16.7
Euro bonds					
US dollar	—	77.9	56.1	59.7	39.6
Japanese yen	—	0	0.4	7.5	12.7
Swiss franc	—	0	0	0.01	0
Deutsche mark	—	17.8	28.4	9.0	13.6
Total EU	—	22.1	37.5	24.7	41.2

Source: OECD, *International Capital Market Statistics,* 1996 and *Financial Statistics* Monthly, June.

denomination and home-country relationship in the selection of a bond underwriter. UK institutions lead 44% of all pound issues, but only 4% on other currencies; French institutions lead 77% of all French franc issues, but only 2% in other currencies; German institutions lead 39% of mark issues, but only 4% in other currencies; Japanese institutions lead 84% of all yen issues, but only 8% in other currencies; US institutions lead 64% of all dollar issues and 16% in other currencies, a much higher share than competing key currencies (BIS, August 1997, p. 27; Savona and Maccario, 1998). In analyzing these data the BIS (p. 28) concludes that

> ...the US dollar sector is the most competitive... the US underwriters have less of an edge from their access to US end-investors... As a result, the ability to place dollar bonds is more widely shared among underwriters of various nationalities than for other currencies.

In more specialized segments of the market, such as syndicated loans, the dollar dominance remains extremely high at approximately 80% of the market (BIS, August 1997, p. 29). Loan markets tend to be more segmented than

Table 7. Cross-border positions of banks in industrial countries vis-à-vis all sectors: currency breakdown of assets in foreign currencies (% at end-December).

	US $	DM	Yen	Pound ster.	Swiss franc	Other
1977	71.1	17.0	0.4	1.3	5.7	4.5
1978	69.1	18.1	0.9	1.4	5.1	5.4
1979	68.6	18.2	0.9	1.7	5.6	5.0
1980	70.8	15.0	1.3	1.6	6.1	5.2
1981	72.1	13.1	1.7	1.5	6.6	5.0
1982	72.4	12.9	1.6	1.3	6.1	5.7
1983	74.0	12.0	1.7	1.2	5.7	5.4
1984	73.5	11.1	2.1	1.4	5.0	6.9
1985	65.6	13.2	4.1	1.9	6.6	8.6
1986	63.0	13.0	5.3	2.0	6.9	9.8
1987	58.4	14.5	7.2	2.4	6.8	10.7
1988	59.0	13.5	7.3	3.2	5.2	11.8
1989	57.5	14.1	6.9	3.6	4.3	13.3
1990	52.9	14.1	6.7	4.4	4.5	17.4
1991	51.6	13.6	5.9	3.8	4.4	20.7
1992	53.3	15.1	4.5	3.4	4.1	19.6
1993	53.3	15.3	4.4	3.0	3.2	20.8
1994	51.2	16.0	5.2	3.2	3.3	21.1
1995	49.2	15.8	6.2	3.0	3.4	22.4
1996	49.2	14.9	6.4	3.4	3.0	23.1
1997 (Sept.)	51.3	13.6	6.3	3.5	2.9	22.4

Source: BIS, International banking activity and financial market developments, various issues.

bond markets. US banks have a larger market share of the international loan market than of the bond market. The reason for this is that, in addition to the importance of the currency, the asymmetry of information underlying the loan market places a premium on the relationship between lead bank and borrower. Hence, US banks do better in the international loan market than in international bond market.

1.5. Debt invoicing of developing countries

The debt of developing countries, in almost all cases, is denominated in foreign currencies. Table 8 shows the share of external assets denominated in the three key currencies vis-à-vis the various regions of the world, as they are reported by banks to the BIS. Since the data include OPEC countries, they cannot be strictly interpreted as developing countries' debt. Furthermore, banks located

Table 8. The share of selected currencies in external assets of reporting banks vis-à-vis four regions.*

	US dollar			Deutsche mark			Japanese yen			Other		
	1983	1988	1996	1983	1988	1996	1983	1988	1996	1983	1988	1996
Asia	73.0	48.5	66.5	4.0	5.3	3.6	9.1	28.5	17.6	13.9	17.7	12.2
Middle-East	73.3	54.4	57.1	6.4	11.5	21.8	5.0	8.6	2.8	15.3	25.5	18.3
Africa	51.9	41.0	43.8	7.6	6.8	9.3	3.2	6.1	4.6	37.3	46.1	42.3
Latin-America	91.1	76.7	84.7	2.6	5.1	5.0	1.4	6.5	1.6	4.9	11.7	8.7

*Including OPEC countries.

Table 9. Currency composition of long-term debt in developing countries (in %).

Currency	1970	1980	1990	1995
US dollar	45.6	47.2	40.3	44.3
Japanese yen	2.2	5.8	9.9	11.6
Deutsche mark	8.6	6.4	8.6	7.3
French franc	5.3	5.3	5.4	4.5
Pound sterling	11.6	3.3	2.2	1.4
All EU currencies	25.5	15.0	16.2	13.2
Multiple currencies	12.1	10.3	14.3	14.2

Source: World Bank, *Global Development Finance* (1997).

in Singapore are not included among the reporting banks, thus biasing the data of Table 8 in favor of the dollar and against the yen. This bias is not likely to be the same across regions since Japanese banks are more involved in Asia than in other regions of the world. Abstracting from these considerations, the dollar's share declined in the 1980s and bounced back in the 1990s, especially in Asia and Latin America. For long-term debt the dollar's share has been fairly stable over the years, much larger than the yen's and the mark's (Table 9).

1.6. Summary

In the last two decades the US dollar has lost some market share, yet it remains the dominant currency in the world. The German mark, more, and the Japanese yen, less, have gained market share at the expense of the dollar. Our findings of an increased role of the mark and the yen in private portfolios stands in contrast with their decline as official reserves in the last five years. This is especially astonishing for the DM, given its leadership in the EMS and the fact that it acts as the nominal anchor for East European countries (e.g., Poland, the Czech Republic and Hungary). The growth of trade brought about by the opening of the Asian economies (e.g., China) explains the ascendancy of the American currency in the compartment of official reserves. These economies tend to peg to or shadow the dollar. The increasing debt invoicing in yen, as well as the transition of Asian countries from a pure dollar peg to a basket peg, consisting of dollar, mark and yen suggests further diversification away from the dollar in the future.

2. Will the euro challenge the supremacy of the dollar?

The United States and the European Union are comparable in economic size, accounting for approximately 20 to 21% each of the world GDP and 15% of the world's exports; yet, the dollar is much more important than the sum of the EU currencies in the international money and capital markets. Approximately 47% of world trade is invoiced in dollars against 32% in EU currencies (Table 1); 42% of foreign exchange transactions involves dollars against 34% involving EU currencies (Table 2); over 60% of official foreign reserves is constituted by dollar assets (Tables 3 and 4); 59% of international money market instruments is priced in dollars; 40% of Eurobonds is denominated in dollars against 41% in EU currencies (Table 6); 33% of foreign bonds is denominated in dollars against 17% in EU currencies (Table 6); 80 of syndicated loans are priced in dollars; and 44% of developing countries' long-term debt is expressed in dollars against 13% in EU currencies (Table 9). In sum, the dollar is over represented in the international money and capital markets in relation to the US share of world output and world exports. On the contrary, the sum of the EU currencies are underrepresented, again in relation to the same criteria. The biggest differences occur in the categories of official reserves and developing countries' debt.

On the basis of these statistics, should the euro get a share of the international money and capital markets that reflects the economic weight of EMU in the world, private and public portfolios will have to be reweighted in favor of the euro and against the dollar. But for the euro to achieve this it must compete with the dollar in terms of cost savings and/or purchasing-power reliability. We begin by looking at the case for the euro in terms of transaction-cost theory and then review a few studies that have ventured estimates on the relative size of the euro in the international money and capital markets.

2.1. The euro and transaction costs

The hypothesis that lower transaction costs will be the engine driving the euro towards the destination of a dominant currency goes as follows (Portes and Rey, 1998). The creation of EMU will consolidate the process of financial markets integration in the EU. With a larger domain, liquidity in these markets would rise and transaction costs would fall, a process that would endow the euro with the micro characteristics for competing with the dollar and possibly replacing it as the dominant currency in the world.

The proposition that money emerges as a process of minimizing transaction costs was first formalized by Niehans (1971). In that framework individuals trade, with a transaction cost, pairs of goods at different trading posts. Money is the commodity with the highest frequency of exchanges. Should one observe that commodity i is exchanged for commodity j, through the intermediation of commodity k, one can infer that commodity k acts as money. The longer, or indirect, chain of exchanging i against k and k against j achieves a lower transaction cost than the shorter, or direct, chain of exchanging i against j. The intervention of commodity k in the exchange process enables traders to save on costs; this is the reason why commodity k emerges as the medium of exchange.

The same insight can be applied to the international economy, subject to a few modifications. To begin with, each country has already "discovered" its own money. In reality, money is a paper commodity, with no alternative uses, issued by the government under monopoly conditions. The exchange of commodity i against j occurs through the designated money which enjoys legal-tender status. In the international economy, legal tender has no value and traders and investors select monies according to purely economic considerations. According to the transaction-cost hypothesis, the national currency with the lowest costs emerges as the dominant, or vehicle, money. Using the same set-up of trading posts, the exchange of currency i against vehicle currency k and the exchange of k against currency j entails lower costs than the direct exchange of i against j.[3]

Portes and Rey (pp. 315–316), relying on Rey's (1997) work, claim that the source of transaction cost saving resides in the liquidity of domestic financial markets. The euro—backed by large, deep, and liquid domestic financial markets—is a viable candidate to challenge the dominance of the dollar:

> The internationalization of the euro will depend mainly on the liquidity of the euro financial markets (the analysis is made under the assumption that the ECB has established its anti-inflationary credentials and that monetary policy is "neutral" in all countries). The driving force towards internationalization will come from the financial market side and then will expand the vehicle currency function.

Thus, the critical conditions for the euro to challenge the dollar as the dominant currency are that financial markets in the EMU become at least as liquid and efficient as US financial markets and that the ECB establish anti-inflationary credentials. We shall look at each one of these two conditions.

2.2. *Size and thickness of financial markets*

Data on the relative size of financial markets in EMU, the United States, and Japan are shown in Table 10. The size of the financial markets is defined as the

Table 10. Size of financial markets in EMU, US, and Japan billions of US dollars, 1995.

Areas	M2	Debt securities	Stock mkt. capitaliz.	Total	Population (millions)	Assets/pop. ($)
EU-15	5,738	8,673	3,779	18,190	369	49,295
EMU	4,343	6,993	2,119	13,455	286	47,045
USA	4,246	11,007	6,858	22,111	263	84,072
Japan	5,339	5,326	3,667	14,332	125	114,656

Sources: M2 from IMF, International Financial Statistics; the rest from Prati and Schinasi (1997, Table 1).
Notes: M2 = money (line 34 in IFS) plus quasi-money (line 35); EMU consists of the eleven member countries that will form Economic and Monetary Union on January 1, 1999: Austria, Belgium, Finland, France, Germany, Ireland, Italy, Luxembourg, the Netherlands, Portugal, and Spain.

sum of the broad money aggregate, M2, debt securities, and stock market capitalization. The US has larger financial markets than the sum of the financial markets of the eleven countries constituting EMU and of the entire EU. Furthermore, the composition underlying the total figure confirms the well-known fact that the United States relies more heavily on security markets than on bank credit, whereas the opposite is true for the EU (with the exception of the UK) and Japan.[4] The latter two have developed bank-intermediated financial markets.

For our purposes integration is more important than size. Unlike the highly integrated US financial markets, markets in the EU, in particular those of EU-11, are more segmented than integrated. How will EMU affect financial market integration? To answer this question we will consider, first, the market for government securities and, then, the market for private debt.

Recent data (May, 1998) show that the yields on long-term government securities of EMU "ins" have purged the exchange rate risk relative to one another; what remains are differences in credit risk (see Table 11). The countries with the highest credit rating—France, Germany, and the Netherlands—trade with virtually same yields. Italian and Portuguese governments bonds have the lowest credit ratings and trade within 20 basis points of the highest credit-rating-group yields. Will EMU push integration to the point that the eleven national securities markets will behave like the market for US treasury securities? On this point, McCauley (1997, p. 37) expresses a widely held view:

> Market participants want, and thoroughgoing integration would require, European treasuries to cooperate in establishing common market practices and conventions... Joint auctions would not be necessary to build large benchmark issues; instead, European treasuries could simply match each other's terms, in effect "reopening" each other's issues.

Complete market integration must need more than harmonizing auction practices. So long as investors perceive that creditworthiness differs among the "ins", yield differentials will persist. The EMU-11 government bond market

Table 11. The yield curve on 15 May, 1998 (in %).

Countries	Overnight	Benchmark government bonds	Foreign-currency rating	
			Moody's	S&P
Belgium	3.5	5.09	Aa1	AA+
Netherlands	3.375	5.00	Aaa	AAA
Germany	3.34	5.02	Aaa	AAA
France	3.41	5.03	Aaa	AAA
Italy	5.59	5.21	Aa3	AA–
Ireland	6.31	5.22	Aa1	AA+
Spain		5.15	Aa2	AA
Portugal		5.16	Aa3	AA–

Source: Financial Times, 18 May, 1998.
Notes: Benchmark government bonds have a maturity of approximately 10 years (2007, except for Ireland for which the closest maturity was 2006); bond yields are those calculated on the bid side of the market and for Italy are net of the 12.5% withholding tax payable by nonresidents.

cannot be as integrated as the US treasury market, unless either of two conditions is satisfied. The first is that investors will have deemed the "Excessive Deficit Procedure," codified in the Maastricht treaty (Article 104c) and reinforced by the "Stability and Growth Pact" to have real bite.[5] In that case, the yields on Italian and Portuguese government securities will converge to the level of the most credit worthy member countries. The alternative condition is that investors will have reached the belief that neither the "Excessive Deficit Procedure" nor the "Stability and Growth Pact" are enforceable and that solidarity, instead, will prevail. In this case, uniformity of government yields will be achieved at levels above those of the most credit worthy countries. The long-run repercussions of the second scenario will depend on the degree of opportunistic behavior: the stronger this behavior and the stronger the feeling of solidarity among the "ins", the higher will the uniform yield on securities paid by member governments.

Moving from public to private debt, the creation of EMU is bound to encourage more placements; liquidity will improve and transaction costs will decline. The important question is whether EMU corporations will switch significantly from bank to market financing. Current consensus indicates that corporate financing in the EMU will converge to the size and mix prevailing in the United States. Yet, some caution is in order because the "ins" still retain national regulations and tax laws that act as borders in the financial markets. This point is emphasized by Prati and Schinasi (1997, pp. 287, 289):

> Although outstanding debt securities issued by EU private entities totaled about $4 trillion (about 87 percent of the size of the US corporate debt market,), about 25 per cent of this total was issued in international markets...

> Excessive regulatory burdens have simply prevented these markets from developing in some countries. For example, tax policy and issuance requirements prevented the development of commercial paper and bond markets in Germany until very recently. More generally, regulators in virtually all EU countries have stifled corporate debt securities markets by discouraging issuance of lower-grade corporate debt securities.

Undoubtedly, there will be pressure on the high regulation and tax member countries to align with the competition, but this process will be slow and contentious. Similar considerations hold for the equity markets. There, however, the leadership of London—the capital of an "out" country—augurs well for a Euro equity market.

2.3. *Anti-inflation credibility of the ECB*

The second condition for the euro to challenge the supremacy of the dollar is that the new European Central Bank establish its low-inflation credibility.[6] Here, the received wisdom is that the ECB will be as averse to inflation as the German Bundesbank. Kenen (1998, p. 372) goes even further and ventures the hypothesis that the preferences of the national governors have become homogeneous:

> The policies and statements of Antonio Fazio at the Banca d'Italia and Ángel Rojo at the Banco de Espana are virtually indistinguishable from those of Jean-Claude Trichet at the Banque de France or Hans Tietmeyer at the Bundesbank.

We would like to advise, here as well, some caution. The ECB is an untested institution and will operate in a different political environment than the Bundesbank in Germany or the Federal Reserve System in the United States. The critical distinction is that both the Bundesbank and the Federal Reserve System are central banks within a well-defined political union, whereas the ECB is the monetary authority of 11 (and eventually more) sovereign states linked together economically and financially, but not politically. This difference implies that country interests will weigh heavily in the decisions of the ECB. Furthermore, the fear of financial crises spilling over from one country to another will reduce the credibility of the no-bailout clause.

On the voting behavior of the ECB, the potential for conflicts in the Governing Council will have less to do with personal preferences of the governors than with structural differences in their national economies. EMU monetary policy will have a differentiated impact on the participating countries, depending on differences in price and wage rigidities, openness, and industrial and financial structures (Dornbusch et al., 1998). Asymmetric shocks and asynchronous cyclical conditions will further add to the inclination of Council members to vote as French, Germans, and Italians rather than as Europeans. The upshot is that such differences will imply that the Council, on most monetary policy issues, will be divided in at least two groups, one representing the inflation hawks and the other representing the inflation doves. Where will each national representative gravitate depends very much on how a monetary policy action affects his or her country. The history of the Federal Reserve System illustrates well the extent to which regional effects influence voting (Woolley, 1988; Dornbush et al., 1998, pp. 25–27). In predicting that the ECB will be as averse to inflation as the Bundesbank one must assume that all Council members have Bundesbank-like preferences and that the common monetary policy has undifferentiated effects across Euro land. Since neither of these assumptions, but especially the second, is likely to hold, the safer prediction is that the ECB will have a hard time in matching the long-run inflation performance of the Bundesbank.

The second implication of being a central bank of many sovereign states is that this cannot be completely insulated from opportunistically behaving governments. It is true, as we have already mentioned, that the Treaty explicitly exonerates a member state from the debts of another member state and constrains national fiscal finances to the straight jacket of the excessive-deficit procedure. It is also true that the Stability and Growth Pact was signed to accentuate the preoccupation against fiscal profligacy. But how practical are these provisions in handling a financial crisis that is sparked by an unsustainable debt in a member country and can quickly spill over to the rest of the EMU? The markets may come to the conclusion that the no bail-out clause is not operational in a world of integrated finance. Despite what the Treaty says, solidarity may be the modus operandi; and the ECB may have to swallow some credibility losses.

2.4. Summary

Financial markets in the EU member countries will be "pulled in" by EMU centripetal force and, as a result, these markets will acquire depth, breath, and liquidity close to those in the United States. On this conclusion there is wide agreement. However, according to the transaction-cost hypothesis, the euro needs deeper and more liquid domestic financial markets than their US counterparts to challenge the supremacy of the dollar as a vehicle currency. This condition is much harder to be satisfied. In the market for government securities, the absence of a Federal government in the EU puts a ceiling on the integration process. Transaction costs may remain lower in the US financial markets than in the EMU financial markets for quite some time. The euro will rise in importance but not enough to displace the dollar as primus inter pares, at least not for a few years. This conclusion is reinforced by the fact that the ECB is a new and untested central bank, serving eleven sovereign states. The "Excessive Deficit Procedure" and the "Stability and Growth Pact" are a poor substitute for the missing political integration. The latter places a second ceiling on the anti-inflation credibility of the new ECB. National interests will weigh in heavily in monetary policy decisions. The differentiated effects of monetary policy across Euro land and the likelihood of asymmetric shocks and asynchronous cyclical movements raise the potential for conflicts in the Governing Council of the ECB and raise the odds that the long-run inflation performance of the ECB will not match the Bundesbank's. So, we are left with a middle-of-the-road prediction that the euro will be a big international currency, but not big enough to dislodge the dollar from pole position.

3. Portfolio shifts and the euro-dollar exchange rate

The creation of EMU is a big innovation in the international monetary system: established currencies from eleven industrialized countries will be replaced by a brand new one. Such a change is destined to alter the portfolios of public and private actors. In this section we discuss the likely portfolio consequences due to the introduction of the euro and the impact these portfolio shifts may have on the exchange rate between the euro and the dollar.

We start with three studies that make "quantitative" predictions on the size of portfolio reallocations. Bergsten (1997, pp. 26–27) generalizes the Eichengreen and Frankel's statistical result that the elasticity of the dominant currency's share of official reserves with respect to its world output share ranges from 0.5 to 1.3 to all international assets, public as well as private. The author himself warns the reader in not taking his work too seriously; even as a back-of-the-envelope exercise it is extremely unsatisfactory. Nonetheless, Bergsten—a euro enthusiast—calculates the mid-point "estimate" of the euro's share of private and official markets at 42.5% and ventures the strong conclusion:

> Assuming that most of the increase in the euro's role came 'at the expense' of the dollar, the euro could eventually achieve parity with the dollar.

McCauley (1997, p. 50) arrives at virtually opposite conclusions from Bergsten with an undisclosed methodology:

> Broad monetary union in Europe would introduce a euro that would generally carry more weight as an international money than the mark carries but less weight than currently adheres to the sum of the euro's constituent currencies.

Consequently, EMU would raise the dollar's share in official reserves, international assets, foreign-exchange transactions, and trade denominations (see Table 12). These predictions appear inconsistent with the other McCauley (pp. 39–40) prediction of a $85–200 billion shift from dollar to euro-denominated official reserves. In light of the fact that the methodology is not revealed, McCauley's estimates fall in the same category of Bergsten's.

Table 12. Shares of the dollar, euro, and the yen; according to McCauley (1997, Table 13) (in %).

	Official reserves		International assets		Foreign exchange transactions*		Denomination of trade	
	Pre-EMU	EMU	Pre-EMU	EMU	Pre-EMU	EMU	Pre-EMU	EMU
Dollar	69	76	40	53	84	92	48	59
Euro	24	16	34	13	70	56	34	22
Yen	7	8	12	15	24	26	5	6

Source: McCauley (1997, Table 13).
*Percentages sum to 200, including currencies not shown.

Frenkel and Sondergaard (1997) estimate eclectic demand functions for official reserves, international bonds, and international bank deposits and, under the strong assumption that EMU will not alter the underlying stochastic structure—i.e., ignoring the Lucas' critique—they forecast the impact of EMU on the demand for those assets. The variable that does most of the work in the prediction is the relative economic size of the EMU; the other variables, the inflation differentials and interest rate differentials, play no role in the forecast on the ground that the euro is assumed to be as stable as the mark. The over-all conclusion of these two authors is that EMU would produce a shift of $457 billion out of dollar-denominated assets and $66 billion out of yen-denominated assets, representing 14% and 10%, respectively, of pre-EMU assets. Unlike in McCauley, dollar shares fall across all assets after EMU inception, except for official reserves held by this area (see Table 13). EMU, in fact, will have a smaller (in absolute value) current-account imbalance than the sum of the national current-account imbalances, justifying a decline in the demand for official reserves; call this the income effect. On the other hand, marks, francs, and liras no longer can function as foreign reserves and their role would have to be replaced by dollar and yen assets; call this the substitution effect. The external demand of dollar and yen assets will reflect these two opposing forces.

Table 13. Shares of the dollar, euro, and the yen; According to Frenkel and Sondergaard (1997) (in %).

	EMU official reserves		Non-EMU official reserves		International bonds		International bank deposits	
	Pre-EMU	EMU	Pre-EMU	EMU	Pre-EMU	EMU	Pre-EMU	EMU
Dollar	58.4	71.5	63. 7	51.5	36.8	31.2	43.7	40.2
Euro			14.00	32.4		23.5		47.6
Yen	4.4	9.2	6. 2	6.0	14.7	14.1	4.8	3.2

Source: Frenkel and Sondergaard (1997, Tables 4, 7, 10, and 13).

Empirically, the income effect is larger than the substitution effect, leading EMU to be a net seller of dollar assets. Yet, the proportion of dollar assets in EMU official reserves would ultimately rise.

The predictions by Frenkel and Sondergaard are consistent with the middle-of-the-road scenario outlined above: the euro will challenge the dollar, but not displace it from pole position. It is worth repeating that the relative economic size of EMU is what drives the results. This may well be the true relationship in the long run. But other factors are at work. For example, portfolio diversification can also work against the euro. With the German mark being the same as the French franc and the Italian lira, the euro will replace less than the sum of the individual EMU country currencies (OECD, 1997, p. 26). The typical German investor will have fewer reasons to hold Italian assets as a result of the fact that the covariance between German assets and Italian assets will rise following currency unification. On the other hand, the German investor will have more reason to increase his or her holdings of dollar-denominated assets and yen-denominated assets so long as the ECB pursues an independent monetary policy relative to the Fed and the Bank of Japan.

Financial integration will increase more rapidly within EMU than between EMU and other blocs. For example, the correlation coefficient between the French and German stock markets has steadily risen since the sixties, whereas the same two markets have retained a constant trend correlation with respect to the US stock market (Solnik et al., 1996, figures 1 and 3). The Franco-German integration is even deeper in the bond market (with a correlation coefficient of 0.8, Solnik et al., figure 5), suggesting little gains from diversifying across these two markets. Also US, French and German bond markets have become more integrated, reducing the value of diversifying out of euro-denominated bonds.

It is hard to push the diversification story too far. It looks as if country weights derived from a global minimum-variance portfolio (see, for example, Erb et al., 1996, Table 7) overstate the importance of country diversification. For large economic areas, such as the United States and the future EMU, the bias to invest at home may prevail over purely diversification considerations.

3.1. Portfolio effects vs. fundamentals

On balance, analysis and empirical research point in the direction of a nontrivial shift out of dollar into euro-denominated assets. Will the euro appreciate relative to the dollar, as a consequence of this shift? Bergsten (1997), Alogoskoufis and Portes (1997), and Portes and Rey (1998) answer in the affirmative. For them the appreciation of the euro will result from net capital inflows into Euro land. A simple two-asset model, with fixed supplies, predicts as much: an exogenous shift into domestic, euro-denominated assets will require either a fall in the euro interest rate, or a rise in the dollar interest rate, or a higher forward premium of the dollar. Assuming unchanged interest rates and forward rate, the dollar must depreciate in the spot market to re-equilibrate the asset markets.

This prediction, however, depends on asset supplies being rigid. But is it a tenable assumption? McCauley (1997, p. 45) correctly objects to the euro appreciation view by noting that:

> ...one should not attempt to calculate the effects of the greater attraction of the euro for official and private asset managers without considering that it might exert a similar attraction for debt managers.

Similar considerations are echoed by the BIS (1997, pp. 93–94):

> ...the behaviour of global liability managers may change in a manner that could partly offset, or more than offset, shifts by private asset managers. Debtor countries, for instance, appear to have a very small fraction of their liabilities denominated in the euro's predecessor currencies. Larger and more liquid fixed income markets in euros, as compared with current European markets, could encourage debt issuance in the euro.

More importantly, the portfolio-shift hypothesis underlying euro appreciation disregards fundamentals such as expectations of prospective monetary and fiscal policies, reputation of the central banks, net foreign indebtedness, and business cycles. EMU fiscal policy will be constrained by the excessive-deficit procedure. EMU monetary policy, as we have argued in the paper, should not be interpreted as being very conservative, or at least not as conservative as a reading of the Maastricht treaty suggests. Furthermore, the ECB will be a young and untested institution compared to the Federal Reserve System. In sum, it would seem premature at this point to state that, on the strength of the under representation of the EU currencies in the international money and financial markets, the euro is bound to appreciate relative to the dollar. The effects of the expected portfolio shift in favor of euro-denominated assets will occur against the background of fiscal and monetary policies in the United State and the EU. Even assuming comparable fundamentals, the appreciation of the euro relative to the dollar is bound to take place over several years. Domestic and foreign investors are not likely to replace all of DM, pound, and lira assets in euro-denominated assets. A wait-and-see attitude is the appropriate strategy when one faces a new and untested player.

Acknowledgement

We would like to thank Benjamin Cohen and Dominick Salvatore for very helpful comments on an earlier draft of the paper.

Notes

1. According to a survey of international invoicing practices of Belgium, France, Italy, Germany, Switzerland, Spain and Ireland (see SanPaolo, 1990, Table 14), the dollar accounted for the lion's share of the vehicle currencies (79.4% of exports and 77.9% of imports), followed by the Deutsche mark and the European Currency Unit, ECU. The latter, however, has had a role mostly in intra-European trade and no role in raw material invoicing.
2. In Tables 3 and 4 the share of SDR and ECU holdings are subsumed in the column "Other". As of 1994, the ECU share was 7% and the SDR share 2% (Eichengreen and Frankel, 1996, Table 2).
3. On the costs and benefits of a monetary union see also Hamada (1998), "The Choice of International Monetary Regimes in a Context of Repeated Games," in this volume.
4. M2 is a proxy for bank credit, since bank deposits equal bank reserves plus bank credit minus other bank liabilities minus bank net worth.
5. The reference values set by the "Excessive Deficit Procedure" are the same as the fiscal convergence criteria: 3% for the ratio of government deficit to GDP and 60% for the ratio of government debt to GDP. The "Stability and Growth Pact" was agreed by the European Council at its Dublin meeting of December, 1996 and further expanded by the European Council at its Amsterdam meeting of June, 1997.
6. For a review of the issues on central bank credibility refer to Salvatore (1998).

References

Alogoskoufis, G. and R. Portes (1997) "The Euro, the Dollar, and the International Monetary System." In P.R. Masson, T.H. Krueger, and B.G. Turtelboom (eds.), *EMU and the International Monetary System*. Washington, D.C.: The International Monetary Fund.

Bank of International Settlements (1997) *67th Annual Report*. Basle, June.

Bank of International Settlements (1989, 1992, 1996) *Central Bank Survey of Foreign Exchange Market Activity*. Basle.

Bank of International Settlements (various issues) *International Banking Activity and Financial Market Developments*. Basle.

Bergsten, C.F. (1997) "The Impact of the Euro on Exchange Rates and International Policy Coordination." In P.R. Masson, TH Krueger, and B.G. Turtelboom (eds.), *EMU and the International Monetary System*. Washington, D.C.: The International Monetary Fund.

Cipolla, C.M. (1956) *Money, Prices, and Civilization in the Mediterranean World*. Princeton, NJ.: Princeton University Press.

Dal Bosco, E. (1998) "Central Bank's Management of Foreign Exchange Reserves." in this volume.

Dornbush, R., C., Favero, and F. Giavazzi (1998) "Immediate Challenges for the European Central Bank." *Economic Policy* 26, 15–64.

ECU Institute (1995) *International Currency Competition and the Future Role of the Single European Currency*. Kluwer Law International.

Eichengreen, B. and A.J. Frankel (1996) "The SDR, Reserve Currencies, and the Future of the International Monetary System." In M. Mussa, J. Boughton, and P. Isard (eds.), *The Future of the SDR in Light of Changes in the International Monetary System*. Washington, D.C.: International Monetary Fund.

Erb, C.B, C.R., Harvey, and T.E. Viskanta (1994) "Forecasting International Equity Correlations." *Financial Analysts Journal*, 32–45

European Council, Presidency Conclusions, Dublin European Council, 13 and 14 December, 1996; European Council, Presidency, Amsterdam European Council, 16 and 17 June, 1997.

Fratianni, M. (1998) "Maxi vs. Mini EMU: The Political Economy of Stage II." *The Columbia Journal of European Law*, 4(2), 375–393.

Fratianni, M. (1992) "Dominant and Dependent Currencies." *Palgrave Dictionary*.

Frenkel, M. and J. Sondergaard (1997) "The Effects of European Monetary Union on the Dollar and the Yen as International Reserve and Investment Currencies." Working Paper Series 97-030, Georgia Institute of Technology, School of Management, Atlanta, Georgia.

Grassman, S. (1973) *Exchange Reserves and the Financial Structure of Foreign Trade*. Westmead: Saxon House.

Hamada, K. (1998) "The Choice of International Monetary Regimes in a Context of Repeated Games." in this volume.

Kenen, P. (1983) *The Role of the Dollar as an International Currency*. Group of Thirty Occasional Paper No. 13, New York: Group of Thirty.

Kenen, P. (1998) "The Transition to EMU: Issues and Implications." *Columbia Journal of European Law*, 4(2), 359–374.

Kindleberger, C.P. (1973) *The World in Depression, 1929–1939*. Berkeley and Los Angeles: University of California Press.

Klein, B. (1974) "The Competitive Supply of Money." *Journal of Money, Credit and Banking*, 6, 423–453.

International Monetary Fund (1997) *World Economic Outlook* (Oct.). Washington, D.C.: International Monetary Fund.

McCauley, R.N. (1997) "The Euro and the Dollar." *Essays in International Finance* Vol. 205, International Finance Section, Princeton University.

Niehans, J. (1971) "Money and Barter in General Equilibrium with Transaction Costs." *American Economic Review*, 773–783.

OECD. (1997) *Economic Outlook*, June.

Portes, R. and H. Rey (1998) "The Emergence of the Euro as an International Currency." *Economic Policy* 26, 305–343.

Prati, A. and G.J. Schinasi (1997) "EMU and International Capital Markets: Structural Implications and Risks." In P.R. Masson, TH Krueger, and B.G. Turtelboom (eds.), *EMU and the International Monetary System*. Washington, D.C.: The International Monetary Fund.

Rey, H. (1997) "International Trade and Currency Exchange." Centre for Economic Performance, London School of Economics.

Salvatore, D. (1998) "Present International Monetary and Financial Arrangements." in this volume.

SanPaolo (1990) "The Commercial Use of the ECU: Invoicing and Import-Export Practices." *ECU Newsletter* 31, 16–30.

Savona P. and A. Maccario (1998) "On the Relation between Money and Derivatives and its Application to the International Monetary Market." in this volume.

Solnik, B., C. Boucrelle, and Y. Le Fur. (1996) "International Market Correlation and Volatility." *Financial Analysts Journal*, 17–34.

Treaty on European Union (1992) *Protocol on the Statute of the European System of Central Banks and of the European Central Bank*.

Woolley, J.T. (1988) *Monetary Politics: The Federal Reserve and the Politics of Monetary Policy*.

Wyplosz, C. (1997) "EMU: Why and How It May Work." CEPR Discussion Paper No. 1685.

Open economies review **9:S1** 493–531 (1998)

Central Bank Policy in a More Perfect Financial System

JÜRGEN VON HAGEN AND INGO FENDER
Zentrum für Europäische Integrationsforschung (ZEI), University of Bonn, Indiana University, CEPR, Walter Flex Strasse 3, 53113 Bonn, Germany

Key words: financial innovation, derivatives, effectiveness of monetary policy, transmission mechanism, financial crises, and financial regulation

JEL Classification Numbers: E41, E42, E44, E52

Abstract

Financial innovation increases markets' liquidity and provides economic agents with new instruments to better handle risks, but it reduces the efficacy of monetary policy while strengthening the logic and force of the "unholy trinity". Increased liquidity of financial markets and increased leverage of financial positions imply that speculators can attack unsustainable fixed exchange rates faster and more powerfully than ever. The rapid innovation of new financial instruments in these markets also implies the futility to "throw sand in the wheels" through regulation or the introduction of transaction taxes. The higher asset substitutability generated by the emergence of derivatives makes the definition of "money," particularly of broad monetary aggregates, increasingly difficult. In a more complete financial market system central banks find it harder to predict the effect of a given monetary impulse on real output and employment with any reasonable precision. Discretionary monetary policies aimed at output and employment become more uncertain. Consequently, central banks should focus on the long-run goal of price stability.

Introduction

Financial markets, national and international, have witnessed a daunting expansion in recent decades. Their rapid growth has been accompanied by massive deregulation in many countries and a process of financial innovation, most notably the development of new types of markets for financial derivatives. This has made existing asset markets more liquid and has created new opportunities for trading financial market risks, enabling investors to achieve a better degree of hedging against these risks and, in doing so, to increase the value of the underlying assets. Financial innovation and deregulation have also allowed financial institutions to move beyond the borders of their traditional activities, making the differences between *banks*, *securities dealers*, *mutual funds*, and *insurance companies* increasingly blurred.[1]

As these developments change the nature and operation of financial markets, an important question to ask is, what do they imply for the conduct and effectiveness of monetary policy. The conventional answer offered in the literature holds that they have but marginal implications. According to this view, financial innovations such as derivatives allow banks to react faster to monetary policy shocks and, at the same time, allow nonbanks to protect themselves against such shocks to some extent. As a result, the transmission of monetary impulses to the economy may become somewhat weaker, but it remains unchanged in principle. A more radical view would argue, however, that financial innovations, and the development of derivatives in particular, have important implications for the nature of an economy's monetary system. More specifically, they imply a move towards a more perfect financial market system, and one in which central bank money and its close substitutes lose their unique role as generally accepted means of transaction. A relatively new literature has begun to speculate about the nature of an economy where that occurs, and its monetary policy implications.

The rapid expansion of derivatives markets has also caused policy makers and economists to worry about the potential threat they might pose to the stability of the financial system. Popular views regard derivatives traders as players engaged in risky bets and counter-bets, creating excess volatility of asset prices and interest rates and threatening to disrupt the orderly functioning of the markets. More sophisticated observers realize that derivatives enable financial institutions to circumvent traditional regulation and to engage in new types of risky activities, and fear that they might create excessive systemic risk. Furthermore, derivatives allow financial institutions to circumvent regulation and assume more risk than their regulators would realize from considering their balance sheets. Another important question is, therefore, how derivatives markets should be integrated into the framework of financial regulation. Since financial derivatives markets are global markets, an important aspect of this question is, how such regulation can be implemented on an international scale.

These are the main issues discussed in this paper. To set the tone, we begin with a characterization of the evolution of financial derivatives markets, the most visible aspect of financial innovation, over the past 20 years in Section 2. In Section 3, we discuss the economic functions of derivatives and derivatives markets. In Section 4, we turn to the monetary policy consequences of the development of a more perfect financial system, assuming that the growing trend of derivatives markets will continue. We argue that in a more perfect financial system, central bank money and fixed-price bank deposits will eventually lose this role as the predominant means of transaction. Hysteresis and the role of government in modern economies, however, will make sure that central bank money retains its unit-of-account function. As a result, central banks will lose much of their ability to use monetary policy to affect the real economy and their attention will shift mainly to securing price stability. In Section 5, we discuss the implications of an emerging, more perfect financial system for banking regulation. In light of the conclusions in Section 4, we argue that systemic risk will eventually decline as a concern of regulatory policies, while the potential instability of individual financial institutions, due to the classical principal-agent problems between depositors and bank owners, will move to the forefront.

1. Derivatives and derivatives markets

Derivatives are agreements between two counterparties specifying the exchange of cash payments based on changes in the price of a particular asset or differences in the returns to different securities (e.g., Kuprianov, 1993).[2] They do, therefore, derive their value from an underlying instrument. Derivatives can be grouped into three categories, futures and forwards, options, swaps and other derivative instruments.[3] As the latter can be decomposed into combinations of forwards and options, the first two are considered "basic" instruments. A forward contract is an obligation to buy or sell an underlying asset at a specified forward price on a known date in the future. If the cash price at the expiration date of the contract is higher than the specified forward price, the holder incurs a profit on her long position, otherwise she incurs a loss. Forwards and futures thus generate symmetric risk structures between the two counterparties to the contract. In contrast, an option is the right to buy or sell (call vs. put option) an underlying asset at the strike price at a known date in the future. The owner can always choose not to exercise the contract. Thus, options create asymmetric risk between the two parties to the contract. The possible gain of the buyer is theoretically unbounded, while possible losses are restricted to the size of the option premium. The seller, on the other hand, incurs a potentially unlimited risk of loss and is compensated by a fixed premium (e.g., Issing and Bischofberger, 1996).

A swap is an agreement between two parties to swap, i.e., to exchange, future cash flows based on different returns to or changes in the price of a specified underlying. This is equivalent to the simultaneous selling and purchasing of the respective cash flows.[4] Swaps are predominantly customized instruments, although some swaps are now exchange-traded. The most common type is the so-called "fixed/floating swap", in which the "fixed-rate payer" agrees to make payments based on a fixed, long-term interest rate to the so-called "floating-rate payer". The latter, analogously, makes payments indexed to a variable, short-term market interest rate. The respective amounts to be paid are calculated on the basis of a specified principal, which is commonly a notional amount. It is common to exchange the net difference of payments only.

According to their degree of standardization, derivative contracts can be divided into fully standardized, exchange-traded (ET) contracts and more customized, over-the-counter (OTC) instruments that are traded in informal markets. Organized markets cut the direct link between the seller and buyer. They have clearing houses serving as the standard counterparty for all contracts traded. To reduce credit risk and provide collateral for settlement payments, existing ET contracts are revalued at current market values on a daily basis and market participants are required to make cash deposits (margin requirements)[5] before they are allowed to undertake transactions. Daily losses and gains (variation margins) are then deducted or added to the deposit, while a certain minimum deposit must be maintained. These procedures together with a high degree of standardization are designed to provide high fungibility and market liquidity. Measures to reduce credit risk, such as third party guarantees, collateral requirements and marking-to-market of existing contracts, have arisen in OTC markets as well, but the less formal nature of these markets implies that they are less standardized and less developed than those in organized markets. Finally, derivatives can be distinguished according to the underlying assets: Foreign exchange instruments, (single currency) interest rate contracts, equity, and commodity contracts (BIS, 1996).

Since the mid-1980s, growth of turnover and notional amounts outstanding in both the OTC and organized markets for financial derivatives, have outperformed the growth in most other financial markets. From year-end of 1995 to year-end 1996 notional amounts of globally outstanding interest rate swaps grew by 49% while currency swaps grew by 45% (BIS, 1998). International Swap and Derivatives Association (ISDA) figures for the first half of 1997 indicate that outstanding notional principal on OTC markets grew by about 42% and 22% against end-June 1996 for interest rate swaps and currency swaps respectively. The markets for interest rate futures and exchange-traded options, on the other hand, grew 26% and 11% during 1997. The average annual growth rate of the combined markets for OTC- and exchange-traded derivative instruments has been 40% over the ten years up to 1996 (IMF, 1997, 1996a). Measuring the size of financial markets is necessarily an elusive concept. Here, we follow established practice and look at three aspects of market size: notional contract values, gross market value of existing contracts, and turnover.

1.1. Over-the-counter markets for derivatives

According to the 1995 survey conducted by BIS among the central banks in twenty-six countries, and after adjustment for double-counting, the global notional amounts outstanding in OTC foreign exchange, interest rate, equity, and commodity derivative contracts accounted for a total of US $40.6 trillion at the end of March 1995. Including estimated gaps in reporting the figure even reaches a total of US $47.5 trillion (see Table 1). All but 2% of this total is accounted for by interest rate and currency instruments. Single-currency interest rate derivatives account for 60.7% of the global OTC notional amount, whereas foreign exchange contracts make up another 37.2%. Contracts based on equity and commodities account for only 1.3 and 0.8%, respectively. The increasing linkage between domestic and international markets and, hence, the global nature of trade in financial derivatives is accentuated by a share of 55% of reported notional amounts outstanding involving counterparties from different countries (BIS, 1996).

Table 1. Global derivatives markets at end-March 1995 (billions of US $).

Contract category	Over-the-counter (OTC)[6]	Exchange-traded[7]
Notional amounts[8]	47530 (100%)	8186 (100%)
of which		
foreign exchange	17700 (37.2%)	60 (0.7%)
interest rate contracts	28850 (60.7%)	7835 (95.7%)
equity contracts	630 (1.3%)	221 (2.7%)
commodity contracts	350 (0.8%)	71 (0.9%)
Gross market values	2205 (100%)	NA
of which		
foreign exchange	1420 (64.4%)	NA
interest rate contracts	700 (31.7%)	NA
equity contracts	55 (2.5%)	NA
commodity contracts	30 (1.4%)	NA

Source: BIS (1996) and own calculations.

Banks and other financial institutions account for a large share of the combined OTC markets, partly performing their role as suppliers of financial derivatives and increasingly also trading on their own behalf.[9] Interdealer business in local and cross-border trading accounted for about 57% of global notional amounts outstanding in March 1995 (BIS, 1996). In terms of notional amounts outstanding, interest rate swaps, accounting for a share of 69%, appear to be the largest component of the OTC markets for interest rate derivatives, followed by forward rate agreements, FRAs (17%), OTC options (13%), and swap options (1%), respectively. Forwards and swaps together account for 83% of the notional amounts outstanding in the foreign exchange markets for derivatives, followed by options with a share of 17% (see Table 2 and figure 1).

The gross market value of outstanding OTC derivatives amounted to US $2.2 trillion on 31st March, 1995 (or roughly US $1.8 trillion without correction for estimated gaps in reporting). Although this is equivalent to only about 4.6% of the notional amounts outstanding, it is nevertheless more than three times the capital of the world's 75 largest banks (IMF, 1996a). These global gross market

Table 2. Turnover in notional amounts; April 1995 (daily averages; billions of US $).

Category	Over-the-counter (OTC)	Exchange-traded
Foreign exchange	720 (82%)	7 (1%)
Interest rate contracts	160 (18%)	563 (99%)
Total	880 (100%)	570 (100%)

Source: BIS (1996) and own calculations.

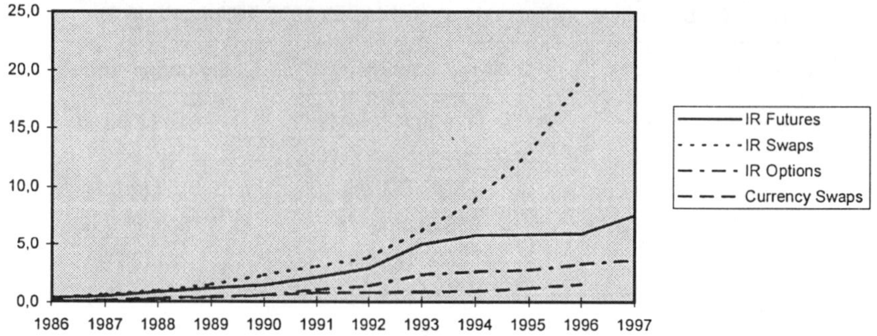

Figure 1. Selected derivatives markets; notional amounts outstanding in trillions of US $.

values serve as an indicator for the overall cost which would have been created had contracts had to be replaced at market prices prevailing on 31st March 1995.

Foreign exchange products accounted for 64.4% of the gross market value, interest rate contracts for about 31.7% and those contracts involving equity and commodity prices 2.5% and 1.4%, respectively. While forwards and swaps together account for 93% of the gross market value of OTC foreign exchange derivatives, swaps alone contribute a share of 87% to the replacement value of outstanding OTC interest rate contracts (BIS, 1996), see Table 3.

Table 3. Breakdown by OTC instrument type and indicator.

Instrument type	Notional amounts (%)	Gross market values (%)	Share[10] (%)	Turnover[11] (%)
Foreign exchange	100	100	8.0	100
Forwards & swaps	83	93	9.1	94
Options	17	7	3.0	6
Other	0	0	16.4	0
Interest rates	100	100	2.4	100
FRAs	17	3	0.4	43
Swaps	69	87	3.0	41
Options	13	9	1.7	14
Other	1	1	3.2	2
Equity	36	50	8.6	NA
Forwards & swaps	9	14	13.5	
Options	91	86	8.2	
Commodities	100	100	8.8	NA
Forwards & swaps	66	78	10.1	
Options	33	22	5.5	

Source: BIS (1996) and own calculations.

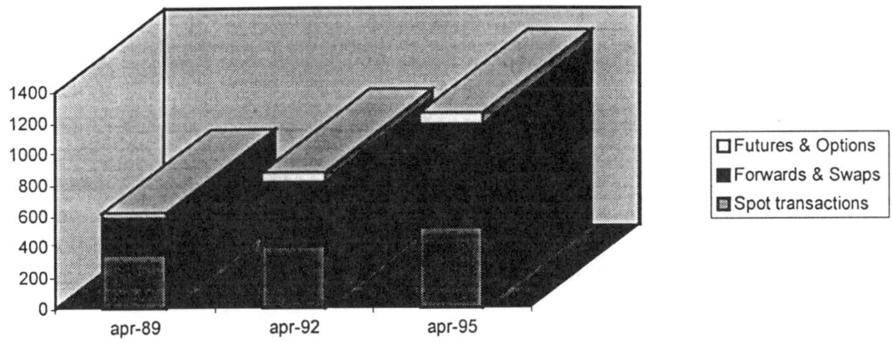

Figure 2. FOREX market turnover.

The BIS survey estimates total average daily turnover (new transactions) in notional amounts of OTC foreign exchange and interest rate derivative contracts at US $880 billion in April 1995, about 82% of which was accounted for by foreign exchange contracts (see figure 2). This runs counter to the relative size of the respective notional amounts outstanding and is due to the longer maturities of interest rate products (BIS, 1996).

1.2. Exchange-traded derivatives

Reported notional amounts outstanding on exchanges totalled about US $16.4 trillion at end-March 1995. To adjust for double-counting the amount must be halved and therefore reduced to a notional value of US $8.2 trillion. The global market for financial derivatives, i.e., the combined markets for OTC and exchange-traded contracts, amounted to US $55.7 trillion and was therefore roughly twice as large as 1995 world output.

Between the end of 1986 and the end of 1997, the total notional amount of outstanding ET derivative contracts grew at an annual average rate of 31% and stood at $12.3 trillion at end-1997. During the same period, annual turnover rose from 315 million contracts to some 1.2 trillion contracts, or at an average annual rate of about 13%. Until recently, markets for ET products generally grew in line with OTC markets (figure 1). In recent years, however, the growth of exchange-trade in derivatives has been outpaced by the development in the markets for OTC instruments, which grew at an annual average rate of about 45% (notional amounts outstanding) over the ten years up to 1997, although figures for the first half of 1997 indicate a slowdown in growth. (BIS, 1998; ISDA, 1997).

Markets for ET derivatives are even more dominated by products involving interest rates than OTC markets (figure 3). Interest rate derivatives account for about 96% of notional amounts outstanding in the markets for exchange-traded instruments. Nonetheless, OTC interest rate markets are by far larger than

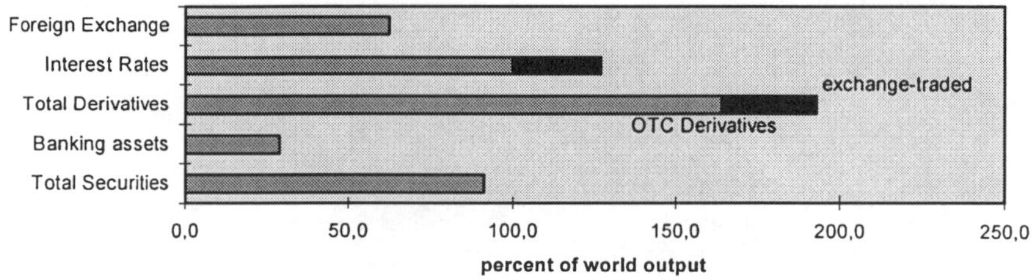

Figure 3. Derivatives in comparison.

interest rate business involving exchange-traded derivatives. A share of 79% of organized interest rate business falls to futures, while options account for the rest. In terms of daily averages of reported turnover, interest rate instruments make up 99%, of which 89% fall to futures. Generally, futures seem to be traded more actively than options. Interest rate and foreign exchange futures account for 89% of daily April 1995 average turnover in the combined markets for exchange-traded foreign exchange and interest rate derivatives. Dealers seem to use futures to offset their net OTC exposures. Thus, cross-market hedging using exchange-traded derivatives serves to meet hedging demands generated by OTC activities.[12]

1.3. *Interest rate derivatives: Counterparties*

Figure 4 illustrates the growth in the market for interest rate derivatives using ISDA data on the market for interest rate swaps. A large and growing share of the notional amounts outstanding in global interest rate swap markets is contributed by the interbank (ISDA member) business, whose share increased from 30% of the total volume in 1987 to 53% in 1996. Nonfinancial end-users account for 11% (down from 18%), while the contribution of financial end-users declined from 44% of the total amount to a share of about 33% over the same period (actually recovering from a low of 27% in 1995). The share of the

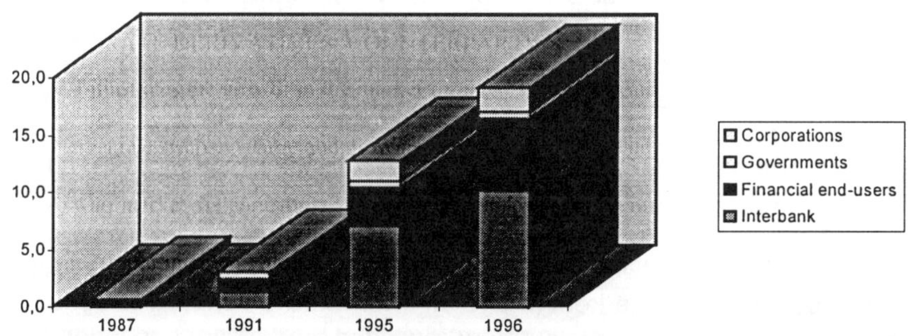

Figure 4. Interest rate swaps by counterparty.

Table 4. OTC interest rate contracts by type and counterparty (reported notional amounts; billions of US $).

Product	Total	Financial institutions (%)	Nonfinancial institutions (%)	Interdealer (local & abroad) (%)
FRAs	6559.5	13.8	4.9	81.3
Swaps	24389.8	17.9	12.8	69.3
OTC options	4390.9	27.9	19.5	52.6
Total	35340.2	18.4	12.2	69.4

Source: BIS (1996) and own calculations.

government sector, the least important player on international markets for interest rate swaps, drops from 7% to a mere 3%.

Table 4 sheds some light on the counterparty breakdown for all OTC interest rate instruments. Reported notional amounts outstanding at end-March 1995 net of local double-counting have been structured by type and counterparty. The table provides figures for interdealer contracts and contracts between dealers and different end-users. It is apparent that markets for OTC interest rate derivatives are dominated by interdealer business, with the market for FRAs being the segment of all OTC markets which is most dominated by contracts between dealers.

Turning to contracts involving dealers and end-users, the share of nonfinancial customers is especially small for FRAs, while options and swaps are used to a greater extent. In contrast, end-users from the financial sectors are heavily engaged in the OTC options business, with FRAs and swaps accounting for smaller shares. But although significantly smaller than their options activities, their shares are nevertheless bigger than the respective contributions of nonfinancial end-users.

The *Survey of Industry Practice* conducted by the Group of Thirty (1993) provides additional data on the use of derivatives by financial institutions. About 92% of the reporting financial firms indicated that they used interest rate swaps, with 54% and 46% of the same group using FRAs and currency swaps, respectively.[13] In the same survey, more than 83% of the reporting financial firms considered the use of derivatives either very important (24%) or even imperative (58%) for risk management. A small survey conducted by GAO (1996) yields similar results.[14] The Group of Thirty survey indicates that banks have become the dominant, though not the only group of dealers on derivatives markets, and that there is a tendency of market concentration among dealers. This is indicated by the observation that about 75% of the notional turnover of each domestic derivatives market are covered by an average of only 10 market makers. Furthermore, some dealers fall in the group of top 10 dealers in more than one country, confirming the tendency towards global concentration (Vrolijk, 1997). Requirements of technology, know-how and expertise in appraising capital and credit quality all contribute to this tendency. In this regard, Campbell and Kracaw (1991) highlight the role of market making, i.e., the pooling of offsetting risks in large derivatives portfolios. Gonzales-Hermosillo (1994) and Board et al. (1995) argue that the tendency for market concentration is characterized by a growing market share of high-quality dealers. They note that more than 90% of swap counterparties are triple-B rated or above, while an increasing share of the market falls to so-called, structured derivative product companies (SDPC) or special purpose vehicles (SVP). These highly specialized OTC derivatives dealers are legally separate subsidiaries of parent firms and endowed with enough capital and operational procedures sufficient to gain a triple-A credit rating (Remolona et al., 1996).

1.4. Interest rate derivatives: Maturity structure

The maturity breakdown of global notional amounts of reported OTC derivatives contracts outstanding points at a predominance of short- and medium-term instruments. Table 5 provides information regarding the maturity structure of OTC interest rate derivatives. The table shows a share of 44% for short-term interest rate instruments, with medium-term contracts accounting for another 43%. The proportion of interest rate contracts of maturities less than one year is the smallest for interest rate swaps, while FRAs are predominantly short-term with a share of 88% falling to the respective instruments.

This fact is supported by the data in Table 3 and seems to reflect the widespread use of FRAs for hedging purposes related to short-term interest rate risks. Breaking down the maturities of the other OTC derivatives markets reveals that foreign exchange instruments are even more dominated by short-term contracts, with shares of 79% and 16% for maturities up to one year and between one and five years, respectively. The same is true for equity and commodity based products, where the respective shares amount to 44% and 43% for the equity based markets, and 75% and 24% for commodity derivatives. Finally, breaking down the maturity structure for the combined OTC derivatives markets yields that only 10% of the notional amounts outstanding were for more than five years, while 56% were for less than one year.

Table 5. OTC interest rate derivatives by maturity.[15]

Contract-type	Up to 1 year (%)	Over 5 years (%)	$1 < \text{year} \leq 5$ (%)
FRAs	88	0	12
Swaps	35	16	49
Options	36	14	50
Total	44	13	43
All OTC instruments	56	10	34

Source: BIS (1996).

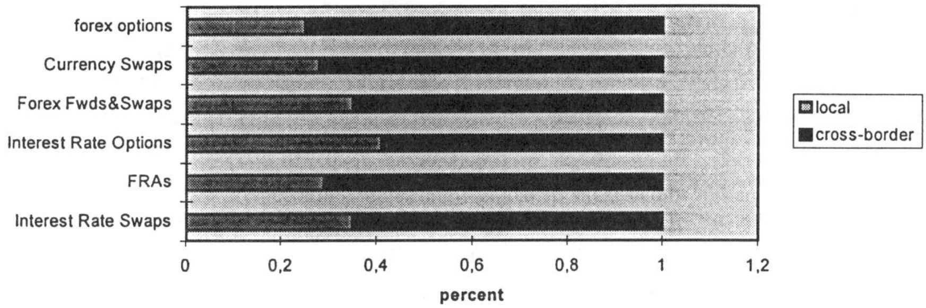

Figure 5. Notional amounts; OTC markets.

1.5. Summary

Derivatives markets are becoming increasingly global, as suggested by a share of 55% of reported notional amounts and about 75% of average daily turnover involving counterparties from different countries. Figure 5 indicates the shares of cross-border trades in the different OTC markets.[16] The data suggest that transactions in swaps and FRAs are overwhelmingly between banks. Banks, therefore, seem to use short-term interest rate swaps and FRAs to manage the interest rate risks created by their portfolios.[17]

Brewer et al. (1994) and Heinecke and Shen (1995) provide empirical evidence showing that banks use derivatives in order to extend their traditional lending activities. Specifically, they demonstrate a positive association between the use of interest rate swaps and the growth in bank loans, concluding that derivatives are complements to banks' loan portfolios. Furthermore, however, banks seem to engage in derivatives in order to offset the shortfall in profits coming from their traditional business (Edwards and Mishkin, 1995).

2. Economic functions of derivatives

Financial derivatives allow investors to assume or lay off certain risks attached to an underlying financial asset. Until recently, derivatives were used exclusively to address market risks of the underlying assets, i.e., changes in the value of the asset due to changes in markets prices and interest rates. More recently, "credit derivatives" have emerged, allowing investors to assume or hedge credit risk, i.e., the risk of default in the underlying asset. Examples are "credit default swaps" and "total-rate-of-return (TROR) swaps." Trading in credit derivatives is dominated by a small number of highly rated banks and largely restricted to a fairly narrow range of sovereign and quasi-sovereign instruments.[18]

In general economic terms, derivatives thus serve to achieve a more complete financial system. Previously fixed combinations of the risk properties of loans and financial assets can be bundled and unbundled into new, synthetic assets. Individual risk attributes of financial assets, thus, acquire separability and mobility (Bisignano, 1998). Repackaging risk properties in this way can provide a better match between an investor's risk preferences and the effective risk of her portfolio or cash-flow. In addition, derivatives allow individual risk elements of an asset to be priced and traded separately. This implies a more efficient price system in the asset markets, as derivatives prices can signal changes in individual aspects of the pay-off profile of the underlying asset that were previously merged with all other aspects.

Beyond these general considerations, derivatives fulfill a number of more specific economic functions (BIS, 1994a; Issing and Bischofberger, 1996). First, they save transaction costs and allow a better exploitation of comparative advantage. For example, two borrowers who can each obtain a better interest rate in one market but need a loan in the other market can swap their interest payments, allowing each to exploit the other's cost advantage. In doing so, the use of derivatives increases the value of the investors' assets.

Second, they provide opportunities for hedging and better and cheaper portfolio diversification. Investors, both end-users and financial institutions can use derivatives to stabilize interest payments over time and reduce their exposure to interest rate and exchange rate shocks. Regarding the allocation of risks in the economy, three cases can be distinguished (Issing and Bischofberger, 1996). The use of derivatives facilitates the elimination of economic risks, when the parties to a contract—or the end users in a chain of contracts—use it to hedge against opposite risk exposures. Empirical evidence from the BIS (1996) survey of OTC markets suggests that the vast majority of derivatives contracts serves to channel exposures to price risks from one end-user to another with offsetting demands, leaving dealers with only small exposures to price risks in the aggregate (Kambhu et al., 1996; IMF, 1996a). The resulting credit risks seem to be rather small. The net credit exposure on swaps, for example, is only about 1% of its notional principal (Hentschel and Smith, 1997). Derivatives serve to achieve a more efficient distribution of risks between private agents, if one party to a contract hedges against a risk and the other, the speculator, assumes the corresponding exposure. Specializing in the acquisition and processing of relevant information, the speculator will generally be better able to assume that risk than her counterpart, so that the redistribution of risks enhances the economy's efficiency in coping with economic uncertainties and the aggregate risk is effectively reduced (Darby, 1994). Both risk reduction and redistribution have positive welfare and wealth effects in the economy.

New risk is created if the parties to a contract are two speculators with different expectations. The positive economic aspect of this case is that trade among speculators with different expectations facilitates competition among agents with different information sets and different specializations in gathering and evaluating new information. Competition among profit-maximizing speculators assures that, in the longer run, only those with efficient information technologies survive.

Third, by unbundling risks, derivatives create additional liquidity in asset markets. Santomero and Trester (1998) investigate whether the increased liquidity together with reduced communications cost leads to riskier lending by banks. The authors find that banks are willing to provide riskier lending to finance real sector investment as a result of increased liquidity. However, they argue that this does not imply that banks are higher risk. Rather, banks have moved from greater exposure to external shocks to greater risk taking on the returns of their assets. Futhermore, the possibility of tying derivatives notionally to a specific asset implies that trading opportunities are not limited by the existing stock of the underlying asset. The result is, again, a positive wealth effect for the investor.

Fourth, derivatives enable investors to devise investment strategies bridging market segments that were previously separated. This implies an increase in the substitutability of financial assets across a wide range of market segments and a broader scope of arbitrage possibilities between markets (Deutsche Bundesbank, 1994). As a result, shock spill-overs from one market to another are magnified, but the impact of an individual shock on the originating market is reduced.

Finally, financial institutions can use credit derivatives to avoid a concentration of their credit risk on particular groups of customers without severing customer relationships, and to diversify portfolios by assuming risk exposures to different borrowers without entering into new customer relationships. Thus, credit derivatives allow banks to focus more keenly on their role as initiators of credit, and other financial institutions to use the resulting credit risks to achieve a more suitable risk structure of their portfolios.

Deregulation together with the greater liquidity and substitutability of financial assets provided by derivatives markets have triggered important institutional changes in the financial system. On the one hand, it has fostered disintermediation, i.e., the tendency of borrowers to access capital markets directly rather than through the use of a bank. On the other hand, nonbank financial institutions have ventured into business areas traditionally reserved for commercial banks. Responding to the resulting loss of traditional business, banks have become the dominant players in the derivatives markets (see above). Corresponding to the greater substitutability of financial assets, then, institutional differences have become more blurred. The emergence of large financial conglomerates in Europe over the last decade confirms this point.

An important question regarding the economic function of derivatives is whether they stabilize financial markets. There are several aspects to the answer. One is that the unbundling of different types of risk attached to an underlying asset and the creation of separate markets for each of them implies that there are now more prices to consider. Creating a price for a specific type of risk means that news regarding this particular type has a larger impact on this particular price, but a smaller one on other prices; it is thus both stabilizing and destabilizing. Furthermore, the increased liquidity of asset markets and the greater substitutability of financial assets lead to stronger links between individual markets and more efficient shock absorption. From this perspective, derivatives should reduce market volatility. A related point is that greater arbitrage possibilities between forward and spot markets should facilitate the incorporation of new information into spot market prices, making the reaction of the latter to unexpected market developments less disruptive. This is supported by the observation that forward market prices typically "lead" spot prices over time (Board et al., 1995). At the same time, derivatives allow traders to take speculative positions with greater financial leverage, since they can buy and sell risks without having to acquire or sell the underlying assets. Traders can react faster and with larger trading volumes to news and shocks affecting asset price expectations, and engage in more complex investment strategies that may exacerbate excess demands or excess supplies of assets in times of turbulence (BIS, 1994). As a result, even small shocks can trigger large changes in asset holdings. In this sense, the development of derivatives markets can destabilize markets.

Empirical evidence suggests that the emergence of derivatives markets has not caused additional volatility in spot markets (IMF, 1997; Cohen, 1996; Board et al., 1995). In fact, official reports on the 1987 crash indicate that the low volume of derivatives slowed down the recovery from the crash.[19] However, BIS (1994) suggests that trading in derivative markets may occasionally have had destabilizing effects on the underlying securities markets during periods of unusual stress, as some trading strategies may amplify excess supplies of assets in times of falling prices. The US General Accounting Office (GAO, 1994) argues that increased market links and the concentration on a small number of traders raises the risk of "chain events," i.e., crises that spread from one market to another. The main concern is the potential effect of a sudden withdrawal of one large trader from the market, making the market very illiquid. To avoid destabilizing effects of derivative-based, automated trading strategies, exchanges today have implemented circuit breakers that stop trading in the case of sudden, large price movements. Kambhu et al. (1996) report from simulation exercises that price shocks cause less volatility in OTC derivatives markets than in securities markets.

3. Monetary policy consequences of derivatives

Section 2 has illustrated the rapid growth of the new financial instruments. Section 3 has reviewed their economic functions and interpreted them in terms of the emergence of a more efficient financial market system. What implications can one draw for the effectiveness and conduct of monetary policy? We answer this question in two steps. First, we consider the implications of derivatives for the design of monetary strategies, given the transmission mechanism of monetary policy. Next, we discuss their implications for the monetary transmission mechanism. This corresponds approximately to a distinction between medium-run and long-run effects. To lay out a long-run scenario, we assume that the growth of financial derivatives markets will continue and eventually create a much more complete financial system.

3.1. Implications for monetary strategies

For a given monetary transmission mechanism and a given set of goals, a monetary strategy is a set of rules regarding instrument choice and the reaction to current events enabling the central bank to best reach its objectives. Since the link between monetary policy actions and target variables—the price level, output and employment—are "long and variable" (Friedman, 1968), the strategy design involves the choice of an intermediate target. An intermediate target strategy focuses on how the intermediate target should be controlled over a medium-run time horizon, during which the target variables themselves cannot be or can only imperfectly be observed.

One implication of a more complete financial market for any monetary strategy is the availability of a broader range of observable asset prices conveying information about the current and expected state of the economy. In addition to inflation, interest rate and exchange rate expectations contained in interest rates and futures prices, derivatives prices in particular contain new types of information a central bank can use to improve its monetary strategy. For example, the Black-Scholes (1973) model of option pricing implies that market expectations about asset price volatility can be extracted from option prices (Söderlind and Svensson, 1997). Furthermore, comparing call and put prices and volumes yields information about market expectations of changes in the prices of the underlying assets and their volatility. At a general level, derivatives markets can help central banks to obtain a more complete picture of market sentiments (BIS, 1994).

The discussion of the choice of an intermediate target focuses on the source of the dominant shocks in an economy and the stability of the link between the intermediate and the ultimate targets of monetary policy. The first issue was raised by Poole (1970) who argues that a central bank should choose the interest rate (more generally, an asset price), if the dominant shocks arise from the financial sector (shocks to the money demand function), and a monetary aggregate, if the dominant shocks arise from the real sector.

The emergence of new financial instruments can be interpreted as creating instability in the money demand function. As new financial instruments are being developed, the public's demand for money changes, and this in a way that is often difficult to predict with any reasonable degree of precision. In a period of rapid development of derivatives markets, central banks should, therefore, give preference to asset prices over monetary aggregates as intermediate targets. But the argument has less strength than it looks at a first glance. On the one hand, the preference for asset prices is only a transitional one. On the other hand, the introduction of financial instruments allowing the stabilization of cash flows and the reduction of exposure to interest rate shocks should affect an economy's investment demand function as much as its money demand function. If so, the net effect on the desirability of asset prices as intermediate targets is unclear.

In the longer run, the emergence of a more complete asset market contradicts the assumption, central to Poole's analysis, that the economy has only "one" interest rate. More generally, a reliable interest rate target then requires that the central bank can target an interest rate index representing the whole range of interest rates over the yield curve. In this regard, the implications of a more perfect financial environment are ambiguous. Monetary policy necessarily operates on the short end of the yield curve. The transmission of monetary impulses from the short to the long end depends on how changes in inflation expectations triggered by monetary policy actions translate into changes in long-term interest rates. On the one hand, the availability of a broader range of arbitrage opportunities suggests that expectation effects "travel faster" along the yield curve (see, e.g., Vrolijk, 1997; Cottarelli and Kourelis, 1994). This results in a more rapid adjustment of financial asset prices to monetary shocks. It is usually argued that this effect is of minor importance, as the speed of financial market adjustment is already high (Issing and Bischofberger, 1996). However, for less liquid assets like mortgages and bank loans price adjustment might be significantly increased.

On the other hand, the greater asset substitutability and the more efficient price system suggest that long term rates are more strongly affected by expectations (and information) from other sectors of the economy. With a greater information set underlying the inflation expectations in long-term interest rates, a given monetary impulse will have a smaller effect on these rates. Hentschel and Smith (1997) argue that the greater information set available should help agents to distinguish between real and monetary shocks, thus reducing the real effects of monetary policy.

Exchange rate policies, the other version of a monetary strategy based on asset prices, are more strongly affected by the emergence of more complete asset markets. After the breakdown of the Bretton Woods System in 1973, many central banks, particularly among the G7 reverted to "sterilized interventions" to combine a monetary strategy geared at domestic policy goals with an exchange rate target. Sterilized interventions, in which the liquidity effect of the central bank's foreign exchange market operations is immediately offset by opposite transactions in the domestic money, can only influence the exchange rate, if domestic and foreign financial assets are imperfect substitutes. From this perspective, the emergence of a more perfect financial market system should decrease the effectiveness of sterilized interventions.[20]

The "unholy trinity" describes the inconsistency of high international capital mobility, a fixed exchange rate, and a monetary policy dedicated to domestic policy goals. With high capital mobility, fixed exchange rates become highly exposed to speculative attacks, leaving the central bank no room for a policy that might raise even slight doubts about the sustainability of the exchange rate target. Thus, national monetary authorities have no choice but to make monetary policy completely subservient to the exchange rate target, and, hence, accept the rate of inflation of the currency to which they peg; alternatively, they must renounce the exchange rate target. The experience of the European Monetary System (EMS) in 1992–93, when the system collapsed after a period of mounting imbalances between national monetary policy goals and the requirements of the fixed rate, has forcefully demonstrated this point (von Hagen, 1996). Eichengreen et al. (1998) point to the potential role played by specific institutional investors (hedge funds) and, hence, by derivatives contracts during the 1992–93 EMS and the recent Asian currency and financial crises. These authors do not find, however, any strong evidence for the hypothesis that hedge funds precipitated such crises either directly, through the sheer size of their positions, or indirectly, via herding behavior of other market participants.

One might, of course, turn the argument around and suggest that central banks themselves could make use of derivative instruments rather than outright purchases and sales in the spot market to stabilize exchange rates. While this is possible in theory, and central banks have occasionally used forward market interventions, central banks would then take speculative positions in the same way private speculators do.[21] One may argue that this is an efficient way of sending credible signals about future central bank intentions—after all, the central bank should not speculate against its own future actions. But, if the spot rate later moves in the wrong direction the central bank would take large losses and be accused as engaging in unprofitable and unpopular speculative activities. If, in contrast, the central bank made large profits on speculative positions, other market participants would accuse it of using its own power to manipulate spot prices in order to make its own bet come true at the cost of private market participants. Institutions like central banks fear such accusations and refrain from using derivatives on a large scale.

Thus, the rapid development of derivatives markets has strengthened the logic and force of the "unholy trinity". Increased liquidity of financial markets and increased leverage of financial positions imply that speculators can attack unsustainable fixed exchange rates faster and more powerfully than ever. The rapid innovation of new financial instruments in these markets also implies the futility of attempts to "throw sand in the wheels" through regulation or the introduction of a "Tobin tax" on speculative transactions (Salvatore, 1998). As a result, the new financial environment has increased the vulnerability of fixed exchange rate systems.

As the European example teaches, one way out of this dilemma is to move to a full-fledged monetary union. But the European Monetary Union will remain the exception on the international scene as it requires the political willingness to accept the loss of national sovereignty over a broad range of policies. The example of Argentina in recent years teaches that the other solution is a currency board, i.e., to give up monetary policy independence completely and to accept the possibility of domestic recessions in times of large capital outflows, even if these are generated by external events, e.g., the 1994–95 "Tequila crisis." Since this solution also is politically unattractive for most countries, the likely consequence of the development of derivatives markets is a strong decline in the interest countries take in fixed exchange rates.

Turning to monetary aggregates, the higher asset substitutability and the increased liquidity provided by derivatives makes the definition of "money," particularly of broad monetary aggregates, increasingly difficult (Savona and Maccario, 1998). Simple-sum monetary aggregates are based on the assumption that their components are perfect substitutes and that the aggregate as a whole has only a very low degree of substitutability with other financial assets. This may remain true for cash and pure transactions accounts (more on this below), but it is increasingly questionable for time deposits, savings deposits, and certificates of deposit. The standard response of central banks is to broaden the simple-sum aggregate used as intermediate target; but this is inappropriate because it disregards the intermediate range of substitutability between zero and perfect. Furthermore, the broader the aggregate, the more a monetary target becomes equivalent to targeting the entire balance sheet of the banking sector, leaving little hope to control the intermediate target.

The more sophisticated response, using aggregation theory, is to construct monetary Divisia indices (Barnett, 1978, 1980). By construction, Divisia indices imbed different degrees of substitution among financial assets by incorporating relative prices. Empirical evidence has shown that Divisia indices do indeed yield superior measures of the money supply than broad simple-sum aggregates (Mullineux, 1996). Yet, they are unsatisfactory as intermediate targets, because they are difficult to explain to the public. Targeting Divisia indices requires a forecast of the effect of monetary policy actions on relative asset prices, a task that remains exceedingly difficult.

In sum, there is a preference for narrow simple-sum monetary aggregates, which remain valid even under Divisia aggregation. Since such aggregates are notoriously more volatile in the short run than in the long run, targeting horizons need to be stretched (two or more years) shifting the focus on trend growth of money (von Hagen, 1997). Hentschel and Smith (1997) argue that use of derivatives should reduce demand for excess reserves by improving banks' liquidity risk management. This, in turn, should also reduce the volatility of the money multiplier, which would increase the central bank's effective control over narrow monetary aggregates.

More recently, the debate over monetary policy strategies has contrasted monetary targets with inflation targets. While monetary targets can be, and in practice have been, combined with inflation rate targets (von Hagen, 1995), the substantive difference between the two approaches is in the choice of the intermediate target. Specifically, inflation targeting involves the use of a much broader range of variables as inputs than a monetary target. Thus, Svensson (1996) speaks about "inflation forecast targeting". But since there is nothing in the concept of monetary targeting preventing the central bank from using all available information to update its monetary target and interpret deviations from it, the mere scope of information variables yields no convincing argument in favor of inflation forecast targeting (von Hagen, 1997). This is confirmed by the observation that, on the basis of the central banks' reactions to current events, there are hardly any differences between the two (Mishkin and Posen, 1997). Similarly, the fact that inflation forecasts in practice use a host of economic relationships does not imply a superior strategy, except under very narrow assumptions about the stochastic nature of the shocks.

3.2. Implications for the transmission of monetary policy

Do more complete financial markets change the effectiveness of monetary policy? The answer to this question depends critically on the underlying theory of the monetary transmission mechanism.

One answer—one that remains within the scope of the traditional IS-LM paradigm—recognizes that financial derivatives allow their users to obtain insurance against interest rate and exchange rate shocks. Smith and Stulz (1985) and Froot et al. (1993), among others, show why firms should use derivatives as part of their risk management strategies. To the extent that monetary policy actions are a source of interest rate and exchange rate shocks, the widespread use of financial derivatives should reduce their immediate impact on investment decisions and, hence, on aggregate demand. However, the finite maturity of all financial derivatives implies that the user cannot shield himself against interest rate or exchange rate changes forever (Hausler, 1996). Thus, monetary policy actions are bound to exert an effect sooner or later (Deutsche Bundesbank, 1994; Issing and Bischofberger, 1996). But this conclusion is weaker than it may first seem. Empirically, changes in central bank interest rates are themselves rarely of a permanent nature.[22] Furthermore, in an international environment firms can use financial derivatives to trade domestic for foreign interest rate risk. The possibility that domestic and foreign interest rate shocks offset each other implies a reduced effect of domestic interest rate shocks on domestic investment decisions. In sum, under the IS-LM paradigm one should conclude that the power of monetary policy to affect aggregate demand is eroded by the emergence of a more complete financial markets.

The IS-LM paradigm, however, has long come under attack, since it does not fit well with empirical evidence of how monetary policy affects the economy (Mishkin, 1995; Bernanke and Gertler, 1995). A more convincing explanation of the transmission mechanism is provided by the *credit-market view* of monetary policy transmission (Bernanke, 1993; Bernanke and Gertler, 1995), which introduces credit market imperfections into the Keynesian macroeconomic framework. This view refutes the assumptions of the *Modigliani-Miller theorem*, instead it argues that internal and external finance are imperfect substitutes and that firms rely critically on external funding to finance investment projects. Among the sources of external funding, bank loans are imperfect substitutes for corporate securities; and there is a class of borrowers in the economy, e.g., small businesses, that rely exclusively on bank loans. When interest rates rise in the economy, banks face an outflow of short-term deposits, which cannot be easily substituted for by issuing certificates of deposits or other sources of funds. Under such circumstances, banks prefer to invest in marketable securities rather than bank loans, as the former are more liquid and less risky than the latter. Thus, the supply of bank credit decreases, and borrowers constrained to this source of funding cut their investment expenditures, leading to a decline in aggregate demand. Another version of the credit market view holds that businesses relying on bank loans as the only source of funding face credit constraints that depend on the value of their marketable collateral (Kiyotaki and Moore, 1997). As interest rates rise, the value of collateral declines and with it the availability of credit. Again, aggregate demand falls by a larger amount than is warranted by the rise in interest rates.

Since financial derivatives increase substitution, the strength of the monetary transmission mechanism is weakened (Issing and Bischofberger, 1996). Specifically, the possibility to trade variable for fixed interest rate payments and to hedge against fluctuations in asset prices should protect businesses against variations of their creditworthiness due to variations in short-term interest rates (e.g., Titman, 1992). Furthermore, the increased liquidity of bank loans provided by derivatives increases the substitutability between these and other forms of credit and, therefore, reduces the strength of the mechanism. Thus, the use of derivatives should reduce the effect of changes in central bank interest rates to the pure IS-LM effect which is otherwise small, as suggested by empirical evidence on the interest elasticity of investment demand.

The credit view still remains within the boundaries of the IS-LM paradigm as the general macroeconomic framework.[23] A central tenet of this paradigm is that the financial markets of an economy can be usefully summarized in a two-assets structure in which "money" is a substitute only for "bonds", implying that all nonmonetary assets are perfect substitutes, and the interest rate is the only relative price in the financial system. A change in the money supply then has a straightforward impact on this interest rate, which, in turn, affects aggregate demand. The more complete a financial market system, the less tenable this view of the economy is. The *monetarist* critique of the IS-LM framework in the 1960s and 1970s already demonstrated that, even considering no more than three financial assets—money, bonds, and equity, and, hence, two asset prices—raises the complexity of the analysis considerably and makes predictions of the effects of monetary policy actions on aggregate demand more complex (Brainard and Tobin, 1968; Brunner and Meltzer, 1976; Meltzer, 1995). The larger the number of assets, the more information is required on the degrees of substitutability between money and other assets to make predictions. This, of course, reinforces our observation about the consequences of financial innovations for the measurement of money.

In a more complete financial market system, then, central banks find it harder to predict the effect of a given monetary impulse on real output and employment with any reasonable precision. While it remains true that a monetary expansion ultimately raises the price level, its short-run real effect is much more difficult to determine. Thus, discretionary monetary policies aiming at moving output and employment closer to some target levels become more uncertain. The important policy implication is that central banks operating in a more complete financial environment should refrain from active monetary stabilization of short-run real fluctuations and focus on the more long-run goal of price stability instead. Thus, the emergence of financial derivatives "disciplines" monetary policy in the sense of inducing a shift of the policy makers' attention to low inflation.

3.3. Nonmonetary payment systems

The extension of the analytical framework discussed above still follows the traditional paradigm of monetary economics in assuming that money, and money alone, is the economy's general medium of transaction and unit of account. Banks play a special role in monetary economics, because, by definition, their liabilities are "money" (Tobin, 1963). Proponents of the "New Monetary Economics" (Cowen and Kroszner, 1987) have long pointed out that this assumption is by no means a natural one: Payment technologies can be conceptualized on the exchange of financial assets other than money, and where the medium of exchange does not coincide with the unit of account (Fama, 1980, 1983). Wallace (1983) argues that the special role of money and, hence, monetary policy is due entirely to legal restrictions, making money artificially the only unit of account.

New Monetary Economics takes an economy with an unregulated, competitive banking system as its paradigm (Black, 1970; Fama, 1980; Hall, 1983). Competitive banks offer transaction services and manage portfolios of interest bearing, risky assets. Bank accounts are shares in such portfolios, pay competitive interest rates and have variable prices in terms of the economy's unit of account.[24] Depending on the depositor's preferences, banks offer accounts of different interest-rate risk combinations. Transactions involve transfers of assets from the payer's account to the recipient's account. Since they provide an extra service, banks charge a competitive fee for them. Apart from that, an arbitrage-free equilibrium demands that such accounts pay the same interest rate as any other asset of the same risk-return characteristic.

In the purest form of such a system, there is no need for a special asset to serve as a generalized medium of payment. Hence, transaction accounts create no need for a bank to hold reserves—voluntary or required—of such a medium against them. This is the main difference compared to the traditional monetary economy, where payments are settled in a medium provided by the central bank (central bank reserves and currency) and where the amount of reserves and currency made available by the central bank—or their price as determined by the central bank—puts a limit on the banking sector's ability or willingness to make loans and create deposits, which is the cornerstone of monetary policy. The implication is that the aggregate volume of these accounts is determined entirely by the private sector's demand (Fama, 1980; Black, 1987). As Greenfield and Yeager (1983) put it: "No longer, then, could there be too much of it [of central bank money in a regulated economy], causing price inflation, or too little, causing depression, or a sequence of imbalances, causing stagflation. A wrong quantity of money could no longer cause problems." Thus, there is no role for government policy trying to affect output and employment in such an economy.

Derivatives can take the modern economy a long way to the environment envisioned by the New Monetary Economics (Bisignano, 1998). To begin with, derivatives allow to circumvent existing legal restrictions in financial markets, making regulations less binding. A second reason relates to the demand for transaction accounts. One reason why variable-price transaction accounts have not been widely used, even after two decades of financial regulation, is probably that private households and firms value planning certainty for their daily transactions. A high degree of certainty about the purchasing power available in a transactions account reduces information and transactions cost. Obviously, this demand for certainty relates much more to the short run than the long run. In this regard, the development of financial instruments allowing banks to offer transaction accounts based on interest-bearing assets with low short-run volatility should make such accounts much more attractive as an alternative to traditional, fixed-price deposits. One should expect, therefore, that such accounts would become increasingly popular as derivatives markets evolve, particularly since financial deregulation increases competition in the banking industry. The decline of the traditional banking industry and traditional bank deposits as a source of funding and the rising role of banks in the derivatives markets clearly supports that expectation (Edwards and Mishkin, 1995).

A third reason for the demise of central bank money as medium of transaction relates to the supply side of the economy. For a given stock of fixed-price transactions accounts, the increased liquidity of nonmonetary assets provided by financial derivatives allows banks to improve the efficiency of their reserve management. That is, interest-bearing assets can be substituted for central bank money as liquid reserves. While the banks' demand for reserves will not disappear completely, the likely consequence is that the quantity of central bank money, or the price of central bank money, will decline in importance in determining the amount of loans banks are willing to extend and the interest rates they charge. This, in turn, will reduce the power of monetary policy in controlling the volume of money and credit. Obviously, the extent of this substitution process depends on the conduct of monetary policy itself, since the choice between central bank money and other liquid reserve assets is an endogenous one. For example, frequent and unexpected changes in central banks' lending conditions to commercial banks will reduce the attractiveness of central bank money as a reserve asset compared to alternatives. Thus, the more variable and less transparent is central bank behavior, the more central bank money will lose ground as a reserve asset and the more the central bank will lose control over the supply of money.

One might argue that central banks can prevent that from happening by setting sufficiently high required reserve rates and by extending the coverage of reserve requirements to a broader range of bank liabilities, beyond fixed-price deposits. Fama (1980), for example, shows how the central bank can create a demand for money by imposing a reserve requirement in terms of central bank money on a completely nonmonetary asset serving as medium of transaction. However, in a world of high international capital mobility, reserve requirements affect the competitive position of the national banking industry; competition for market shares in the international financial markets will put pressure on central banks to reduce reserve requirements. There is a close parallel to international competition in capital taxation: high capital mobility puts strong downward pressure on reserve requirements. The reduction of required reserve ratios in recent years, even in countries where the central bank traditionally regards reserve requirements as indispensable for monetary policy, like Germany, indicates the force of this competition.

Despite these tendencies to replace money by other means of transaction, however, the demand for government-issued money will not disappear completely, as envisioned by proponents of the New Monetary Economics. One reason is quite simple that governments themselves can secure a demand for the money they issue by insisting that all tax payments be made using it.[25] As long as governments uphold this requirement, central bank money will stay. Since taxation pervades all sectors of the economy, the demand for central bank money will respond to aggregate real income and real wealth, although it will likely be much less interest elastic and much more seasonal than traditional money demand. Even if all private transactions were executed without using central bank money, banks would have to hold some central bank money to serve their customers' demand for executing transactions with the government.

Furthermore, a demand for government-issued cash as a medium of transaction in very small denominations will remain. New Monetary Economics focuses entirely on payments from bank accounts and disregards the fact that economic agents execute small payments in their daily shopping activities. The desire to make informal, nonmarket exchanges of a medium of transaction (gifts and payments in the shadow economy) contributes further to this demand for cash.[26]

Nevertheless, even with these qualifications it is plausible to expect that the demand for government-issued money will decline substantially as banks develop more attractive types of transaction accounts. The degree to which new media of transaction will replace money is ultimately an endogenous variable.

Taking the unregulated financial system and a fully demand-determined quantity of transactions accounts as the reference point suggests that it will depend largely on the central banks behavior in controlling the supply of money. The more frequently the central bank exploits its role as provider of a medium of transaction, the more these institutions will be induced to seek alternative means of payment and offer them to the nonbank public. Similarly, uncertainty about central bank actions constraining financial institutions will induce banks to move out of money. From this perspective, the emergence of a more perfect financial market system induces central banks to refrain from short-run oriented, macroeconomic activism in favor of a more long-run oriented, predictable monetary policy.

Expecting a diminished role of monetary policy in controlling monetary aggregates is not equivalent to expecting that aggregate demand will no longer be exposed to shocks originating in the financial sector. Here, we disagree with the proponents of the New Monetary Economics, who claim that, in an unregulated financial environment, financial institutions will not be able to actively create credit, and, hence, macroeconomic fluctuations caused by an excess supply of (demand for) credit which must be met by an excess demand for (supply of) goods cannot arise (Black, 1970; Tobin, 1963). As Krüger (1997) shows, this view mistakes an unregulated economy to be necessarily one of perfect information. As long as information asymmetries prevail between lenders and borrowers, and information advantages make banks "local" monopolists in their loan relationships, the potential for credit creation, hence macroeconomic fluctuations remains. Nevertheless, the declining role of money as the general medium of transaction implies a declining role of monetary policy as an independent source of such fluctuations and as a policy tool to combat them. Whether macroeconomic fluctuations will, in the end, be more or less pronounced than in a traditional monetary economy remains an empirical question.

The possible emergence of a financial system where central bank money largely loses its role as medium of transaction raises the question, discussed in the New Monetary Economics, of what will be the unit of account in such an economy. As pointed out by Fama (1980), there is nothing that requires an economy's medium of transaction to coincide with its unit of account.[27] While competition and market forces can drive the economy towards using more efficient transactions technologies, the choice of a unit of account is a matter that markets cannot solve easily. A unit of account is an important element of communication among market participants, and its attractiveness for an individual economic agent depends on how many other agents use the same unit of account. Thus, the choice involves important economies of scale and network externalities. Empirical evidence suggests that economies switch from one unit of account to another only in times of hyperinflation, when the value of this unit is uncertain and eroding rapidly. Hysteresis thus plays a large role in answering the question. A suggestive answer then is that government-issued money would retain its role as unit of account even in economies where it no longer serves as the dominant medium of transaction, as long as central banks secure its stable value in terms of goods and services.

In sum, we have argued that the development of a more complete financial market system has important consequences for monetary policy and its role in the economy. It allows banks to offer shares in interest-bearing asset portfolios as transaction accounts with relatively little short-run price volatility. Central bank money will remain the medium of transaction with the government and retain its unit of account function, but monetary policy will lose its power to affect the real side of the economy by actively restraining the amount of loans banks are willing to extend. By itself, this should induce central banks to shift attention away from trying to achieve short-run oriented goals of output and employment stabilization and from short-run oriented, discretionary activism. As central banks realize that the banking sector's choice between central bank money and other, highly liquid reserve assets depends critically on the stability of the central bank's lending conditions, and that the publics use of central bank money as unit of account depends critically on the stability of its value, the focus on the long-run goal, price stability, will also be reinforced.

Note that, even if monetary policy loses its power to affect output and employment in the short run, price stability remains a reasonable goal of monetary policy.[28] Since the demand for money remains well-defined, a positive price of money in terms of other goods exists. Monetary policy will then have to combine a high degree of elasticity of the money supply to accomodate seasonal variations in the demand for money in the short run with a long-run money growth trend that follows the trend growth rate of aggregate output. A monetary strategy based on multiannual targets for narrow monetary aggregates would be an appropriate strategy to achieve that.

The demise of short-run, macroeconomic stabilization as a monetary policy objective contributes to the declining importance of exchange rate considerations in monetary policy. This, in turn, will make central banks less interested in pursuing international policy coordination, since the benefit from policy coordination comes mainly from international spill-overs of monetary surprises generated by central banks responding to aggregate demand and supply shocks (Canzoneri and Henderson, 1991). This development will be reinforced by the fact that in a more complex financial environment the design of optimally coordinated central bank strategies becomes increasingly difficult.

4. Regulatory policies

The rapid emergence of derivatives markets has raised fears about their potential damaging effect on the stability of the financial sector, exemplified by the statement of Henry Gonzalez, chairman of the Banking Committee of the US House of Representatives: "I have long believed that growing bank involvement in derivatives trade is, as I say and repeat, like a tinderbox waiting to explode."[29] Likewise, the GAO (1994) report concludes that there was some reason to believe that derivatives created a threat to the financial system and that additional regulation was required, although the GAO saw the increasing activities of unregulated nonbank financial institutions in these markets as the main reason to worry (Bothwell, 1994). In contrast, Greenspan (1994a) warns that increasing regulation might create the false impression that federal regulation would remove all risk, inducing private agents to engage in ever riskier activities. Similarly, Goodhart et al. (1997) warn that regulation would be excessive and overly expensive if it tried to reduce the risk facing small investors and consumers to unduly low levels. The Group of Thirty (1997) insists that, while it is not sensible to eliminate all risk, the risk of large disruptions of the financial system as a whole should be eliminated through regulatory initiatives.

Apart from the sheer size of the new markets (Edwards and Mishkin, 1995), two factors are behind these fears: derivatives (i) allow to take speculative positions with greater leverage and more complex strategies, and (ii) are not visible in the balance sheets of financial institutions, often span across international borders, and are difficult to monitor. The existing empirical evidence suggests that the first factor may be a valid concern for individual financial institutions engaging in excessively risky activities (witness the Barings crisis), but not so for the financial system as a whole, since the net exposure of the banking system to credit risks stemming from derivatives trade is rather small (IMF, 1996a; Edwards and Mishkin, 1995; Kambhu et al., 1996).[30] Recognition of the second factor has triggered a discussion about changes in the regulatory approach.

Traditional, corporatist arrangements for banking regulation have emphasized restricted market access, limited competition and the imposition of regulatory standards based on financial accounting, balance sheets and income statements (Goodhart and Schoenmaker, 1993). These arrangements relied heavily on a strict institutional separation of different types of financial activities, such as commercial banking, real estate finance, insurance, etc. This separation was reflected in a division of regulatory responsibilities among different regulatory bodies, each concerned with one particular financial industry. With restricted market access and competition, regulatory functions could often be implemented on the basis of semiprivate industry arrangements or in cooperation between industry organizations and government agencies rather than through direct government intervention.

Financial innovation and the emergence of a more complete financial system have eroded the boundaries between different markets and spurred more intense competition, including international competition, among financial institutions. Corporatist arrangements become much more difficult to maintain in such an environment, because competition tends to destroy the traditional, insider-club nature of industry relations, and because the branching out of financial institutions into new markets has created a more fuzzy industry structure than the traditional one. At the same time, the use of derivatives and other innovations has facilitated the circumvention of barriers to market entry and limits to competition. The traditional arrangements have, therefore, both lost effectiveness in constraining management behavior and created inefficiencies as the same financial activities came to fall under different regulatory jurisdictions. Regulatory bodies are notoriously bad in cooperating with each other (Goodhart, 1996a; Goodhart and Schoenmaker, 1993). Regulatory responses to these challenges include a shift towards more market-friendly modes of regulation, the consolidation of regulatory functions, and attempts at international cooperation (Padoa-Schioppa, 1995).

4.1. Motivations for banking regulation

There are three basic reasons why financial institutions are regulated,[31] each leading to different modes and instruments of regulation. The first is the protection of (small) depositors against the risk of bank failure (Dewatripont and Tirole, 1994). Small depositors find it hard and excessively costly to monitor the lending activities of their bank and are, therefore, unable to prevent banks from pursuing too risky lending strategies. While banks can, in principle, offer to insure their deposits to solve this problem, information asymmetries between the insurer and the bank make it impossible to price deposit risk in an actuarially fair way, and mispricing risk induces moral hazard on the part of the insured (Chan et al., 1992). Where it exists, deposit insurance is, therefore, commonly compulsory and provided by the government which uses further regulatory tools to address the moral hazard problems created by the insurance.

The second reason for financial regulation is to prevent financial contagion. The mismatch in maturities between bank assets and liabilities creates the risk that depositors want to withdraw their funds from a bank in the event of even a slight suspicion that the bank is unable to repay its liabilities (Diamond and Dybvig, 1983). As each depositor wants to be first in line to obtain his deposit before the bank has used up its liquid reserves, bank runs are self-generated. If depositors at other banks read the closing of one bank as a signal that their banks are equally in financial trouble, the run can spread to other banks. Regulatory strategies to prevent bank runs involve measures to convince depositors of the financial soundness of the banking sector, such as, prudential rules limiting the risk exposure of the banks and forcing them to hold reserves sufficient to meet sudden increases in the demand for cash. Furthermore, bank panics can be prevented by a credible lender of last resort. If depositors are assured that banks can obtain the reserves to pay out their deposits, the value of being first in line disappears and bank panics do not arise.

The third reason for financial regulation is to preserve the integrity of the payments mechanisms.[32] Payments systems can help economize on central bank money and avoid long delays in payments if they limit actual settlement between the participants to the net positions at the end of a specified settlement period. In doing so, they create credit relations among the participants during the time interval between the initiation and the final settlement of all payments. In contrast to a bank's ordinary lending business, a payments system makes banks extend credit to other banks without choice or assessment of their counterparts (Angelini and Passacantando, 1992; Goodhart and Schoenmaker, 1993). If a participant proves unable to meet its obligations, all other participants may be affected as they are interconnected in a cobweb of credit relations. The system would then have to grind to a halt and all payments be unwound to isolate the failing institution from the other participants, a procedure that would be lengthy, costly, and often impossible. In an international context, this liquidity risk is augmented by "Herstatt risk", the settlement risk resulting from the fact that national payment systems in different countries may not be open during the same hours of a day. The smooth operation of payments systems can be assured by an agent who guarantees the execution of all payments initiated during a settlement period, another lender-of-last-resort function. Regulatory provisions surrounding this function focus on the quality of a bank's risk controls, computing and back-up facilities and network technologies (Goodhart and Schoenmaker, 1993).

Among the three modes of banking regulation, the first is akin to consumer protection and the latter two address systemic issues. Although there is a large degree of variation across countries in this regard (von Hagen, 1997), central banks are typically charged with either one or both types of lender-of-last resort functions. The reason is that systemic risks are themselves the result of the use of central bank money as a medium of transaction. Bank runs and financial contagion only arise because bank deposits have a fixed price in terms of money and bank reserves of central bank money are only a fraction of their nominal value. If bank accounts were simply shares in asset portfolios with variable prices, being first in line to withdraw funds would have no value. A rumor that a bank might be financially unsound might still induce its customers to withdraw shares from their bank accounts, but this would simply produce a decline in the value of their shares (Cowen and Kroszner, 1994). Payment systems can still be devised in the money-less economy envisioned by New Monetary economists, but since payments would be exchanges of portfolio shares with variable prices, they would have to be executed on a gross-settlement basis. Thus, if the emergence of a more complete financial system entails the demise of central bank money as medium of transaction, it reduces the importance of systemic risk. Financial regulation to protect consumers against the principal-agent problems from asymmetric information then moves to the forefront.

Technical and institutional developments in recent years have reduced the importance of the risks related to the viability of payment systems (IMF, 1996b). A number of countries have adopted real-time gross-settlement (RTGS) systems in which settlement is executed continuously and on a gross basis. The European Monetary Union's payment system, TARGET, will be of that type, too. The straightfoward way to eliminate "Herstatt" risk is the introduction of "payment versus payment" (PVP) systems, in which a third party assures that both parties to a transaction have made their payments before the funds owed to them are simultaneously released (IMF, 1996a, 1997). One way to facilitate this is to extend business days in at least one market so that business hours of markets in different time zones overlap. For this purpose, the Federal Reserve Bank of New York started operating the Fedwire system for a full 18 hours a day in 1997. Obviously, however, this approach has practical limits. Alternatively, PVP systems can be operated by global clearing banks that bridge the time gaps between business hours, e.g., through a cooperative arrangement among national central banks (Emmons, 1997). A major difficulty with that approach is that it requires close international coordination of regulatory arrangements which we discuss below.

4.2. Regulatory approaches

The central focus of current regulatory standards is to assure the solvency of financial institutions by maintaining a sufficiently high capitalization. High capitalization insures the creditors against adverse shocks to the value of the institution's portfolio of assets. This is exemplified by the capital-asset ratios laid down in the Basle Accord of 1988. Regulators wish to assure sufficient capitalization by imposing minimum capital asset ratios on banks. To take into account the different risk properties of different bank assets, regulators define fixed weights for different types of assets and different classes of bank capital (Dewatripont and Tirole, 1994).

The basic problems with this approach are widely discussed in the literature.[33] Regulatory arrangements are incentive contracts between bank managers and regulators. The imposition of capital standards on banks changes the incentives and constraints under which managers seek to optimize bank portfolios; and in ways that are not necessarily conducive to achieve the regulators' objectives. Focusing on balance sheet ratios moves the attention away from other important aspects of bank management, such as internal risk controls and management incentives. Capital asset ratios may induce banks to choose a higher share of risky assets in their portfolios. While portfolio theory can find correct risk-weights for different assets, these weights vary with changing market conditions. More importantly, inconsistent risk weights, i.e., weights that are different from the theoretically correct ones, create incentives that result in an increase rather than a mitigation of systemic risk. Similarly, minimum capital asset ratios must be distinguished from optimum capital asset ratios. Minimum ratios, while easily verifiable, should only be used as a first-line tool to monitor bank performance. In a more perfect, yet more complex financial environment, these considerations gain increasing weight, implying that alternative regulatory approaches should move to the forefront (Goodhart, 1996a).

Recent experience with bank failures, including large international banks, suggests that weaknesses in the management procedures and risk controls of a bank are more important than noncompliance with balance sheet ratios (Goodhart et al., 1997). Specifically, Goodhart (1996b) explains how misguided pay schemes and bonus arrangements for bank managers can induce excessively risky management behavior. The Group of Thirty reports survey results among bank managers that indicate inadequate management procedure, failure of internal controls and actions of rogue employees as the three most likely causes of bank failure. This suggests that regulation should focus more on management practices and internal risk controls (GAO, 1994). In line with this, the Group of Thirty (1993) report put forth a set of management standards as a guide for good practice. In the US, the Federal Reserve System and the Office of the Comptroller of the Currency have issued guidelines for bank examinors incorporating some of these recommendations. Key ideas are to ensure that derivatives activities are (1) consistent with the bank's overall risk management philosophy and strategy, (2) conducted in a safe and sound manner, (3) overseen by an independent risk-management group with clear authorities (GAO, 1994).

Turning this insight to mean that regulators should draw up requirements for formal management procedures, rules, and organizational structures would miss the point. Such formalities can easily be implemented, but rather than their mere existence what matters is that the spirit of the intended procedures is being followed. This is much harder for regulators to verify (Goodhart, 1996a). Different institutions have different corporate cultures of risk management and different comparative advantages. Turning away from simple balance sheet ratios, therefore, involves a sufficient degree of flexibility of the regulatory arrangement to allow for specialization and competition. Institutions equipped with better risk management techniques should be subject to lower capital requirements. Two proposals have emerged. The first, incorporated in the proposed amendment to the Basle Accord (Hartmann, 1997), requires banks to choose a particular model of market risk management from a set of allowable options approved by the supervisory authority. Using the model and historical or simulated data to evaluate the riskiness of its portfolio regularly, banks can determine the capital requirement needed to achieve a minimum level of return over a given holding period. This eliminates the need to define fixed asset weights as in the standard approach. However, the approach still demands very complex choices regarding the minimum level of return, the relevant holding period, the parameters of stress-testing models and the like. Furthermore, it demands very specialized expertise from the regulators and, where this is absent, the requirement of official approval may hamper the development of new and better risk management models.

The second proposal, developed at the Federal Reserve Board, relies on precommitment to standards on the outcome of bank management decisions rather than regulating management tools (Hartmann, 1997; Goodhart et al., 1997). Under this approach, banks precommit to maximum cumulative trading losses over a certain time horizon and are obliged to hold enough capital to cover those maximum losses. Violation of the maximum loss is then subject to financial penalties. The advantage of this approach is that it leaves the choice of risk management techniques entirely to the financial institutions and, hence, frees the regulators from the burden of verifying compliance with the approved techniques. The proposal also allows institutions to choose from a broader range of models and techniques and, therefore, promotes competition. One difficulty with the approach is that the threat of financial sanctions may not be credible, if the fines are large enough to push an already troubled financial institution over the brink of insolvency; and may not be effective, if the fines are small or their payment can be postponed. A related difficulty is that the proposal might lead to fines imposed on all financial institutions in times of a general market disruption.

4.3. Institutional arrangements

At the national level, division of regulatory responsibilities among industry-specific agencies is obviously inefficient, when the boundaries between these agencies become increasingly blurred. On the one hand, it creates competitive distortions if the same business activity is regulated in different ways under different regulatory competencies. On the other hand, getting a complete picture of the risk exposure of a financial institution requires insight into the potential for spillovers from one functional branch of the institution to another. Subjecting, say, the insurance branch of a financial conglomerate to one regulatory body and the banking branch to another runs the risk that both regulators may miss important information about the true risk of the branch they are responsible for. To avoid such inefficiencies calls for a comprehensive regulatory approach and for equal regulatory treatment of the same activities (Padoa-Schioppa, 1995). The obvious solution would be the creation of a single regulatory body with authority over all financial institutions, and the allocation of supervisory functions at the level of the consolidated conglomerate rather than its branches. The recent proposals for unified regulatory authorities in Britain (Securities and Investment Board, SIB) and Korea (Financial Supervisory Board) reflect those principles (OECD, 1998; SIB, 1997).

There are, however, a number of difficulties with this. In practice, the appropriate domain of a unified financial regulator may be difficult to define in view of the fact that financial and nonfinancial firms are often closely intertwined and that applying strictly the principle of equal regulation for the same activity would call for a consolidation also of the regulators of financial institutions and of financial markets (Padoa-Schioppa, 1995). A unified regulatory super-authority may be regarded as an institution too powerful and, therefore, not subject itself to sufficient accountability. Abuse of regulatory power and internal administrative inefficiency would easily replace the inefficiency of the current, fragmented setup, with little hope for better outcomes. A second problem is that a unified authority may end up using inappropriate regulatory tools to solve specific problems. For example, an authority administering both a lender-of-last resort function and overseeing risk management controls may be drawn into using the former too frequently to save troubled financial institutions, both because it would develop a more friendly view of the management problems facing a bank than a lender-of-last-resort concerned entirely with systemic issues, and because it may want to cover up failures of its own oversight functions.

A related problem with a unified authority is that it suppresses competition among regulatory agencies. Where several agencies work side by side, institutional competition can work and create incentives for each agency to work efficiently. With regard to institutional competition on an international level, Herring and Litan (1995), therefore, argue that given the minimum standards in place, individual countries should be left with sufficient discretion over additional standards for other types of risk not covered by international standards like the Basle Accord. While this would certainly not provide a level playing field, it would facilitate regulatory competition and the discovery of superior mechanisms. Institutional competition also serves as a safeguard against regulatory capture. A unified regulatory authority would be more exposed to regulatory capture.

Thus, there are a good reasons also to refrain from full consolidation of regulatory authorities. One way to strike a balance between consolidation and division of authorities is to define the borders of regulatory domains according to functional responsibilities rather than industry structures (Goodhart, 1996a). As discussed above, financial regulation can be functionally separated into consumer protection and systemic risk prevention; the latter, in turn, can be divided into financial contagion and payments system risk.

4.4. International coordination

In an increasingly interdependent international environment, financial regulation raises new difficulties. International effects of national financial troubles have raised the awareness to coordinate regulatory activities (e.g., GAO, 1994; Group of Thirty, 1997). But given the diversity of national regulatory practices, little if any progress has been made in this direction beyond the Basle Accord. The most efficient solution, in theory, would be to set up a global regulatory authority internalizing all spill-overs between national financial systems. But regulation must, ultimately, be based on national legislation; hence, the coordination of national policies is the best achievable solution.

International coordination of regulatory activities faces two basic problems. The first starts with recognizing that regulation imposes costs on the regulated institution. Differences in regulatory regimes are, therefore, the basis for competitive advantages and disadvantages in international markets. Thus, in a system of open financial markets, governments have an incentive to reduce regulatory burdens on their own industries to strengthen their competitiveness. This makes credible commitments to a common set of rules and standards difficult.

Second, the administration of regulatory tools such as deposit insurance and lender-of-last-resort functions entails potentially large expenditures of tax money to the creditors of financial institutions. In view of this, governments have a bigger incentive to protect domestic depositors against the risk of bank failure than foreign depositors. Since a transfer of tax revenues to foreigners is not politically attractive, governments can be expected to be reluctant to rescue foreign bank depositors and delay payments or refrain from honoring their obligations altogether if the deposit losses are large. The failure of the Italian Banco Ambrosiano, controlled by a Luxembourg holding company, illustrates the point. When the failure of the holding company brought down the Italian bank in 1983, creditors of Banco Ambrosiano were treated more favorably than creditors of the holding company (Herring and Litan, 1995). Furthermore, governments do have an incentive to offer lender-of-last-resort protection to foreign banks operating in their countries, since a run on or the illiquidity of a foreign bank operating in the domestic market may spill over to the domestic banking sector. Goodhart and Schoenmaker's (1993) survey of bank failures supports that point by illustrating governments' interest in rescuing foreign-owned banks operating in their domestic markets. However, governments are unlikely to care much about the ripples that financially troubled, domestic banks may cause in foreign markets, as illustrated by the Herstatt case (von Hagen, 1992). By implication, governments will be reluctant to stand by as providers of lender-of-last-resort functions to domestic banks operating mainly in foreign economies. This, in turn, means that the incentive to enforce domestic regulation on banks operating abroad is weak, since the benefit of the enforcement falls on the foreign government.

These considerations put a narrow limit on the scope for international cooperation; in practice it reduces to a case-by-case approach to joint actions. One implication is that international coordination entails too many costly rescue operations when financial institutions or systems come under stress, and too little preventive action.

Realizing the narrow scope for international coordination, the Group of Thirty (1997) stresses the potential for cooperative arrangements among international financial institutions. In a cobweb of international, interdependent financial relations, each participating institution has an interest in understanding how its partners-competitors manage their business as a condition to better understanding and managing its own risk exposure. The Group of Thirty thus argues that the "core" institutions of the global financial markets should subject their operations to an expanded review by a single, independent, external auditor, or agree on more consistent and meaningful disclosure of financial and risk information, and cooperate with national regulators to improve their monitoring capabilities of financial institutions and their international activities. The relatively large degree of concentration of global business activities on a small number of "core" institutions should facilitate such an industry arrangement. Interestingly, the very process that undermines industry arrangements at the national level would, in this view, promote an industry arrangement at the global level. Private sector financial institutions have already responded to outside pressures to publish additional information on their risk-taking activities. A number of banks voluntarily disclosed more than is legally required. Thus, there is a tendency towards regulatory mechanisms that are relying on self-regulation and reinforcement of market discipline (IMF, 1997). The BIS (1997) reports that disclosure practices improved during 1996, particulary with respect to value-at-risk data. While industry arrangements like this are certainly desirable, one may doubt that they would go much beyond rules for a more standardized disclosure of financial information in practice.

Structured derivative product companies offer another example for market-based regulation and supervision. As discussed above, these specialized OTC derivatives subsidiaries are constructed so as to gain a triple-A credit rating. Rating agencies, therefore, are used to assess counterparty credit-risk in the derivatives markets. The fact that the recent Asian crisis did not signal any credit scoring warning underscores the weaknesses and limitations of such an approach.

In the end, then, coordination among governments in the area of financial regulation will remain quite limited. This is the price paid for a more global and more complete financial system within an environment of national governments and national legislation. The recent financial market crises in Mexico and Asia, however, suggest that stricter enforcement of regulatory rules, already in place at the national level, could have prevented much, if not all, of the damage. In fact, bad government behavior, such as nepotism, deliberate lax supervision of financial institutions to avoid taking unpopular action, and the extension of implicit guarantees to financial institutions as part of ambitious industrial and development policies, seems to be a large factor behind the financial crises in Asia. Peer pressure on governments to enforce existing rules effectively, combined with advice and incentives to do so, may, after all, be more promising than efforts to coordinate the activities of national regulators.

Notes

1. See Bisignano (1998) for an extensive discussion of the causes and possible consequences of institutional change in the financial sector from the viewpoint of an evolutionary theory of innovation and institutional survival.
2. Although their recent growth has attracted attention, derivatives themselves are not new. An early derivative product was a dual-currency bond offered by the Confederate States in 1863, with optional convertibility of the principal into 40,000 pounds of cotton delivered on the Gulf of Mexico (Raisler, 1997). An even earlier example are Japanese rice futures, which have been introduced in 1610 during the first Shogunate (McKenzie, 1993).
3. The first futures traded at the Chicago Board of Trade (CBOT) in 1972 were foreign exchange contracts. The CBOT also introduced the first interest rate future in 1975 (Federal Reserve Bank of Richmond, 1993).
4. See Federal Reserve Bank of Atlanta (1993): The first ever swap contract was a currency swap involving IBM and the World Bank in 1981. The first ever interest-rate swap was entered into by the US Student Loan Marketing Association in 1982.
5. Bisignano (1998, p. 21) points to the interesting fact that techniques similar to margin accounts were introduced by the Dutch financial industry as early as by the mid-17th century.

6. Notional amounts outstanding and gross market values of OTC contracts net of interdealer double-counting (including estimated gaps in reporting).
7. NA = not available; amounts have been halved to approximate for double-counting. See BIS (1996, p. 3).
8. Notional amounts outstanding are an indicator for market size and may also serve as an indicator for the amount of potential exposure to price-risk being exchanged in the derivatives markets. Gross markets values, however, measure the replacement values of the different derivative positions and do therefore indicate credit risk. Because of netting arrangements (e.g., ISDA Master Agreement) credit exposure is probably even lower than replacement values suggest. See BIS (1996, p. 24).
9. See GAO (1996, Appendix VII) and Edwards and Mishkin (1995, pp. 35–37).
10. Reported gross market values as a percentage share of reported notional amounts outstanding. The "share" rises in the length of maturities and is smaller for lower volatilities of the respective underlying.
11. Percentage shares are based on reported turnover net of local and cross-border double-counting without adjustment for estimated gaps in reporting.
12. See Kambhu et al. (1996, pp. 10, 11); Federal Reserve Bank of Richmond (1993, p. 199).
13. The respective shares for private sector corporations are 87% and 64% for interest rate and currency swaps, respectively. 44% consider the use of derivatives very important, 37% imperative (Group of Thirty, 1993).
14. GAO (1996) reviews the use of derivatives by 12 major end-user banks and thrifts. 64% of the notional amounts of derivatives held were interest rate contracts, about 42% of which were used for hedging. Of all instruments used for hedging, 99% were based on interest rates. While all reviewed firms were using derivatives for hedging activities, 75% of them were also using derivatives for the purpose of dealing.
15. Total notional amounts outstanding net of interdealer double-counting.
16. Notional amounts (as of March 1995) net of local interdealer double-counting.
17. See BIS (1992, pp. 48–58); GAO (1996, Appendix VII).
18. Credit derivatives are not necessarily part of the swap market. The above mentioned credit default swap is actually a put option on a portfolio of assets. See Federal Reserve Board (1996) and Neal (1996).
19. Board et al. (1995) refer to the Bank of England and Stock Exchange reports on this issue.
20. The alternative mechanism how sterilized interventions can affect exchange rates is if they are understood by the market as credible signals about future central bank actions (Mussa, 1986). In this context, the emergence of a more complete financial market system has no clear implications for their effectiveness.
21. This could be avoided if the central bank closes its derivatives position by an appropriate operation in the spot market. This however, makes the operation equivalent to a sterilized intervention (e.g., BIS, 1994).
22. Bernanke and Gertler (1995) estimate that federal funds rate shocks in the US generally peter out after six to nine months.
23. Proponents of the credit market view have so far been more interested in empirical research than in developing a model of general macroeconomic equilibrium incorporating their arguments. Although the underlying model is usually claimed to be of a three-asset type (money, bonds, and bank credit), the interaction of these markets is not analyzed. This is in contrast to the earlier literature led by Brunner and Meltzer, where the bank loan market was at the heart of the analysis.
24. As Fama (1980) points out, deposits might alternatively have a fixed price in terms of the unit of account and a variable interest rate.
25. The importance of the government's power to tax as a basis for the demand for government-issued money is discussed extensively in Goodhart (1997).
26. See Rogoff (1998) for a theory of the demand for cash based on informal exchanges.
27. It is worth noting in this context that the introduction of European Monetary Union as currently planned introduces a separation of the unit of account and the (dominant) medium of

transaction. Specifically, the Euro will be the sole medium of transaction in wholesale financial transactions immediately upon the start of EMU, while the national currency units will remain units of account in retail business for the first few years.
28. See Cowen and Kroszner (1994). Woodford (1997) shows that the central bank can control inflation even if the demand for central bank money tends to zero in the limit.
29. Congressional Record 18 June 1993, H 3322.
30. Even the Barings crisis, after all, did not result in problems regarded as systemic.
31. We ignore some secondary reasons related to the smoothness of the money supply process and credit allocation schemes driven by social policy goals.
32. See Goodhart and Schoenmaker (1993) and Hartmann (1994) for a review of these issues.
33. See Dewatripont and Tirole (1994), and Hartmann (1994, 1997) for reviews of this debate.

References

American Institute of Public Accountants AICPA (1994) "Derivatives—Current Accounting and Auditing Literature." New York: AICPA.

Angelini, Paolo and Franco Passacantando (1992) "Central Banks' Role in the Payment System and its Relationship with Banking Supervision." *Giornale degli Economisti e Annali di Economia* 51, Oct./Dec., 453–491.

Bank for International Settlements (1992) "Recent Developments in International Interbank Relations (Promisel Report)." Basle.

Bank for International Settlements (1994a) "Macroeconomic and Monetary Policy Issues Raised by the Growth of Derivatives Markets (Hannoun Report)." Basle.

Bank for International Settlements (1994b) "A Discussion Paper on Public Disclosure of Market and Credit Risks by Financial Intermediaries (Fisher Report)." Basle.

Bank for International Settlements (1996) "Central Bank Survey of Foreign Exchange and Derivatives Market Activity." Basle.

Bank for International Settlements (1997) "Survey of Disclosures About Trading and Derivatives Activities of Banks and Securities Firms." Basle.

Bank for International Settlements (1998) "International Banking and Financial Market Developments." Basle.

Barnett, W.A. (1978) "The User Cost of Money." *Economics Letters* 1, 145–149.

Barnett, W.A. (1980) "Economic Monetary Aggregates: An Application of Index Number and Aggregation Theory." *Journal of Econometrics* 14, 11–48.

Benston, G. and G.C. Kaufman (1996) "The Appropriate Role of Bank Regulation." *The Economic Journal* 106, 688–697.

Bernanke, B.S. (1993) "How Important is the Credit Channel in the Transmission of Monetary Policy?: A Comment." *Carnegie-Rochester Series on Public Policy*, Fall, 47–52.

Bernanke, B.S. and M. Gertler (1995) "Inside the Black Box: The Credit Channel of Monetary Policy Transmission." *Journal of Economic Perspectives* 9, 27–48.

Bisignano, J. (1998) "Towards an Understanding of the Changing Structure of Financial Intermediation: An Evolutionary Theory of Institutional Survival." SUERF Working Paper, Amsterdam.

Black, F. (1987) "Banking and Interest Rates in a World Without Money: The Effects of Uncontrolled Banking." In F. Black (ed.), *Business Cycles and Equilibrium*. New York: Basil Blackwell, pp. 1–20.

Black, F. and M. Scholes (1973) "The Pricing of Options and Corporate Liabilities." *Journal of Political Economy* 81, 637–654.

Board, J. et al. (1995) "Derivatives Regulation." Financial Markets Group, Special Paper No. 70, London School of Economics.

Bothwell, J.L. (1994) "Response to the International Swaps and Derivatives Association Position Paper." US GAO/T-GGD-94-163, Washington, DC.

Brainard, W.C. and J. Tobin (1968) "Pitfalls in Financial Model Building." *American Economic Review*, Papers and Proceedings, 58, 99–122.

Brewer, Elijah III., B.A. Minton, and J.T. Moser (1994) "The Effect of Bank-Held Derivatives on Credit Accessibility." Federal Reserve Bank of Chicago Working Paper WP-94-5, Chicago.

Brunner, Karl and A.H. Meltzer (1976) "An Aggregative Theory for a Closed Economy." In J.L. Stein (ed.), *Monetarism*. Amsterdam: North Holland.

Campbell, T.S. and W.A. Kracaw (1991) "Intermediation and the Market for Interest Rate Swaps." *Journal of Financial Intermediation* 1, 362–384.

Canzoneri, M.B. and D.W. Henderson (1991) *Monetary Policy in Interdependent Economies*. Cambridge: MIT Press.

Chan, Y.S., S.I. Greenbaum, and A.V. Thakor (1992) "Is Fairly Priced Deposit Insurance Possible?" *Journal of Finance* 47(1), 227–245.

Cohen, B.H. (1996) "Derivatives and Asset Price Volatility: A Test Using Variance Ratios." BIS Working Paper No. 33, Basle: BIS.

Cottarelli, C. and A. Kourelis (1994) "Financial Structure, Bank Lending Rates, and the Transmission Mechanism of Monetary Policy." *IMF Staff Papers* 41(4), 587–623.

Cowen, T. and R. Kroszner (1987) "The Development of the New Monetary Economics." *Journal of Political Economy* 95, 567–590.

Cowen, T. and R. Kroszner (1994) *Explorations in the New Monetary Economics*. Oxford.

Darby, M. (1994) "OTC Derivatives and Systemic Risk to the Global Financial System." NBER Working Paper 4801, Cambridge: NBER.

Deutsche Bundesbank (1994) "Geldpolitische Implikationen der Zunehmenden Verwendung Derivativer Finanzinstrumente." *Monatsbericht*, Nov., 41–57.

Dewatripont, M. and J. Tirole (1994) *The Prudential Regulation of Banks*. Cambridge: MIT Press.

Diamond, D.W. and P.H. Dybvig (1983) "Bank Runs, Deposit Insurance, and Liquidity." *Journal of Political Economy* 91, 401–419.

Edwards, F.R. and F.S. Mishkin (1995) "The Decline of Traditional Banking: Implications for Stability and Regulatory Policy." *Federal Reserve Bank of New York Economic Review*, July, 27–45.

Eichengreen, B. et al. (1998) "Hedge Funds and Financial Market Dynamics." IMF Occasional Paper No. 166, International Monetary Fund, Washington, DC.

Emmons, W.R. (1997) "Recent Developments in Wholesale Payments Systems." *Federal Reserve Bank of St. Louis Review*, Nov./Dec., 23–43.

Estrella, Arturo (1995) "A Prolegomenon to Future Capital Requirements." *Federal Reserve Bank of New York Economic Review*, July, 1–12.

Fama, E.F. (1980) "Banking in the Theory of Finance." *Journal of Monetary Economics* 6, 39–58.

Fama, E.F. (1983) "Financial Intermediation and Price Level Control." *Journal of Monetary Economics* 12, 7–28.

Federal Reserve Bank of Atlanta (1993) "Financial Derivatives: New Instruments and Their Uses." Atlanta.

Federal Reserve Bank of Richmond (1993) *Instruments of the Money Market*. 7th ed. Richmond.

Federal Reserve Board (1996) "Supervisory Guidance for Credit Derivatives." Supervision and Regulation Letter SR 96-17, Washington, DC.

Friedman, M. (1968) "The Role of Monetary Policy." *American Economic Review* 58, 1–17.

Froot, K.A., D.S. Scharfstein, and J.C. Stein (1993) "Risk Management: Coordinating Corporate Investment and Financing Policies." *Journal of Finance* 48, 1629–1658.

General Accounting Office (1994) "Financial Derivatives: Actions Needed to Protect the Financial System." Washington, DC.

General Accounting Office (1996) "Financial Derivatives: Actions Taken or Proposed Since May 1994." Washington, DC.

Gonzalez-Hermosillo, B. (1994) "The Microstructure of Financial Derivatives Markets: Exchange-Traded versus OTC." Technical Report No. 68, Bank of Canada, Ottawa.

Goodhart, C.A.E. (1995) "Price Stability and Financial Fragility." In K. Sawamoto, Z. Nakajima, and H. Taguchi (eds.), *Financial Stability in a Changing Environment*. Bank of Japan, pp. 439–497.

Goodhart, C.A.E. (1996a) "Some Regulatory Concerns." *Swiss Journal of Economics and Statistics* 132, 613–636.

Goodhart, C.A.E. (1996b) "An Incentive Structure for Financial Regulation." *Swiss Journal of Economics and Statistics* 132, 637–648.

Goodhart, C.A.E. (1997) "The Two Concepts of Money and the Future of Europe." Paper presented at the 1997 Konstanz Seminar on Monetary Theory and Policy, Konstanz.

Goodhart, C.A.E. et al. (1997) "Financial Regulation: Why, How, and Where Now?" London.

Goodhart, C.A.E. and D. Schoenmaker (1993) "Institutional Separation between Supervisory and Monetary Agencies." Special Paper No. 52, LSE Financial Markets Group.

Greenfield, R.L. and L.B. Yeager (1983) "A Laissez-faire Approach to Monetary Stability." *Journal of Money, Credit, and Banking* 15, 302–315.

Greenfield, R.L. and L.B. Yeager (1986) "Competitive Payments Systems—Comment." *American Economic Review* 76, 848–849.

Greenspan, A. (1994a) "Statement to Congress." *Federal Reserve Bulletin*, July, 594–605.

Greenspan, A. (1994b) "Testimony before the Committee on Banking, Housing, and Urban Affairs." Washington, DC: US Senate.

Group of Thirty (1993) "Derivatives: Practices & Principles." *Global Derivatives Study Group*, Washington, DC.

Group of Thirty (1997) "Global Institutions, National Supervision, and Systemic Risk." Washington, DC.

Hall, R.E. (1983) "Optimal Fiduciary Monetary Systems." *Journal of Monetary Economics* 12, 33–50.

Hartmann, P. (1994) "Foreign Exchange Risk Regulation: Issues for Industrial and Development Countries." IMF Working Paper 94/141, Washington, DC: IMF.

Hartmann, P. (1997) "Capital Adequacy and Foreign Exchange Risk Regulation." *Kredit und Kapital* 30, 186–218.

Hausler, G. (1996) *Derivatives and Monetary Policy*. Washington, DC: Group of Thirty.

Heinecke, K. and P. Shen (1995) "Bank Derivative Activity in the 1990s." Federal Reserve Bank of Kansas City Research Working Paper 95-12, Kansas City.

Hentschel, L. and C.W. Smith, Jr. (1997) "Derivatives Regulation: Implications for Central Banks." *Journal of Monetary Economics* 40, 305–346.

Herring, R.J. and R.E. Litan (1995) "Financial Regulation in the Global Economy." Washington, DC: Brookings Institution.

International Monetary Fund (1997, 1996a) "International Capital Markets: Developments, Prospects, and Key Policy Issues." Washington, DC: IMF.

International Monetary Fund (1996b) "IMF—World Economic Outlook: May 1996." Washington, DC: IMF.

International Swap and Derivatives Association (1997) "Summary of Recent Survey Results: 1997 First Half and 1996 Year-End ISDA Market Survey." New York: ISDA, Mimeo.

Issing, O. and K. Bischofberger (1996) "Derivate und Geldpolitik." In D. Duwendag (ed.), *Finanzmärkte, Finanzinnovationen und Geldpolitik*. pp. 111–137.

Kambhu, J., F. Keane, and C. Benadon (1996) "Price Risk Intermediation in the Over-the-Counter Derivatives Markets." Federal Reserve Bank of New York *Economic Review* 4, 1–15.

Kiyotaki, N. and J. Moore (1997) "Credit Cycles." *Journal of Political Economy* 105(2), 211–248.

Krüger, M. (1997) "The Moneyless Economy—Not as Brave as it may Seem." University of Cologne, Mimeo.

Kuprianov, A. (1993) "Over-the-Counter Interest Rate Derivatives." Federal Reserve Bank of Richmond *Economic Quarterly* 79(3), 65–94.

McKenzie, S. (1993) "Futures and Options." In S. McKenzie (ed.), *Risk Management with Derivatives*. Basingstoke, pp. 17–44.

Meltzer, A.H. (1995) "Monetary, Credit (and Other) Transmission Processes: A Monetarist Perspective." *Journal of Economic Perspectives* 9, 49–72.

Mishkin, F.S. (1995) "Symposium on the Monetary Transmission Mechanism." *Journal of Economic Perspectives* 9, 3–10.

Mishkin, F.S. and A.S. Posen (1997) "Inflation Targeting: Lessons from Four Countries." Federal Reserve Bank of New York *Economic Review* 3, 9–110.

Mullineux, A. (1996) "Financial Innovation, Banking, and Monetary Aggregates." Cheltenham.

Mussa, Michael (1986) "Nominal Exchange Rate Regimes and the Behavior of Real Exchange Rates: Evidence and Implications." *Carnegie Rochester Conference Series on Public Policy*, 25, Autumn, 117–213.

Neal, R.S. (1996) "Credit Derivatives: New Financial Instruments for Controlling Credit Risk." Federal Reserve Bank of Kansas City *Economic Review*, 1996(2), 16–27.

OECD (1998) "Financial Market Trends." No. 69, Feb. 1998, Paris.

Padoa-Schioppa, T. (1995) "Cooperation between Banks and Market Regulators." Paris: International Organisation of Securities Commissions, Mimeo.

Poole, W. (1970) "Optimal Choice of Monetary Policy Instruments in a Simple Stochastic Macro Model." *Quarterly Journal of Economics* 84(2), 197–216.

Quinn, B. (1994) "Derivatives—A Central Banker's View." *Bank of England Quarterly Review*, Aug., 277–280.

Raisler, K. (1997) "The Risks of Financial Derivatives." In R.C. Effros (ed.), *Current Legal Issues Affecting Central Banks*. Washington, DC: IMF, pp. 474–481.

Remolona, E.M., W. Bassett, and I.S. Geoum (1996) "Risk Management by Structured Derivative Product Companies." *Federal Reserve Bank of New York Economic Review*, April, 17–37.

Rogoff, K. (1998) "Foreign and Underground Demand for Euro Notes: Blessing or a Curse?" *Economic Policy* 26, 261–304.

Salvatore, D. (1998) "Present International Monetary and Financial Arrangements." in this volume.

Santomero, A.M. and J.J. Trester (1998) "Financial Innovation and Risk Taking." *Journal of Economic Behavior and Organization* 35, 25–37.

Savona, P. and A. Maccario (1998) "On the Relation between Money and Derivatives and its Application to the International Monetary Market." in this volume.

Securities and Investment Board (1997) "Reform of the Financial Regulatory System." London.

Smith, C.W. and R.M. Stulz (1985) "The Determinants of Firms' Hedging Policies." *Journal of Financial and Quantitative Analysis* 20(4), 391–405.

Söderlind, P. and L.E.O. Svensson (1997) "New Techniques to Extract Market Expectations from Financial Instruments." *Journal of Monetary Economics* 40, 383–429.

Svensson, L.E.O. (1996) "Inflation Forecast Targeting: Implementation and Monitoring of Inflation Targets." NBER Working Paper No. 5797.

Thorbecke, W. (1995) "Financial Derivatives: Harnessing the Benefits, Containing the Dangers." Jerome Levy Economics Institute, Working Paper 145.

Titman, S. (1992) "Interest Rate Swaps and Corporate Finance Choices." *Journal of Finance* 47, 261–270.

Tobin, J. (1963) "Commercial Banks as Creators of 'Money'." In D. Carson (ed.), *Banking and Monetary Studies*. Homewood: Richard D. Irwin.

von Hagen, J. (1992) "Herstatt Crisis." In J. Eatwell et al. (eds.), *The New Palgrave Dictionary of Money and Finance*. London: Macmillan.

von Hagen, J. (1995) "Monetary and Inflation Targeting in Germany." In L. Leiderman and L.E.O. Svensson (eds.), *Inflation Targeting*. London: CEPR.

von Hagen, J. (1996) "Credible Roads to EMU." In Marc Uzan (ed.), *The Financial System under Stress: An Architecture for the New World Economy*. London: Routledge.

von Hagen, J. (1997) "Monetary Policy and Institutions in the EMU." *Swedish Economic Policy Review* 4, 51–116.

Vrolijk, C. (1997) "Derivatives Effect on Monetary Policy Transmission." IMF Working Paper WP/97/121, International Monetary Fund, Washington, DC.

Wallace, N. (1983) "A Legal Restrictions Theory of the Demand for 'Money' and the Role of Monetary Policy." *Federal Reserve Bank of Minneapolis Quarterly Review*, Winter, 1–7.

Woodford, M. (1997) "Doing Without Money: Controlling Inflation in a Post-Monetary World." Seminar Paper 632, Institute for International Economic Studies, Stockholm University.

Open economies review 9:S1 533–536 (1998)

Comments on the Papers by Salvatore, Hamada, Capie, Fratianni et al., and Von Hagen and Fender

PAUL DE GRAUWE Paul.deGrauwe@econ.Kuleuven.ac.be
Catholic University of Louvain, Naamsestraat 69, 3000 Leuven, Belgium

It is not easy to find a common theme in five papers that present a rich analysis of the international monetary system. Let me try though, by presenting a story of the main changes and challenges that we are likely to face in the future international monetary system. I will then use that story to make links with the five papers, thereby also demonstrating that I read the papers.

A first fundamental change of the last two decades is the trend towards liberalisation of the financial markets, which started in the US and which spread to more and more countries of the world. This led to unprecedented technological innovations, which in turn helped to boost further liberalisation. These technological changes have made possible a financial revolution, the implications of which are not yet fully understood. They have also created new issues, two of which I want to discuss here.

Does the creation of new financial instruments make monetary policy increasingly irrelevant in affecting real economic conditions? von Hagen and Fender, but also Salvatore, seem to answer this question in a positive way, thereby reflecting a consensus view among economists today. But if that is true, the next issue is whether the move to a cash-less society may not make monetary policy irrelevant. von Hagen defends the view of the "new monetary economics," according to which the means of payments will be totally demand driven. As a result, we may not need a central bank anymore to anchor the price level.

I have doubts. It seems to me that the financial system will often be disrupted by volatility, produced by the fact that the self fulfilling nature of expectations leads to multiple equilibria. In such a world, relatively small disturbances can push the financial markets to a new equilibrium. If that is the underlying model that drives the financial markets, there may be a lot of volatility in the supply of means of payments, and therefore in economic activity. I conclude that in a cash-less society we may still need an anchor that can only be provided by a central bank.

The financial revolution that we are witnessing leads to another important issue, efficiency and stability. The Chicago view is that the creation of new financial instruments helps to complete markets in the Arrow-Debreu sense. For those who do not understand this economist's jargon: the financial revolution allows us to better hedge our risks, and to make us better off. There is another view, however. This is that these new financial instruments may generate new uncertainties. As a result, risk may not decline at all. It may even increase. Thus, risk is not something exogenous that financial instruments help to manage better. It may also be endogenously increased by the proliferation of new financial instruments. Today we still grasp with these issues.

A second major change in the international monetary system is a direct consequence of the technologically induced financial revolution. This is the internationalisation of financial markets. As amply demonstrated by Salvatore in his paper, capital movements have now taken unprecedented proportions. What are its implications? The major one is that fixed exchange rate regimes have become increasingly unsustainable, and are quickly becoming endangered species. As a result, countries now face either the option of accepting a high degree of flexibility of the exchange rate or to move into a much tighter monetary regime, i.e., a monetary union. Anything in between will not be robust, and will face crisis.

There are some economists who believe that we can return to the old system by re-introducing capital controls. The Tobin tax is such a capital control that has been advocated by a number of economists. I share Salvatore's view that such measures cannot fundamentally change the dynamics of financial market integration. As argued earlier, the latter is driven by technological changes. A Tobin tax would do very little to turn around these dynamics. There are now so many new financial instruments available for speculators that do not involve cash transactions, but that achieve the same result. One would have to turn back these new financial technologies to make these traditional instruments of capital control effective.

In addition, financial market integration is intimately linked to trade integration. Countries that want to stay competitive in the goods markets will have to allow their domestic firms to fully use the services provided by international financial markets. Financial protectionism will quickly put domestic firms at a competitive disadvantage very much like trade protectionism does.

From the previous section it follows that the move to monetary union in Europe is the inevitable consequence of the fact that fixing the exchange rates in the EU is not a viable option anymore. To use Hamada's framework of analysis, this has changed the cost-benefit calculus of EU-countries in a fundamental way. As long as countries had the choice between fixing the exchange rate (which made occasional realignments possible) or entering into a monetary union, they preferred the former. Fixing the exchange rate combined stability with some flexibility and was therefore perceived to be more attractive than a monetary union that promised no flexibility at all. Now that the fixed exchange rate option in not available anymore the choice is reduced between floating exchange rates and monetary union. Under those conditions, many EU-countries have selected monetary union.

If the previous analysis is correct, it is simply not true that EMU is a purely political project, as Capie seems to imply in his paper. There is an underlying change in the economic cost-benefit structure of monetary union that, in addition to the political motives, has driven EU-countries to start EMU.

The decision of EU-countries to start EMU now forces us to think about other issues than the issue of whether these countries belong to an optimum currency area. We now have to think about the optimal institutional design of the monetary union. This can also be formulated by a question. Is there a political institutional set-up that will sustain EMU so that it can function efficiently? Capie's historical examination tries to answer this question. It teaches us that political union is a necessary condition (not a sufficient one, remember the Soviet Union) for the long-term survival of monetary unions. From this historical analysis one could conclude, with Capie, that because EMU is not backed by a political union, it is bound to collapse in due time as its predecessors did. But this, in my opinion, is a very superficial reading of history. When one compares EMU with the Latin Monetary Union or with the Scandinavian Monetary Union, it is striking to find how different EMU is in comparison with these past monetary unions. To begin with, both the Latin and the Scandinavian Monetary Unions lacked one central bank. Surely, this was a fatal shortcoming, which is not shared by EMU. Second, backing EMU there is a whole infrastructure of political and economic unification, a feature that was totally absent from the previous monetary unions.

Thus, the argument that EMU will fail because it lacks a political union is wrong. There is already a significant political union in the EU. The only serious issue is whether the political union reached today is sufficient to sustain EMU. And here one could argue that more has to be done to achieve a sufficient level of political integration. Two examples will illustrate this contention.

The future monetary union will be confronted regularly with asymmetric shocks. As a result, the representatives of the different nations in the Board of the ECB will have conflicting desires about the monetary policies for the union as a whole. In the absence of flexible national instruments of economic policies, these conflicts could become so intense that the ECB will be paralysed or be forced to pursue erratic policies as shifting coalitions lead to frequent reversals in monetary policies. This would not only prevent the euro from becoming an international currency at par with the US dollar, as it is stressed by Fratianni et al., but would also endanger the survival of EMU itself. It is, therefore, imperative that a EU-body responsible for the other aspects of economic policies (e.g., budgetary policies) takes over some of the pressure that otherwise would be exerted exclusively on the ECB.

A second example has to do with prudential control. As is well known, the responsibility for bank supervision in EMU remains in the hands of the nation-states, despite the fact that monetary policies are fully centralised at the European level. In addition, the principle of home country control applies. This institutional set-up is not optimally designed to deal with the risks that inevitably will arise, especially when asymmetric shocks occur. Suppose, for example, that a French bank (perhaps Crédit Lyonnais) expands its lending activities in

Spain and Portugal through its local branches to profit from the high rates of returns generated by the booming conditions in these countries. The French authorities are responsible for detecting and discouraging the French bank from taking on excessive risk. In principle, the French authorities can do the job since they will control the consolidated balance sheet of the French bank. In practice, however, the monitoring will be made difficult because the information the French supervisory authorities will want to use to evaluate the risk exposure of the French bank will have to be provided by the host countries. It is unclear whether this transfer of information will be timely and efficient.

There are no existing monetary unions where the monetary policies are centralised while the supervision is decentralised at the regional level. What we do find is that supervision is functionally decentralised, but is invested in federal institutions. This is the model to which Euroland will have to evolve to, which implies a further transfer of sovereignty to European institutions. If it does not do so quickly enough, financial crises may force such a transfer.

The move to EMU can be compared to the move to a house that does not yet have a roof. Two scenarios can occur in such a situation. In an optimistic scenario, the new inhabitants of the house decide to hasten the construction of the roof (political union) so as to live more conformably. In a pessimistic scenario, they get fed up with the discomfort of having to live in a roofless house and decide to disband and to live elsewhere. One can only hope that the optimistic scenario will force itself on the members of EMU.

Open economies review 9:S1 537–567 (1998)

Trade and the Number of OCAs in the World

MICHAEL ARTIS ARTIS@datacomm.iue.it
European University Institute, Florence and CEPR, via dei Roccettini, 9 Badia Fiesolana
50016 San Dominico di Fiesole (FI), Italy

MARION KOHLER
European University Institute, Florence

JACQUES MÉLITZ MELITZ@ensae.fr
CREST-INSEE, Paris, Institut des Etudes Politiques, Ecole Supérieure de Commerce de Paris, and CEPR. Bâtiment Malakoff 2-Timbre j 31, 15 Boulevard gabriel Péri, 92245 malakoff Cedex

Key words: optimal currency areas, trade, business cycles

JEL Classification Numbers: F02, F15, F40

Abstract

This paper employs worldwide data on output and bilateral trade in order to identify optimum currency areas (OCAs) on a global basis. By retaining only two of the many criteria in the literature on OCAs, computer programming could serve to do the identification. The two chosen criteria relate to trade and the symmetry of shocks to output. Based on the first criterion, trade, some large continental OCAs emerge. Adding the second, symmetry, whittles down the size of these OCAs considerably. Nevertheless, some significant examples remain in the Americas, Europe and Asia, of which the European and the Asiatic are the most noteworthy.

Introduction

How many 'optimal currency areas' (OCAs) are there in the world? In this study, we make an attempt to use worldwide trade and output data to answer this question. As a start, we shall discuss the general question itself. Our approach will be to limit ourselves to two of the many criteria that have been proposed in the literature on optimum currency areas in order to identify the ideal participants in a monetary union. The first one relates to bilateral trade between countries; the second to the symmetry in the shocks affecting output in different countries. These two criteria have been translated into five rules, which were then programmed to identify OCAs.

Up to 117 countries or territories come under our searchlight. These entities comprise most of the world outside of Africa, for which the only bilateral trade data we have concern Egypt and Lybia. There are other gaps: Iraq, Afghanistan, and Cambodia, for example. With respect to the former USSR, we shall rely strictly on the data since the collapse of the Soviet Union. In general, we began the analysis in 1965, but shall concentrate on the 1990s.

1. The question

The question of the number of OCAs in the world may seem a bit exotic. The number of currencies in the entire globe today is only moderately inferior to the number of countries. The reason is not that some countries maintain pegged exchange rates, even in the extreme case of currency boards (Argentina or ex-colonial-French Central and Western Africa), since in these instances, there are still separate currencies in most meanings of the term: conversion costs, margins, and possible changes of par value. The genuine reason lies in small states and principalities such as Luxembourg and Liechtenstein. These political entities truly do not maintain a separate currency in any sense: no exchange rate, nothing to peg. Interestingly enough, even when a number of new states were created recently, upon the break-up of the Soviet Union and former Czechoslovakia, almost as many new currencies emerged as did new countries (the exception being Belarus, which is likely to be reintegrated into a greater Russia).

In the same connection, it is often said that unless a currency area coincides with a nation state, serious problems arise (see Goodhart, 1997). From this perspective, the whole issue of the number of OCAs in the world may seem to be something out of Alice in Wonderland.

Yet there are important reasons for an opposite view. Contrary to the principle of one-country-one-money, the examples of Luxembourg and Liechtenstein (of which there are other instances, such as Puerto Rico, Monaco, and a number of other territories of quasi-independent political status), however innocuous they may seem, are actually very significant. These examples mean that we can go too far in equating the optimal number of currencies with the number of countries. As many currencies as square miles, or multiples of one thousand inhabitants, would obviously be too many. But if the disadvantages of not having a separate money were necessarily overwhelming, why would this be so? Why would minor political entities not be overwhelmed by the net disadvantages of lacking a separate money, like all the rest? And if there is some small enough country size below which the costs of a separate money exceed the benefits, how do we know that we do not already have too many currencies in the world today? Given the present state of information about the dimensions of an OCA, the minimal size would seem just as foggy as the maximal one. The prediction that the movement toward a single currency in the European Union must fail without further political integration cannot simply be accepted as fact.

In addition, Eichengreen (1994) offers an important perspective on the current evolution of money in the world which may serve to underline the relevance of the question of the total number and composition of OCAs today. As he points out, greater capital mobility makes pegged exchange rates increasingly difficult to maintain. Apart from capital controls, monetary union may, therefore, become the only viable alternative to flexible exchange rates in the future. Since pressures for freedom of capital movement already exist widely around the globe, and many countries clearly wish to avoid flexible exchange rates (because of problems of exchange rate uncertainty and misalignment), projects for monetary union could arise in parts of the world other than the European Union, all the more so if EMU proves to be a success. Thus, a proper understanding of the composition and the number of OCAs worldwide could help to foresee and even, possibly, shape the future.

2. The two criteria

The main driving force behind the potential welfare-improvement of enlarging a currency area is obviously trade. All the essential benefits of one money—fewer units of account and lower transaction costs—depend on trade. Moreover, several attempts to provide formal treatments of OCAs consider the costs of enlarging a monetary union as rising monotonically with the diminution of external trade in relation to output. Lower ratios of trade to output, or lower openness, raise the value of independent monetary policy for stabilization purposes, and therefore as a monetary union widens, losing independent monetary policy becomes costlier. It follows that trade is not only the motor for the gains of monetary union, but also captures many of the costs of monetary union too (see Krugman, 1990; Mélitz, 1995, 1996).

However, the literature on OCAs, since Mundell (1961), calls attention to a number of other criteria for an OCA besides trade. Two of the most frequently mentioned of these criteria for OCAs are labor mobility and fiscal federalism. International labor mobility is mainly low, even among close trading partners, and fiscal federalism generally does not exist at all on a supra-national level, or does so only minimally, as in the EU. However, labor mobility and fiscal federalism have been used essentially to explain why countries benefit from a single money no matter how large they are, not how much further enlargement would be to their advantage. Since we shall not question here that existing currency areas are not already too large (except possibly in the case of the emerging 11-member EMU), only that they may be too small, putting the two previous criteria to the side might do limited harm.[1]

There are other omissions, however. Trade also fails to cover reputation or anti-inflationary credibility as a criterion of an OCA. Nor does it embrace issues of the political control and political constitution of the common central bank. Yet the sweep of the trade criterion alone may be wider than meets the eye. In particular, trade could well proxy for the criterion that has dominated empirical work on OCAs: namely, the symmetric or asymmetric nature of shocks. A recent study by Frankel and Rose (1997a) discloses a positive correlation between bilateral trade intensity and symmetry in output fluctuations. Similarly, Artis and Zhang (1997a, 1997b) indicate a positive correlation between exchange rate

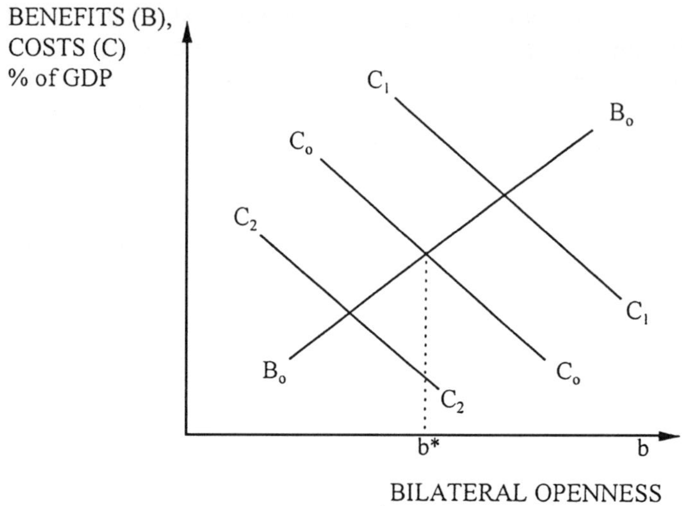

Figure 1. **Benefits and costs as a function of bilateral openness.**

stability and business cycle symmetry. Taken together, these studies seem to suggest that a currency union, formed on the basis of trade alone, would not contain many members who would fail to meet the symmetry-of-shocks criterion. In any case, the number of incorrect candidates would likely decline over time. If so, the symmetry-of-shocks criterion can be regarded as 'endogenous', to use Frankel and Rose's term.[2]

Figure 1, based on Krugman (1990), illustrates the matter. The benefits of joining a currency union with other countries are shown (by the curve B_0B_0) as an increasing function of bilateral trade in relation to output, or 'bilateral openness'. The costs of entering such a union are shown (by the curve C_0C_0) as a decreasing function of bilateral openness, since the value of the exchange rate (independent monetary policy) as a stabilization instrument decreases with the degree of integration. The intersection of C_0C_0 and B_0B_0 for the 'representative' country determines a threshold value for openness above which ($b > b^*$) the benefits of membership exceed the costs. However, the position of the C_0C_0-curve depends on the importance of the asymmetric shocks calling for a stabilization effort. A higher degree of asymmetry, represented by the higher curve C_1C_1, would then lead to a higher critical value of b^*. If participation in a monetary union in itself reduces the frequency and size of asymmetric shocks, then the C-curve itself would drift downwards following entry into a union. The same factor could cause an upward drift in the B-curve under monetary union, on the assumption that the union may also tend to boost trade integration.

If monetary union would cause a trend diminution in the C-curve, it might be possible to rely strictly on the trade criterion in our investigation. However, the evidence supporting such a downward tendency is still somewhat scanty and the topic deserves further serious investigation. For this reason, we have chosen to test whether currency unions established on a trade criterion will survive the additional test of a symmetry-of-shocks criterion as well.

What about Kenen's (1969) diversification criterion, which is often mentioned in the literature on OCAs, though it has had little empirical success thus far? Indeed, one of the few empirical regularities about the choice of exchange rate systems seems to be that highly specialized countries favor fixed rates, contrary to Kenen's criterion (see Honkapohja and Pikkarainen, 1992). However, the diversification criterion can be interpreted partly as a restatement of the symmetry one, since well-diversified countries may be viewed as less likely to require exchange rate adjustment because sets of such countries will tend to be hit by symmetric shocks. Kenen seemed to have precisely that point in mind in his original essay. So far as this interpretation holds, then, the present study accounts for the diversification criterion as well.

3. The data

Our basic data relate to bilateral trade and output. All of our information about bilateral trade comes from the IMF's *Direction of Trade Statistics*. Unfortunately, these data cover only goods, whereas services are just as relevant. Rather than base the study strictly on goods, we decided to employ the existing information about aggregate trade in goods and services, and to simply decompose the trade aggregates on the basis of the bilateral flow of goods. Doing so naturally assumes that the geographical composition of trade in services is identical to the one in goods. Still, the method has the advantage of taking into consideration the true extent of openness rather than basing this essential aspect on goods alone.

Quite specifically, we collected data for aggregate exports and aggregate imports of goods and services and for Gross Domestic Product (GDP) by individual country. Data on aggregate exports and imports were drawn from the IMF's *International Financial Statistics*, while GDP data came partly from this source, and, in some cases, also from the United Nations' *National Income and Expenditure Accounts*. From these data, we then constructed openness ratios $O_i, i = 1, \ldots, n$, for all of the n countries in the study as the sum of exports and imports divided by twice GDP. Given the matrix of bilateral trade in goods found in the IMF data, we then calculated flow values for exports plus imports of goods only for all countries i in trade with countries $j, i \neq j (j = 1, \ldots, n-1)$. Suppose we designate these next values as t_{ij} and the sum of t_{ij} values for any country i over its $n-1$ possible trade partners as T_i. The ratio t_{ij}/T_i is a measure of trade intensity (as employed for example in Tichy (1992) and Frankel and Rose (1996)). In this study, we use the output-weighted correlate of this measure, $T_{ij} = t_{ij}/T_i$ times O_i, as our basic metric of bilateral trade. The ratio T_{ij} evidently states the trade of country i with country j as a percentage of country i's GDP, and the sum of the T_{ij} values for country i with all possible trade partners equals O_i.

In constructing the t_{ij} terms and the ratios O_i on which our T_{ij} values rest, we compiled the raw data into five-year averages starting in 1965–69 and through 1990–95 (involving a six-year average at the very end). The sample of countries in this exercise grew from 69 in 1965–69 to 117 in 1990–95. In the case of missing annual observations during the five- (or six-) year intervals, we averaged over fewer years, but as a rule required at least two. (Some new countries of the former USSR are represented by only one observation in the data set.) As already mentioned, however, the evolution from 1965 to 1990 yielded nothing of broad enough interest for our purposes. Though this aspect has therefore informed our analysis, the statistical material we present covers essentially the period 1990–95. Trade composition evolves progressively in the absence of dramatic political shifts (such as the break-up of the Soviet Union), and our information for the most recent period is much greater than for the rest.

4. Measures of symmetry

To construct measures of symmetry in output fluctuations, we focused on cross-correlations of the cyclical components (residuals) of the series for annual real GDP. Those components were obtained by fitting a log-linear trend to the data for the period 1980–1996 and then detrending. Alternatively, we applied Hodrick-Prescott filters with dampening parameters of either 100 or 400. As a further precaution, we inspected the results of detrending and using Hodrick-Prescott filters for the entire available period, which often exceeded the 1980–1996 time stretch and sometimes started as early as 1965. The required GDP data series were available for only 90 countries (data from IMF: *International Financial Statistics*), the most notable exclusions coming from Central and Eastern Europe.

5. Identifying currency unions: The procedure

Given our data set, the formal procedure for identifying currency unions comes in two parts. The first part, consisting of four steps or rules, concerns the trade criterion alone, while the second part incorporates the symmetry-of-output-fluctuations criterion as well. First we set out these steps in a formal fashion, next we discuss some general features of their application, and then we present the empirical results. In the empirical discussion, we organize the material by geographical area, as it is possible to do. We also facilitate informed judgment by providing detailed trade data for each geographical area.

5.1. *Identification by the trade criterion*

The application of the trade criterion rests on the following four rules:

(1) *Sample selection.* Countries eligible for monetary union must have a high enough degree of openness O_i, that is, one which exceeds a threshold level O^*.
(2) *Partner ordering.* For each country i in the sample, partners j are selected from the sample in descending order of T_{ij} values, and are progressively added to the union, subject to steps (3) and (4).
(3) *Stopping rule.* The process (2) stops when the openness of the union falls to O^*.
(4) *Reciprocity.* Every additional member of the union must accept every insider and must be accepted by every insider based on the preceding rules.

These rules operationalize the basic idea that high values of bilateral trade relative to GDP increase the benefits of a currency union as long as the overall openness ratio of the union O stays above a certain limit. Evidently, the lower the critical lower bound of O, O^*, the larger the currency unions that can be advantageously formed. In applying the rules, we stuck to values of O^* either higher than, or at least close to, the O levels displayed by the world's two largest economies, both of which are relatively closed by general international standards: the United States having an openness ratio of 10.6%, and Japan having one of 9.6%.

Two major consequences of the application of our rules do not necessarily meet the eye and should be mentioned at once. First, when the critical level of union openness O^* is set at the relatively low value typical of the larger countries, adding one of these larger countries to the union immediately triggers the 'stopping rule' (3). Second, alternative monetary unions with partly overlapping memberships will often occur. They can do so for three major reasons. First, adding a number of small members may have the same effect on O for the union as a whole as adding a single large one. Second, though the exports of country A toward country B are necessarily the imports of country B from country A, bilateral exports and imports between A and B differ in our work because we weigh trade by output, and therefore the bilateral trade weight of the smaller country is higher. As a result, many small countries frequently "wish to join" a large country (typically, Germany, the United States, or Japan) while the large country is not interested in them. Third, the ordering of partners tends to differ between countries (independently of the preceding point). Thus, Italy may be high on the list of a country that is low on Italy's list.

We report results for values of O^* a little below the US and Japanese levels, 0.09, a little above these levels, 0.11, and much higher, 0.15. Whenever $O^* = 0.9$ holds, we always consider the alternative of excluding both the US and Japan as potential partners.

5.2. *Adding the output-shock-symmetry criterion*

Adding the criterion of output-shock-symmetry requires a fifth 'rule':

(5) *Business cycle symmetry.* Countries identified as putative union members based on steps (1)–(4) are eliminated if the cross-correlation of their business-cycle output components with those of the largest producer, or the 'center country', in the putative union, falls below a critical level.

In deciding on the critical level of cross-correlation in rule (5), we took note of related earlier work. Based on US data for 1977–1995, Hess and Shin (1997) report an average correlation of Gross State Product (GSP) for individual states with the rest of the Union of about 0.75 (excluding the negative correlations for Texas and Louisiana). Van Wincoop (1995) finds an average pairwise cross-correlation of output of only 0.42 among the 47 Japanese prefectures in 1975–1988. Both of these studies use the Hodrick-Prescott filter with a dampening parameter of 100. The presence of lower cross-correlations in Japan than the United States is perhaps not surprising, since the average size of the Japanese region is much smaller than that of the average US state.

All things considered, we opted for a critical value of the cross-correlation coefficient of 0.6. But since this choice could seem arbitrary, we also report on cross-correlations in the 0.5–0.6 range under any of our de-trending methods and sample periods. Broadly speaking, only moderate revisions would be needed if the critical value was reduced to 0.4, whereas setting this value as high as 0.7 would merely cause the monetary unions we identify to shrink (except those with Mexico or Venezuela as center countries, which would then disappear). Our cross-correlations, it may be noted, all rest on GDP statistics, whereas much existing work (including that reported by Artis and Zhang, 1997a, 1997b) is based on industrial production data. Even though the latter series have the advantage of appearing at higher frequencies than those we use, GDP series may be preferred, since industrial production often accounts for as little as 25–30% of GDP in developed economies.

6. The results

6.1. Western Europe

Figure 2 displays the basic bilateral trade data for Western Europe. Along each horizontal axis there appear the output-weighted trade intensities (from here on referred to as 'trade weights') of a particular Western European country in relation to 16 others. The trade weights obviously tend to peak for Germany. The United Kingdom, France and Italy represent less important, though still notable, poles of attraction for trade. Table 1 provides a summary of Western European countries' world trade relations. The countries are uniformly highly open economies. Even apart from the extreme openness of the Benelux countries and Ireland, the openness ratios are frequently above 30%. Moreover, about one half of this openness comes from trade with or among the EU6. This would seem to suggest that the application of the trade criterion

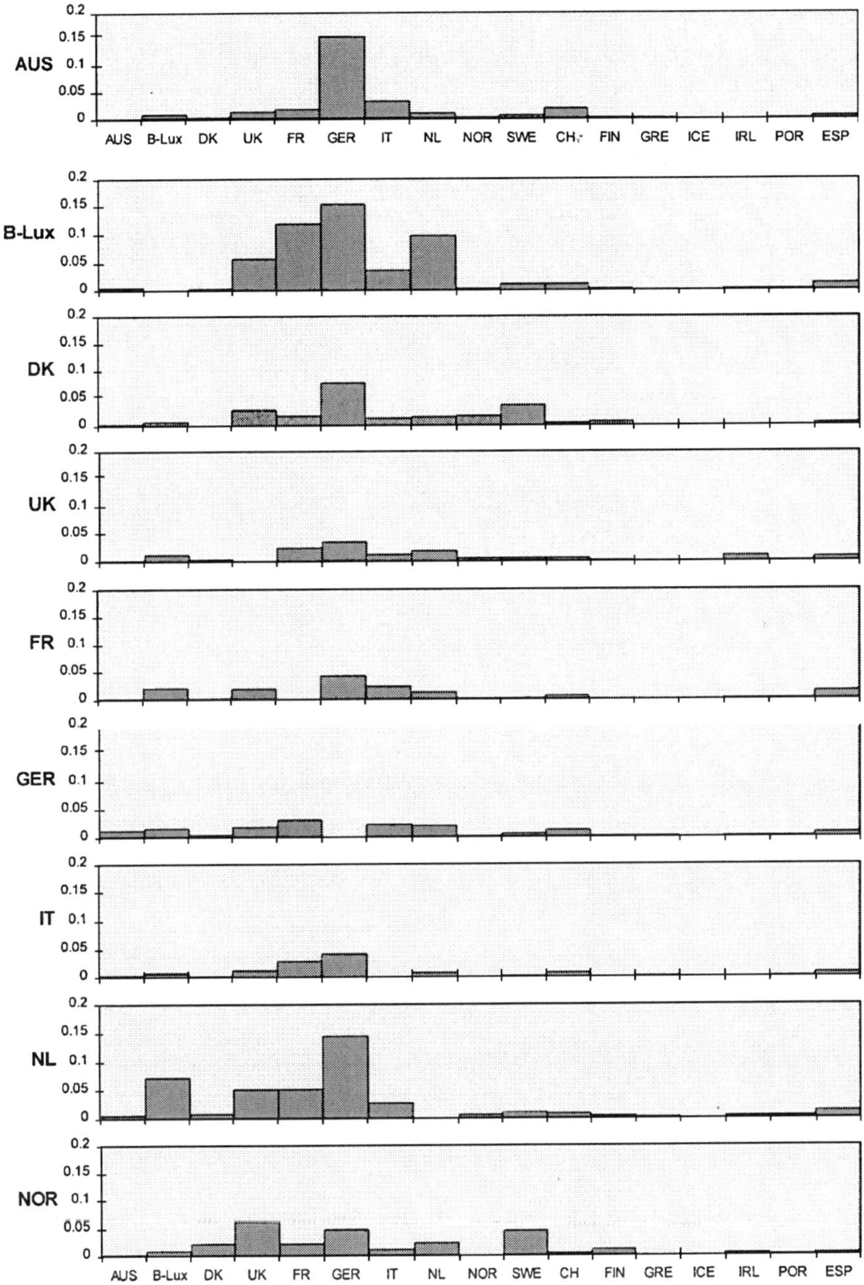

Figure 2. Western Europe: bilateral trade intensities.

(*Continued on next page.*)

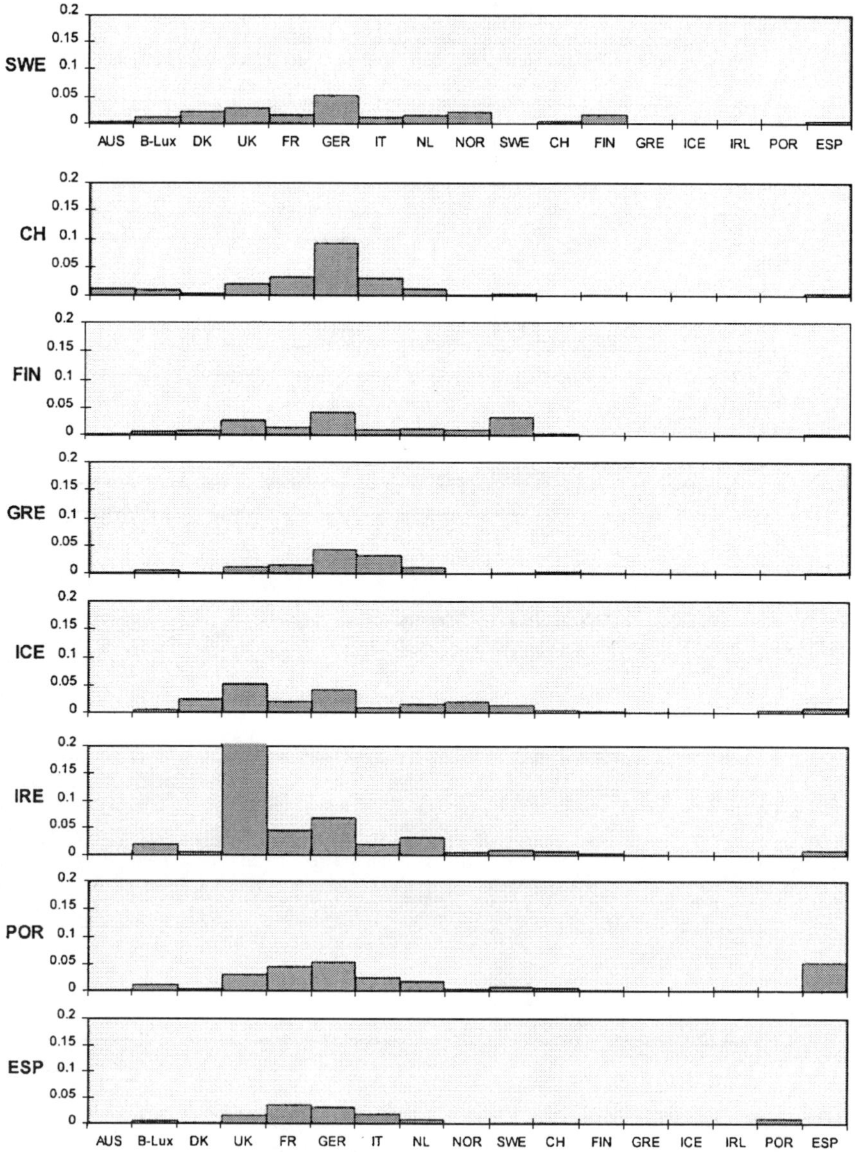

Figure 2. (*Continued*).

Table 1. Trade weights in Western Europe 1990–95.

	US	EU6	Japan	Openness
I. *EU6*				
Germany	1.8	10.8	1.0	26.0
France	1.8	11.9	0.7	23.4
UK	3.1	10.6	1.1	26.2
Italy	1.3	10.0	0.5	20.9
Netherlands	3.4	34.7	1.3	56.3
Belgium-Lux	3.8	46.9	1.4	70.4
II. *Iberia*				
Spain	1.3	11.9	0.6	20.6
Portugal	1.3	18.4	0.7	34.0
III. *Scandinavia*				
Sweden	2.6	14.2	1.1	32.3
Denmark	1.8	16.9	1.3	35.0
Norway	2.4	17.5	1.2	36.2
Finland	1.9	11.1	1.0	28.9
Iceland	3.8	14.6	2.5	33.5
IV. *Other*				
Austria	1.4	23.5	1.2	39.1
Greece	0.9	12.9	1.0	23.4
Switzerland	2.5	20.0	1.3	33.2
Ireland	7.6	40.5	2.6	64.3

might yield a significant return in identifying a large currency union. And so it is.

Table 2 shows the results of applying the trade criterion based on our algorithm. Setting the critical value for openness at 0.09, or a little below the value characteristic of the United States (0.106) and Japan (0.096), the "big four"—France, Germany, Italy and the United Kingdom—and the Benelux would wish to form a monetary union. The only combinations of the other countries that would also join in a monetary union in Western Europe (the EU + 3) are either Scandinavian or Iberian. But these results are critically affected by the eligibility of the United States. As soon as the US is admitted by others in a union based on the first three rules, the value of openness for the union falls below O^* (while the US, of course, 'opts out' under the reciprocity criterion) and the stopping rule comes into effect. As indicated above, we alleviate this problem in two ways. One is to keep the critical value of O^* just above the US level, at 11%. The other is to retain a O^* at 9% but simply rule out the US as a possible union partner. In the case of Europe, the two methods yield similar results.

Table 2. West European OCAs produced by the program: Trade criterion only.

I. The EU + 3

$O^* = 0.09$

1. France, Germany, Italy, UK, and Benelux
2. France, Germany, Italy, Switzerland
3. Belgium-Luxembourg, France, Italy, Spain
4. Austria, Germany, Italy
5. Denmark, Norway, Sweden
6. Ireland, UK
7. Spain, Portugal
8. Finland, Norway, Sweden

$O^* = 0.9$ minus US and Japan

1. All of the EU + 3 except Iceland plus Malta
2. Same plus Russia and Turkey
3. UK, Ireland, Portugal, Sweden, Canada, Mexico, Australia, New Zealand

$O^* = 0.11$

1. France, Germany, Italy, UK, Benelux, Spain, Switzerland
2. Sweden, Norway, Finland, Denmark
3. France, Spain, Portugal

$O^* = 0.15$

1. France, Germany, Italy, UK
2. Germany, Italy, UK, Netherlands
3. France, Belgium-Luxembourg
4. Denmark, Norway, Sweden
5. Finland, Norway, Sweden
6. A few two-country unions (apart from those implicit) arise

Once the United States and Japan are excluded despite $O^* = 0.09$, 16 of the 17 countries in the EU + 3 sample (all of them except Iceland) would form an OCA. In addition, Russian membership would suit everyone, as would Turkish membership. Only one alternative *large-scale* OCA emerges in Europe that would interfere with this big one. It would consist of the United Kingdom, Ireland, Canada, Australia, New Zealand, Sweden, Mexico, and Portugal. But this octet, which obviously evokes memories of the British Commonwealth, would disappear from view at $O^* = 0.11$. The other, larger, and strictly European OCA would not. Eight of the countries in the latter grouping, including the "big four", would still hold together (while Russia would no longer be accepted). Notably, though, the four Scandinavians would form a separate block.

At a 15% threshold for openness, our strictest setting for O^*, the only potential unions are naturally smaller. Those composed of three or more countries belong to one of three types: the "big four" alone; a selection of these four countries plus either Belgium-Luxembourg or the Netherlands; and a Scandinavian grouping (see Table 2).

The initial result, pertaining to 0.09 openness, is worth highlighting. On trade grounds alone, and assuming that the union becomes little more closed than the United States or Japan, the optimal area is Western Europe as a whole (without Iceland). Thus, the distinctions that often prevailed in discussion of the European Monetary Union between 'Ins', 'Pre-ins' and 'Outs' are not well reflected in the trade data, except perhaps by the presence of a fairly coherent 'Scandinavian' grouping.

Things change when we bring into account the business cycle symmetry criterion (of Table 3). The large OCA, based on $O^* = 0.9$ in the absence of the

Table 3. European OCAs produced by the program: Trade and business cycle symmetry criteria.[a]

I. The EU + 3

$O^* = 0.09$

1. *Germany*, Belgium, Netherlands (0.52)
2. —
3. *France*, Spain, Belgium, Italy
4. *Germany*, Austria
5. *Sweden*, Denmark
6. —
7. —
8. *Sweden*, Finland

$O^* = 0.9$, minus US and Japan

1. *Germany*, Austria, Belgium, Netherlands (0.52), Malta
2. Same as preceding
3. *UK*, Sweden, Canada, Australia

$O^* = 0.11$

1. *Germany*, Belgium, Netherlands (0.52)
2. *Sweden*, Finland, Denmark
3. *France*, Spain

$O^* = 0.15$

1. —
2. *Germany*, Netherlands (0.52)
3. *France*, Belgium
4. *Sweden*, Denmark
5. *Sweden*, Finland

[a]Countries shown are those remaining from the unions identified by trade alone in Table 2; except where otherwise indicated, a cross correlation of 0.6 or higher between the cyclical component of output with the center country was required. The center country is in italics.

United States and Japan, dwindles down to two possibilities: (1) a 'greater deutschmark' core consisting of Germany, Austria, Belgium and the Netherlands, to which Malta could be added; and (2) a more 'Mediterranean' core consisting of France, Italy, Spain and Belgium. Quite notably, France and Germany do not mix together. As indicated above, business cycle symmetry was tested on six alternative definitions, using three de-trending techniques and two different sample periods. In four of these six alternatives, the cross-correlation between output in France and Germany was less than 0.45. The other two instances were the ones where the long (1965–95) data sample served.[3] Less surprisingly perhaps, the application of the business cycle symmetry criterion eliminates the United Kingdom from all the potential unions identified on trade grounds, except for the one with Sweden, Canada and Australia. In addition, the business cycle symmetry criterion underscores the coherence of the various Scandinavian groupings. Broadly speaking, once we bring output into consideration, Germany does not seem as good a 'center' country as it does in regard to trade. In a number of European countries (including Italy, the United Kingdom and Sweden), business cycle correlations with the United States and Canada are much higher than the similar correlations with Germany.

In sum, by applying the business cycle symmetry criterion, we encounter a lot of the divisions that have been witnessed in the European debate on EMU, most notably in relation to the United Kingdom and Scandinavia.[4] The fact that a large union is now under way might then suggest the widespread assumption that the trade criterion is most important and possibly the further idea that the cost of business cycle asymmetry will fall (if not the view that political considerations prevail).

6.2. The rest of Europe

The basic trade data summarized in Table 4 indicate that for most countries in the rest of Europe, trade with the EU6 occupies a much more important place than trade with the United States or Japan. At the same time, most of these economies are highly open and do a lot of trade among themselves. The algorithm identifies only small monetary unions of two or three members at $O^* = 0.09$ in this next part of Europe (see Table 5), including ex-Yugoslavia (with a question mark regarding Serbia, for which we have no data), the Baltic countries, and ex-Czechoslovakia. Once again, the exclusion of the United States and Japan yields an enlargement. Specifically, the following monetary unions of four or five members appear:

1. Czech Republic, Hungary, Poland, Ukraine, Russia
2. Czech Republic, Slovakia, Hungary, Russia
3. Poland, Estonia, Latvia, Belarus, Russia
4. Estonia, Latvia, Lithuania, Belarus
5. Romania, Bulgaria, Russia, China

Table 4. Trade Weights in the rest of Europe 1990–95.

	The EU6	Japan	US	Openness
I. Ex-USSR				
Belarus	6.7	0.1	1.0	18.7
Bulgaria	12.3	0.5	1.4	41.9
Czech Republic	27.1	0.5	1.3	57.8
Estonia	15.2	1.2	2.3	77.2
Hungary	13.2	0.6	1.1	37
Latvia	11.2	0.3	0.7	49
Lithuania	25.5	0.7	1.5	71.1
Poland	11.8	0.3	0.7	24.6
Romania	6.8	0.2	0.8	22.5
Russia	9.6	1.3	1.7	31.9
Slovakia	19.2	0.1	0.7	63.8
Ukraine	20.4	1.3	5.4	50.4
II. Ex-Yugoslavia				
Bosnia/Herzegovina	4.2	—	1	19.6
Croatia	21.2	0.2	1.1	40.4
Slovenia	33.0	0.7	1.9	60
III. Southeast				
Albania	10.7	0.2	0.9	22.6
Malta	70.4	2.2	5.2	98.6
Turkey	6.7	0.5	1.5	16.3

Once the threshold level of openness rises to 15%, however, the only monetary unions remaining in the region consist of only two countries.[5] We lack the requisite output data to apply the business cycle symmetry criterion to these countries.

6.3. *The Americas*

The trade data for the Americas suggest a sharp distinction between three regions: (1) North America, Central America, and the Northern ring of South America; (2) the rest of South America; and (3) the Caribbean. Trade ties to the United States reign supreme for countries in the first region, including Venezuela, Colombia and Ecuador or the Northern ring of South America. As a scrutiny of Table 6 will show, if the European "hard core" or the EU6 can be seen as an OCA based on trade alone, so can this area. But our algorithm is more demanding. The problem stems from the reciprocity rule and the centrality of relations with the United States. To put it simply, the US is simply not interested in such a union.

Table 5. OCAs identified by the program in the Rest of Europe.

$O^* = 0.09$

1. Latvia, Lithuania plus either Estonia or Belarus
2. Czech Republic, Slovakia and Hungary
3. Czech Republic, Poland
4. Croatia and Slovenia, Bosnia/Herzogovina
5. Romania plus either Bulgaria or Ukraine
6. Russia, Turkey

$O^* = 0.09$ minus the US or Japan (four or more members)

1. Czech Republic, Hungary, Poland, Russia, Ukraine
2. Hungary, Slovak Republic, Russia plus either Czech Republic or Romania
3. Poland, Estonia, Latvia, Belarus, Russia
4. Romania, Bulgaria, Russia, China

$O^* = 0.11$

Same first four as with $O^* = 0.09$ (but excluding Czech Republic and Poland) with some additions containing Russia (specifically, Russia plus Bulgaria, Russia plus Ukraine and China, and Russia plus Ukraine, Czech Republic and Hungary)

$O^* = 0.15$

Only pairs remain: Belarus and Latvia, Russia and China, Czech and Slovak Republics, Estonia and Latvia, Croatia and Slovenia, Croatia and Bosnia/Herzegovina, Latvia and Lithuania.

Unlike Germany, or the "center country" in Europe, the United States is only moderately open and does less than a third of its trade with the rest of the countries of North, Central, and the relevant Northern part of South America. In addition, most of the US trade with those countries is with Canada and the rest, predominantly, with Mexico, while Japan is the United States' second-most important trading partner, after Canada. Of course, the US should have no objection if the others in the hypothetical OCA simply adopted the dollar as their home currency, and any objection by the rest would fall outside of our analysis. But based on the strict application of our program (Tables 7 and 8), the only viable monetary union with the US includes Canada and, possibly, also (on trade grounds alone and given a low enough O^*) Japan. As the program now stands, there are only two other OCAs in the first region: a Central American one consisting of Costa Rica, El Salvador, Guatemala and Nicaragua (whose contiguity is broken by the omission of Honduras); and another between the two South American neighbors, Columbia and Venezuela.

But if we exclude the United States and Japan, while keeping O^* at 0.09, then all of the countries in Central America, except for Honduras or Haiti, plus Venezuela and Columbia could form a single OCA (while Honduras and Haiti would object to one another but everyone else would be willing to admit both of them). Peru, Bolivia, and Chile almost enter too. Another large grouping, involving Canada, would also be possible. With O^* at 11%, however, the large

Table 6. Trade Weights in the Americas 1990–95.

	US	EU6	Japan	Openness
I. North, Central and Northern ring of South America				
Canada	21.4	2.1	1.6	29.7
Columbia	7.5	3.7	1.2	19.6
Costa Rica	21.1	6.7	1.5	43
Dominican Republic	12.5	3.2	1.7	27.6
Ecuador	10.4	3.7	1.6	26.9
El Salvador	10.2	2.8	0.9	24.7
Guatemala	9.3	2.4	0.9	22.3
Haiti	8.7	1.9	0.3	14.2
Honduras	18.8	4.5	1.9	34.3
Mexico	11.3	1.2	0.6	15.3
Nicaragua	8.9	3.9	1.6	33
Panama	13.6	3.4	2.1	36.5
US	—	1.9	1.6	10.6
Venezuela	13	3.4	0.9	27.2
II. South America				
Argentina	1.2	1.8	0.3	7.6
Bolivia	4.8	4.5	1.4	21.5
Brazil	1.3	1.6	0.4	6
Chile	5.6	6.2	3.7	29.6
Paraguay	3.6	5	2.1	31.2
Peru	2.6	2.2	0.9	11.1
Uruguay	1.9	3.8	0.5	21
III. The Caribbean				
Antigua & Barbuda	25.2	20.2	—	96.8
Bahamas	26.9	13.5	11.1	78.9
Barbados	15.4	8.2	2	48.3
Belize	31.2	11.9	0.6	59.8
Bermuda	9.5	3.1	0.8	19.8
Dominica	12.4	19.7	2.3	72.3
French Guiana	0.9	15.9	0.4	22.8
Grenada	13.1	12.3	2.2	52.5
Guadeloupe	1.2	16.6	0.4	27.3
Guyana	30.7	32.1	6.3	110.1
Jamaica	28.6	9.3	2.1	60.3
Martinique	0.5	18.1	0.3	23.5

(*Continued on next page.*)

Table 6. (*Continued*).

	US	EU6	Japan	Openness
Dutch Antilles	47.2	23.3	4.5	170.3
St. Kitts & Nevis	41.2	18.6	2.1	75.2
St. Lucia	25.6	33.2	3	76.2
St. Vincent & Grenadines	13.5	21.5	2.7	62.9
Suriname	10.2	13.5	2.1	43.7
Trinidad & Tobago	18.3	4.3	1	39.8

Table 7. North and Latin American OCAs produced by the program: Trade criterion only.

I. North, Central and Northern Ring of South America

$O^* = 0.09$

1. US, Canada (marginally Japan)
2. Costa Rica, El Salvador, Guatemala, Nicaragua
3. Columbia, Venezuela

$O^* = 0.09$ minus US and Japan

1. All plus Chile and minus Canada, Haiti and Ecuador (or Chile, Columbia, Costa Rica, Dominican Republic, El Salvador, Guatemala, Honduras, Mexico, Nicaragua, Panama, Venezuela)
2. Haiti can be substituted for Honduras, and Ecuador, Bolivia and Peru can be substituted for Honduras, Nicaragua and Dominican Republic
3. Canada, Colombia, Costa Rica, Ecuador, Mexico, Peru, Venezuela.

$O^* = 0.11$

1. El Salvador, Guatemala, Honduras, Nicaragua, Costa Rica, Panama, Venezuela (central branch of the first OCA mentioned under the preceding heading)
2. Mexico, Dominican Republic, El Salvador, Guatemala, Costa Rica, Panama, Venezuela (northerly branch)
3. Costa Rica, Panama, Columbia, Ecuador, Venezuela, Peru, Mexico (southerly branch, except for Mexico)
4. Canada, Mexico, Venezuela, Columbia, Chile (North-South combination)

$O^* = 0.15$

1. Costa Rica, El Salvador, Guatemala, Nicaragua (same as under 0.09)
2. El Salvador, Guatemala, plus either Costa Rica and Panama or Honduras
3. Columbia, Ecuador, Panama
4. Columbia and Venezuela (same as under 0.09)
5. Canada, Australia, China, Korea
6. Canada, Mexico

II. South America

$O^* = 0.09$

None

(*Continued on next page.*)

Table 7. (Continued).

$O^* = 0.09$ minus US and Japan

1. Bolivia, Chile, Peru and Paraguay plus Mexico, Panama, Ecuador and Venezuela
2. Bolivia, Chile, Peru plus Columbia, Costa Rica, Dominican Republic, Ecuador, El Salvador, Guatemala, Mexico, Panama, Venezuela (already mentioned under section I)

$O^* = 0.11$

1. Chile, Peru, Paraguay, Uruguay
2. Chile, Peru, Bolivia, Columbia
3. Bolivia, Peru, Paraguay, Costa Rica
4. Chile enters a number of North-South combinations of 4 or 5 countries in the Americas

$O^* = 0.15$

None

III. The Caribbean

$O^* = 0.09$

1. Trinidad & Tobago, Barbados
2. Trinidad & Tobago, Netherlands Antilles
3. Guadeloupe, Martinique

$O^* = 0.09$ minus US and Japan

1. Antigua & Barbuda, Belize, Dominica, Grenada, Guyana, Jamaica, Barbados, St. Vincent & Grenadines
2. Bahamas can be substituted for Dominica and Grenada, Bermuda can be substituted for Grenada and St. Vincent & Grenadines, St. Kitts can be substituted for Antingua & Barbuda, Trinidad and Tobago added.
3. Various other combinations of other Caribbeans with five or six of the preceding are possible.

$O^* = 0.11$

1. Antigua & Barbuda, Barbados, Dominica, Guyana, Jamaica, St. Vincent & Grenadines
2. Guyana & Jamaica can be replaced by Grenada
3. Guyana, Jamaica, Netherland Antilles, Suriname, Trinidad
4. Trinidad, Belize, Jamaica, Netherland Antilles
5. Various other 4–5 country combinations are possible.

$O^* = 0.15$

1. Barbados, Dominica, Grenada, St Lucia, St. Vincent & Grenadines
2. Dominica, Grenada, St Kitts, St. Vincent & Grenadines
3. A large number of smaller OCA's are possible. All three of those mentioned above under $O^* = 0.09$ survive.

Table 8. North and Latin American OCAs produced by the program: Trade and business cycle symmetry criteria.[a]

I. North, Central and Northern Ring of South America

$O^* = 0.09$

1. *US*, Canada
2. *Guatemala*, Costa Rica, El Salvador
3. *Venezuela*, Columbia (0.56)

$O^* = 0.09$, minus US and Japan

1. *Mexico*, Chile (0.54), Guatemala
2. *Mexico*, Bolivia, Chile (0.54), Guatemala, Ecuador
3. —

$O^* = 0.11$

1. *Venezuela*, Costa Rica, Guatemala, Honduras
2. *Mexico*, Guatemala
3. *Mexico*, Ecuador
4. —

$O^* = 0.15$

1. *Guatemala*, Costa Rica, El Salvador
2. See Part 1; (Panama drops out) or *Guatemala*, El Salvador, Honduras
3. —
4. *Venezuela* (as under 0.09), Columbia (0.55)
5. *Canada*, Australia, Korea
6. —

II. South America

$O^* = 0.09$

None

$O^* = 0.09$ minus US and Japan

1. *Mexico*, Bolivia, Chile (0.54), Paraguay, Ecuador
2. *Mexico*, Bolivia, Chile (0.54), Ecuador, Guatemala. *But* using Guatemala as center country (3rd largest after Mexico and Peru): *Guatemala*, Bolivia, Chile, Colombia, Costa Rica, Ecuador, El Salvador, Mexico, Venezuela.

$O^* = 0.11$

1. —
2. —
3. —
4. Only *Mexico*, Chile (0.54), Ecuador

$O^* = 0.15$

None

(*Continued on next page.*)

Table 8. (*Continued*).

III. The Caribbean

$O^* = 0.09$

1. —
2. — (no data for Netherlands Antilles)
3. — (no data for Guadeloupe)

$O^* = 0.09$ minus US and Japan

1. *Jamaica*, Belize
2. Same as preceding
3. Other combinations... *Trinidad & Tobago*, Suriname, *Jamaica*, Suriname

$O^* = 0.11$

1. —
2. *Barbados*, Antigua & Barbuda, Dominica (0.58), Grenada
3. *Jamaica*, Suriname
4. —

$O^* = 0.15$

1. *Barbados*, Dominica (0.58), Grenada, St. Lucia
2. *Grenada*, St. Kitts

[a]Countries shown are those remaining from the unions identified by trade alone in Table 7; except where otherwise indicated, a cross correlation of 0.6 or higher between the cyclical component of output with the center country was required. The center country is in italics.

groups break up into three alternative sets of seven. With O^* equal 15%, these large groupings disappear from view and we are back to monetary unions barely bigger (and economically more significant) than those with $O^* = 0.09$ in which the United States is present. The most striking difference at $O^* = 0.15$ is a distinctly Pacific-orientation of Canada, which now looks out toward the distant shores of Australia, Korea and China.

The remainder of South America, below the Northern ring, has stronger trade links to the EU6 than the United States on the whole, except for Peru. Brazil and Chile are also fairly evenly divided in their trade between the EU6 and the US. In addition, a number of countries in this next part of the globe are surprisingly closed: namely, Argentina, Brazil and Peru. This was not always true. Brazil had an openness ratio of around 15% in the earlier period of 1970–85, and Peru's had been around 17% in 1965–85. But for the last ten years, those two countries have been relatively closed, while Argentina has been steadily so in the postwar era. Even if we examine the trade relations of the seven countries in our Latin American grouping with a fine-tooth comb, they would seem to be little interested in monetary union with the US, regardless of who else in the Americas joins.

The program with $O^* = 0.09$ and the exclusion of the United States and Japan shows two possible monetary unions in the southern region involving a core of Bolivia, Chile and Peru. Additionally, Mexico, Panama, Ecuador and Venezuela always belong to one of these unions, but in one case (mentioned above) so would most of the rest of Mesoamerica, while in the other, Bolivia's Southern neighbor, Paraguay, would be present instead. However, either union would break up quickly if we set O^* slightly higher than 0.09.

The third section of Table 6, dealing with the Caribbean, takes us to a region of the world consisting of very small countries, or in some cases territories with no separate currencies at all. The three French-related areas, Guadeloupe, Martinique, and French Guiana, fall into this last category: they all use the French franc as their currency, and correspondingly do the bulk of their trade with mainland France. Some of the other islands and territories in the Caribbean also have close political ties to Europe. Yet, in these cases, trade with the United States often dominates. This applies to Antigua & Barbuda, Barbados, Grenada, Guyana, and St. Kitts & Nevis, all of whom have some British affiliation, and it holds in both examples of a Dutch connection, Netherlands Antilles and Suriname. But St. Lucia and St. Vincent & Grenadines, with British political ties, do as much trade with the United Kingdom as with the United States. In areas where no European government plays any active role, as in the Bahamas, Bermuda, Jamaica and Trinidad & Tobago, trade with the United States greatly dominates trade with all of the EU6 combined.

In general, the Caribbean presents an unusually varied and complicated picture. None the less, one monetary union in the zone, the East Caribbean Currency Area (ECCA), can provide a point of reference. It consists of Antigua & Barbuda, Dominica, Grenada, St. Kitts & Nevis, St. Lucia, and St. Vincent & Grenadines.[6] The only other monetary union in the Caribbean is the aforementioned one with France. Our program (Tables 7 and 8) would indeed identify the East Caribbean Currency Area as an OCA at $O^* = 0.09$ without the United States (with a single qualification for Antigua & Barbuda, which would not admit either St. Kitts & Nevis or St. Lucia). This OCA would then stretch beyond the ECCA to include Belize, Guyana and Jamaica. It could also include Trinidad & Tobago, the largest country in the group (in terms of GDP), which is acceptable to all the other members except Antigua and Barbuda. Even if we set O^* at 0.15, the only two currency unions consisting of as many as four members that would still survive in the Caribbean would be composed exclusively of members of the ECCA or harbor strictly one outsider. Thus, our program would essentially detect an OCA in or around the ECCA. Finally, the program easily discerns Guadeloupe and Martinique as an OCA but does not recognize French Guiana as a member (even at $O^* = 0.09$).

How well do the preceding potential currency areas in the Americas withstand the test of the business cycle symmetry criterion? The answer can be seen by comparing Tables 7 and 8. If anything, in fact, the American unions appear somewhat more robust than the European ones. The union between the

United States and Canada in the North is confirmed, as is the Central American union (shorn of Nicaragua) and the combination of Colombia and Venezuela. Excluding the US and Japan, but maintaining O^* at 0.09, one of the three large groupings in the area survives the application of the business cycle symmetry criterion. The smaller unions suggested by the trade criterion when O^* is 0.11 or 0.15 also survive this next test. On down in South America, we find that quite large groupings stand up to the application of the business cycle criterion—though, naturally, none of them include Argentina or Brazil, the big-country participants in Mercosur, which, as mentioned above, are relatively 'closed'. The picture in the Caribbean is complicated by missing data points; however, little remains of the currency areas suggested by the trade criterion.

6.4. The Near and Middle East

The analysis of the Near and Middle East points out an important limitation of the trade criterion. As a rich oil-importing country, Japan figures heavily in trade in this part of the world. But the oil trade is in US dollars, and the US dollar best reflects the monetary concerns of the middle-east exporters of oil to Japan. It is therefore potentially dangerous to draw conclusions from the trade data about membership in an OCA in this part of the world. This problem also applies to the trade of the region with Europe to some extent, but less so—as witnessed by the trade data in Table 9 for the non-oil-producing countries, Cyprus, Egypt, Israel, Jordan, Lebanon and Syria. All of these states display markedly stronger ties to the EU6 than the United States or Japan, singly or combined. In general, a lot of European trade in the Near and Middle East does not concern oil.

Quite significantly, however, our reciprocity criterion avoids any conceptual anomalies in defining OCAs in the region (see Tables 10 and 11). Japan would

Table 9. Trade Weights in the Near and Middle East 1990–95.

	US	EU6	Japan	Openness
Bahrain	5.1	8	4.3	105.6
Cyprus	3.8	19.5	3.6	53.3
Egypt	3.9	8.2	0.1	24.8
Israel	8.4	14.2	1.8	36.9
Jordan	6.5	16.1	2.5	71.4
Kuwait	9.2	12.4	8.4	56.7
Lebanon	2.8	16	1.3	43.8
Lybia	0.1	60	1.2	91.7
Oman	2.5	6	10.5	43.5
Qatar	1.8	4.9	15.4	35
Saudi Arabia	9.2	10	6.9	44.2
Syria	0.6	5.6	0.5	14.3
United Arab Emirates	3.3	9.1	16.3	57.2

Table 10. Near and Middle Eastern OCAs produced by the program: Trade criterion only.

$O^* = 0.09$

1. Lebanon and Syria

$O^* = 0.09$ minus US and Japan

1. Bahrain, Jordan, Kuwait, Oman, Qatar, Saudi Arabia, United Arab Emirates (UAE)
2. Bahrain, Cyprus, Jordan, Kuwait, Lebanon, Saudi Arabia, Syria
3. Egypt plus two of the preceding (never Bahrain)

$O^* = 0.11$

1. Bahrain, Saudi Arabia, UAE, plus Pakistan
2. Kuwait, Saudi Arabia, plus *either* Korea, Pakistan and Singapore *or* plus Korea, and the Philippines
3. Saudi Arabia, the UAE, Pakistan, China, Hong Kong, Korea, Malaysia, Thailand and Singapore or Indonesia, *or else* Oman, UAE, Korea, Singapore, Thailand and China.

$O^* = 0.15$

1. Saudi Arabia, Korea, Singapore
2. Oman, UAE, Korea
3. Bahrain, Saudi Arabia
4. Kuwait, Pakistan
5. UAE plus either Pakistan or Singapore

Table 11. Near and Middle Eastern OCAs produced by the program: Trade and business cycle symmetry criteria.[a]

$O^* = 0.09$

1. —

$O^* = 0.09$ minus US and Japan

1. *Saudi Arabia*, Bahrain, UAE
2. *Saudi Arabia*, Bahrain, Syria (0.54)
3. —

$O^* = 0.11$

1. *Saudi Arabia*, Bahrain, UAE
2. *Saudi Arabia* plus Singapore (0.52) or plus the Philippines
3. —

$O^* = 0.15$

1. —
2. —
3. *Saudi Arabia*, Bahrain
4. —
5. *Singapore*, UAE

[a]Countries shown are those remaining from the unions identified by trade alone in Table 10; except where otherwise indicated, a cross correlation of 0.6 or higher between the cyclical component of output with the center country was required. The center country is in italics.

not join any Near and Middle Eastern countries that might wish to hook up with it in a monetary union because of inadequate trade interests with those countries, and the same is true, with minor qualifications, for the Europeans. Saudi Arabia or, alternatively, Israel would be accepted by the EU at $O^* = 0.09$ if we excluded the United States and Japan, but only marginally and with exceptions. At 0.09 and without the US or Japan, our program treats all of the oil producers but Lybia as a single OCA. This last OCA could well include Cyprus, Lebanon and Syria instead of Omar, Qatar and the UAE. But quite importantly, the grouping dissolves readily with higher values of O^*. Smaller alliances then arise, distinctly pointed toward the East: Pakistan, Singapore and Korea in particular. Those three Asiatic countries feature in all of the OCAs in the region at O^* equal 15%, except for the one between Saudi Arabia and Bahrain (Tables 10 and 11).

As seen in Table 11, adding the business cycle symmetry criterion causes many of the earlier unions in the area to dissolve or shrink. The output fluctuations of the largest economy in the potential OCAs in the region, Saudi Arabia, are closely attuned to those of Bahrain and the UAE. Apart from this one example, output fluctuations among Near and Middle Eastern countries are not markedly synchronized.

6.5. Asia and Oceania

Consideration of Asia obviously raises the issue of the possible range of a yen currency area. Accordingly, we have isolated a "yen core" on the basis of trade alone, consisting strictly of some other members of the Association of Southeast Asian Nations (ASEAN) besides Japan. The group includes Indonesia, Laos, Malaysia, Singapore, Thailand and Vietnam. Myanmar (formerly Burma) might belong to this group as well, since one third of its total trade is with these countries. However, Myanmar trade is extremely low: the country is very closed. Unfortunately, we have almost no data for Cambodia, and cannot say whether this ASEAN member also belongs in the core. In the case of Indonesia, Thailand and Vietnam, the dominance of Japanese trade over that with the United States or the EU6 is clear from Table 12. For Laos, Malaysia, and Singapore, however, our reasoning is not obvious, since these three countries trade as much or more with either the United States or the EU6 than with Japan. Yet if we include those countries in the "yen core", then their trade with the rest of the yen bloc (which goes beyond Japan, of course) greatly dominates their trade with either the US or the EU6.

But, evidently, Japan poses a similar problem to the one of the United States in the Americas: the country does not trade predominantly with the rest of the "yen core." Its trade with this group only matches that with the EU6 and is about half as large as its trade with the US. In addition, Japan is relatively closed. Thus, as in the earlier example of the US in the Americas, the "center" country would only be interested in monetary union (apart from wider political

Table 12. Trade Weights in Asia and Oceania 1990–95.

	US	EU6	Japan	Yen core	Openness
I. Yen core					
Indonesia	3.5	4	7.8	10.2	26.4
Japan	2.6	1.3	—	1.2 (1.6)	9.6
Laos	0.4	2.9	2.4	19.6	26.8
Malaysia	14.9	11.1	16.9	36.5	85
Singapore	29.8	19.9	25	59.9	168.4
Thailand	6.7	6.3	10.4	16.1	43.1
Vietnam	0.1	2.9	4.7	11.5	29.5
II. Rest of Asia					
Bangladesh	2.3	3	1.1	2.6	16.4
Brunei	4.9	8.9	18.4	33.5	55.2
Myanmar	0.0	0.0	0.1	0.5	1.5
China	2.5	2.2	3.5	4.5	19.9
Hong Kong	17.8	13.7	12.8	20.6	116.6
India	1.4	2.8	0.8	1.5	10.3
Korea	7.2	3.4	6.4	9.2 (10.1)	31.2
Maldives	5.2	15.6	4.5	62.2	113.2
Nepal	2.7	6.3	2.2	6.3	25.3
Pakistan	2.5	5.1	2.2	3.7	21.1
Philippines	8.9	4.3	6.7	10.1 (10.9)	33.8
Sri Lanka	6.1	8.1	3.3	7.3	39
III. Oceania					
Australia	3	3	4.2	6.1 (7.1)	19.5
Fiji	6.5	8.1	5.1	9.3 (25.8)	60.9
Kiribati	47.3	16.4	11.5	11.5 (29.8)	109.9
New Zealand	4.5	4.6	4.6	6.2 (11.8)	30.2
Papua New Guinea	2.2	4.7	9.6	13.7 (34.9)	48.3
Solomon Islands	4.7	8.3	28.1	38.1 (56.4)	84.9
Tonga	4.5	0.8	6.5	9.4 (26)	42
Vanuatu	1.3	11.3	19.5	20.6 (32.7)	54.3
Western Samoa	8.3	3.3	6.7	7.5 (54.3)	84.7

considerations which are outside of the analysis) if the others in the organization simply allowed it to dictate joint monetary policy.

The next section of Table 12 extends the analysis to the remainder of Asia and Oceania. In the central section, dealing with the rest of Asia, we find that the entire Indian subcontinent, consisting of Bangladesh, India, Nepal, Pakistan and Sri Lanka, would not be particularly attracted to the yen zone. Those five countries do more trade with the EU6 than with either Japan or the United States. In addition, India, in particular, is too closed to be greatly interested in monetary union with anyone. On the other hand, Korea and the Philippines represent interesting cases: both are more drawn to the US than Japan through trade, but in the event of a monetary zone embracing the entire "yen core", would trade more with the "yen zone" than the US. The resulting swing in their trade toward the yen zone, however, would be far smaller than that of the ASEAN countries classified earlier in the "yen core". China also belongs to a yen zone based on trade, it would seem, as do the two tiny states of Brunei and the Maldive Islands.

As concerns Oceania, the trade of Australia and New Zealand is particularly evenly balanced between the EU6, the United States and Japan. Indeed, these two countries' trade tilts more toward Japan than does that of Korea and the Philippines, which represent two points of comparison. Thus, in the event of a currency area comprising the entire "yen core", Australia and New Zealand would be very much in the same ambiguous position as Korea and the Philippines, as their trade with the yen area would then exceed their trade with either the United States or the EU6. Australia would feel the pull toward the yen zone more than New Zealand, but should Australia join the yen bloc, then New Zealand could no longer hesitate about doing so too, based on the trade criterion alone. The parenthetical figures in the "yen core" column, which include Australia and New Zealand in the core, show as much.[7] Except for Kiribati, which remains attracted to the US in any event (yet uses the Australian dollar as its currency), some of the small states in the Pacific, east of Australia, would also have an interest in joining the yen zone. Indeed, all of them would if Australia and New Zealand did so.

When we apply our program to the Far East Asian part of the world, a large OCA, stretching across the entire surface, emerges. With O^* set at 0.09 and both Japan and the United States excluded as possible partners, an OCA emerges stretching from China and Hong Kong to Korea, embracing the entire "yen core", the Philippines, and extending further south to Australia and New Zealand (see Table 13). Even India and Bangladesh belong. The major qualification regarding the membership of the entire "yen core" in this OCA concerns Laos, which is accepted only by Thailand, Vietnam and the Philippines. The alternative monetary unions in the region are much smaller. One of them, comprising Brunei and Nepal, would equally admit Korea, but then be limited to the "yen core" (because Brunei and Nepal are not of wide enough trade interest). Similarly, a number of monetary unions could be formed between Australia and New Zealand and the small Pacific islands, but these would then be confined to Oceania.

Quite significantly, at O^* of 11%, the previous large Asiatic OCAs remain evident. Even when O^* equals 15%, when Malaysia drops out, the OCA does

Table 13. Asian and Oceanian OCAs identified by the program: Trade criterion only.

$O^* = 0.09$

1. China and Hong Kong
2. Malaysia and Singapore

$O^* = 0.09$ minus US and Japan

1. Bangladesh, China, Hong Kong, India, Indonesia or Singapore, Korea, Malaysia, Philippines, Thailand, Australia, New Zealand, Vietnam or Sri Lanka and Pakistan
2. Brunei, Korea, Malaysia, Nepal, Philippines, Indonesia or Singapore, Thailand,
3. Australia, New Zealand, Fiji, plus either Papua New Guinea and Solomon Islands, or Western Samoa and Tonga, or Papua New Guinea, Tonga and Vanuatu
4. Australia, Fiji and Kiribati

$O^* = 0.11$

1. China, Hong Kong, Indonesia, Korea, Malaysia, Philippines, Thailand, Vietnam, Australia or with Singapore replacing Indonesia and Vietnam
2. Somewhat smaller unions with Singapore

$O^* = 0.15$

1. China, Hong Kong, Korea, Singapore, Thailand, Australia
2. China, Indonesia, Korea, Malaysia, Australia
3. There are a few distinct, smaller OCAs

Table 14. Asian and Oceanian OCAs identified by the program: Trade and business cycle symmetry criteria[a].

$O^* = 0.09$

1. Not sufficient data on Hong Kong
2. *Singapore* and Malaysia

$O^* = 0.09$ minus US and Japan

1. Not sufficient data on Hong Kong. If China and Korea excluded as center countries, then *Indonesia*, Bangladesh, Malaysia, Philippines, Thailand
2. —
3. —
4. —

$O^* = 0.11$

1. Excluding China and Korea as center countries, *Indonesia*, Malaysia, Philippines, Thailand
2. —

$O^* = 0.15$

1. *Thailand* and Singapore if China, Korea, Australia excluded as center countries
2. *Indonesia*, Malaysia, if other center countries excluded
3. —

[a]Countries shown are those remaining from the unions identified by trade alone in Table 13; except where otherwise indicated, a cross correlation of 0.6 or higher between the cyclical component of output with the center country was required. The center country is in italics.

not vanish from view: three of its major members—China, Korea and Australia—remain present along with two or four others. There is therefore plainly a large OCA in Far East Asia without Japan on the basis of our program.

Adding the business cycle symmetry criterion causes this large OCA to shrink considerably (see Table 14). Only Indonesia, Bangladesh, Malaysia, the Philippines and Thailand hold together as a group. Singapore is a likely additional member of this OCA, but we cannot be sure because of a data problem.[8]

Conclusions

This paper has applied the theory of optimal currency areas on a worldwide basis. To achieve this aim, we retained a stripped-down version of the theory, wherein only two of the many criteria that have been mentioned in the literature on the subject remain. We also made a case for choosing these two criteria. It was then possible to use computer programming to identify OCA's. Trade is our first criterion. According to the traditional literature, high levels of bilateral trade provide a potential source of benefits from a common currency. Our other criterion relates to symmetry of shocks. The lack of such symmetry can make the abandonment of independent monetary policy costly. A small, recent literature also suggests that the first criterion may even suffice in itself, since the second one will tend to be progressively met under monetary union. But we have taken no position on the issue.

Our results suggest that four large OCAs can be identified in the world based on the most liberal application of the trade criterion that we admitted, which permits openness to fall slightly below the US and Japanese level. Of these four large unions, one covers virtually all of Western Europe; a second encompasses all of Mesoamerica and the Northern ridge of South America; a third occupies a good part of the Middle East, and a fourth stretches across the entire ASEAN area, including China and Australia. Two of these large OCAs—the ones in the Americas and the Middle East but especially the latter—are not too robust. They depend too much on allowing a critical level of openness low enough to admit the United States and Japan while excluding both countries nevertheless, and they dissolve too easily when those conditions are tightened.[9] The other two OCAs in our analysis withstand a similar test. Of the two, the East Asian OCA may be the more interesting, since efforts to promote exchange rate stability have not gone nearly as far in that part of the world. Those efforts have also centered on the dollar rather than the yen (see Frankel and Wei, 1992). However, the question of dollar or yen can be put aside here since the OCA we envisage does not include either Japan or the US. stated differently, our Asiatic OCA could well dispose of a separate currency (cf. Bénassy-Quéré, 1997).

Of considerable interest as well, our program displays a marked tendency to identify monetary unions on a geographical basis, and, quite pronouncedly, in line with the gravity model of trade. There are exceptions, mostly concerning

Canada, Australia, Saudi Arabia and Singapore, which show traces of earlier days of eminent British influence on world trade.

On trade grounds alone, then, the world may seem ripe for further consolidation into large currency areas; but the shock-symmetry criterion sounds a qualifying note. Its application would even suggest that the 11-member country European Monetary Union may already be too large. However, giving credence to the 'endogeneity' of the criteria could reverse this judgement.

Acknowledgment

The authors would like to acknowledge the useful suggestions of Andrew Rose.

Notes

1. Quite independently of the previous two criteria, there are powerful reasons to think that no unified political entity could live happily with two or more central banks issuing separate currencies within its boundaries. The different central banks might engage in competitive devaluation not only in order to gain a trade advantage, but also in order to shift the tax burden to the other's region. This point also underlies our unwillingness even to consider the possibility that existing currency areas may already be too large.
2. See Frankel and Rose (1997b) for a further application to European Monetary Union.
3. Note that in their study of the eligibility of European countries for monetary union with Germany based on OCA-type considerations, Bayoumi and Eichengreen (1997) also exclude France from the "converged group" on the grounds of the country's "structural characteristics and cyclical performance" (p. 769).
4. In its "Five Tests" for acceding to the EMU, the UK government has formally included a better convergence of cyclical conditions in the UK with those in the Union-countries (cf. UK Treasury, 1997).
5. Compare Honohan (1997), who discusses the prospect of European countries outside of EMU forming miniblocs based on trade alone. Interestingly too, Tichy (1992) uses trade data in order to identify an "optimum customs union" in Europe.
6. Anguilla is also a member, but we have no data for this country.
7. The parenthetical figures for Korea and the Philippines in this column (Table 12) show how much more these two countries would also be drawn toward the yen zone if Australia and New Zealand were included.
8. Our data show Singapore as Indonesia's third largest trading partner, while Singapore is reported as having no trade at all with Indonesia.
9. On the other hand, the American OCA holds up rather well to the application of the business-cycle-symmetry criterion.

References

Artis, Michael and W. Zhang (1997a) "International Business Cycles and the ERM: Is There a European Business Cycle?" *International Journal of Finance and Economics* 2, 1–16.

Artis, Michael and W. Zhang (1997b) "On Identifying the Core of EMU: An Exploration of Some Empirical Criteria." CEPR Discussion Paper No. 1689.

Bayoumi, Tamim and Barry Eichengreen (1997) "Ever Closer to Heaven? An Optimum Currency Area Index of European Countries." *European Economic Review* 41, 761–770.

Bénassy-Quéré, Agnès (1997) "Optimal Pegs for Asian Currencies." CEPII Document de Travail, No. 97–114.

Eichengreen, Barry (1994) *International Monetary Arrangements for the 21st Century*. Brookings Institution.

Frankel, Jeffrey and Andrew Rose (1997a) "The Endogeneity of the Optimum Currency Area Criteria." *Swedish Economic Policy Review* 4, 487–512, also CEPR Discussion Paper No. 1473, 1996.

Frankel, Jeffrey and Andrew Rose (1997b) "Is EMU More Justifiable Ex-Post Than Ex-Ante?" *European Economic Review* 41, 753–760.

Frankel, Jeffrey and Shang-Jin Wei (1992) "Yen Bloc or Dollar Bloc: Exchange Rate Policies in East Asian Economies." In Ito and Krueger (eds.), *Macroeconomic Linkages*. University of Chicago Press.

Goodhart, Charles (1997) "The Two Concepts of Money, and the Future of Europe." London School of Economics, Mimeo.

Hess, Gregory and Kwanko Shin (1997) "International and Intranational Business Cycles." *Oxford Review of Economic Policy* 13(3), 93–109.

Honkapohja, Seppo and Pentti Pikkarainen (1992) "Country Characteristics and the Choice of Exchange Rate Regime: Are Mini-skirts Followed by Maxis?" CEPR Discussion Paper No. 744.

Honohan, Patrick (1997) "Miniblocs and Fringe Currencies of the EMU." CEPR Discussion Paper No. 1704.

Kenen, Peter (1969) "The Theory of Optimum Currency Areas: An Eclectic View." In Mundell and Swoboda (eds.), *Monetary Problems of the International Economy*. University of Chicago Press, pp. 42–60.

Krugman, Paul (1990) "Policy Problems of a Monetary Union." In Paul De Grauwe and Lucas Papademos (eds.), *The European Monetary System in the 1990s*. London and New York: Longman, CEPS and Bank of Greece, pp. 48–64.

Mélitz, Jacques (1995) "A Suggested Reformulation of the Theory of Optimum Currency Areas." *Open Economies Review* 6, 281–298.

Mélitz, Jacques (1996) "The Theory of Optimum Currency Areas, Trade Adjustment, and Trade." *Open Economies Review* 7, 99–116.

Mundell, Robert (1961) "A Theory of Optimum Currency Areas." *American Economic Review* 51, 657–698.

Tichy, Gunther (1992) "Theoretical and Empirical Considerations on the Dimension of an Optimum Integration Area in Europe." *Aussenwirtschaft* 47, heft I, 107–137.

UK Treasury (1997) "UK Membership of the Single Currency—An Assessment of the Five Economic Tests." *HM Treasury*. London: HMSO.

Van Wincoop, Eric (1995) "Regional Risk-Sharing." *European Economic Review* 39(8), 1545–1567.

Open economies review **9:S1** 569–607 (1998)

Exchange Rate Stability and Financial Stability

BARRY EICHENGREEN eichengr@econ.berkeley.edu
University of California, Berkeley, Department of Economics, Berkeley, CA 94720-3880

Key words: exchange-rate regime, banking crisis, financial stability, lender of last resort

JEL Classification Numbers: E44, E58, F33, F36

Abstract

Historical evidence reveals no monocausal explanation for banking crises, including one which would emphasize the maintenance of a currency peg. To some extent this follows from the standard textbook wisdom: whether fixed or flexible exchange rates are preferable depends on the source of disturbances. If threats to the stability of the banking system come from the "outside," there is a case for exchange rate flexibility to discourage the banks from relying excessively on external sources of finance and to enhance the capacity of the domestic authorities to act as lenders of last resort. Conversely, if the main threats to the stability of the banking system emanate from "inside" (e.g., erratic monetary policies at home), there is an argument for attempting to peg the exchange rate in order to discipline domestic policymakers and vent shocks via the external sector. From this point of view, it is no surprise that there is no simple correlation between the exchange rate regime and the prevalence of banking crises.

Introduction

Most of the literature on the choice of exchange rate regime pays little mind to implications for financial stability. Contributions typically focus on factors emphasized by the theory of optimum currency areas: economic size and openness to trade, the flexibility of labor markets, and the incidence of macroeconomic shocks (Mundell, 1961). McKinnon (1963) hints at the importance of financial factors, suggesting that countries with deep financial markets will prefer to float. Heller (1976) argues the opposite that countries with integrated and developed financial markets will prefer to peg. But neither these nor other authors systematically analyze the significance of financial structure for the optimality of exchange-rate arrangements or the implications of the exchange rate regime for the stability of the financial system.

In this paper I consider these connections, focusing on the implications of international monetary arrangements for the stability of the banking system. I ask questions like the following. Under what conditions can a currency peg jeopardize the stability of the banking system? Can adopting a peg set in motion processes that weaken the banks, themselves the linchpin of the financial system? Once the banking system weakens, how serious an obstacle is the currency peg to lender-of-last-resort intervention?

The timeliness of these questions is clear. Since the 1970s banking crises have been endemic in both developing and advanced industrial economies. Casual observation suggests a connection between exchange rate policy and banking problems. The Argentine banking crisis of 1980 and the Chilean crisis of 1981, two early examples, occurred in countries pursuing exchange-rate-based stabilizations (Sundararajan and Balino, 1991). Finland, Norway and Sweden experienced banking crises in the eighties and nineties while operating ecu or basket pegs (Goldstein and Folkerts-Landau, 1993). The banking systems of the CFA franc zone deteriorated in the 1990s, culminating in 1994 in the first devaluation of the franc-zone currencies in nearly 50 years. Mexico and Argentina, which experienced banking crises in 1994–95, both entered the period committed to policies of exchange-rate pegging (though Mexico was soon compelled to abandon its crawling peg). The banking-cum-financial crises experienced by Thailand, South Korea and Indonesia all occurred in the context of exchange rate regimes characterized by limited flexibility (although Korea and Indonesia both moved toward greater flexibility just before or just when the crisis struck).

While cases such as these would appear to establish a presumption that countries pegging their exchange rates are especially prone to banking crises, counterexamples also exist. The savings-and-loan crisis in the United States and the Japanese banking crisis of the 1990s, for example, both occurred under floating rates. These cases flag the fact that the relationship between exchange rate and banking stability is complex.

Here I employ historical evidence to shed light on the relationship between banking crises and exchange rate arrangements. This makes it possible to do more than simply compare banking crises under pegged and floating rates; in addition, we can compare countries with tightly and loosely regulated financial systems, with and without controls on international capital flows, and with histories of high and low inflation. We can compare countries with and without central banks and with and without deposit insurance. We can compare countries which have recently pegged their currencies as part exchange-rate-based stabilizations against countries, long-lived currency pegs, and countries, in which the behavior of wages, prices and interest rates suggests that the markets vest different degrees of credibility in the government's commitment to stabilizing the nominal rate.

These more detailed comparisons lead one to question any monocausal explanation for banking crises, including one that would emphasize the maintenance of a currency peg. To some extent this follows from the standard textbook wisdom: whether fixed or flexible exchange rates are preferable depends on the source of disturbances. For example, when threats to the stability of the banking system take the form of fluctuations in world interest rates that make it more difficult for banks to fund themselves offshore, there will be a case for exchange rate flexibility to discourage the banks from relying excessively on external sources of finance and to enhance the capacity of the domestic authorities to act as lenders of last resort. Conversely, when the main threats to the stability of the banking system emanate from erratic monetary policies at home, there will be an argument for attempting to peg the exchange rate in order to discipline domestic policymakers and vent shocks via the external sector. From this point of view, it is no surprise that there is no simple correlation between the exchange rate regime and the prevalence of banking crises.

The paper develops these ideas in four steps. Section 1 introduces the issues. Section 2 discusses banking crises under the 19th century gold standard, a prime hunting ground for anyone investigating the connections between exchange rate and financial stability. Section 3 contrasts the interwar period, the heyday of financial instability and an obvious contrast with the classical gold standard. Section 4 then provides a selective survey of recent experience with banking crises and exchange rate policies. The conclusion, Section 5, summar izes the implications.

1. Analytical issues

Any discussion of the connections between exchange rates and banking crises must start by defining variables.

1.1. Definitions

I distinguish two aspects of exchange arrangements: the flexibility of the domestic-currency price of foreign exchange, and the convertibility of the currency. Exchange rate flexibility can range from pegged to freely floating.[1] And whether the exchange rate is pegged or allowed to vary, the domestic currency can be freely convertible into foreign exchange by market participants, or convertibility can be limited by statute.[2] Internal convertibility may be limited or free; that is, the right to convert bank liabilities into gold or foreign exchange at par (or, for that matter, at any price) may or may not be restricted.

Following Bordo (1985, 1986) and Caprio and Klingebeil (1997), I define a banking crisis as a situation where actual or incipient bank runs or failures lead banks to suspend the internal convertibility of their liabilities or force the government to intervene to avert this by replacing a significant share of bank capital.

1.2. The exchange rate and the causes of banking crises

Gavin and Hausmann (1996) provide a catalog of macroeconomic factors that can contribute to banking crises, distinguishing shocks to bank assets from shocks to bank liabilities. Shocks to asset quality include recession (which can cause insolvency among borrowers, adversely affecting their ability to repay), adverse terms of trade movements (which will similarly undermine creditor solvency), erratic fiscal policies (which will affect borrowers' ability to repay by raising interest rates), and bubbles in financial markets (like markets for real estate). Factors affecting bank funding include expected depreciation (which will reduce the demand for domestic-currency deposits), the availability of domestic credit (which will affect the liquidity of the interbank market), and world interest rates (which affect the ability of banks to borrow abroad).

Given the heterogeneity of this list, it is hardly surprising that no single exchange rate arrangement is necessarily best for contending with shocks to the banking system. Standard models suggest that floating exchange rates will be advantageous when disturbances are primarily monetary and primarily foreign, since in this case exchange rate changes can largely insulate the domestic economy. They suggest that pegged rates are preferable when shocks are associated mainly with unstable domestic monetary and financial policies, since pegged rates will then work to discipline erratic policymakers. This textbook logic is directly applicable to the case at hand. If shocks to the banking system are associated with changes in the level of world interest rates, exchange-rate flexibility can help to insulate the economy and the banks. It introduces an element of risk that limits the magnitude of the capital inflows when world interest rates are unusually low and enhances the capacity of the domestic authorities to act as lenders of last resort.

On the other hand, if shocks to the banking system are domestic and associated mainly with erratic monetary policies, there may be a case for pegged rates. A propensity toward erratic monetary policies will be discouraged when the government is committed to a currency peg (and capital markets are open). There is less scope for policy to disturb interest rates when the exchange rate is credibly pegged and capital controls are absent.[3] This is the logic for currency boards and other strategies of binding policymakers' hands by tying the exchange rate to the mast.

This discussion assumes that the currency peg is credible. In countries where the exchange rate is used as a nominal anchor in disinflation programs, this is not necessarily the case. In such cases the transition to price stability can be accompanied by large capital inflows. Residents borrow abroad to finance consumption and imports of durable goods for fear that the stabilization of prices is only temporary. Households borrow from banks, which fund loans by borrowing offshore. Foreign investors are willing to lend insofar as interest rates remain high (in part reflecting the incomplete credibility of the program). The currency peg limits exchange risk for foreign banks and other lenders confident of their ability to repatriate their funds before the stabilization breaks down. Thus, foreign funds flow into the domestic banking system in the early stages of stabilization, leading to a lending boom and deterioration in asset quality. The lending-based consumption boom means a current-account deficit and dependence for balance-of-payments equilibrium on the continued inflow of foreign funds. If that inflow dries up for any reason (including doubts about the permanence of the stabilization), an exchange rate crisis will ensue in which investors withdraw their money from the banks to avoid capital losses on domestic-currency-denominated assets. The exchange rate crisis can lead to a banking crisis, which magnifies the impact of the former (Goldfajn and Valdes, 1995).[4]

The next section, in discussing the response to financial crises, considers the lender of last resort. It is worth anticipating that discussion insofar as last-resort lending can itself affect the incidence of crises. One argument to this effect, due to Diamond and Dybvig (1984), is that the existence of a lender of last resort eliminates the scope for self-fulfilling bank panics. These authors emphasize that even banks solvent in the absence of a run can fail when a run occurs, for the simple reason that bank liabilities are more liquid than bank assets. Bank deposits are demandable, but loans can be liquefied only with time or at a loss. When some depositors queue up at the till, others have an incentive to do likewise to avoid being denied redemption of their claims; if information is asymmetric, a bank run can be self-fulfilling. And banks being linked by the interbank market and the payments and clearing system, bank runs can spread contagiously and degenerate into panics. But if depositors are confident that the central bank or government will provide the liquidity the bank needs to meet the demands of its creditors, depositors will have no incentive to withdraw their funds. The prevalence of self-fulfilling runs and panics may thus depend on the presence or absence of a lender of last resort. Hence, a rigid currency peg, which limits the scope for last-resort lending (under circumstances discussed in Section 1.3 below), can increase the incidence of banking panics.

The counter-argument is that last-resort lending is a source of moral hazard that itself increases the prevalence of banking problems. Insured depositors having little incentive to scrutinize bank balance sheets, depositor discipline is weakened. Banks will bias their portfolios toward risky investments, since the distribution of returns will be truncated downward. Moral hazard can be limited by bailing out depositors but not banks (by being sure that bank management suffers consequences), by making last-resort loans costly (obeying Bagehot's rule), and by extending last-resort loans only to banks that submit to regulatory surveillance. Only then will the presence of a lender of last resort prevents banking panics without at the same time encouraging other equally costly financial problems.

1.3. The exchange rate and the response to banking crises

Under a rigid currency peg, the central bank has no capacity to undertake lender-of-last-resort operations. The textbook currency board law, for example, requires that each unit of domestic currency issued by the central bank or currency board be backed by a unit's worth of foreign exchange. While Bagehot's rule instructs the central bank to support the banking system by lending freely at a penalty rate, statute or constitution prohibits the textbook currency board from issuing the domestic currency unless it possesses foreign exchange. If it does not possess excess reserves, it may be precluded from providing liquidity to the banks.

A similar constraint can bind countries with less rigid currency pegs. There may be one supply of central bank credit to the economy consistent with exchange rate stability but another larger supply needed to prevent the collapse of distressed financial institutions. Injecting credit into the financial system may therefore undermine confidence in the currency peg and provoke a balance-of-payments crisis, deterring a central bank which values the peg from aiding the banks even when it is not legally prevented from doing so.[5]

More realistically, the monetary authority may have some, limited room for maneuver even under a currency board. Reserves in excess of the statutory minimum may enable it to increase the supply of domestic credit without violating its currency board statute. A central bank with only the desire, not the statutory requirement, of pegging the exchange rate may be able to do the same. But while it may be able to increase the supply of domestic credit without exhausting its reserves, it may not be able to simultaneously peg the exchange rate.[6] There are reasons to think that both velocity and output might be affected by banking crises, velocity insofar as ease of transactions is different for currency and deposits, output insofar as bank panics reduce the efficiency of the financial sector. Miller (1996) considers a case where asset market equilibrium (and therefore prices) depend on high-powered money rather than the money stock broadly defined, and shows that there are conditions under which bank runs can lead to reserve inflows and strengthen the exchange rate, but that particular specification does not appear relevant to the general case under discussion here.[7]

In general, only if instruments like sterilized intervention are effective for stabilizing the exchange rate in the face of changes in the money supply is there scope for last-resort lending under pegged rates. The central bank can offset the exchange-rate effects of the additional domestic credit by selling foreign-currency-denominated bonds from its portfolio for their domestic-currency equivalent (where the foreign-currency-denominated bonds are the excess reserves) so long as sterilized intervention works. Unfortunately, the evidence on sterilized intervention is mixed, many observers questioning its effectiveness. If it is ineffectual, there will be no way for the central bank to avoid having to choose between exchange rate stability and financial stability (for a survey of the literature see Dominguez and Frankel, 1993).

If the central bank is precluded from lending, the government may still intervene in its stead. It may have balances with the central bank that it can transfer to the commercial banks. This can be thought of as an increase in the demand for deposits and for money (on the part of the government), which will help to restore bank liabilities to pre-crisis levels. Thus, under the early-20th century gold standard, the U.S. government transferred deposits from U.S. treasury accounts to the commercial banks in periods of financial stringency (see Section 2 below). The Argentine Government helped to recapitalize the banking system in the wake of the 1994–95 tequila crisis (see Section 4).

These options are open not just to governments and central banks with resources in reserve, but also to those that can borrow abroad. A government or central bank obtaining a foreign loan can replenish bank capital without changing the balance-sheet position of the consolidated public sector (aside from increasing its external obligations). Examples of the use of foreign loans to finance last-resort lending under a pegged exchange rate include loans to the Bank of England by the Bank of France and the Russian Government in 1890 (Section 2) and the loan to the Argentine Government by the International Monetary Fund in 1995 (Section 4).

Finally, there is the possibility of invoking an exchange-rate "escape clause" to reconcile the exchange rate commitment with last-resort lending. If the disturbance provoking the crisis is verifiable by third parties and not of the authorities' own making, then the latter may be able to suspend their defense of the currency peg without damaging the credibility of their commitment to its long-term maintenance (Canzoneri, 1985; Obstfeld, 1993). Investors will know that the authorities are suspending defense of the exchange rate only until they sort out the banking system's problems. Although the exchange rate may depreciate temporarily, capital will flow in from abroad in anticipation of the restoration of the previous parity when the additional domestic credit is eventually withdrawn from the financial system. These stabilizing capital flows will limit the currency depreciation associated with the temporary provision of additional domestic credit.

Thus, the escape-clause provision can help to reconcile an exchange rate commitment with last-resort lending. But that escape clause can be invoked without damaging the credibility of the exchange rate commitment only under the limited circumstances detailed in the preceding paragraph. Recourse to the escape clause will not be available to governments and central banks at all times and places.

2. The gold standard

If pegged exchange rates were conducive to banking crises, then one would expect to see a proliferation of the latter in the gold standard years. In fact, crises were not uncommon, although their frequency varied across countries. This points to the importance of institutional arrangements as a determinant of the success with which exchange rate stability and financial stability were reconciled.

2.1. Institutional arrangements

Exchange rates were widely though not uniformly pegged to gold and hence to one another under the classical gold standard.[8] 34 of the 39 countries studied by Eichengreen and Flandreau (1996a) were on some form of gold standard in 1908.[9] In all but three of those 34 countries, banks issuing paper money were obliged to redeem their notes for specie. Where the currency was inconvertible—in Austria, Italy, and pre-1910 Greece—additional issues could produce a premium on specie; that is, the price of notes in terms of currency could vary, introducing an element of exchange rate flexibility. But the exchange rate was pegged within narrow bands vis-a-vis other gold standard countries.[10]

Gold standard pegs, like all pegged rate systems, still offered a limited degree of exchange rate flexibility. Fluctuation bands under the gold standard were made up of two components.[11] One reflected transaction costs, the other "the gold devices." In England these devices included the Bank of England's right to pay out old Sovereigns (whose foreign exchange value was less than that of newly minted, full-bodied coins). The central banks of formerly bimetallic countries like France, Belgium and Italy had the further option of redeeming their notes in depreciated silver. This allowed them to maintain wider fluctuation bands, although some central banks made only limited use of this freedom.[12]

Institutional arrangements also differed along a number of further dimensions.[13] While in some countries domestic financial conditions were tightly linked to the gold and foreign exchange reserves of the banks under rules specified by the gold standard statutes, elsewhere this link was loosened by the practice of holding excess reserves, by provisions that allowed the reserve ratio to slip below the legal minimum under specified conditions, and by the practice of suspending the convertibility of currency into gold in the event of exceptional circumstances.[14] Some countries had central banks in which those reserves were concentrated, others (such as Canada, Australia, New Zealand) not. Some central banks were aware of their lender-of-last-resort responsibilities, while others denied their existence.

Various authors have tabulated the incidence of banking crises under the gold standard. For the United States, Schwartz (1988) identifies bank panics in 14 of the 141 years between 1790 and 1930. Bordo's (1985, 1986) chronology covers six countries (the United States, Britain, France, Germany, Sweden and Canada) for six decades (1870–1933): he identifies 16 banking crises (characterized by bank runs or failures) and four panics (in which runs and failures forced the suspension of payments). In the classical gold standard period, the major crises were 1873, 1884, 1890, 1893 and 1907 in the United States, 1882 and 1889 in France, 1901 in Germany, and 1914 in both the U.S. and Canada.

2.2. *The United States*

The dominance of the United States in lists of 19th century banking crises points to the structure of the country's monetary and financial system as a determinant of crisis incidence. The literature on financial crises in the U.S. can be traced back to the studies conducted for the National Banking Commission (e.g., Sprague, 1910). In accounting for the prevalence of banking and financial problems this literature points to the fragmented structure of the banking system, such as prohibitions on interstate branching, which limited banks' ability to diversify their portfolios and risks.[15] It highlights the magnitude of cyclical and seasonal fluctuations in the demand for money and credit, which led to sharp fluctuations in bank assets and liabilities.[16] It emphasizes the absence of a central bank that limited the ability of the federal government to manage credit conditions.[17]

Given the strength of agrarian and silver-mining interests, the country's commitment to defending its fixed dollar parity was less than complete. Inflationist interests lobbied for the free coinage of silver, making the gold standard a political issue in the 1892 and 1896 presidential elections. Suspending convertibility temporarily threatened to reinforce investors' doubts about the depth of the exchange rate commitment and to destabilize expectations; hence, the escape clause provision of the gold standard was not available until the Gold Standard Act of 1900 removed remaining doubts about the country's commitment to the regime.

With no central bank to operate a discount window or to engage in open market operations, using monetary policy to head off panics would have been awkward in any case. Contemporaries like Kemmerer (1910) complained of the "inelasticity" of the currency—that supply did not accommodate demand, causing interest rates to spike up in the spring and the fall, when planting and crop moving augmented money demand. Banking panics were concentrated in those same seasons, when the banks were least liquid (reflecting the increase in credit demand on the part of their customers). The inelasticity of the currency provided one motivation for the founding of the Federal Reserve System in 1913.

The U.S. Treasury had some capacity to ameliorate these strains. It could borrow abroad to augment the resources that it could marshal in defense of the dollar and the banking system. In 1895 Treasury Secretary J.G. Carlise negotiated a contract with a syndicate of international bankers, led by the Morgan and Rothschild houses in London, to borrow some $60 million of gold from foreign countries. The Belmont-Morgan Syndicate, as this consortium was known, also agreed to protect the Treasury against gold withdrawals and continued doing so for nearly a year and a half (Garber and Grilli, 1986; Eichengreen, 1992).

In addition, in the first decade of the 20th century, Treasury Secretary Shaw restored the earlier practice of running down the Treasury's cash balance when the money market tightened. Each autumn he transferred government deposits from subtreasuries to national banks designated as depositories for public funds and augmented the public's currency holdings by purchasing government bonds or prepaying interest due. Most experts believe, however, that Treasury operations made only a modest contribution to relieving financial strains (see e.g., Timberlake, 1963, 1978).

More important were the banks' self-help measures. The major urban banks had established clearinghouses for netting claims on one another; these devel oped into mechanisms for exchanging information and dealing with difficulties that might prevent particular banks from making good on their debts. In the event of a serious crisis, the members of the clearinghouse might suspend the convertibility of their deposits into gold and currency. The suspension of the convertibility of deposits into currency relieved distressed banks of the need to obtain liquidity from other banks to meet the demands of their depositors, which in turn prevented the crisis from spreading through the financial system. During the period of suspension, banks might make payments with specially issued clearinghouse certificates (which traded at a discount relative to currency and gold).[18] These certificates were issued in every major financial crisis from 1857 through 1914. A bank obtained certificates from the clearinghouse upon submitting acceptable (if illiquid) collateral and the other members stood ready to accept them in payment of intraclearing-house debts. Thus, under clearing house cooperation, strong banks effectively provided liquidity to their weaker counterparts.[19]

Moreover, because the suspension of internal convertibility was regarded as temporary, it attracted international capital flows. Foreign investors would buy domestic bank deposits at a discount relative to currency in anticipation of reaping capital gains once internal convertibility was restored (Miller, 1996).

The U.S. under the gold standard thus provides an example of an inflexible currency peg, which provided the authorities little scope for last-resort lending. Seasonal and cyclical shifts in the demand for money repeatedly strained the banking system. The absence of a central bank constrained the management of money and credit. Limited credibility precluded recourse to temporary suspensions of the dollar parity. While Treasury operations, foreign loans and clearing house cooperation prevented financial difficulties from precipitating a complete breakdown of the banking system, as in the 1930s, they did not preclude repeated crises.

2.3. Great Britain

The Bank of England and British Government, having effectively been on the gold standard since 1717, enjoyed a level of credibility matched in few other countries. They therefore found it straightforward to invoke the escape clause provision of the gold standard in times of crisis. In 1847, 1857 and 1866 they suspended the statute linking the Bank of England's note issue to the gold reserve held by the Issue Department.[20] Clearing banks which saw asset quality deteriorate could discount at the Bank of England, which financed these operations using excess gold reserves in the Banking Department. If the Banking Department ran dry, a Treasury letter relieved the Bank of England of the need to back each additional currency note with gold, enabling it to continue discounting. Because there was no question that the relevant provision of the 1844 Bank Act would be restored as soon as the crisis passed, capital flowed in stabilizing directions, and the exchange rate hardly weakened.[21]

Recourse to a Treasury letter would be taken only under exceptional circumstances. At other times the Bank of England could head off problems by altering its discount rate. Raising the discount rate attracted gold from abroad, augmenting the reserves of the Banking Department. Lowering the rate encouraged the clearing banks to rediscount and raise their liquidity. In times of crisis the Bank discounted freely at a penalty rate, combining the two procedures. Thus, while financial crises were anything but absent from Britain in the gold standard years, the presence of a central bank that could adjust its discount rate to moderate seasonal and cyclical strains meant that such crises were relatively few and far between.[22]

The Bank of England did not always respond in the manner of a modern central bank. It was criticized in the 1866 crisis for refusing to meet the demand for discounts and for failing to grant advances against government securities.[23] Still a profit-oriented, officially private entity, it could succumb to the temptation to sell securities in periods of stringency to raise cash for itself.

The "up side" of the Bank of England's ambiguous status was that it could cooperate with other private banks in arranging lifeboat operations. In 1890, for example, not only did the Bank borrow abroad to replenish its reserves, enabling it to freely discount Baring's bills, but it cooperated with Rothschilds and other merchant banks to support the price of Baring's securities. The members of the syndicate promised to make good any loss sustained by the Bank in the course of liquidating Baring's position (establishing a guarantee fund) in return for the power to effectively assume control of Barings' affairs. Thus, the fact that it was at the same time a central and private bank allowed the British financial system to be supported both by countercyclical central bank operations, as in other Continental European countries, and by intrabank cooperation, as in the United States.

The Bank of England's ability to shape financial conditions was limited by the fact that it commanded a shrinking share of transactions on the London market over the course of the 19th century. The Bank's reserve was a mere 3% of the British money supply from the 1860s and fell to less than 2% at times of crisis. In the wake of the 1866 crisis the Bank therefore sought to augment its reserve; it made similar efforts in the aftermath of the 1890 crisis. While additional reserves meant additional room for maneuver, the reserve constraint might still bind, prompting the Bank to solicit foreign assistance. Faced with the Baring Crisis, Rothschilds negotiated on the Bank's behalf a L3 million gold loan from the Bank of France against Treasury bills and William Lidderdale of the Bank of England obtained half that sum from Russia to ensure that the gold reserve ratio would not be violated (Pressnell, 1968). In 1906 and 1907, again faced with financial stringency, the Bank once more obtained foreign assistance from the Bank of France and, this time, from the German Reichsbank. In 1909 and 1910 the Bank of France again discounted English bills, making gold available to London.

Thus, the British case is one where the exchange-rate commitment and management of the domestic financial system were relatively well reconciled. The credibility of the country's commitment to the gold standard facilitated use of

Treasury letters and bills of indemnity, relieving the Bank of the consequences of violating provisions of the 1844 Act and allowing the exchange-rate escape clause to be invoked and domestic financial problems to be addressed. The existence of a central bank that accumulated excess reserves and actively managed domestic credit conditions minimized crises in the final third of the 19th century. Repeated recourse to foreign assistance allowed the central bank to adjust policies in ways that might otherwise have been impossible owing to the inelasticity of reserves.

3. The interwar gold standard

During World War I these institutional arrangements were placed in abeyance. The gold standard as restored in the 1920s was a very different creature.

3.1. Institutional arrangements

Friedman and Schwartz (1963, p. 346) note that "[t]he more extensive use of deposits [was] widely regarded during the twenties as a sign of the great progress and refinement of the American financial structure..." Where in 1907 the American public had held $6 of deposits for every $1 in currency, by March 1931 the deposit/currency ratio had risen to more than 10. The same trend was evident in other countries. This increased the excess reserves that governments and central banks had to hold in order to accommodate panic-induced shifts from deposits to currency. Unfortunately, there was no commensurate rise in the reserve backing of the currency (and, by implication, in the authorities' capacity to issue additional gold-backed currency if investors shifted out of deposits).[24] To the contrary, the excess of gold reserves over the statutory minimum fell from $5.0 billion to $3.6 billion between 1913 and 1927.[25] While the scope for a shift from deposits to currency was now greater, central banks' capacity to accommodate it was less.

The standard remedy, according to those concerned to create an elastic currency, was to establish central banks where they did not exist. The United States had founded one, the Federal Reserve System, in 1913. To prevent this new institution from issuing credit too liberally, its statutes required the Federal Reserve to back monetary liabilities not collateralized with gold (or silver dollars, silver certificates and greenbacks) with "eligible" paper, namely commercial, agricultural and industrial securities and bankers acceptances. These and not government bonds were the only securities that could be discounted or purchased in open market operations when the Fed lacked "free gold" above that required by statute. How tightly the free-gold constraint bound prior to its abolition 1932 (under the provisions of the first Glass-Steagall Act) is a disputed issue. The fact that legislators saw it as important to eliminate this provision in the depths of the slump suggests that eligible securities might grow scarce when economic activity turned down, making it difficult for the Fed to discount such securities in order to support the financial system.

The lack of an adequate investment portfolio initially prevented the Federal Reserve from employing open market operations, while an overhang of short-term government debt discouraged it from actively manipulating the discount rate until the debt had been funded in 1920. But by the mid-twenties the Fed had emerged as a leading player in international financial markets. Whether this dominant player had a clear conception of its lender-of-last-resort responsibilities is another question. Confusion about its priorities may have been a consequence of institutional inexperience.[26] But it is also true that different factions within the Federal Reserve System had different views of the causes and consequences of bank failures and of the desirability of last-resort lending; some viewed commercial and financial failures as a healthy corrective which purged financial excesses from the economy and were therefore disinclined to engage in lender-of-last-resort operations.[27]

An indirect effect of the creation of a U.S. central bank was the decline of self-help by American financial institutions. The restriction of payments, emission of clearing house certificates, and assistance for weak banks by their stronger clearing house partners that had been commonplace before 1913 were not repeated between the wars. Friedman and Schwartz (1963, pp. 311–312) attribute the decline of lifeboat operations to the advent of the Fed. Establishing a central bank created a presumption that concerted action by commercial banks was no longer necessary. The Fed's existence weakened the incentive for stronger banks to aid their weaker counterparts, since they could now replenish their liquidity through alternative channels—namely, at the Fed's discount window—and hence were not in the same boat as the weaker banks.

Similar trends were evident elsewhere, for example in Western Europe. The expectation that central banks would intervene to stabilize the clearing system meant that strong banks no longer saw it necessary to support their weaker counterparts in order to protect themselves. In some cases the authorities sought to engineer shotgun marriages between banks as a substitute for lifeboat operations: the merger of the Austrian Kreditanstalt with the Bodenkreditanstalt is one example; the Austrian government imposed this merger on the reluctant chairman of the Kreditanstalt to protect the National Bank from losses on the rediscounts it had previously extended the now insolvent smaller bank.[28]

Governments elsewhere—in Latin America and Eastern Europe—established central banks along similar lines, often following the model of the United States.[29] But where one justification for founding the Fed had been to establish an elastic currency, many of these other central banks created in its image operated under gold-standard statutes which rigidly linked their note issues to their international reserves. This reflected the desire to create a central bank as a device for insulating monetary policy from political pressures (Simmons, 1994). The experience with floating exchange rates in the early 'twenties reinforced the belief that the alternative to autonomous central banking was monetary chaos, exchange-rate volatility and, ultimately, hyperinflation. Even countries like France, which had long possessed central banks, reformed their monetary statutes to limit the ability of those entities to undertake discretionary open market operations. Hence, the restored gold standard was characterized by an element of rigidity not shared by its prewar predecessor.[30]

Nor was the gold standard escape clause invoked as readily as before World War I. The credibility of the authorities' commitment to the maintenance of convertibility was now tempered by political and economic developments that shattered the constellation of political power upon which the prewar policy regime had been based.[31] Adopting the corporatist strategy for securing labor peace, wartime governments encouraged the spread of unionism. Issues that had previously remained outside the political sphere, such as the determination of wages and employment, became politicized. Extension of the franchise and the growth of political parties dominated by the working classes intensified the pressure to adapt policy toward employment targets. When employment and balance-of-payments goals clashed, it was no longer clear which would dominate. Doubt was cast over the credibility of the commitment to gold. No longer did capital necessarily flow in stabilizing directions; now it might do the opposite, intensifying the pressure on countries experiencing a loss of reserves.[32]

This rendered governments and central banks reluctant to invoke the exchange-rate escape clause. With the credibility of their commitment to convertibility in doubt, a temporary suspension could permanently damage their reputation for defending the exchange rate peg. By allowing the rate to depreciate they might be thought to be manipulating it under cover of their contingent rule, announcing the existence of exceptional circumstances when these did not exist or producing those circumstances themselves. Reassurances that the suspension was temporary might be dismissed, and capital would no longer flow in to cushion the currency's fall. Governments and central banks consequently hesitated to invoke the escape-clause provision of the gold standard for fear of damaging their reputations.[33]

The difficulty of resorting to temporary suspensions placed a premium on foreign assistance to replenish reserves. Unfortunately, the requisite level of cooperation was not forthcoming. Three obstacles blocked the way: domestic political constraints, international political disputes, and incompatible conceptual frameworks. Special interest groups with the most to lose were able to stave off adjustments in economic policy that would have facilitated international cooperation. Disputes over war debts and reparations contaminated efforts to redesign and cooperatively manage the gold standard system. Incompatible conceptual frameworks prevented policymakers from reaching a common understanding of their economic problem, let alone agreeing on a solution.

3.2. The exchange rate and the interwar financial crisis

The global expansion of the second half of the 1920s was driven by capital flows from the principal financial centers, notably New York, to countries in earlier stages of economic development and to those where postwar reconstruction and adjustment were still underway. Latin America and East-Central Europe, two leading destinations of U.S. funds, were representative of these two groups of countries. Although much of the literature on foreign lending in the 1920s (e.g., Lewis, 1938) focuses on bond and stock markets, considerable quantities of foreign capital in fact flowed through the banks. Banks in East-Central Europe and Latin America borrowed offshore, soliciting foreign deposits and floating bonds under their own names. In the depths of the interwar depression German banks (other than the Reichsbank) had nearly $1 billion of short-term liabilities to foreigners, nearly half of all German short-term debt. The banks accounted for a third of all short-term debts in Hungary, a quarter in Bulgaria, half in Romania, and four-fifths in Poland (League of Nations, 1933, p. 269). Given the fractional-reserve structure of these banking systems, the foreign funds that flowed through these institutions had a magnified impact on economic activity.

All the while, the gold standard's pegged exchange rates worked as a powerful magnet for foreign funds. As before the war, the gold standard was regarded as a "good housekeeping seal of approval" for countries seeking to borrow abroad (Bordo and Rockoff, 1996). It signaled that they had returned to sound and stable policies. It suggested that exchange risk was minimal. In some cases, like Germany in the aftermath of the war, foreign funds anticipated the return to gold (Holtfrerich, 1986), but in most they waited on stabilization and the resumption of gold convertibility.

This dependence on foreign funds proved problematic when U.S. lending fell off in the summer of 1928 and global economic activity declined. Not only did the banks experience a funding shock (foreign markets displaying a sudden reluctance to lend), but also they were simultaneously exposed to a shock to asset quality (as farm loans fell into delinquency and industrial concerns began failing). Declining agricultural commodity prices led to farm mortgage delinquencies and weakened the condition of rural banks. The rise in U.S. interest rates made it increasingly difficult for banks outside the United States to borrow offshore and fund their loans. And the collapse of prices and production in the Depression led to a dramatic deterioration in asset quality and performance.

Banking crises were widespread: by Grossman's (1994) count, they occurred in Austria, Belgium, Estonia, France, Germany, Hungary, Italy, Latvia, Norway, Poland, Romania, Switzerland, Yugoslavia and the United States.[34] Yet they were not universal: Bulgaria, Canada, Czechoslovakia, Denmark, Finland, Greece, Lithuania, Portugal, Spain, Sweden and the UK proved immune. There is no shortage of explanations for the contrast: Grossman cites bank branching, size and concentration, the condition of the macroeconomy, and the prevalence of lender-of-last-resort intervention. But the single most important variable in his econometric tests of crisis incidence is the exchange rate. Countries, which depreciated their currencies starting in 1931, had a significantly lower probability of experiencing banking crises than those that remained on gold. Revealingly, all of the countries listed in the second sentence of this paragraph as escaping banking crises abandoned the gold standard at a relatively early date.

Grossman suggests several reasons why the maintenance of a currency peg adversely impacted the banking system. Most countries imported the destabilizing macroeconomic impulse from abroad; and countries with pegged exchange rates quite logically enjoyed less insulation from this shock.[35] Such countries had less leeway for responding with expansionary monetary and fiscal policies. And their central banks had less capacity to engage in last-resort lending.

As explained above, the combination of imperfect credibility, which discouraged resort to the exchange-rate escape clause, and obstacles to international cooperation rendered the scope for central bank action especially limited. The German case illustrates the point.[36] While the German Bank Law authorized the General Council of the Reichsbank to reduce the cover ratio to less than the 40% minimum required by statute under exceptional circumstances, this measure was not invoked for fear of damaging confidence in Germany's commitment to gold. The government's budgetary problem was conspicuous, and the association of budget deficits with inflation had been burned into investors' consciousness by the hyperinflation ten years before. The Social Democrats opposed all cuts in unemployment benefits; the military objected to cuts in defense spending; agriculture demanded subsidies to offset the collapse of farm prices; and the Reich Association of German Industry pressed for cuts in corporate taxes.

Under such circumstances, anything less than strict adherence to the gold standard encouraged the fear that deficits would reignite inflation. The markets had no confidence that an abridgement of Germany's gold standard would be temporary. The psychological effect of breaching the 40% cover requirement, Hans Luther, Reichsbank President warned, might be "absolutely fearful." Hans Schaeffer, Reich State Secretary, warned that breaching the 40% limit could "precipitate a massive flight from the mark." German officials found it difficult to argue that the disturbance to the financial system was not of their own making (as would have been necessary to avoid damaging their credibility). Among Bruning's priorities were a reparation settlement, and the weaker Germany's payments position, the stronger the case for concessions by the Allies. Bruning was therefore accused of pursuing policies that aggravated Germany's payments problem.

For all these reasons, the Reichsbank's ability to act as lender of last resort was severely constrained. The 1931 financial crisis did not take long to reveal this fact. When the failure of the Austrian Credit-Anstalt spilled over to the German banking system, the Reichsbank responded initially by injecting liquidity. But the faster funds were poured into the banking system, the faster they leaked back out. Providing liquidity signaled that the authorities attached as much weight to propping up the banking system as to defending the gold standard.

Realizing that convertibility might be compromised and that with devaluation they would incur capital losses on domestic assets, investors rushed to get their money out of the country. Reserves were depleted, forcing the authorities to drain liquidity from the banking system in order to defend the exchange rate. By the end of the third week of June, the Reichsbank was forced to ration credit. Almost immediately a full-fledged banking panic ensued.

A couple of weeks passed before the government finally closed the banks, during which it sought foreign support. Luther solicited a $100 million loan from the Bank of England, the Federal Reserve and the Bank for International Settlements. Although this money was made available in a matter of days, no further credits were granted. Montagu Norman of the Bank of England insisted that this was impossible so long as there remained uncertainty about Germany's willingness to pay reparations. Clement Moret of the Bank of France demanded as a condition for assistance that the German government renounce Bruning's request to reopen reparation negotiations. George Harrison of the Federal Reserve Bank of New York made his support for further credits contingent on an extensive list of financial and economic conditions. Here, then, was a clear case where the deterioration of the international political climate prevented central bank cooperation and heightened the conflict between exchange rate stability and financial stability.

While other national cases were less dramatic, the same underlying forces were at work. The gold standard heightened the banking system's exposure to the foreign shock. Not only did it constrain lender-of-last-resort intervention, but also it rendered it counterproductive insofar as the provision of liquidity excited devaluation expectations. Countries prepared to abandon the currency peg were better able to stabilize economic activity and support their banking systems.[37] It is noteworthy that no major banking crises occurred after countries left the gold standard.[38]

4. The 1980s and 1990s

The end of World War II inaugurated four decades of tranquility in the global banking system.[39] White (1992) identifies several factors contributing to this stability.[40] Economies were growing buoyantly prior to the first the OPEC oil-price shock. The fact that a stable world price level was maintained through the 1960s, as a corollary of the operation of the Bretton Woods System, enhanced the transparency of loan and collateral evaluation (Schwartz, 1988). With prices and interest rates relatively stable, the book and market values of bank assets and liabilities never moved far out of line. Competition from nonbank intermediaries developed only slowly, reflecting the relative stability of financial service technologies. Finally, banks were protected from excessive competition by a heavy layer of regulation. Thus, banking stability was sustained by a combination of favorable microeconomic and macroeconomic circumstances.[41]

4.1. *Recent experience*[42]

All this changed in the 1970s. Inflation increased the difficulty of assessing credit quality, while the two OPEC oil shocks undermined borrowers' ability to repay. Rising interest rates accentuated adverse selection, as safer borrowers dropped out of the market. Petro-dollar recycling encouraged money-center banks to seek out higher yielding investments abroad. Much of this money was channeled through developing-country banks who acted as agents for their national governments or as independent borrowers. This same ample supply of funds weakened the incentive for the money-center banks to carefully scrutinize the quality of the customers approaching them for loans.

The Volcker disinflation brought this lending boom to a halt. Interest rates rose, and U.S. economic growth slowed. The large and growing budget deficits of the first Reagan Administration placed additional upward pressure on interest rates. It is no coincidence that the Savings & Loan (S&L) crisis followed on the heels of these events. Eighty per cent of the industry's assets were fixed rate mortgages, the return on which no longer matched the cost of attracting funds (BIS, 1989, p. 94).[43] The decline in agricultural land prices (by as much as 30%) in the succeeding five years, itself a function of tighter credit conditions, then compounded the plight of S&Ls in the American West.[44] Although restrictions on the geographical diversification of S&L investments had been phased out in the 1960s, tradition and limited management competence left their investment portfolios regionally concentrated, allowing regional economic cycles to disproportionately affect bank balance sheets.

But while these financial difficulties were associated with macroeconomic factors, they were not associated with pegged exchange rates. The exchange rate was not a precipitating factor in the S&L crisis, nor was it a constraint on lender-of-last-resort intervention. Throughout the 1980s the dollar fluctuated (in the first-half of the decade, in the virtual absence of intervention by the U.S. authorities).[45] Nor did concern for the exchange rate prevent the government and the Fed from launching the most expensive bank bailout in history in the second-half of the 1980s. Owing largely to this response, the macroeconomic disturbances of the late seventies and early eighties did not culminate in a full-scale financial meltdown like that of the Great Depression.

The developing countries were on the other end of the lending boom of the 1970s. The debt crisis in which that boom culminated is too well known to be recounted here. What are relevant for present purposes are the role of the exchange rate and the consequences for the banks. The typical sequence of events was financial liberalization followed by exchange-rate-based stabilization and large-scale foreign borrowing. In many cases the maintenance of pegged rates predictably amplified the ebb and flow of foreign funds. Argentina, for example, used a crawling peg as a stabilization tool from late 1978 through early 1981. With exchange risk minimized, residents were able to borrow offshore: there was a boom in real estate markets, apartment prices in

Buenos Aires rising by 50% between 1977 and 1980. Inevitably, however, the exchange-rate peg together with inertial inflation resulted in overvaluation, and the competitive difficulties of Argentine exporters set the stage for recession. When the Argentine economy turned down in early 1980, a banking crisis erupted almost immediately. As capital inflows fell off, real lending rates turned strongly positive, leaving borrowers financially strapped and banks saddled with an overhang of nonperforming loans. By the end of 1982, 43 financial institutions, including the country's largest commercial bank, had been liquidated.

Chile in 1981 is another case where capital-account liberalization and exchange-rate-based stabilization unleashed a surge of capital inflows. In the second half of the 'seventies the banks were freed to borrow abroad in dollars (but not to assume exchange risk). Pegging the exchange rate encouraged the money-center banks to lend. Capital inflows fueled a consumption boom (partially in the form of consumer durable goods purchased by households skeptical of the durability of liberalization and stabilization), until the banking crisis in neighboring Argentina put sudden upward pressure on interest rates. The financial position of borrowers had already been undermined by a long period of overvaluation. As those borrowers experienced growing distress, the position of the banks was undermined. Eleven Chilean financial institutions accounting for 15% of total loans had to be liquidated in 1981–82. Clearly, macroeconomic factors (and exchange rate policy in particular) aggravated the difficulties of the Chilean banking system, although Edwards (1995) convincingly argues that lax regulation and supervision also played a role by allowing the banks to succumb to adverse incentives.[46]

While banking problems in Argentina and Chile preceded the developing-country debt crisis, the opposite was true in Colombia, Mexico, Peru and Uruguay. There, banking crises were precipitated by the curtailment of foreign financing in 1982. In each case the capital account had been liberalized and the exchange rate stabilized, encouraging inflows of foreign funds. The rise in the cost of borrowing and decline in credit availability consequent on the debt crisis in turn provoked loan defaults and bank insolvency. In most cases, the government responded to its deteriorating financial position by pressuring the central bank to print money. The resulting inflation further depressed the ratio of deposits to national income, which in turn undermined the banks' ability to fund loans and withstand runs.[47]

The sequence typical of Latin America—capital-account-cum-financial liberalization, followed by exchange rate pegging, macroeconomic disturbance, and banking crisis—was also evident in muted form in Northern Europe. For the Nordic countries the eighties were a decade of deregulation and relaxation of restrictions on cross-border financial transactions.[48] Encouraged by stimulative monetary and fiscal policies, the banks, responded by lending freely, fueling a consumption boom and soaring real estate and equity prices.[49] When central banks and governments finally retrenched to counter the inflationary consequences, bank borrowers and the banks themselves ran into the wall.

The Norwegian crisis, starting in 1986–87, was precipitated by a sharp decline in the price of oil (akin to that experienced by the U.S. Southwest on the eve of the S&L crisis), which raised the rate of corporate bankruptcy by nearly half between 1986 and 1989. A recession followed the drop in oil prices and led to sharp falls in commercial property prices (in 1987) and housing prices (in 1988). The Finnish crisis of 1990–91 was similarly precipitated by monetary tightening (in 1989) and by the collapse of trade with the Soviet Union.[50] Sweden's crisis, which showed up in that country's finance companies in 1990–91, was affected by many of the same factors as in neighboring Finland and in addition by a tax reform introduced in the late 1980s which limited the tax deductibility of interest payments and put a damper on the housing market.[51]

Having entered the 1980s poorly capitalized, Nordic banks had little cushion against loan losses; encouraged by lax supervision, they responded to problems with their portfolios by doubling up their bets.[52] In doing so they only dug themselves a deeper hole. Thus, in the Nordic countries, as in Japan, the banks' substantial stakes in the equity and real estate markets were a source of serious problems when asset prices collapsed.

Exchange-rate pegging was the final ingredient in this combustible mix. Norway, Finland and Sweden all pegged their currencies from 1983. Each operated a trade- (in the case of Norway, payments-) weighted peg until the early nineties, when they shifted to ecu pegs. Capital inflows were discouraged by limited exchange risk, and all three countries imported the higher level of European interest rates consequent upon German unification.[53] In Finland, banking and macroeconomic problems forced the government to devalue in 1991 and then abandon the peg in 1992. The devaluation of the markka undermined the financial position of Finnish corporations, which had taken out foreign currency loans but had few foreign currency earnings, in turn aggravating the problems of the banks. In Sweden, there were widespread doubts about the durability of the exchange rate peg; as early as 1990 devaluation expectations led to a decline in deposits amounting to 5% of GDP (Gavin and Hausmann, 1996). Desperate attempts to defend the exchange rate peg in the autumn of 1992, which forced the central bank to raise lending rates to as much as 500%, then increased the cost of funding loans relative to the return on assets (Wihlborg et al., 1994). In neither Finland nor Sweden were major banks allowed to fail; in both cases the government opted rather to abandon the currency peg, freeing it to run budget deficits and recapitalize the banks. Still, it can be argued that following a more flexible exchange rate policy previously would have averted some of the subsequent problems. Had the markka been allowed to float more freely, Finnish corporations without foreign-currency earnings would not have taken out unhedged foreign-currency loans to the same extent. Had the Swedish krona not been pegged so rigidly, it would not have been necessary to subject the country's banks to 500% interest rates. Given the circumstances of the early nineties—German unification, a weak dollar, and uncertainty about the prospects for European monetary unification—a unilateral currency peg meant an unstable macroeconomic environment and, potentially, problems for the banks.

A summary evaluation would thus be that the Nordic banking crises were compounded but not caused by exchange-rate policy. Their seeds were lax supervision and overly accommodating monetary and fiscal policies, and the crisis was precipitated by macroeconomic shocks emanating from Germany and the Soviet Union. While the Swedish and Finnish authorities ultimately abandoned their currency pegs in order to prop up their banking systems, their initial efforts to defend those currency pegs worked to magnify the effects of those external shocks.[54]

The latest round of banking problems has been in emerging markets.[55] In Mexico, the confidence crisis associated with the December 1994 devaluation of the peso ratcheted up interest rates to the high double digits; firms relying on short-term bank credit and with dollar-denominated loans outstanding experienced severe distress, undermining the position of the banks. Bank balance sheets were already weak, reflecting the familiar combination of deregulation and lax supervision (Desmet and Mann, 1996); the need to recapitalize the banking system was a major factor in the Mexican government's decision not to repeg the exchange rate in early 1995. The larger banks (led by Banamex and Bancomer) were better able to cope with the shock by virtue of their relatively ample reserves. To contain the spread of problems, the Mexican government purchased subordinated debt from the banks in order to raise their capitalization; in addition it provided dollar loans to banks with dollar-denominated liabilities on relatively liberal terms. Finally, it liberalized rules governing the acquisition of Mexican banks by foreign financial institutions and encouraged large banks to absorb their smaller, weaker counterparts (although the large banks have been understandably reluctant to ascend the alter). This has forced the Zedillo Government to agree to buy bonds issued by troubled banks in an effort to recapitalize them without resorting to direct intervention.[56]

Without question, macroeconomic policy—notably the overvaluation associated with the deadly combination of inflation and exchange-rate pegging—contributed to both Mexico's banking problems (by undermining the competitiveness of firms in the traded-goods sector and adding to nonperforming loans) and its balance-of-payments problems (again through deteriorating competitiveness but also by rendering the central bank reluctant to defend the currency by raising interest rates if that meant further worsening the condition of the banks). But the now-familiar combination of financial deregulation and lax supervision set the stage: the financial condition of many banks was already weak as early as 1992, prior to the recent episode of real appreciation.

Argentina's banks found themselves in the same position when they felt the reverberations of the Mexican crisis; in addition, banks in Buenos Aires held large stocks of Brady bonds, whose prices collapsed with Mexico's difficulties. Sensing that the exchange rate might have to be devalued, deposit withdrawals, amounting to some $2 billion in two weeks, began in early 1995. Overnight rates reached 30% in Buenos Aires in mid-January.[57] By the end of March, deposits in Argentine banks had fallen by $7.5 billion (or 17%), the most serious losses being suffered by smaller provincial and cooperative banks.

The convertibility law requiring the central bank to peg the exchange rate severely limited its ability to undertake lender-of-last-resort operations. The monetary authorities could reduce the banks' reserve requirements (from 33 to 30%) to make liquidity available for meeting depositor demands and use their excess reserves to extend some $2 billion extraordinary liquidity assistance above the limits of bank capital (Caprio, 1997). They authorized banks with excess reserves to loan these to their weaker counterparts and persuaded the top five banks to provide some $250 million. The government for its part loaned to the banks out of its own financial reserves, but the $1 billion allocated for this purpose was exhausted by the end of April.[58] Only a major package of international assistance from the IMF, IBRD and IDB along with President Menem's reelection in mid-May 1995 quieted fears about the future of the convertibility law and the stability of the banks, leading a third of the deposits which had flowed out of Argentina's banks following the Mexican crisis to flow back in. Public funds were then used to finance the closure or privatization of the main provincial banks.

This episode has been taken as confirming that developing countries vulnerable to sudden shifts in capital flows cannot afford to peg their currencies (e.g., Sachs, 1995). If the confidence of investors is disturbed, such countries can find themselves threatened by banking and balance-of-payments crises which will feed on one another in a vicious circle. Their central banks will have few options for responding to these crises. The counter-argument is that the problem in Mexico was not the exchange rate per se but the failure of the authorities to appropriately harmonize monetary and fiscal policies with the exchange rate peg. And, the critics continue, the case of Argentina shows that a government can undertake lender-of-last-resort operations even when maintaining a rigid currency peg.

Both objections are too simple. For Mexico it is now widely agreed that monetary and fiscal policies were only a minor part of the problem. Also important were a currency peg that offered one-way bets to speculators and large amounts of short-term, foreign-currency-denominated debt that offered scope for a debt run (Sachs et al., 1996). Argentina for its part was able to support both its exchange rate peg and its banking system only because it received some $8 billion of foreign financial assistance, mainly from the IMF, part of which was used to recapitalize the banks and fund a deposit insurance scheme. Thus, while Argentine experience confirms that a currency peg can be consistent with lender-of-last-resort intervention, it underscores the need for international cooperation.[59]

In the wake of its 1995 crisis, the Argentine government has taken steps to secure lines of credit with foreign banks upon which it will be able to draw in the event that another crisis again compels it to inject liquidity into the banking system. In addition, it has imposed high reserve and capital requirements which limit the banks' ratios of liquid liabilities to liquid assets and therefore the resources that must be raised in the event of a run. High reserve requirements can also be lowered in the event of stringency, freeing up resources to meet depositors' demands. Thus, recent experience, like that of a hundred years ago, suggests that a rigid exchange rate peg and last-resort lending can be rendered compatible, but only in the presence of institutional arrangements specifically tailored to reconcile them.

4.2. The Asian crisis

These same points are driven home by Asia's experience in 1997–98. The critical ingredients of that crisis were the familiar combination of lax supervision and regulation, implicit guarantees for bank creditors, and pegged exchange rates. Investors had again been encouraged to establish and maintain positions in emerging markets by the low level of interest rates in leading money centers. They funded themselves in mature markets and invested in Asia, the ample credit of which they made use reflecting the low level of interest rates in Japan and the United States.

Much of this was bank-to-bank lending. Asian banks with implicit guarantees had an incentive to fund themselves abroad and invest in high-yielding securities. Hence, the stories of Korean banks obtaining funds from Japanese banks and investing in Indonesian corporate paper, Russian GKOs, and Brazilian Brady bonds. And Asian governments, having long regarded their financial systems as central to their national economic development strategies, were loath to let their banks fail. Aware of the tendency for governments in this position to guarantee the liabilities of distressed domestic financial institutions, international investors were not deterred from lending by the riskiness of the banks' assets.[60]

The exchange rate peg is critical to this story, comprising as it did a key link in the chain of implicit guarantees. The government purported to guarantee that the exchange rate would not be devalued, relieving foreign investors of all exchange risk. It purported to guarantee all bank deposits, relieving foreigners lending short to the financial system of all credit risk. These distortions created a one-way bet encouraging excessive capital inflows.

But, as in earlier episodes, the situation was not sustainable. The carry trade was susceptible to being disrupted by a modest move toward more restrictive global credit conditions. In the spring of 1997 this took the form of interest rate increases in the United Kingdom and Germany. Japanese long rates moved up from 2 to 2.5% when the outlook for the Japanese economy appeared to brighten, and short rates firmed with talk that the Bank of Japan might raise rates by the end of the year.[61] Together with the appreciation of the dollar against the yen, which undermined the competitiveness of Asian countries that placed heavy weights on the dollar in their basket pegs, a slowdown in the global electronics industry, and mounting problems in some of the recipient countries, most notably Thailand, these developments curtailed the carry trade. The ability of the Thai government to honor its exchange rate commitment was cast into doubt. International banks and other investors closed out their long positions in Asian fixed-income securities and began shorting the baht as Thailand's vulnerability became apparent. What had previously been an excessive capital inflow became an unmanageable capital outflow.

The Mexican crisis had already led some far-sighted observers to suggest that the dominant source of financial crises in emerging markets was likely to be weak banking systems and weak bank supervision.[62] In Thailand, the failure of the finance companies appears to have been the trigger that set off the run on the currency. In other Asian countries, the timing of events was generally the reverse—currency depreciation undermined the balance-sheet positions of banks and bank customers with unhedged foreign exposures, helping to precipitate a run on the banking system, which then further weakened the position of the banks—but the weakness of financial systems and financial supervision was again key.

What lessons can be drawn from this most recent episode? While the advocates of pegged exchange rates have not fallen silent—some of those alarmed by the instability of currencies in Asia continue to plump for currency boards and common basket pegs, and a few have even suggested that Asia may eventually be driven to emulate Europe in attempting to banish exchange rate instability from the region by establishing a common currency—the dominant conclusion would nonetheless appear that the Asian crisis is simply more evidence of the irresistible pressures for greater exchange rate flexibility as a way of reconciling monetary stability with banking stability. Governments, in other words, need to introduce greater currency flexibility earlier rather than later as a way of encouraging banks and others to hedge their foreign exposure and of introducing an element of risk that will work to moderate excessive capital flows.

The other lesson drawn is the importance of stricter prudential supervision and regulation of banking systems in both lending and borrowing countries (Savona and Maccario, 1998).[63] Unfortunately, this is easier said than done. Political pressure for regulatory forbearance is intense. The specialized knowledge required to assess bank balance sheets is in short supply, nowhere more so in emerging markets. Efforts to loosen this bottleneck through technical assistance by the World Bank and banking-system surveillance by the IMF run up against personnel and expertise constraints of their own. The problem grows more intense as banks branch into new lines of business and with the proliferation of exotic, thinly traded derivative financial instruments.

The alternative is to rely on simple rules, limiting, inter alia, banks' foreign-currency exposures as a way of containing risk. Unfortunately, simple rules can have complex consequences, including unintended ones. Restricting the open foreign exchange positions of banks, for example, may simply cause the latter to pass on that exposure to their domestic customers (who are even less able to handle it) in the form of foreign-currency-denominated loans.

Similarly, capital requirements higher than the Basle standards are a deterrent to excessive risk taking only if bank capital is ultimately written down. Political pressure may lead the authorities to recapitalize an otherwise insolvent bank on concessionary terms or to establish a special public facility that takes nonperforming loans off the banks' books in return for government bonds in excess of those loans' marked-to-market value. If so, capital requirements will have little deterrent effect.

These dilemmas have motivated the search for additional options for regulating and restructuring the banking sector. One such option is narrow banking, under which banks, or at least insured banks, are permitted to invest their liquid liabilities only in liquid assets (Litan, 1987; Burnham, 1990). Eligible assets could be limited to deposits with other banks and to interest-bearing assets like short-term government securities, the market in which is deep and broad. Since narrow banks are still exposed to interest-rate risk and small depositors will still have difficulty in evaluating banks' portfolios, there may still be a case for deposit insurance. But narrow banks would have little scope for taking on additional risk.[64]

The demand for other banking services would not disappear, of course. Firms with a demand for external finance would supply increasing amounts of commercial paper and junk bonds, the demand for which would be provided by the expansion of mutual funds.[65] But only relatively creditworthy borrowers are able to issue the kind of publicly traded securities attractive to mutual-fund-like vehicles.[66] The demand for commercial, industrial, real estate and consumer loans by less creditworthy borrowers would presumably shift to finance companies and finance-company-like organizations, which were not offered deposit insurance.[67] The latter would then have an incentive to offer deposit-like liabilities.[68] Thus, many of the risks presently associated with banks would simply shift to nonbank intermediaries, which might themselves have a tendency to affiliate with narrow banks (through, inter alia, holding companies). The question would then become whether the authorities' ex ante commitment not to apply too-big-to-fail arguments to these entities would be politically sustainable ex post. Insofar as financial distress in these entities gave rise to bank-like externality problems, this might not be the case. The hope of narrow-banking proponents is that the authorities could head off threats to systemic stability by undertaking lender-of-last-resort operations (following sound central bank practice, lending only at penalty rates against acceptable collateral), but not necessarily compensating investors for their losses, who would then have an incentive to exert stronger market discipline against unsound lending practices. But in a sense, the proponents of narrow banking are simply assuming a convenient answer to the fundamental question; were it really so simple for governments to limit depositor bailouts in this way, they could simply limit the provision of those bailouts to existing financial institutions, obviating the need to create narrow banks.

A second option is to internationalize the banking system. A banking system with an internationally diversified asset base is less likely to be destabilized by a domestic economic crisis and in turn to worsen crisis conditions. Domestic branches of foreign banks effectively possess their own private lenders of last resort in the form of the foreign head office. And the institution as a whole can count on last-resort lending by the central bank of the country in which the home office resides, where that country is likely to be a more stable mature market. Finally, where competent management is in short supply, allowing entry by foreign banks can be a means of importing expertise. Parent banks with hard-earned reputations for financial probity have an incentive to apply to their foreign branches state-of-the-art internal controls and accounting standards.

All this provides an argument for internationalizing national banking systems. To be sure, the elimination of statutory barriers to the establishment of foreign branches and subsidiaries will not produce a single global banking system overnight. Domestic banks have an advantage when seeking to defend their market share as a result of having invested in proprietary sources of information. And, however, invigorating the chill winds of international competition, suddenly opening domestic banking to foreign entry can be a sharp shock to previously sheltered financial institutions. In the absence of an orderly exit policy, it may encourage gambling for redemption and other perverse short-run responses. This argument for phasing in the internationalization of banking suggests that this solution will take time to implement.

A final option is to place taxes or quantitative limits on the short-term foreign-currency borrowing of banks. Banks, it has already been argued, are a special source of vulnerability to the stability of the financial system. Knowing that the importance the authorities attach to the maintenance of confidence will ultimately induce them to make good on the banks' liabilities, international investors attracted by high domestic interest rates will be inclined to freely provide short-term foreign-currency funding in the expectation of being able to get their money out. At the same time, allowing the banks to borrow freely short term, in foreign currency, greatly heightens the risk of crisis, since the domestic authorities cannot print the foreign exchange needed by a lender of last resort seeking to make good on these liabilities and can only pay off the banks' creditors by putting the domestic economy through a wrenching internal and external adjustment.

These are arguments for placing limits on the banks' short-term foreign-currency borrowing. Each bank could be restricted to borrowing no more than a certain percentage of its liabilities. Alternatively, the total short-term foreign-currency borrowing of the banks could be limited to a certain percentage of total banking-sector liabilities, and banks could auction entitlements to borrow among themselves.

Limiting the ability of banks to borrow abroad would, however, simply encourage nonbanks to do the borrowing for them. Domestic corporations could borrow offshore in foreign currency and deposit the proceeds with domestic banks which, their access to external funding restricted, would presumably offer relatively attractive deposit rates; the banks would then lend the proceeds to other customers. If corporations hedged their exposure by making foreign-currency denominated deposits the banks would end up with the same short-term foreign currency exposure as when there were no limits on their ability to fund themselves abroad. Assuming no change in the pressure on the authorities to provide the banks with guarantees, foreigners would have the same incentive to freely supply short-term foreign-currency funding, since there would still be little question about their ability to get their money back. The vulnerabilities to which the financial system was subject would remain essentially unchanged.[69]

The logical result of starting down this road is therefore a tax or tax equivalent on all foreign capital inflows, not merely on inflows into the banking system. If it was intended to target short-term capital inflows, it could be structured as a holding period tax; for example, like the Chilean measure which requires all nonequity foreign investment to be accompanied by a one year, noninterest-bearing deposit (whose tax equivalent therefore declines with the duration of the investment).

4.3. European prospects

Looking forward, it is in Europe where the exchange rate commitment and the lender-of-last-resort function may conflict most strongly. The danger is that European monetary unification and the creation of a European Central Bank (ECB) will heighten the tension between these two imperatives.

When Stage III of the monetary unification process commences on January 1st, 1999, the exchange rates of the participating countries will be locked, and the ECB will be committed to exchanging their currencies for one another at par.[70] The ECB's mandate, stated in the central bank's statute, is to maintain price stability and advance the general economic interests of the EU without jeopardizing the primary objective of price stability. In particular, that statute states that the ECB is responsible for overseeing the operation of the payments system, a provision which can be interpreted as preventing problems of bank illiquidity and insolvency from spreading contagiously through the financial system.

Under what conditions might an exchange rate commitment prevent the ECB from discharging this function? One circumstance would be when the ECB was obligated to peg the Euro against the dollar or a basket of foreign currencies, in which case the same kind of conflict that arose in Finland and Sweden in the early nineties between the exchange rate peg and the lender-of-last-resort function might force it to choose between defending the peg and the banking system. This can be dismissed as a short-run possibility on the grounds that the adoption of an external peg for the Euro is unlikely. While the Council of Ministers is free under the provisions of the Maastricht Treaty to provide "general orientations" for exchange rate policy the ECB is not obliged to act upon them. It is not likely to embrace a commitment to a "quiet target zone" for the Euro against the dollar or the yen while it is still establishing the credibility of its commitment to price stability (Fratianni and Hauskrecht, 1998). The Council of Ministers has the power to negotiate a formal agreement with countries outside Europe for the establishment of a Bretton-Woods-like exchange rate regime and to require the ECB to adapt policy to its dictates. But any such agreement is unlikely. With the inauguration of Stage III, the Euro zone will come to more closely resemble the relatively large, relatively closed economy epitomized by the United States, which has been disinclined, on standard optimum-currency-area grounds, to peg its currency against those of other countries.[71]

While its statute states the ECB's responsibility for the payments system and, by implication, the banks, it also puts barriers in the way of central bank operations in support of the public finances. The "no-bailout" clause of the treaty (Article 21 of the Protocol on the European System of Central Banks) states that the ECB cannot acquire public debt directly from the issuer.[72] Article 21 is designed to shelter the ECB from pressure to monetize public debts and thereby encourage fiscal profligacy. Knowing that the ECB is prohibited from purchasing public debt directly from the issuer and otherwise subsidizing the issue of public debt by governments, those governments will be deterred from issuing excessive debt and running excessive deficits, while the ECB will be deterred from inflating away existing debts.

A complication is that in many European countries commercial banks have substantial investments in public debt. Fear of default, which caused the prices of those securities to plunge, could therefore create problems of solvency for the banks and undermine depositor confidence. Precisely this problem arose in Mexico in 1994–95, where the banks held large amounts of government paper and the run on *tesobonos* and *cetes* damaged their balance-sheet position. Were the ECB forced to stand back from the public-debt market in the event of a meltdown, it could then find itself faced with very serious problems in the banking system.

In fact, Article 21 only precludes ECB purchases of public debt *directly from the issuer*. Nothing prevents it from purchasing public debt on the secondary market and from the banks in particular. In doing so it can help to restore the liquidity of the latter. But if debt prices have collapsed, the banks will be selling their government securities to the ECB at a loss. While the transaction will enhance their liquidity, the collapse in debt prices will still eat into commercial bank capital, potentially undermining investor confidence. It may be necessary for the ECB to inject additional liquidity to stabilize the situation.

The question then becomes whether the ECB will hesitate to do so for fear of undermining the credibility of its commitment to price stability. Credibility will require acquiring a track record for pursuing anti-inflationary policies. Buying up the public debt holdings of the banks and more generally engaging in last-resort lending could be seen by the markets as the ECB taking its eye off the ball. In particular, if the ECB was targeting the narrow money supply, providing liquidity in support of the banking system in violation of those targets and as a credibility-damaging signal.

Other central banks have been able to engage in lender-of-last-resort operations without damaging the credibility of their commitment to price stability; the Fed in 1987 springs to mind. Its injection of liquidity in the wake of the October stock market crash did not excite inflationary expectations or throw monetary policy off course. Once the panic passed, it withdrew the additional funds and restored policy to its previous trajectory. The Banco de Mexico in 1995 is an example of the opposite, where the injection of liquidity necessary to support the financial system was associated with an acceleration of inflation to the mid-double digits. Two factors help to explain the contrast. First, the Fed's 1987 operation occurred against a backdrop in which aggregate supply and demand conditions were well balanced and there were few inflationary expectations to excite, whereas the Banco de Mexico's 1995 operation took place in a more unbalanced macroeconomic environment in which the climate for inflation was ripe. Second, the Fed's superior credibility, accumulated over many years, made for a better outcome.

The first of these two considerations suggests that the ECB should be willing and able to undertake lender-of-last-resort operations. In its early reputation-building years, it will take seriously the pursuit of price stability, so any banking problems should occur in a relatively benign inflationary climate. But the second consideration suggests that the ECB may be reluctant to lend on the grounds that it has not yet built the requisite reputation. Which consideration will dominate is uncertain, which gives grounds for concern about how the ECB will respond to banking problems in its early years.

Can European governments, as opposed to the central bank, assist the banks, as the Argentine government did in 1995?[73] Yes, if the governments in question have financial reserves or the ability to borrow. The danger here is that European governments will be constrained by the Excessive Deficit Procedure of the Maastricht Treaty and the Stability Pact. Under their provisions, countries with deficits in excess of 3% of GDP may be subject to fines and sanctions unless they are exempted on grounds of an exceptionally severe recession. For governments with balanced budgets or current surpluses, this constraint will not bind. But most European governments, with their recent history of large deficits, will be up against their Stability Pact limits when Stage III commences. They may lay themselves open to fines if they expend additional resources to bail out the banks. And depositors, knowing the disincentive this provides for a government bailout, may not be deterred from running on the banks.

Thus, both the ECB and Europe's national governments should have the capacity to intervene to stabilize their banking systems once Stage III of the EMU process has been underway for some time. In the short run, however, the constraints of imperfect credibility and the Stability Pact may limit their room for maneuver. This is one of several grounds for thinking that the early years of Stage III may prove exciting.

5. Conclusions and implications

While this review of the historical record shows that there is no simple mapping between exchange rate stability and financial stability, it confirms that the textbook insight about the origin of disturbances and the advantages of fixed and floating rates is still the obvious place to start. When foreign monetary disturbances are important, a flexible rate provides useful insulation, but when such disturbances originate at home, exchange rate stability allows them to be shared with the rest of the world and disciplines domestic policymakers. This logic applies directly to the stability of the banking system. When changes in global monetary and financial conditions are an important source of disturbances to the banking system, as has repeatedly been the case, exchange rate flexibility can help to insulate the banks from shocks to their funding and investments and give the authorities the opportunity to act as lenders of last resort. The Great Depression provides perhaps the clearest illustration: in the 1930s most countries experienced the contraction of credit and collapse of activity as an imported shock, and those which allowed their exchange rates to adjust, decoupling domestic monetary and financial conditions from those abroad, were best able to avert banking panics and to engage in lender-of-last-resort operations. Conversely, when monetary and financial shocks jeopardizing the stability of the banking system are home grown, as has also often been the case, pegging the exchange rate imposes valuable discipline on domestic policymakers. Argentina in the 1990s illustrates the point: by adopting a rigid currency peg it has prevented domestic policymakers from succumbing to the monetary excesses that long destabilized its banking system.[74]

But this experience also illustrates the problems created for banking stability if the source of disturbances changes, as it did in Argentina at the beginning of 1995. An exchange-rate arrangement that had contributed positively to banking and financial stability so long as disturbances were primarily monetary and primarily domestic proved to be a liability once an external financial shock—the Tequila crisis—came to dominate Argentina's financial affairs.

This case also highlights the positive role for policy in shaping the link between exchange rate and banking stability. A government or central bank can reconcile a commitment to peg the exchange rate with a readiness to act as lender of last resort by establishing credit lines abroad: this was the expedient used by Argentina to recapitalize its banks without jeopardizing its currency peg. Additional devices include encouraging lifeboat operations among the banks (as in the Nordic countries) and invoking the exchange-rate escape clause (abandoning the peg temporarily). To be sure, encouraging mutual-support operations, like establishing foreign credit lines, is easier said than done; if there is a government or a central bank in the background concerned that some financial institutions are too big to fail, strong banks may be reluctant to support their weaker counterparts, as in the United States in the Great Depression. This is a lesson of U.S. experience in the Great Depression. And for countries like Argentina, whose pegged rates are less than fully credible, invoking the exchange-rate escape clause is not an option.

Thus, where lack of domestic monetary discipline is the problem, pegged rates retain obvious appeal. But countries adopting pegged rates, for this or other reasons, must take care to tailor financial arrangements affecting their banking systems to accommodate this additional constraint.

Notes

1. As in Eichengreen (1994), I use the term "pegged" rather than "fixed" on the grounds that supposedly fixed exchange rates can always be "unfixed."
2. Universally or for specified transactions.
3. By implication of the interest parity condition.
4. By implication, the idea that pegged exchange rates are desirable where macroeconomic disturbances are domestic in origin needs to be qualified where the response to those internal dislocations is exchange-rate-based stabilization. An elegant theoretical treatment of the point is Edwards and Vegh (1997). After first establishing that a temporary stabilization is likely to ignite a domestic consumption boom financed in part by large capital inflows, they then show that in a model in which the creation of bank credit and deposits is costly and has real effects, exchange-rate-based stabilization cycles also lead to cycles in output and employment.
5. A model of this relationship is Miller (1996), who considers bank failures and currency crises under the gold standard. In her model, a deterioration in bank asset quality leads households to shift from deposits to currency. The increase in currency demand prompts an inflow of capital and reserves, with which the monetary authority backs additional note emissions. Because that additional liquidity merely satisfies household demand, it does not offset the decline in deposits, a source of distress among financial institutions. If the monetary authority provides still more liquidity with the objective of aiding the banks, reserves will flow out, and intervention on behalf of the banking system may jeopardize the currency peg.
6. Imagine a banking panic that leads investors to withdraw x dollars from the banking system and to hold instead an additional x dollars of domestic currency. The x dollars of foreign capital flows in, is added to the central bank's stock of reserves, and backs the emission of x additional dollars of currency. The money supply (currency plus deposits) is unchanged. If output and velocity are unchanged, domestic prices are unchanged (by the quantity equation: $MV = PY$).
7. If the exchange rate is given by purchasing power parity, then the exchange rate is unchanged. But if the central bank now issues additional domestic currency (above and beyond x) in order to recapitalize the banking system, M will begin to rise, along with the price level and the exchange rate.
8. For present purposes, 1890 to 1913. Prior to 1890 adherence to the gold standard was spotty (Eichengreen and Flandreau, 1996a, Table 1).
9. The term "standard" refers to the asset—in this case, gold—that was legal tender in unlimited amounts and could be freely coined.
10. The remaining five countries in the Eichengreen-Flandreau sample (Guatemala, Honduras, Salvador, China and Persia) were on silver standards (Persia was officially bimetallic but no gold circulated). While their exchange rates could vary against the gold-based currencies, those exchange rates depended mainly on aggregate supplies and demands in global markets for precious metals, not on economic policies or conditions in any one country. For present purposes these countries too can be thought of as operating exchange rate pegs.
11. As described at more length by Eichengreen and Flandreau (1996b).
12. In France, for example, it was thought that the central bank should not more than double the size of the fluctuation band, while Italy used its room for maneuver more liberally.

13. The definitive account of these arrangements is Bloomfield (1959).
14. Thus, in Belgium reserves could slip below the legal minimum upon the authorization of the finance minister, while in Austria-Hungary, Germany, Italy, Japan and Norway they could do so if the central bank paid a tax.
15. Thus, it is revealing that the Canadian monetary system shared many features with that of the United States—including no central bank and an inelastically supplied currency—and yet experienced a minimum of serious financial crises before 1914 (Rich, 1989), a contrast that is plausibly attributable to its more widely branched and concentrated banking system.
16. On the role of seasonal factors, see Eichengreen (1984) and Miron (1986). On the role of cyclical instability in precipitating financial crises, see Gorton (1988).
17. Although some central banking operations were, in fact, undertaken by the Treasury (see text).
18. Meanwhile, the banks, in the words of Friedman and Schwartz (1963, p. 328), "continued to make loans, transfer deposits by check, and conduct all their usual business except the unlimited conversion of deposits on demand." Armaos (1992) analyzes suspensions of convertibility from a theoretical perspective and shows conditions under which they can be an efficient response to a bank run.
19. In the words of Cannon (1910, p. 12), "In times of panic it is not infrequently the case that a bank in good standing becomes temporarily embarassed. Unfortunate report may cause a run upon it, and, being unable to call in a sufficient amount of its outstanding loans to meet the demands of frightened depositors, it must either secure a loan or fail. In such an emergency the other members of the clearing house are usually willing to render assistance until the strain is relaxed."
20. As emphasized by Bordo and Kydland (1995). Horsefield (1953) notes that the Bank itself had suggested that an explicit escape clause be built into the 1844 Bank Act, but Peel omitted it from the final legislation. The first occasion on which this was done, the financial crisis of October 1847, is studied in depth by Dornbusch and Frenkel (1984).
21. As Hughes (1984) put it, "Once the London financial world realized that a Treasury letter could always be counted on to be forthcoming, the Bank's crisis-proven management technique conceivably added long-term stability to expectations and thus to the gold standard itself." He continues "Conceivably." Hughes suggests that this crisis-management technique remained untested for the remainder of the gold standard period because growth slowed and therefore financial fluctuations moderated relative to earlier years.
22. Especially in the final third of the 19th century, and especially in comparison with the United States.
23. Bagehot (1873, repr. 1902, p. 64) observed that in 1866 there was "an instant when it was believed that the Bank would not advance on Consols, or at least hesitated to advance on them. The monment this was reported in the City and telegraphed to the country, it made the panic indefinitely worse." Schwartz (1986) calls 1866 the last real financial crisis in Britain. Still, the Bank did lend freely enough to prevent the failure of Overend and Gurney from bringing down the entire nation's banking system.
24. In fact, the ratio of reserves (including both gold and foreign exchange) to the currency and other sight liabilities of central banks was little changed from 1913.
25. On the assumption that central banks held as much foreign exchange as they were legally permitted. League of Nations (1930), p. 98.
26. A point to which I return in my discussion of the European Central Bank in Section 4.
27. As I have argued elsewhere, the Fed's failure to respond to bank failures cannot be fully understood without reference to this "liquidationist view".
28. Another example is the Royal Bank of Scotland's take-over of Williams Deacons in 1929–30, with Bank of England assistance (see Sayers, 1976, pp. 235–259). The German Government was involved in the Dresdner Bank's absorption of the Danat Bank and the merger of the Commerz- und Privat-Bank A.G. with the Barmer Bank-Verein Hinsberg, guaranteeing the Danat Bank's foreign obligations and injecting funds into the Commerz- und Privat-Bank. Friedman and Schwartz (1963) discuss the Canadian authorities' resort to preventive bank merger in

1930. And the Italian authorities relied on forced merger and reorganization in dealing with that country's 1931–32 banking crisis.

29. And with the advice of American apostles of central banking like the Princeton professor Edwin Kemmerer (the same Kemmerer whose 1910 book is cited in the text).
30. Grossman (1984) notes that the Reichsbank, the Netherlands Bank and certain other continental central banks were also limited in their ability to conduct open market operations.
31. This is a subject about which I have written previously. The version of the argument here is from Eichengreen (1995).
32. Those responsible for fiscal policy enjoyed even less insulation from political pressures than their counterparts in central banks, the war having shattered earlier understandings regarding the distribution of the fiscal burden. The level and composition of taxes had been radically altered, while incomes had been redistributed. Economic interest groups now fought a fiscal war of attrition, resisting any and all increases in taxes and all reductions in transfer payments. Even in countries where central bankers had retained considerable independence from political pressures, fiscal policy became politicized. And without a fiscal consensus, there was no guarantee that taxes would be raised or government spending cut when required to defend the gold standard.
33. Temporary suspensions of the sort observed in the 19th century thus did not take place under the interwar system. The closest approximation was Roosevelt's abandonment of gold convertibility in 1933, which was restored in January 1934, but not at the pre-suspension parity.
34. An alternative list, which is broadly overlapping, is provided by Bernanke and James (1991).
35. As in the standard textbook model. This point is perhaps most persuasively documented by Choudri and Kochin (1980).
36. I draw this discussion from Eichengreen (1994b).
37. Hori (1996) estimates monetary policy reaction functions for a panel of 24 countries, using annual data from 1929 to 1937. Dividing his sample into observations for countries on and off the gold standard, he detects no tendency for countries on the gold standard to reduce their discount rates in response to a banking crisis, but a significant tendency in this direction for countries off gold.
38. Only the United States might be thought be different. There the macroeconomic disturbance was home grown rather than imported. And authors like Friedman and Schwartz deny that the exchange-rate constraint significantly constrained lender-of-last-resort intervention. The argument that it did emphasizes the free gold constraint prior to the Glass-Steagall Act (Wicker, 1966; Eichengreen, 1992), fears of declining reserves in the summer of 1932 (Epstein and Ferguson, 1984), and doubts about Roosevelt's commitment to defending the dollar parity in the winter of 1932–1933 (Wigmore, 1987). Hori (1996) documents a break in the Fed's monetary-policy reaction function in March 1933 when the country left gold. Before that there was no tendency for the Fed to reduce the discount rate in response to an increase in the deposits at suspended banks; thereafter it does so in a statistically significant way. This evidence suggests that the U.S. was not all that different from other countries in which exchange-rate stability and financial stability were at odds.
39. Tranquility **relative** to the periods before and after.
40. While his analysis focuses on the United States, his conclusions are applicable more broadly.
41. On the recent developments in the international financial system see Salvatore (1998).
42. The one important industrial-country case that is not considered under this heading is the Japanese banking crisis, which is still unfolding at the time of writing.
43. Commercial bank failures also soared in the 1980s, suggesting that this was not just a mortgage-related phenomenon.
44. The fall in oil prices in 1985 made for further difficulties for S&Ls in the Southwest in particular.
45. Indeed, some authors have argued that an exchange-rate constraint, had it existed, would have forced the United States to reign in its budget deficit and stem the rise in interest rates and the dollar, thereby relieving the problems of the banks. See e.g., Bergsten and Henning (1996).

46. Especially in the Southern-Cone countries, inadequate information-disclosure requirements generated situations of adverse selection in which good and bad risks were not distinguished. As interest rates rose, riskier borrowers were the only ones still willing to borrow, and the quality of bank loan portfolios deteriorated. Macroeconomic instability exacerbated this situation by increasing the variance of project yields and making it particularly difficult for banks to rate risks (McKinnon, 1991).
47. Inflation caused a fall in deposits by depressing the demand for money. In many of these countries the authorities capped the interest rates at which the banks could lend as a way of guaranteeing the provision of cheap credit to the government; interest rate caps together with inflation were a deadly combination for deposits (Rojas-Suarez and Weisbrod, 1996). BIS (1996) notes that a number of chronically high inflation Latin American countries continue to have ratios of bank credit to GDP well below those of other countries at similar stages of economic development, reflecting the instability of their macroeconomic environments.
48. Measures motivated by the desire to retain the option of entering the European Union and the need to place growing amounts of public debt.
49. In Sweden, for example, these reduced unemployment to the lowest levels in a decade and raised inflation significantly relative to levels in the country's principal trading partners. Jonung and Stymne (forthcoming, p. 37).
50. As well as by declining paper and pulp prices.
51. An introduction to the Nordic banking crises is Moeller and Nielson (1995).
52. Consistent with this interpretation, Danish banks, which had the strongest capitalization, survived the crisis of the eighties most easily despite having the largest losses and provisions as a percentage of lending.
53. Jonung and Stymne (forthcoming) show that real interest rates in these countries climbed sharply after 1990.
54. Another interesting parallel is with earlier efforts, discussed in previous sections of this paper, to rely on self-regulation. Traditionally, the Nordic banking industry has dealt with the problem of weak banks by arranging marriages with stronger partners. Self-regulation and mutual support may have worked less well in the 1980s than in earlier decades both because deregulation disrupted the cozy atmosphere in which the banks had previously operated but also because strong banks had no incentive to support their weaker counterparts once they came to believe that the government regarded them all as too big to fail (in parallel with Friedman and Schwartz's argument about the U.S. in the 1930s).
55. One should probably include under this heading banking crises in the transition economies, although bad loans made by state-owned banks to state-owned enterprises make these a somewhat special case (Anderson et al., 1996).
56. If those bonds are not redeemed upon maturity they will be converted into shares.
57. At the same time, smaller banks saw their loan portfolios deteriorate as a result of currency overvaluation, slow growth and mounting unemployment.
58. In addition, a deposit insurance scheme was implemented in April in an effort to restore depositor confidence.
59. Like that in which the Bank of England, the U.S. Treasury and other governmental institutions engaged in the 19th century.
60. Guarantees were not limited to the borrower side. Thus, it was European banks enjoying implicit guarantees, including state savings banks in Germany and institutions like Credit Lyonnais in France, that moved most aggressively into high-risk, high-yielding Asian loans. They were late to the party: even while American banks were winding down their exposure in Asia, European banks were continuing to build up their's. And Japanese banks, for their part, invested in high-yielding Asian securities as a way of gambling for redemption.
61. See Aliber (1998).
62. See, for example, Goldstein (1996), and Kaminsky and Reinhart (1996).
63. In particular, supervisors should monitor the adequacy of internal controls, internal and external audits, loan and investment policies, and risk-management techniques. They should

verify that banks have adequate management information systems in place to identify loan and investment concentrations in their portfolios. They should make a particular effort to prevent abuses associated with connected lending and require banks to lend on an arm's-length basis. They should require realistic valuation of bank assets while imposing appropriate capital adequacy, liquidity, credit diversification, foreign exchange exposure, and nonbank activity requirements and limits. Bank supervisors should be granted political independence, financial autonomy, legal immunity, and the right to conduct on-site inspections. Banks for their part should be required to provide adequate and accurate information to their supervisors, who should have the power to impose remedial and punitive measures, including revocation of the license to operate, in the event of noncompliance. Other desirable elements include limiting public sector distortions (by limiting public sector guarantees, restricting deposit insurance to small deposits, and establishing a credible exit policy) and raising the quality of public disclosure as a way of strengthening market discipline. This list is essentially drawn from the Core Principles for Effective Banking Supervision (Basle Core Principles).

64. They would be competitive with other financial institutions in the same sense as money-market mutual funds. And were there any doubt about this, giving them exclusive access to the payments system operated by the central bank would give them a special advantage in terms of convenience in carrying out transactions for their customers.
65. As well as insurance companies, pension funds, and hedge funds.
66. For a theoretical explanation, see Diamond (1991).
67. Finance companies typically fund themselves with capital (significantly more capital than commercial banks) and long-term debt.
68. Unless this was prohibited and prevented in practice by detailed and rigorously enforced regulatory restrictions.
69. If, on the other hand, corporates made domestic-currency deposits, they would assume the foreign-exchange exposure and be subject to similar insolvency risk from exchange rate chan ges as the banks in the no-restriction scenario. It seems likely that they authorities that had previously felt impelled to extend guarantees to the banks would now extend similar support to nonbanks, having induced the latter to take on financial-intermediation responsibilities.
70. National currencies will be replaced by the single European currency three years later, at the beginning of 2002.
71. An external exchange rate commitment for the Euro, in the form of a new international monetary system of pegged rates or target zone, is simply not in the cards, a position that I have argued at more length in Eichengreen (1994a).
72. In a sense, this rule is an exchange rate constraint, since Germany and other signatories of the Maastricht Treaty required its inclusion as a prerequisite for agreeing to the creation of a European Central Bank empowered to peg intra-European exchange rates once and for all.
73. Or Secretary Shaw did before 1913?
74. And led to one of the lowest ratios of bank deposits to GDP for a country at its stage of economic development.

References

Aliber, Robert Z. (1988) "Transforming Korean Values." *Korea's Economy 1998*, New York: Korea Economic Institute of America, pp. 28–32.

Anderson, Ronald, Erik Berglof, and Kalman Mizsei (1996) *Banking Sector Development in Central and Eastern Europe*. London: Centre for Economic Policy Research.

Armaos, John (1992) "Bank Runs and Partial Suspension of Convertibility." Working Paper FB-92-34. Graduate School of Business, Columbia University.

Bagehot, Walter (1873 [1902]) *Lombard Street*. New York: Scribner's.

Balino, Tomas J.T. (1991) "The Argentine Banking Crisis of 1980." In V. Sundararajan and Tomas J.T. Balino (eds.), *Banking Crises: Cases and Issues*. Washington, D.C.: International Monetary Fund, pp. 58–112.
Bergsten, C. Fred and C. Randall Henning (1996) *Global Economic Leadership and the Group of Seven*. Washington, D.C.: Institute for International Economics.
Bernanke, Ben and Harold James (1991) "The Gold Standard, Deflation, and Financial Crisis in the Great Depression: An International Comparison." In R. Glenn Hubbard (ed.), *Financial Markets and Financial Crises*. Chicago: University of Chicago Press, pp. 33–68.
Bloomfield, Arthur (1959) *Monetary Policy Under the International Gold Standard*. New York: Federal Reserve Bank of New York.
Bordo, Michael D. (1985) "The Impact and International Transmission of Financial Crises: Some Historical Evidence, 1870–1933." *Rivista di Storia Economica* 2, International Issue, pp. 41–78.
Bordo, Michael D. (1986) "Financial Crises, Banking Crises, Stock Market Crashes and the Money Supply: Some International Evidence, 1870–1913." In Forrest Capie and Geoffrey Wood (eds.), *Financial Crises and the World Banking System*. London: Macmillan, pp. 190–248.
Bordo, Michael D. (1990) "The Lender of Last Resort: Alternative Views and Historical Experience." *Economic Review*. Federal Reserve Bank of Richmond (Jan./Feb.), pp. 18–29.
Bordo, Michael D. and Kynn Kydland (1995) "The Gold Standard as a Rule: An Essay in Exploration." *Explorations in Economic History* 32, 423–465.
Bordo, Michael and Hugh Rockoff (1996) "The Gold Standard as a Good Housekeeping Seal of Approval." *Journal of Economic History* 56, 389–428.
Burnham, James B. (1990) "A Financial System for the Year 2000." Center for the Study of American Business, Formal Publication Number 97.
Cannon, James G. (1910) *Clearing Houses*. Washington, D.C.: Government Printing Office.
Canzoneri, Matthew (1985) "Monetary Policy Games and the Role of Private Information." *American Economic Review* 75, 1056–1070.
Caprio, Gerald, Jr., Michael Dooley, Danny Leipziger, and Carl Walsh (1997) "The Lender of Last Resort Function Under a currency Board: The Case of Argentina." *Open Economies Review* 7, 625–650.
Caprio, Gerald, Jr., and Daniela Kinglebeil (1997) "Bank Insolvencies: Cross-Country Experience." Policy Research Working Paper No. 1620. Washington, D.C.: The World Bank.
Choudri, E. and Levis Kochin (1980) "The Exchange Rate and the International Transmission of Business Cycle Disturbances." *Journal of Money, Credit and Banking* 12, 565–574.
Desmet, Klaus and Thomas Mann (1996) "Lessons from the Mexican Banking Crisis." Stanford University of and University of Cologne, unpublished manuscript.
Diamond, Douglas (1991) "Monitoring and Reputation: The Choice Between Bank Loans and Directly Placed Debt." *Journal of Political Economy* 99, 689–721.
Diamond, Douglas and Phillip Dybvig (1984) "Bank Runs, Deposit Insurance and Liquidity." *Journal of Political Economy* 91, 401–419.
Dominguez, Kathryn and Jeffrey A. Frankel (1993) *Does Foreign Exchange Intervention Work?* Washington, D.C.: Institute for International Economics.
Dornbusch, Rudiger and Jacob A. Frenkel (1994) "The Gold Standard and the Bank of England in the Crisis of 1847." In Michael D. Bordo and Anna J. Schwartz (eds.), *A Retrospective on the Classical Gold Standard*. Chicago: University of Chicago Press, pp. 233–264.
Edwards, Sebastian (1995) *Crisis and Reform in Latin America*. Oxford: Oxford University Press.
Edwards, Sebastian and Carlos A. Vegh (1997) "Banks and Macroeconomic Disturbances Under Predetermined Exchange Rates." NBER Working Paper No. 5977.
Eichengreen, Barry (1984) "Currency and Credit in the Gilded Age." In Gary Saxonhouse and Gavin Wright (eds.), *Technique, Spirit and Form in the Making of the Modern Economies*. Westport, Conn.: JAI Press, pp. 87–114.
Eichengreen, Barry (1992) *Golden Fetters: The Gold Standard and the Great Depression, 1919–1939*. New York: Oxford University Press.
Eichengreen, Barry (1994a) *International Monetary Arrangements for the 21st Century*. Washington, D.C.: The Brookings Institution.

Eichengreen, Barry (1994b) "Wages and the Gold Standard: Perspectives on the Borchardt Debate." In Christoph Buchheim, Michael Hutter and Harold James (eds.), *Zerrissene Zwischenkriegszeit: Wirtschaftshistoriche Beitrage: Knut Borchardt zum 65, Geburtstag*. Baden-Baden: Nomos Verlagsgeselleschaft, pp. 177–204.

Eichengreen, Barry (1995) "Central Bank Cooperation and Exchange Rate Commitments: The Classical and Interwar Gold Standards Compared." *Financial History Review* 2, 99–117.

Eichengreen, Barry and Marc Flandreau (1996a) "The Geography of the Gold Standard." In Jorge Braga de Macedo, Barry Eichengreen, and Jaime Reis (eds.), *Currency Convertibility: The Gold Standard and Beyond*. London: Routledge, pp. 113–143.

Eichengreen, Barry and Marc Flandreau (1996b) "Blocks, Bands and Crawls: International Monetary History in Light of Recent Theoretical Developments." *Scottish Journal of Economics* 43, 389–418.

Epstein, Gerald and Thomas Ferguson (1984) "Monetary Policy, Loan Liquidation and Industrial Conflict: The Federal Reserve and the Open Market Operations of 1932." *Journal of Economic History* XLV, 957–984.

Fratianni M. and A. Hauskrecht (1998) "From the Gold Standard to a Bipolar Monetary System." in this volume.

Friedman, Milton and Anna J. Schwartz (1963) *A Monetary History of the United States, 1863–1960*. Princeton: Princeton University Press.

Garber, Peter M. and Vittorio U. Grilli (1986) "Belmont-Morgan Syndicate as an Optimal Investment Banking contract." *European Economic Review* 30, 649–677.

Gavin, Michael and Ricardo Hausmann (1996) "The Roots of Banking Crises: The Macroeconomic Context." In Richardo Hausmann and Liliana Rojas-Suarez (eds.), *Banking Crises in Latin America*. Washington, D.C.: Inter-American Development Bank.

Goldfajn, Ilan and Rodrigo O. Valdes (1995) "Balance of Payment Crises and Capital Flows: The Role of Liquidity." MIT unpublished manuscript.

Goldstein, Morris (1996) *The Case for an International Banking Standard*. Washington, D.C.: Institute of International Economics.

Goldstein, Morris and David Folkerts-Landau (1993) *International Capital Markets: Part II: Systemic Issues in International Finance*. Washington, D.C.: International Monetary Fund.

Gorton, Gary (1988) "Banking Panics and Business Cycles." *Oxford Economic Papers* 40, 751–781.

Grossman, Richard S. (1994) "The Shoe that Didn't Drop: Explaining Banking Stability During the Great Depression." *Journal of Economic History* 54, 654–682.

Heller, H. Robert (1978) "Determinants of Exchange Rate Practices." *Journal of Money, Credit and Banking* 10, 308–321.

Horsefield, J.K. (1953) "The Origins of the Bank Charter Act, 1844." In T.S. Ashton and R.S. Sayers (eds.), *Papers in English Monetary History*. Oxford: Clarendon Press, pp. 109–125.

Hughes, Jonathan (1984) "Comment on Dornbusch and Frenkel." In Michael D. Bordo and Anna J. Schwartz (eds.), *A Retrospective on the International Gold Standard*. Chicago: University of Chicago Press, pp. 265–271.

International Monetary Fund (1994) "The Nordic Banking Crises: Pitfalls in Financial Liberalization?" IMF, unpublished manuscript.

Jonung, Lars and Joakim Stymne (1996) "The Great Regime Shift: Asset Markets and Economic Activity in Sweden, 1985–93." University of Lund, unpublished manuscript.

Kaminsky, Graciela and Carmen Reinhart (1996) "The Twin Crises: The Causes of Banking and Balance of Payments Problems." Federal Reserve Bank, unpublished manuscript.

Kemmerer, Edwin (1910) *Seasonal Variations in the Relative Demand for Money and Capital in the United States*. Washington, D.C.: GPO.

Krugman, Paul (1979) "A Model of Balance-of-Payments Crises." *Journal of Money, Credit and Banking* 11, 311–325.

League of Nations (1930) *Interim Report of the Gold Delegation*. Geneva: League of Nations.

League of Nations (1933) *Economic Survey 1932/33*. Geneva: League of Nations.

Litan, Robert (1987) *What Should Banks Do?* Washington, D.C.: The Brookings Institution.

Lewis, Cleona (1938) *America's Stake in International Investments*. Washington, D.C.: The Brookings Institution.

McKinnon, Ronald (1991) *The Order of Economic Liberalization: Financial Control in the Transition in a Market Economy*. Baltimore: Johns Hopkins University Press.

Miller, Victoria (1996) "Exchange Rate Crises with Domestic Bank Runs: Evidence from the 1890s." *Journal of International Money and Finance* 15, 637–656.

Mundell, Robert A. (1961) "A Theory of Optimum Currency Areas." *American Economic Review* 53, 717–725.

McKinnon, Ronald (1963) "Optimum Currency Areas." *American Economic Review* 51, 657–665.

Miron, Jeffrey A. (1986) "Financial Panics, the Seasonality of the Nominal Interest Rate, and the Founding of the Fed." *American Economic Review* LXXVI, 125–140.

Moellere, Michael and Niels Chr. Nielsen (1995) "Some Observations on the Nordic Bank Crisis." Copenhagen Business School Working paper 95–98, Institute of Finance.

Obstfeld, Maurice (1993) "Destabilizing Effects of Exchange Rate Escape Clauses." NBER Working Paper No. 3603.

Pressnell, L.S. (1968) "Gold Reserves, Banking Reserves, and the Baring Crisis of 1890." In C.R. Whittlesey and J.S.G. Wilson (eds.), *Essays in Money and Banking in Honour of R.S. Sayers*. Oxford: Oxford University Press, pp. 167–228.

Rich, Georg (1989) "Canadian Banks, Gold, and the Crisis of 1907." *Explorations in Economic History* 26, 135–160.

Rojas-Suarez, Liliana and Steven R. Weisbrod (1996) "Banking Crises in Latin America: Experiences and Issues." In Ricardo Hausmann and Liliana Rojas-Suarez (eds.), *Banking Crises in Latin America*. Washington, D.C.: Inter-American Development Bank, pp. 3–22.

Sachs, Jeffrey A. (1995) "Do We Need an International Lender of Last Resort?" Harvard University, unpublished manuscript.

Sachs, Jeffrey A., Aaron Tornell, and Andres Velasco (1995) "The Collapse of the Mexican Peso: What Have We Learned?" *Economic Policy* 22, 15–56.

Salvatore D. (1998) "Present International Monetary and Financial Arrangements." in this volume.

Savona, P. and A. Maccario (1998) "On the Relation between Money and Derivatives and its Application to the International Money Market." this volume.

Sayers, Richard S. (1976) *The Bank of England, 1891–1944*. Cambridge: Cambridge University Press.

Schwartz, Anna J. (1986) "Real and Pseudo Financial Crises." In Forrest Capie and Geoffrey Wood (eds.), *Financial Crises in the World Banking System*. New York: St. Martin's, pp. 11–31.

Schwartz, Anna J. (1988) "Financial Stability and the Federal Safety Act." In W.S. Haraf and R.M. Kushmeider (eds.), *Restructuring Banking and Financial Services in America*. Washington, D.C.: American Enterprise Institute, pp. 34–62.

Simmons, Beth (1994) *Who Adjusts? Domestic Determinants of International Economic Policy in the Interwar Years*. Princeton: Princeton University Press.

Sprague, O.M.W. (1910) *History of Crises under the National Banking System*. Washington, D.C.: Government Printing Office.

Sundararajan, V. and Tomas J.T. Balino (1991) *Banking Crises: Cases and Issues*. Washington, D.C.: International Monetary Fund.

Timberlake, Richard H. (1963) "Mr. Shaw and his Critics: Monetary Policy in the Golden Era Reviewed." *Quarterly Journal of Economics* LXXVII, 40–54.

Timberlake, Richard H. (1978) *The Origins of Central Banking in the United States*. Cambridge: Mass.: Harvard University Press.

Velasco, Andres (1991) "Liberalization, Crisis, Intervention: The Chilean Financial System, 1975–85." In V. Sundararajan and Tomas J.T. Balino (eds.), *Banking Crises: Cases and Issues*. Washington, D.C.: International Monetary Fund, pp. 113–174.

Weichere, John C. (1988) "The Future of the Housing Finance System." In William S. Haraf and Rose Marie Kushmeider (eds.), *Restructuring Banking and Financial Services in America*. Washington, D.C.: American Enterprise Institute, pp. 296–336.

White, Lawrence J. (1992) "Change and Turmoil in U.S. Banking: Causes, Consequences, and Lessons." Salomon Center Working Paper S-92–93, New York University.

Wicker, Elmus (1966) *Federal Reserve Monetary Policy 1917–1933*. New York: Random House.

Wigmore, Barrie (1987) "Was the Bank Holiday of 1933 Caused by a Run on the Dollar?" *Journal of Economic History* XLVII, 739–756.

Wihlborg, Clas, Michael Hutchinson, and Lars Meuller (1994) "Credit Market Deregulation, Asset Prices and Banking Crisis in Sweden." Goteborg University and University of California, Santa Cruz, unpublished manuscript.

Open economies review **9:S1** 609–635 (1998)

From the Gold Standard to a Bipolar Monetary System

MICHELE FRATIANNI fratiann@indiana.edu
Dept. of Business Economics and Public Policy, Indiana University, Kelley School of Business, Bloomington, Indiana 47405, USA

ANDREAS HAUSKRECHT hauskrecht@aol.com
Assistant Professor, Deutsche Bundesbank Foundation, Free University of Berlin, Department of Economics, 14195 Berlin, Germany

Key words: evolution of the international monetary system, currency blocs, hierarchical structure, hegemony, cooperation, inflation rate targeting

JEL Classification Numbers: E42, E52, F33, F36

Abstract

This paper argues that the international monetary system will evolve into a bipolar structure consisting of a dollar area and a euro area, each of which attracting other countries to their gravitational centers. A deepening and widening of NAFTA and the EU will enlarge the sphere of influence of both currencies; trade wars will restrict them. The yen is a big question mark. The deep and still unresolved financial crisis in Japan works against the enlargement of the yen; deregulation of its financial markets, with the attendant decline in transaction costs, goes in the opposite direction. Our conclusion is that the yen area will be much smaller than the dollar and the euro area and, consequently, the two large blocs will shape the international monetary system of the 21st century in a critical way. We also discuss feasible scenarios of interaction between currency blocs. A large EMU works in favor of cooperation because fewer players imply lower decision-making costs in reaching a cooperative solution. The relative closeness of the EMU and the United States, on the other hand, works against cooperation and in favor of benign neglect. Exchange-rate agreements are fragile unless supported by strong commitment to economic policy cooperation, and such a commitment may well be premature. The article advocates that the United States and EMU target common inflation rates, an idea that Keynes proposed back in 1923.

Introduction and summary of conclusions

The creation of Economic and Monetary Union (EMU) and of its currency, the euro, is a historic decision, not only for the European Union (EU) but also for the world at large. The sheer size and economic importance of the countries involved is bound to alter the character of the international monetary system. Historically, there is a positive correlation between relative size and dominant-currency status. On this score the formation of EMU will give the euro a big push in competing against the dollar for the position of dominant currency. On the other hand, the euro will be issued by a new central bank representing a group of countries that have yet not achieved political unification. Historically, political unification tends to occur before monetary unification; there is no precedent for a monetary union of the size and economic importance of EMU. Thus, the benefits from a large economic and financial area will be partly offset by relatively untested institutions.

Our maintained hypothesis is that the international monetary system will evolve into a bipolar structure consisting of a dollar area and an euro area, each of which attracting other countries to their gravitational centers. The dollar sphere of influence stretches to Latin America, South and East Asia, Iraq, Bahrain, Qatar, Saudi Arabia, and United Arab Emirates. That of the euro will most likely encompass Central and Eastern Europe, the CFA zone, and parts of the Middle East and North Africa. These maps will have uncertain boundaries. A deepening and widening of NAFTA and the EU will enlarge the sphere of influence of both currencies; trade wars will restrict them. The yen is a big question mark. The deep and still unresolved financial crisis in Japan works against the enlargement of the yen; deregulation of its financial markets, with the attendant decline in transaction costs, goes in the opposite direction. Our conclusion is that the yen area will be much smaller than the dollar and the euro area and, consequently, the two large blocs will shape the international monetary system of the 21st century in a critical way.

A central theme of the paper is how will these two large blocs interact. To obtain some insight from history we review, in part one of the study, the lessons learnt since the classical gold standard. Our assessment is that exchange-rate unions tend to be more hierarchical than hegemonic. The requirements for hegemony are extremely demanding on the data. The hegemon, not only imparts large effects on the rest of the system, but also is insulated from it. In a hierarchical structure, instead, asymmetries exist but the country at the top of the pyramid is not insulated from the actions taken by countries located at lower levels of the pyramid. Furthermore, the considerable amount of cooperation observed in the gold standard and in Bretton Woods is more consistent with a hierarchical structure than with a hegemonic one.

The hierarchical structure that was successful in the gold standard, Bretton Woods, and the EMS cannot be duplicated in a bipolar world: the United States and EMU are so large that neither is likely to subordinate monetary policy.

Part two of the paper discusses feasible scenarios of interaction. Having ruled out policy subordination, we explore the case for interbloc cooperation. On a first look, the case for cooperation appears ambiguous, resulting from two conflicting forces, the openness of the economy and the reduction of relevant players in desiring a cooperative solution. A large EMU works in favor of cooperation because fewer players imply lower decision-making costs in reaching a cooperative solution. The openness of the economy, on the other hand, works against cooperation and in favor of benign neglect because the EMU will be as closed as the US economy. Using the experience of the Federal Reserve

System, which takes monetary policy decisions more on domestic than international considerations, one arrives at the prediction that also the decisions of the ECB will be heavily influenced by domestic (i.e., inside the EMU) considerations. This line of argumentation ignores the fact that it is large countries that initiate cooperation; the reason is that large countries reap a large share of the benefits and do not suffer from free riding problems. Collective action theory would predict that the incentives for an exchange-rate agreement would be higher in a bipolar world than under current conditions.

Exchange-rate agreements are fragile unless supported by strong commitment to economic policy cooperation, and such a commitment may well be premature. A less demanding alternative is to have the United States and EMU target common inflation rates. This was the proposal advocated by Keynes (1923). Compatible long-run inflation targets do not guarantee that nominal exchange rates will be perfectly stable. Changes in real exchange rates, portfolio shifts, and the inevitable noise, so typical of auction markets, would still impart movements and jolts to the nominal exchange rate. What consistent inflation targets can deliver is long-run exchange rate predictability and this much to the advantage of international trade and long-term capital flows.

1. Lessons from the past

Rules define a regime or an order, that is a "framework of laws, conventions, regulations, and mores that establish the setting of the system and the understanding of the environments by the participants in it." (Mundell, 1972, p. 92). Not all rules are written; some can be informal or based on custom. The important point is that, regardless of the degree of formality, participants behave as if these rules exist (McKinnon, 1993, p. 2). While there are many possible regimes, these can be derived as combinations of two pure regimes, the fixed and the flexible exchange rate. For the latter the rule set reduces to one: the monetary authorities do not intervene in the foreign exchange market. Some authors (Corden, 1983; Hamada, 1998) consider the existing floating exchange-rate regime a nonsystem. A fixed exchange-rate regime, instead, commits participants to specific form policy coordination. The reason is well known in the literature as the *N-degrees of freedom paradigm*. When N countries form an exchange-rate union only $N-1$ central parities can be fixed; the regime as a whole is left with one degree of freedom. This degree of freedom determines the union's common monetary policy. More specifically, it gives the union the ability to respond to fluctuations in the union's aggregate demand and aggregate supply and to common external shocks, e.g., changes in world interest rates. Over the long run, the one degree of freedom sets the union's inflation trend and its rate of depreciation against other nonunion's currencies.

The most important consequence of the *N-degrees of freedom paradigm* is that there can be at most one monetary authority in the union that sets its policy independently of other members. Thus, it is important in the design of an exchange-rate union to determine which member is assigned the authority over the remaining degree of freedom and, consequently, how the burden of adjustment to external shocks is distributed. To a large extent, this is a result of how the institutions of the union are framed: the rules for foreign exchange market interventions and their sterilization, which stipulate whose monetary base is affected by the efforts to maintain the central parities; the tolerance for barriers to international capital flows, which shield monetary conditions in one country from the rest of the system and allow the country to retain some monetary independence even within the union; and the rules for changing central parities (Fratianni and von Hagen, 1992, pp. 43–44).

Combinations of two extreme organizational structures, the hegemonic and the cooperative delimit the resulting range of possibilities. In the hegemonic structure, one country, typically the largest member, unilaterally determines the union's common monetary policy and the other members adjust passively though the fixity of the exchange rate. In the cooperative organizational structure monetary policy is the outcome of a collective process of decision making. This process, in turn, can vary from the strictly democratic—one member one vote—to weighted voting, with weights reflecting the relative economic and/or political power of each member, as for example in the International Monetary Fund.

Much of the debate about the creation and performance of exchange-rate unions boils down to the question of how the Nth degree of freedom is distributed among the participating countries. Hegemonic explanations have dominated the literature, not only in political science, but also in economics. In the classical gold-standard (1880–1914) Britain was the hegemonic country and the pound the hegemonic currency; in the Bretton Woods system (1945–1971) the United States was the hegemonic country and the dollar the hegemonic currency; and in the European Monetary System (1978–1998) Germany was the hegemonic country and the mark the dominant currency.[1] Kindleberger (1973) argues that all stable international monetary arrangements require a hegemon that provides stability as a public good. Eichengreen (1989, p. 287), on the other hand, finds that:

> Collaboration is equally apparent in the design of the international monetary system, its operation under normal circumstances, and the management of crises.

In the rest of this section we will revisit, albeit with broad brushes, international monetary history since the days of the classical gold standard with an eye for fundamental lessons that may be useful to the operation of a bipolar world. Common to these lessons is the tension between hegemony and cooperation.

1.1. The gold standard

The gold standard rested on a decentralized organization in which participants retained their own monetary authorities, their own fiscal autonomy, and their

Table 1. The UK balance of payments (in millions of, stg. current).

	1871 1875	1876 1880	1881 1885	1886 1990	1891 1895	1896 1900	1901 1905	1906 1910	1911 1915
Visible balance	−19.3	−78.9	−56.4	−44.3	−84.4	−118.4	−115.0	−79.1	−61.3
Interest & dividends B balance	50.0	56.3	64.8	84.2	94.0	100.2	113.0	151.4	188.0
Total current account balance	75.6	23.7	56.5	85.4	55.5	28.6	41.2	147.5	211.8

Source: De Cecco (1974, p. 233).

own political sovereignty; in essence, monetary integration without fiscal and political integration. According to the Humean tradition, the common price level was endogenously determined by the interaction of the global supply of and demand for gold. The fixed money price of gold was the primary coordinating device among participants. A balance-of-payments deficit would force a gold flow out of the country and a proportional decline of the domestic monetary base, resulting in a downward pressure on prices and wages. Gold flows would be directed towards countries with balance-of-payments surpluses. These would experience a rise of the domestic monetary base and rising prices and/or economic activity (absorption). Under the assumption of price and wage flexibility, the system was symmetric and self-adjusting. The rules of the game called for central banks not to sterilize gold flows; actually, according to some authors (e.g., Bloomfield, 1959), central banks were to reinforce gold flows by appropriately varying the bank rate (e.g., decrease the bank rate in periods of gold inflows).

The practice of the gold standard differed somewhat from the stylized script. The system evolved into a gold reserve standard. Foreign exchange reserves grew more rapidly than gold reserves; by 1913 they accounted for 16% of total reserves (Lindert, 1969, Table 1). These reserves were not only denominated in British pounds, but also in the currency of the two "junior" reserve centers, France and Germany. The amount of international liquidity held in the reserve centers by far exceeded the total gold reserves held by these countries, in particular British official gold (Lindert, Table 2); yet, unlike in Bretton Woods, there were no signs of confidence crises. The "senior" center and the two "junior" centers were net capital exporters (Tables 1 and 2), reassuring reserve holders that the centers were financially solid. All in all, there was a clear tendency for the gold standard to evolve into a gold reserve standard, economizing on gold.

Gold economization was not restricted to international reserves; it took place also in the internal liquidity of the countries, with notes and bank demand deposits accounting for a rising proportion of the national money supplies; this smoothed the volatility imparted by gold and silver coins on output and prices (Table 3).

Table 2. Summary international accounts of Great Britain, France, and Germany, 1900–1913 (annual averages in millions of dollars).

	Great Britain	France	Germany	Three countries combined
1. Trade balance	−736.6	−51.6	−320.7	−1,108.9
2. Private specie transactions	−25.2	−70.2	−47.6	−143.0
3. Invisibles balance	1,330.6	261.9	NA	NA
4. Current-account balance	568.8	140.1	NA	NA
5. Long-term capital movements, net decrease in short-term capital abroad, and many errors and omissions	−589.7 $-E(27.6)$	−142.1 $-F(27.6)$	NA	NA
6. Increase in central-bank gold, silver, and foreign-exchange holdings (increase = −)	−2.0	−15.7	−15.7	−33.4
7. Known increase in liquid foreign liabilities	22.9 $+E(27.6)$	17.7 $+F(27.6)$	8.1 $+G(27.6)$	48.7 $+27.6(E+F+G)$
8. Of which, known increase in liquid liabilities to foreign official institutions	22.9 $+e(10.1)$	17.7 $+f(10.1)$	8.1 $+g(10.1)$	48.7 $+10.1(e+f+g)$
9. Minimum liquidity deficit	29.9 $+E(27.6)$	2.0 $+F(27.6)$	$G(27.6)-7.6$	15.3 $+27.6(E+F+G)$
10. Minimum settlements deficit	20.9 $+e(10.1)$	2.0 $+f(10.1)$	$g(10.1)-7.6$	15.3 $+10.1(e+f+g)$

Source: Lindert (1969, p. 39).

Notes: Rows (4) through (7) add up to zero, Row (5) being the residual.

E = England's share of the unallocated total holdings.
F = France's share of the same.
G = Germany's share.
e, f, g = the corresponding shares of the unallocated official holdings.

Row (2) = private production of gold and silver minus consumption plus the net decrease in private metal holdings, or, exports minus imports plus the net increase in official specie holdings. The net debit (negative) balances in this row are known to be exaggerated, particularly for France, because the import-biased customs statistics of each country have been used in their derivation.

Britain's role had much to do with the "city" being the key financial center and the pound being the dominant currency in the world. Foreign individuals and foreign banks held large amounts of British treasury bills and bank deposits (Yeager, 1966, pp. 255–258; Cleveland, 1976). All countries held short-term assets in Britain, whereas Britain had exclusively long-term claims abroad. These features help explain the asymmetric effects of monetary policy actions throughout the system. But can one interpret asymmetries as hegemony exercised by the "senior" center?

Table 3. Money stock and international reserves, 1885 and 1913.

End of	Three countries[a] 1885	Three countries[a] 1913	Eleven countries[b] 1885	Eleven countries[b] 1913	World 1885	World 1913
	(In billions of US dollars)					
1. Money supply	**6.3**	**19.8**	**8.4**	**26.3**	**14.2**	**33.1**
a. Gold	1.4	2.0	1.8	2.7	2.4	3.2
b. Silver	0.7	0.6	1.0	1.2	3.0	2.3
c. Credit money	4.1	17.2	5.6	22.4	8.8	27.6
i. Currency[c]	*1.6*	*3.8*	*2.3*	*5.9*	*3.8*	*8.1*
ii. Demand deposits	*2.6*	*13.3*	*3.3*	*16.5*	*5.0*	*19.6*
2. Monetary reserves	**1.0**	**2.7**	**1.5**	**4.0**	**2.0**	**5.3**
a. Gold	0.6	2.1	0.9	3.2	1.3	4.1
b. Silver	0.4	0.6	0.6	0.8	0.7	1.2
3. Total gold and silver	**3.1**	**5.4**	**4.3**	**7.9**	**7.4**	**10.8**
a. Gold	2.0	4.1	2.7	5.9	3.7	7.3
b. Silver	1.1	1.2	1.6	2.0	3.7	3.5
	(In % of money supply)					
1. Money supply	**100**	**100**	**100**	**100**	**100**	**100**
a. Gold	23	10	21	10	17	10
b. Silver	11	3	12	5	21	7
c. Credit money	66	87	67	85	62	83
i. Currency	*25*	*19*	*27*	*22*	*27*	*25*
ii. Demand deposits	*41*	*67*	*39*	*63*	*35*	*59*
2. Monetary reserves	**16**	**14**	**18**	**15**	**14**	**16**
a. Gold	9	11	11	12	9	12
b. Silver	7	3	7	3	5	4
3. Total gold and silver	**49**	**27**	**51**	**30**	**52**	**33**
a. Gold	32	21	32	22	26	22
b. Silver	17	6	19	8	26	11

Source: Triffin (1985, p. 134).

Notes:

[a]United States, United Kingdom and France.

[b]United States, United Kingdom, France, Germany, Italy, Netherlands, Belgium, Sweden, Switzerland, Canada and Japan.

[c]Including subsidiary (non-silver) coinage, except in last column.

Orthodox explanation has it that Britain acted as a hegemon. The evidence goes as follows. Increases in the British bank rate were followed, in most cases, by increases in the bank rates of other countries, suggesting Granger causality from Britain to the rest of the system. Furthermore, if other countries were to match the British bank rate increase, capital would still flow to London, suggesting that London and the Bank of England exerted a centripetal force on the system. To stem reserve outflows, and thus to prevent a convertibility crisis, other countries had to more than match the bank rate increase (Lindert, 1969, p. 47 and following). The question of direct interest to us is whether British hegemony may not exaggerate the working of the system. Indeed, a hierarchical hypothesis seems to fit the facts better than the hegemonic hypothesis. A hierarchical structure acknowledges the existence of effect asymmetries, in the sense that the same action imparts different effects on the system depending on where it is initiated—the higher the position of the actor the larger the effect. But asymmetries do not imply zero feedback effects. The actor located at a higher level of the pyramid is not insulated from the effects of the actions taken by actors located at a lower level of the pyramid. Stated differently, the fact that the elasticity of capital flows to the British bank rate was larger than the corresponding foreign elasticity did not imply that British rates were insulated from changes in other countries' interest rates. Indeed, this was the case: Britain reacted to interest rate changes initiated elsewhere, especially by the two countries that immediately followed her in the hierarchy, France and Germany (Lindert, pp. 49–52). Some countries—Argentina, Bulgaria, Chile, Italy, Mexico, and Portugal—were so low in the hierarchy that were unable to compete in retaining reserves during rounds of bank rate increases and they had either to devalue or leave the standard altogether (Eichengreen, 1985). The pressure on the periphery countries was especially intense during times of gold shortage, causing deflationary pressure and relatively high real interest rates (Flandreau et al., 1998).[2]

There is very little evidence of cooperation in terms of lending facilities or pooling reserves. Whenever it happened, it was on ad hoc basis (Flandreau, 1997). Cooperation was more understood as accepting the rules of the game and refraining from converting suddenly reserves into bullion.

Finally, the relative economic power of the "director of the orchestra" diminished as other nations grew more rapidly (Table 4). The same phenomenon occurred after World War II with the other director of the orchestra, the United States.

1.2. The interwar period

The international system lost its order (i.e., set of rules) after World War I. The Brussels conference of 1920 and the Genoa conference of 1922 aimed at resurrecting a set of rules and an environment of cooperation; in particular, to restore fiscal discipline, central bank independence, and the gold reserve standard. The United Kingdom was a strong voice in the conferences, despite the fact that it had lost its preeminent position as the leading country of the international monetary system. On the other hand, the United States—the country anointed to replace the United Kingdom—decided not to participate at Genoa.

Table 4. Distribution of world industrial production, 1820–1963 (in percentages).

Year	Europe total	U.K.	France	Germany	Russia	Belgium	Scandinavia	Italy	Rest of Europe	USA
1820	100	24	20	15					37	4
1840	99	21	18	17					38	5
1860	100	21	16	15					34	14
1870		32	10	13	4	3	0	2		23
1881–1885		27	9	14	3	3	1	2		29
1896–1900		20	7	17	5	2	1	3		30
1906–1910		15	6	16	5	2	1	3		35
1913		14	6	16	6	2	1	3		36

Source: Rostow (1980, p. 52).

The aims of this effort went completely frustrated because of "incompatible conceptual frameworks and the dispute over war debts and reparations" (Eichengreen, 1992, p. 11).

France strongly opposed the results of the Genoa conference establishing a gold reserve standard, seeing in this an attempt by Britain to reassert the dominance of the pound and London "as international banking center without its obligations (of a leading currency)" (Yeager, 1966, p. 285). What followed were a series of ad hoc decisions without a common design. Germany returned to the gold standard in 1924 in the aftermath of its disastrous hyperinflation, Britain in 1925, and France in 1928. Prewar parities were set in Germany and Britain. Why reenter at the old parities? The rules of the game dictated that, should a country leave the standard it should reenter it at the old parity (McKinnon, 1993).[3] This commitment was supposed to enforce credibility and prevent destabilizing speculation. The evidence shows, however, that several countries reentered the standard with a depreciated currency. Alesina (1988) offers an alternative explanation. The rentier class, interested in the preservation of the real value of debt securities, was able to push for a return to prewar parities because it was in charge of policy making. Central bank independence was an important tool to ensure that debts would not be monetized. The burden of adjustment fell on other groups. As Keynes (1923) had predicted, the return of Britain to prewar parity was extremely deflationary, overvalued the pound, and created a deficit in the current account. Contrary to the hopes of the prewar parity advocates, the necessary downward price adjustment, especially of money wages, did not materialize; the adjustment fell primarily on production and employment (Cleveland, 1976).[4] This evidence is consistent with Alesina's distributional hypothesis.

France's new parity undervalued the French franc, causing a surplus in the current account. Furthermore, widespread speculation of a future appreciation of the French franc was responsible for large capital inflows. Consequently, international reserves exploded and the Banque de France sterilized them to prevent a nominal appreciation of the franc. Saddled with large non-gold reserves the French were reluctant to give Britain the privilege of financing current-account deficits with pound-denominated debt (this argument will resurface again in the Bretton Woods). Consequently, the French opted to redeem reserves into gold, causing deflation in the "center" and easing the pressure on home currency's appreciation. In terms of the implied rules of the game, France was no longer willing to accept the pre-WWI hierarchical structure; that is, it was unwilling to cooperate. But, as Kindleberger (1986, p. 302) puts it, France "...had the power to act as a destabilizer, but...was insufficiently powerful to stabilize."

Scepticism about the viability of the gold reserve standard was not limited to France. The influential Benjamin Strong , Governor of the Federal Reserve Bank of New York, feared that a reserve standard would be inflationary (Clarke, 1971). Consequently, the US as well sterilized reserve inflows. Again, the preservation of the reserve standard depended on the willingness of all countries to cooperate by not cashing paper reserves in gold. In that case reserve countries would be placed in the horns of a dilemma: either abandon the standard or deflate at home. Faced with such choices, the United States opted for a more inward oriented policy at the expense of acting as an international lender of last resort (Kindleberger, 1986).[5]

1.3. Bretton Woods

The Bretton Woods Agreement was built on the ashes of World War II. Eichengreen (1989, pp. 263–267) argues that the Agreement was a collaborative exercise between the two victorious countries, even though the final plan resembled more the wish list of the Americans than that of the British. The influence of Keynes on the negotiating process ensured that a return to the pure gold standard would be a nonstarter. Keynes had deemed this system deflationary and imposing larger burdens on (external) deficit countries than on surplus countries. In its place Keynes would have wished an international clearing union with the power to create international money; debtor countries would have obtained international liquidity by resorting to an overdraft facility, a provision that would have leveled the field between deficit and surplus countries. White, leading the US delegation, was keen in creating a system that would promote international trade and avoid competitive depreciation. In the end the more cautious American approach prevailed: the clearing union would give way to a Fund to which members would make contributions and from which they would draw in limited amounts, for limited time and for the specific purpose of correcting external imbalances. Countries could have pegged their currency either to gold or to the US dollar; gold was demonetized for private transactions. The peg could change if the country could demonstrate a fundamental disequilibrium. Finally, Keynes' aversion for short-term capital flows was sanctified by limiting currency convertibility to current-account transactions. In a nutshell, Bretton Woods tried to mix the credibility of the gold standard with the flexibility of an adjustable peg.

From the very beginning the system operated as a dollar-gold standard. According to the N-degree of freedom paradigm, $N-1$ countries pegged their currencies to the US dollar, while the United States, the Nth country, set the common monetary policy under the constraint that it would convert dollars into gold at a ratio of 35 to 1. The gold link disciplined the United States not to misuse the system's one degree of freedom (Gilbert, 1985).

Unquestionably, the United States came out of the war as the undisputed political and economic leader. Bretton Woods reinforced the dollar as the dominant currency in the world. The IMF, with insufficient resources, was not capable of fulfilling the role of international lender of last resort. This role was assumed by the leading country, which extended generously credit to Europe and Japan, thus easing the so-called dollar shortage.[6] Economic growth was more rapid in Europe and Japan than in the United States and by 1958 most European countries had introduced full currency convertibility. The highly reputable Bundesbank that made the mark an increasingly appealing currency supported the speedy German recovery.[7]

Soon the dollar shortage gave way to a dollar glut. This glut exposed a fundamental weakness in the system. Triffin (1960) was the first to recognize it, although we saw traces of this argument in the interwar period. A dollar-gold standard is not stable because the demand for international liquidity is primarily satisfied by the reserve country issuing dollar-denominated liabilities. But as these liabilities rise relative to the US owned gold stock, international holders of dollars become more dubious about the credibility of the gold conversion clause of dollars. The threat of converting dollar reserves was more than a theoretical possibility. France, true to form, called the bluff against the United States as she did in 1928 against the United Kingdom and justified her action claiming that the US dominant position was "an exorbitant privilege" (Cohen, 1977, p. 98).

To remedy the situation, Triffin proposed that dollars held abroad be replaced by a new medium of international liquidity, an idea reminiscent of Keynes' bancor.[8] Despres et al. (1966) who argue in favor of a pure dollar standard offered an alternative solution. According to these authors the United States acted as a bank for the rest of the world, lending long and issuing short-term liabilities to finance the lending. The gold link was simply a technical mistake that needed to be corrected. Balance-of-payment data corroborate this view: the United States had current account surpluses until 1968, strengthening the US credit position vis-à-vis the rest of the world.

It is fair to say that Bretton Woods lacked flexibility. Devaluations came too late and were synonymous of policy failure; appreciations were rare. When they did occur—as in the case of Germany in 1961—they were insufficient to restore external equilibrium. The asymmetry of adjustment, so much feared by

Keynes, was a feature of Bretton Woods. Furthermore, during the second half of the sixties the center was misbehaving by producing an inflation rate that was neither consistent with the gold conversion clause nor with the preferences of major players like Germany. The incentives for cooperation were petering out. In the words of the report written by the Commission on the Role of Gold (1982, p. 86):

> The Bretton Woods system might have been able to survive an end of gold convertibility. It could not survive the inflationary policies of the center country that characterized the decade from the mid-1960s on.

In 1969 the French franc was devalued and Germany allowed the mark to slightly appreciate against the dollar. Subsequently, other countries decided to disconnect their currencies from the dollar. In 1971 President Nixon abrogated the dollar-gold convertibility clause and in 1973 the United States announced a 10% devaluation of the dollar.

1.4. The European Monetary System

In creating the European Monetary System (EMS), their founders were mindful to avoid two undesirable features of Bretton Woods, its inflexibility and its asymmetric burden of adjustment. The EMS, at least until 1987, showed to be very flexible by producing frequent realignments. As to asymmetry, traditional analysis of the EMS (e.g., Giavazzi and Giovannini, 1989) relies on the hegemonic paradigm, with the Bundesbank setting monetary policy for the whole system. This view was first challenged by Fratianni and von Hagen (1992) who find that the data are not consistent with Germany dominating the EMS in the sense that the Bundesbank determines the system's monetary policy independently of the other monetary authorities and that the other central banks passively follow all Bundesbank actions. The evidence, instead, is consistent with a hierarchical or asymmetric structure, whereby the actions of the Bundesbank have a larger impact on other members' monetary policy decisions than other members' actions have on the Bundesbank policy; in essence, the EMS promoted central banks cooperation more than passive submission to a hegemon.

1.5. Summary

These are the main lessons we learn from our brief historical review.

1. The organization of exchange-rate unions tends to be more hierarchical than hegemonic. The requirements for hegemony are extremely demanding on the data. The hegemon, not only imparts large effects on the rest of the system, but also is insulated from it. In a hierarchical structure, instead,

asymmetries exist but the country at the top of the pyramid is not insulated from the actions taken by countries located at lower levels of the pyramid. Furthermore, cooperation is more consistent with a hierarchical structure than with a hegemonic one. In the gold standard Britain was at the top of the pyramid, followed by the junior core countries France and Germany and finally by passive countries in the periphery. In Bretton Woods the United States replaced the United Kingdom and the dollar replaced the pound sterling. In the EMS Germany replaced the United States and the mark replaced the dollar.

2. A key currency is related not only to the economic size of the issuing country, but also to the size and depth of the financial markets and the external credit position of the country. In the gold standard Britain, at least initially, enjoyed relative economic preeminence, the deepest financial markets, and the largest creditor position. In Bretton Woods the United States was the undisputed economic and financial leader and had accumulated large foreign credit. In the EMS Germany was the largest economic unit and had the most stable currency.[9]
3. The reserve country has a large weight in determining the system's inflation rate (in the hegemonic organizational structure the weight goes to unity). This was true for Britain in the gold standard and even more so for the United States in Bretton Woods. This practice was challenged by some countries, especially France, meaning that some members reject the hierarchical structure or are unwilling to cooperate. More importantly, it revealed the difficulty of the reserve country of both managing internal balance and providing the system with an international currency. This conflict delayed the United States in playing a leading role in the interwar period, and Germany in the 1970s (Bundesbank, 1979, 1984, 1988). Although designed to be symmetric, Bretton Woods and the EMS performed asymmetrically. Here too, members located at lower levels of the EMS hierarchy raised objections to policy dominance.

2. A bipolar world

The formation of EMU will transform the international monetary landscape in the fundamental sense that the hierarchical structure that was successful in the gold standard, Bretton Woods, and the EMS will not longer be applicable in the 21st century. The United States and the EU are, at the moment, comparable in economic size and international trade, accounting for approximately 21% each of the world GDP and 15% each of world exports; and have financial markets of comparable size. Furthermore, the dollar area is much larger than the United States and the euro area will also be larger than the EU. The dollar sphere of influence extends to Latin America, South and East Asia, Iraq, Bahrain, Qatar, Saudi Arabia, and United Arab Emirates. To the euro will gravitate Central and Eastern Europe and the CFA zone. The expected enlargement of the EU, not only to the East, but also to the South raises the odds that Middle Eastern and North African currencies will link with the euro (McCauley, 1997, p. 8). These maps have uncertain boundaries, the redesign of which depends on whatever moves the EU and the United States will be making next. A deepening and widening of NAFTA and the EU will enlarge the sphere of influence of both currencies. The yen is a big question mark. On paper, some Asian currencies would do no worse being anchored to the yen; yet, the dollar remains the anchor of choice, possibly because of the "network" effect (McCauley, p. 30). The deep and still unresolved financial crisis in Japan works against the enlargement of the yen; deregulation of its financial markets, with the attendant decline in transaction costs, goes in the opposite direction. Our best bet is that the yen area will be much smaller than the dollar and the euro area and, consequently, the international monetary system of the 21st century will be shaped in a critical way by the interaction between the two large blocs.

2.1. Potential weaknesses of the euro bloc

Before discussing feasible scenarios of interaction, we compare the relative strengths of the monetary authorities in the two currency blocs. The received wisdom is that the ECB was created as a "harder" copy of the Bundesbank and, consequently, will soon establish low-inflation credibility. Fratianni et al. (1998) caution that the ECB is an untested institution and will operate in a different political environment than the Federal Reserve System in the United States (Artis and Winkler, 1997). The fundamental difference is that the United States is a political and fiscal union, the EMU is not. Political and fiscal union is an important ingredient for the success of a monetary union. Capie (1998, p. 10) looks at the evidence of the 19th century monetary unions and concludes that "...they were principally driven by a desire for political union [and] were essentially currency unions in countries using the same metallic standard." Since EMU is not a political union, the more relevant question is whether currency unions formed by sovereign states are stable. Cohen (1993), after reviewing the experience of six such currency unions, identifies two factors for success: the existence of a local hegemon (e.g., Belgium in the Belgium-Luxembourg Economic Union) or the development of a strong sense of solidarity (e.g., the East Caribbean Currency Area).

The Maastricht treaty rules out the hegemonic solution and goes to great length to rule out solidarity in fiscal matters. The Treaty, not only exonerates member governments from the debt obligations of other member governments, but also imposes fiscal discipline: budget deficits must be contained within 3% of GDP, government debt within 60% of GDP, and governments cannot resort to monetary financing (Salvatore, 1998). Should transgression occur, offending sovereign states would be subject to punishment ranging from branding the debt prospectuses with warning statements all the way to the imposition of fines. Are these treaty clauses credible and enforceable? Consider the following scenario (Fratianni, 1998). Country X, with an initially high ratio of debt to GDP, becomes more fiscally profligate. The ECB pursues a high interest rate policy because most of the EMU, but not Country X, is in the expansion phase of the business cycle. Country X's debt, denominated in euro, carries a default premium. This premium discounts the possibility of Country X's government either consolidating its debt—lengthening of maturities—or raising tax rates on interest payments. There is a premium beyond which investors prefer not to hold government debt. At this point the Treasury of Country X could not renew its debt at maturity and would fail to meet financial obligations. Prices of government securities would fall and trading in these securities would be drastically curtailed. Debt holders would incur a wealth loss. Banks would face a liquidity crisis, in addition to a wealth loss. This is because government debt is an asset that credit institutions trade to adjust their liquidity. The financial crisis would embrace the banking system if the total amount of bank reserves were to fall short of the liquidity requirements of the industry. These events would inevitably shake the confidence of bank deposit holders and instigate bank runs.

The crisis could not be contained within the border of Country X, for two reasons. To begin with, holders of other government debt—debt issued by prudent governments—may wonder whether such a crisis may not occur in their markets as well. The higher degree of uncertainty would spill onto other debt markets and force interest rates to rise.[10] The second reason has to do with the banking crisis. No government can tolerate large bank defaults because of their large negative effect on the rest of the economy. A government debt crisis, inevitably, would force the hand of the ECB in providing the necessary liquidity and thus restore confidence in the banking system of Country X. This liquidity injection may not necessarily imperil the quality of monetary policy in the EMU, so long as the liquidity expansion in Country X's money market were compensated by liquidity absorption in the rest of the EMU, or if the injection were temporary. However, it is very likely that a liquidity crisis in Country X would also affect liquidity in the rest of the EMU area. Banks are in the market of the means of payments and settle with one another debits and credits. Liquidity crises in a national banking system would endanger the safety of the euro payment mechanism. In sum, a liquidity crisis started by fiscal imprudence in Country X is likely to spread to the entire EMU money market. The ECB would have no choice but to inject liquidity, possibly for a long period of time.

The absence of political and fiscal union in EMU may have another negative consequence on the quality of monetary policy. Regional shocks or regional economic disparities cannot be compensated by the center with appropriate fiscal instruments (e.g., the Federal income tax in the United States). The affected regions will express dissatisfaction with the EMU and will blame the ECB for their predicament. This problem is acknowledged in the Delors Report (1989, p. 89):

> In all federations the different combinations of federal budgetary mechanisms have powerful 'shock-absorber' effects, dampening the amplitude either of economic difficulties or of surges in prosperity of individual states. This is both the product of, and the source of the sense of solidarity, which all relevant economic and monetary unions share.

The third and final factor working against the EMU is accountability or lack thereof. The Federal Reserve System is an independent branch of government but is accountable to the US Congress, which created it. The ECB, in contrast, is accountable to no one and can act in total vacuum. For Capie (p. 15) "this looks like a deeply flawed institution." The total insulation enjoyed by the ECB may actually work against the very principles that inspired its establishment. Should the people find that the EMU central bank is not representing them, legitimacy will be lost and with it the quality of monetary policy.

There is a factor that works in favor of the euro area and against the dollar area: EMU is a net creditor vis-à-vis the rest of the world, the United States is a large debtor nation. In Part I of the paper we noted that center country and key currency status was associated with the nation being an external creditor. This was true for Britain during the gold standard and the United States during Bretton Woods. As a result of the current-account deficits of the 1980s and the 1990s the United States has moved from being the largest creditor to the largest debtor nation in the world. Other things the same—i.e., holding constant fundamentals and cyclical variables—a large debtor nation faces a prospective devaluation of its currency in relation to the creditor nation's currency.

2.2. *The transition scenario*

Not only will the ECB be an untested institution, but it will also face a new monetary environment in 1999. To begin with, an EMU price level will have to be constructed by weighting national price levels. Differences in national statistical practices and uncertainty about true national weights will make the constructed aggregate less than perfectly reliable. Furthermore, even if the inflation measure turned out to be sufficiently reliable, the ECB will have no practical experience on the transmission mechanism of monetary policy. The expected change in the stochastic structure underlying macro relationships—i.e., the Lucas critique—will render obsolete part of the stock of knowledge accumulated before EMU.

Inflation targeting, in the initial phase of the EMU, would face the disadvantage that an initial mistake (on the high side of the inflation rate) would undermine the credibility the ECB needs to establish itself as an inflation fighter. Monetary targeting would be no better than inflation targeting for similar reasons: old relationships are not likely to hold. The literature of the early 1990s on the European demand for money appeared overly optimistic in its conclusion that the European aggregate would be more stable and more predictable than national money demand functions. Arnold (1994) examines the relationship between money demand stability and size of the currency area. The result that a multicountry aggregate has smaller variance than a national aggregate depends on two conditions: the first condition is that shocks to national money demand functions are independent across countries and the second is that national variances be of equal size. Since these two conditions are difficult to hold in practice, one cannot make strong predictions about the relative stability of the demand for money and size of the EMU (Arnold, Figures 1 and 2).

Increased financial integration is another argument against money targeting. EMU will exert a strong centripetal force on domestic financial markets; these will have depth, breath, and liquidity close to those in the United States (Fratianni et al., 1998). Transaction costs on financial transactions will be falling and individuals and corporations will further economize on money. The process of integration will not take place over night, but rather over a period of months or years. The European demand for money will be declining, not suddenly, but over a period of months or years, complicating the money targeting procedure of the ECB.

In light of these considerations, the ECB may be persuaded to take the prudent course of targeting the exchange rate between the euro and the dollar. As Masson and Turtelboom (1997, p. 215) put it:

> The exchange rate is a particularly visible and publicly recognized indicator. Indeed, since national currencies will remain in circulation during a transition period, EU citizens will be able to compare exchange rates pre- and post-EMU... Indeed, there is much current discussion in Europe of whether the euro will be 'as strong as' the deutsche mark. In order to judge this, the public is unlikely to be guided in the first instance by European inflation, which will be an unfamiliar aggregate to them... Thus the problem of establishing credibility may lead the ECB to pay more attention to the exchange rate than does the Bundesbank at present, not less.

The ECB may find it in its institutional interest to pursue exchange rate targeting without formalizing it into a policy. Impressions count, especially at the beginning of an institution. An open acknowledgment that the US Federal Reserve System determines monetary policy in the EMU would not square well with advocates of central bank independence.

Beyond the transition period, EMU has several alternative courses of actions. It can decide to cooperate on exchange-rate variability with the other major currency bloc and with Japan; it can assume benign neglect; or can adopt Keynes' preferred plan of stabilizing prices and not exchange rates.

2.3. Cooperation or benign neglect

Even if the two blocs had an incentive to cooperate, a major obstacle to this strategy will be posed by the implied institutional design. There are three possible solutions: the US sets the growth rate of money growth and EMU fixes the exchange rate; the EMU fixes money growth and the US pegs the value of the dollar to that of the euro; or the Fed and the ECB decide jointly the value of the target exchange rate and cooperate on monetary policies. Given the economic and political weight of the two blocs, the first two solutions appear far fetched: neither bloc would be willing to relinquish the role of setting monetary policy and passively adjust to the other bloc's monetary policy. Again, we stress the point that the hierarchical structure of the gold standard, Bretton Woods, and the EMS cannot be reproduced in a bipolar world. The cooperative strategy is the only feasible one. Kenen (1995, pp. 122–123) looks at the incentives for cooperation and arrives at an ambiguous answer. EMU will be approximately as open—measured by the ratio of the sum of exports and imports to GDP—as the United States. Assuming that degree of openness and desire for exchange-rate stability are positively correlated, the construction of EMU, *ceteris paribus*, implies more exchange-rate variability. The ECB is bound to follow the path of the Fed, which is known to be more concerned by domestic than international factors. On the other hand, coordination costs fall when club membership shrinks. Hence, the answer to the question of whether exchange rate would be less volatile is ambiguous.

We note, however, that leading countries tend to initiate cooperation. The hierarchical structure of the gold standard and Bretton Woods could not have succeeded without cooperation. The center countries assumed the role of the international lender of last resort (e.g., the United States and the Marshall Plan) and the periphery accepted the rules of the game. The issue of interest is whether a bipolar system has more incentives to cooperate than the hierarchical structures of the past. The United States and EMU will capture a larger proportion of the benefits from cooperation. Should a regime of exchange-rate stability be welfare improving for the world, the United States and the EMU would reap a large share of these benefits. Hence, their incentives for cooperation rise, not fall, as predicted by the theory of collective action (Olson, 1965; Fratianni and Pattison, 1982). This prediction is opposite from the prediction obtained from the degree of openness. Some evidence in favor of the collection action theory comes from currency crises. The United States has been the principal actor in resolving the Mexican crisis of 1994–1995 and has been leading the charge in the more recent Asian currency crisis. One would expect EMU to internalize a larger share of the benefits from exchange-rate stability than the participating countries. Thus, our conclusion is that a bipolar world may actually deliver more cooperation than the present system, not less.

2.4. Keynes and inflation targeting

Exchange-rate stability is not an objective pursued for its own sake, but serves to facilitate trade and capital flows. Intercountry inflation rate differences and exchange-rate stability imply real exchange rate movements and consequent shifts in competitiveness that have distributional and political consequences. Better to let real exchange rates be determined by real factors for which monetary policy cannot be blamed. If two blocs had identical economic structures, inflation rates, productivity improvements, and shocks, nominal as well as real exchange rates would be stable. The desirability of an exchange rate movement occurs either when shocks are asymmetric or when inflation rates between the blocs differ. What are the prospects that inflation rates are the same in the United States and EMU?

Assume a common negative supply shock. Will the two central banks respond in a similar fashion? Much will depend on the short-run tradeoff between inflation and unemployment. Since US labor markets are more flexible than EMU labor markets, the ECB would have a larger incentive to inflate than the Fed (Fratianni, 1998). These differences in incentives would undermine exchange-rate stability. Given the impossibility to impose either a dollar or a euro standard and the inherent instability of a fixed exchange rate between two large economic blocs that enjoy different degrees of labor mobility, the best chance for cooperation is that the Fed and the ECB target the same long-term rate of inflation. This is what Keynes (1923) advocated in *A Tract on Monetary Reform*. Keynes (p. 117) posed the central question:

> "Is it more important that the value of a national currency should be stable in terms of purchasing power, or stable in terms of the currency of certain foreign countries?"

His answer was unequivocally in favor of stabilizing the purchasing power of the currency because the gold standard, especially in the post-World War I experience, had produced undesirable deflation (pp. 117–125). In addition to avoiding unwanted inflation fluctuations, inflation targets, if properly coordinated, would reduce exchange rate fluctuations. Again quoting from Keynes (pp. 158–159):

> If Great Britain and the United States were both embarked on this policy [i.e., pursuing stability of the commodity value of the national currency] and if both were successful, our secondary desideratum, namely the stability of the dollar-exchange standard, would follow as a consequence. I agree with Mr. Hawtrey that the ideal state of affairs is an intimate co-operation between the Federal Reserve System and the Bank of England, as a result of which stability of prices and of exchange would be achieved at the same time. But I suggest that it is wiser and more practical that this should be allowed to develop out of the experience and mutual advantage, without either side binding itself to the other... A collaboration which is not free on both sides is likely to lead to decisions, especially if the business of keeping dollars steady involves a heavy expenditure in burying unwanted gold.
>
> ...we have not yet reached the point when the management can be entrusted to a single authority. The best we can do, therefore, is to have *two* managed

currencies, sterling and dollars, with as close a collaboration as possible between the aims and methods of the management.

Keynes, as noted in part one of the paper, would have wished a world monetary union. Recognizing the implausibility of his proposal, he chose the next-best solution, one where countries set, not only coordinated inflation targets, but also a procedure to ensure that these targets would be achieved. That leads us directly into today's literature on inflation targeting, with its emphasis on transparency and flexibility (Mishkin and Posen, 1997; Laubach and Posen, 1997). Transparency translates in the monetary authorities communicating clearly with the public about goals and strategy. The public outreach policy enhances central bank's legitimacy. Furthermore, it allows the use of discretion (i.e., flexibility) when it is most needed, in time of shocks, without compromising the belief in the validity of the central bank's goals.

Common long-run inflation targets—say at approximately 2%—do not mean automatically that nominal exchange rates will be stable. Changes in real exchange rates, portfolio shift, and the inevitable noise, so typical of auction markets, would cause movements and jolts to the nominal exchange rate. What consistent inflation target can deliver is long-run predictability of the most important exchange rate in the international monetary system. The current philosophical climate in central banking appears very favorable for the implementation of an old proposal.

Appendix: Comparison of monetary and real variables across monetary regimes

We present summary statistics on a few macroeconomic variables of the G-7 group under four different monetary regimes: the gold standard (G) from 1881 to 1913, the interwar period (I) from 1919 to 1938, the Bretton Woods system (BW) from 1946 to 1970, and the subsequent period, spanning from 1974 to 1995, which we conveniently labelled as floating (F). There is a large literature on the relative performance of different monetary regimes and we refer the reader to Bordo (1993a, 1993b).

The data are presented graphically to underscore possible differences across regimes.[11] Chart 1 plots the relationship between inflation and per capita output growth for the period 1881 to 1995. Each observation represents the regime average, for a total of 28 observations. There is no significant association between inflation and output growth. The estimated coefficient of the regression of the latter on the former is 0.18 with a standard error of .096, statistically not different from zero under traditional confidence intervals. The G period had no trend inflation and an average output growth of 1.5%. In the I period the average inflation fell below zero. During the F period inflation rose, relative to BW, for some countries—US, UK, Germany, Canada, and Italy—but fell for others (France and Japan). Output growth fell for all seven countries. To be sure, the

Chart 1: Inflation and Growth in the G7
1881-1995

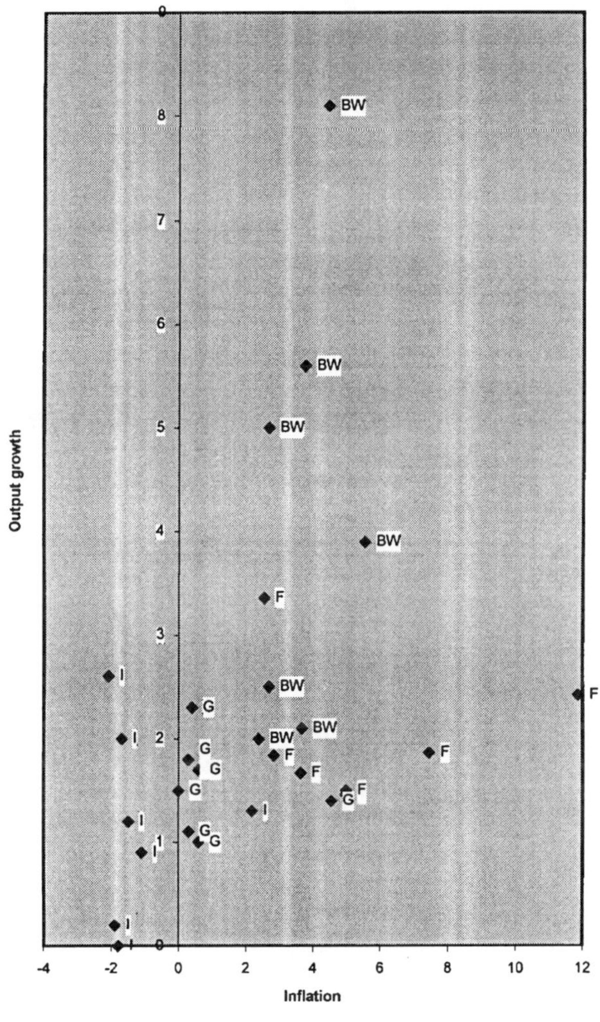

Figure 1.

four regimes are not comparable because the economies were affected by different shocks and because the underlying economic structures were evolving. Yet, the claim that central bank reputation can affect economic growth does not emerge from the historical record of low-to-moderate levels of inflation rates.

Chart 2 plots the relationship between the variability of inflation and the variability of output growth, where variability is measured by the standard deviation around the sample mean. There is a strong, positive relationship between the

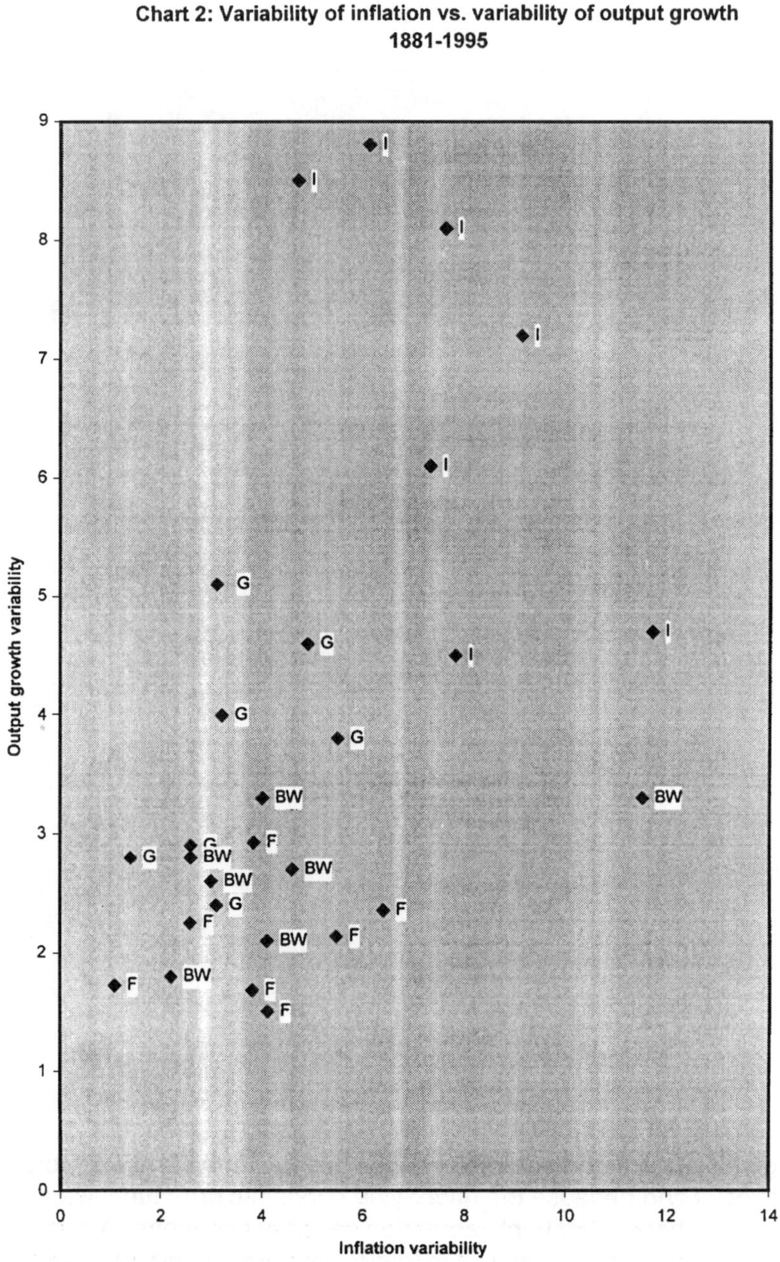
Chart 2: Variability of inflation vs. variability of output growth
1881-1995
Output growth variability
Inflation variability
0
1
2
3
4
5
6
7
8
9
0
2
4
6
8
10
12
14
I
G
BW
F

Figure 2.

Chart 3: Nominal and real exchange rate variability
1881-1995

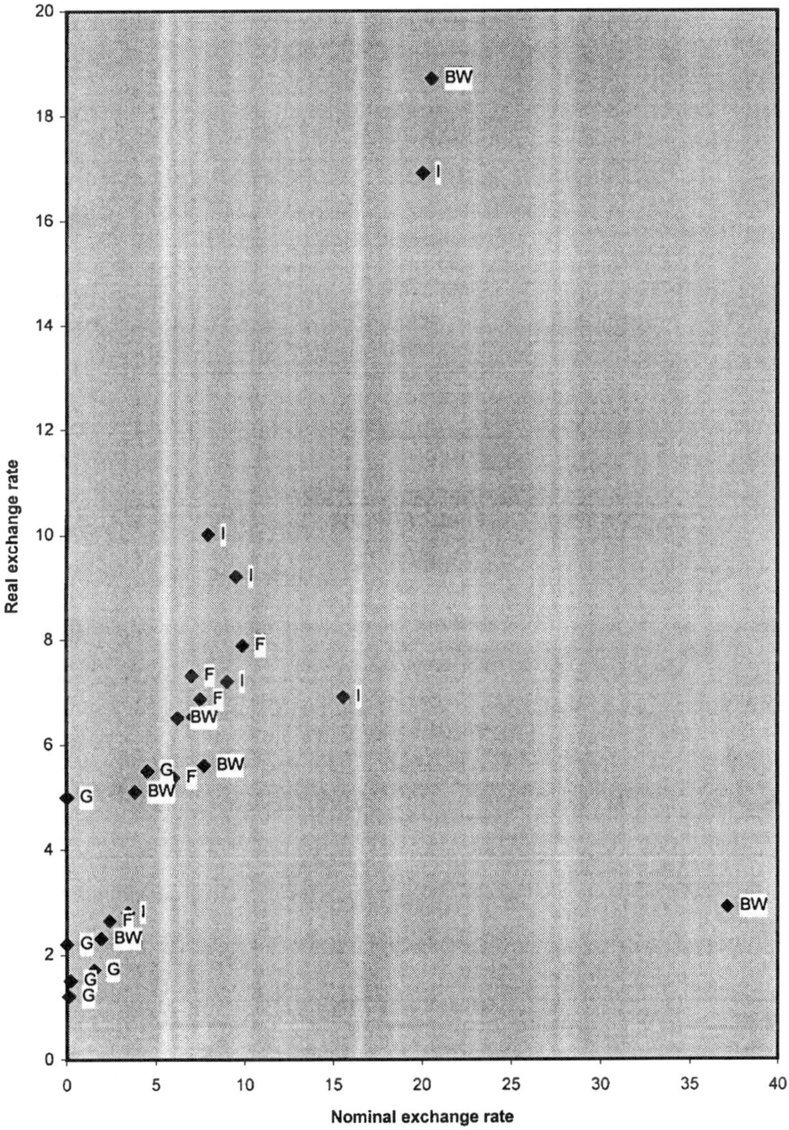

Figure 3.

two: the slope coefficient of the regression of output variability on inflation variability is .36 with a standard error of .136, statistically different from zero under traditional confidence intervals. The BW and F observations tend to be located in the South West corner of the graph; the G and I observations in the North East corner. The G period was one of low average inflation, but of relatively high inflation and output growth variability; the BW period was less volatile than the G period; and the F period was a mixture of cases where variability rose and others where variability declined. The literature deems that supply shocks were more important in the G period than in the BW and F periods. The consensus is that the gold standard was able to absorb the shocks better than other regimes because of more flexible input markets. Also, institutional design may have something to do with the explanation.

Chart 3 plots the variability of nominal exchange rate against the variability of real exchange rate. Since the exchange rates are defined in terms of the US dollar, the United States have been omitted and the number of observations drops to 24. The relationship is strongly positive: the slope coefficient of the regression of the variability of real exchange rate on the variability of the nominal exchange rate is .25 with a standard error of .096, statistically different from zero. This positive correlation is well known and has been interpreted in various ways. One explanation is that price levels are rigid relative to the nominal exchange rate. Another explanation is that productivity shocks affect real exchange rates and these in turn affect nominal exchange rates; under fixed rates monetary authorities resist nominal exchange rate changes.

Notes

1. We have been very selective in an immense literature and refer only to Kindleberger (1973) and Keohane (1984), representing respectively the economics and political science literature, for the hegemonic hypothesis. For the application of the hegemonic hypothesis to the European Monetary System the standard reference is Giavazzi and Giovannini (1989). The reader may want to consult Eichengreen (1989) for a broader set of references.
2. Countries went beyond interest rate changes in influencing capital movements. They manipulated gold points; made redemption from currency to gold only available at their financial center (capital) to impede gold export, or offered redemption at the border to attract gold imports; resorted to moral suasion to prevent export gold although the exchange rate had exceeded the export gold point; and intervened in the foreign exchange to keep the exchange within the bands, though they tried to sterilize the impacts of capital flows in order to insulate the domestic economy (Bloomfield, 1959).
3. Brown (1929, p. 239) summarizes the viewpoint of the Cunliffe Committee as "...it was to be the British policy to *force* the exchange rate to the old parity in any event in a short time even if this involved again overvaluing the pound and causing deflation in England..."
4. It is often argued that increased price rigidity was caused by a higher rate of unionization, enlargement of suffrage, and a swing from an economic policy that emphasized the external balance to another that placed more importance on full employment. Central banks were either nationalized or made dependent on government to ensure that monetary policy would be consistent with the new objectives (Capie, 1998). On the other hand, Triffin (1985) finds no evidence for nominal wage flexibility during the gold standard, while Flandreau et al. (1998) conclude that the process of enlarged suffrage was well under way at the end of the 19th century.

5. This inward oriented policy included restrictions on imports in 1930 and small governmental lending to ease capital shortage, especially in war debt and reparation laden Germany.
6. The two great ventures promoted by the United States were the Marshall Plan and the European Payment Union. The latter guaranteed preferential trade and payment arrangements within Europe to ease the dollar shortage (Cohen, 1977). The hegemonic country was willing to accept temporary measures of discrimination with the prospect of enhancing a freer international trade environment in the longer run. For Keohane (1984) these examples demonstrate that a hegemon neither imposes policies on others nor refuses to engage in cooperation.
7. Up to 1958 the German central bank was called "Bank deutscher Laender" (Deutsche Bundesbank, 1995).
8. Triffin's focus was on money as international reserve and not as a private store of value. This may explain why he did not suggest cutting the link between the dollar and gold and opted, instead, for a new international money, issued under the control of a supranational institution.
9. What does not fit in this picture are the relatively underdeveloped financial markets of Germany.
10. The experience of the Mexican crisis of 1994–1995 is illustrative in this context. Several Latin American countries felt the negative effects of the peso devaluation. Equity prices fell indiscriminately without regard to the underlying fundamentals. Only after some time, investors began to discriminate between fundamentally healthy economies—e.g., Chile—and unhealthy ones. This blind reaction of the public is reminiscent of bank panics, where the public is incapable of differentiating liquid from illiquid banks.
11. Data on the inflation rate, real per capita growth, nominal and real exchange rate for the period 1881–1989 come from Bordo (1993a). We used the International Financial Statistics CD-ROM for the remaining period; the GNP deflator for Italy and Japan was available only up to 1992. Growth rates are the first differences of the natural logarithms and variability is measured by the standard deviation around the sample mean of the growth rates.

References

Alesina, R. (1988) "The End of Large Public Debt." In F. Giavazzi and L. Spaventa (eds.), *High Public Debt: The Italian Experience*. Cambridge, New York, New Rochelle, Melbourne, and Sydney: Cambridge University Press.

Arnold, I.J.M. (1994) "The Myth of a Stable European Money Demand." *Open Economies Review* 5(3).

Artis, M.J. and B. Winkler (1997) "The Stability Pact: Safeguarding the Credibility of the European Central Bank." CEPR Discussion Paper No. 1688 23, London.

Bloomfield, A.I. (1959) *Monetary Policy under the International Gold Standard: 1880–1914*. New York: Federal Reserve Bank.

Bordo, M.D. (1993a) "The Gold Standard, Bretton Woods and Other Monetary Regimes: A Historical Appraisal." *Federal Reserve Bank of St. Louis Review*, March/April, 123–191.

Bordo, M.D. (1993b) "The Bretton Woods International Monetary System: A Historical Overview." In M.D. Bordo and B. Eichengreen (eds.), *A Retrospective on the Bretton Woods System*. Chicago and London: The University of Chicago Press.

Brown, W.A. (1929) *England and the New Gold Standard, 1919–1926*. New Haven: Yale University Press.

Capie, F. (1998) "Monetary Unions in Historical Perspective: What Future for the Euro in the International Financial System." in this volume.

Clarke, S.V.O. (1971) *Exchange-Rate Stabilization in the Mid-1930s: Negotiating the Tripartite Agreement*. Princeton Studies in International Finance No. 41, Princeton University Press.

Cleveland, H. Van B. (1976) "The International Monetary System in the Interwar Period." In B.M. Rowland (ed.), *Balance of Power of Hegemony: The Interwar Monetary System*. New York: New York University Press.

Cohen, B.J. (1977) *Organizing the World's Money. The Political Economy of International Monetary Relations*. New York: Basic Books, Inc., Publishers.

Cohen, B.J. (1993) "Beyond EMU: The Problem of Sustainability." *Economics and Politics* 5, 187–203.

Commission on the Role of Gold in the Domestic and International Monetary System (1982). Report. Washington, DC: Government Printing Office.

Corden, R.N. (1983) "The Logic of the International Monetary Non-System." In F. Machlup (ed.), *Reflection of a Troubled World Economy*. McMillan.

De Cecco, M. (1984) *The International Gold Standard. Money and Empire*. London: Frances Pinter.

Delors Report (1989) Committee for the Study of Economic and Monetary Union, *Report on Economic and Monetary Union in the European Community*. Luxembourg: Office for Official Publications of the EC.

Despres, E., C.P. Kindleberger, and W.S. Salant (1966) "The Dollar and World Liquidity—A Minority View." *The Economist*, Feb., 526–529.

Deutsche Bundesbank (1979) "The Deutsche Mark as an International Investment Currency." *Monthly Report* 31(11).

Deutsche Bundesbank (1984) "The Deutsche Mark as an International Investment Currency." *Monthly Report* 36(1).

Deutsche Bundesbank (1988) "Forty Years of the Deutsche Mark." *Monthly Report* 40(5).

Deutsche Bundesbank (1995) *The Monetary Policy of the Bundesbank*. Frankfurt a.M.

Eichengreen, B. (1985) "Editor's Introduction." In B. Eichengreen (ed.), *The Gold Standard in Theory and History*. New York and London: Methuen.

Eichengreen, B. (1989) "Hegemonic Stability Theories of the International Monetary System." In R.N. Cooper, B. Eichengreen et al. (eds.), *Can Nations Agree*? Washington, DC: Brookings Institution.

Eichengreen, B. (1992) *Golden Fetters. The Gold Standard and the Great Depression, 1919–1939*. New York and Oxford: Oxford University Press.

Eichengreen, B. and A.J. Frankel (1996) "The SDR, Reserve Currencies, and the Future of the International Monetary System." In M. Mussa, J. Boughton, and P. Isard (eds.), *The Future of the SDR in Light of Changes in the International Monetary System*. Washington, DC: International Monetary Fund.

Flandreau, M. (1997) "Central Bank Co-operation in Historical Perspective: A Sceptical View." Paper presented at the International Conference, Economic Globalization and International Organizations, Potsdam.

Flandreau, M., J. Le Cacheau, and F. Zumer (1998) "Stability Without a Pact? Lessons from the European Gold Standard 1880–1914." CEPR, Discussion Paper Series, No. 1872.

Fratianni, M. and J. Pattison (1982) "The Economics of International Organizations." *Kyklos* 35(2), 244–262.

Fratianni, M. and J. von Hagen (1992) *The European Monetary System and European Monetary Union*. Boulder, San Francisco, and Oxford: Westview Press.

Fratianni, M. (1998) "Maxi versus Mini EMU: The Political Economy of Stage III." *The Columbia Journal of European Law* 4(2).

Fratianni, M., A. Hauskrecht, and A. Maccario (1998) "Dominant Currencies and the Future of the Euro." in this volume.

Giavazzi, F. and A. Giovannini (1989) *Limiting Exchange Rate Flexibility: The European Monetary System*. Cambridge, MA: MIT Press.

Gilbert, M. (1985) "The Gold-Dollar System: Conditions of Equilibrium and the Price of Gold." In B. Eichengreen (ed.), *The Gold Standard in Theory and History*. New York and London: Methuen.

Hamada, K. (1998) "The Choice of International Monetary Regimes in a Context of Repeated Games." in this volume.

Kenen, P.B. (1995) *Economic and Monetary Union in Europe. Moving beyond Maastricht*. Cambridge University Press.

Keohane, R.O. (1984) *After Hegemony. Cooperation and Discord in the World Political Economy*. Princeton, New Jersey: Princeton University Press.

Keynes, J.M. (1923) *A Tract on Monetary Reform*. London: Macmillan.

Kindleberger, C.P. (1973) *International Economics*. 5th ed. Homewood, IL: R.D. Irwin.
Kindleberger, C.P. (1986) *The World in Depression, 1929–1939*. Berkley and Los Angeles: University of California Press.
Laubach, T. and A.S. Posen (1997) "Disciplined Discretion: Monetary Targeting in Germany and Switzerland." *Essays in International Finance*, vol. 206, Princeton: Princeton University.
Lindert, P.H. (1969) "Key Currencies and Gold, 1900–1913." *Princeton Studies in International Finance*, vol. 24, Princeton University.
Masson, P.R. and B.G. Turtelboom (1997) "Characteristics of the Euro, the Demand for Reserves, and Policy Coordination under EMU." In P.R. Masson, T.H. Krueger, and B.G. Turtelboom (eds.), *EMU and the International Monetary System*. Washington, DC: The International Monetary Fund.
McCauley, R.N. (1997) "The Euro and the Dollar." *Essays in International Finance*, vol. 205, International Finance Section, Princeton University.
McKinnon, R.L. (1993) "Rules of the Game: International Money in Historical Perspective." *Journal of Economic Literature* 31, 1–44.
Mishkin, F.S. and A.S. Posen (1997) "Inflation Targeting: Lessons from Four Countries." Federal Reserve Bank of New York. *Economic Policy Review* 3(3), 9–110.
Mundell, R. (1972) "The Future of the International Monetary System." In A.L.K. Acheson, J.F. Chant, and M.F.J. Prachowny (eds.), *Bretton Woods Revisited*. Toronto: Toronto Univerity Press.
Olson, M. (1965) *The Logic of Collective Action*. Cambridge: Harvard University Press.
Rostow, W.W. (1980) *The World Economy: History and Prospect*. Austin and London: University of Texas Press.
Salvatore, D. (1998) "Present International Monetary and Financial Arrangements." in this volume.
Triffin, R. (1960) *Gold and the Dollar Crises*. New Haven: Yale University Press.
Triffin, R. (1985) "The Myth and Realities of the So-Called Gold Standard." In B. Eichengreen (ed.), *The Gold Standard in Theory and History*. New York and London: Methuen.
US Gold Commission (1982) *Report to the Congress of the Commission on the Role of Gold in the Domestic and International Monetary Systems*, Washington, D.C.: US Government Printing Office.
Yeager, L.B. (1966) *International Monetary Relations: Theory, History, and Policy*. New York: Harper & Row Publishers.

Open economies review 9:S1 637–664 (1998)

On the Relation between Money and Derivatives and its Application to the International Monetary Market

PAOLO SAVONA pasavona@tin.it
Department of Political Economy, University of Rome "Tor Vergata", Via del Plebiscito, 102 Rome, Italy

AURELIO MACCARIO asscarli@luiss.it
Department of Economics, Luiss University, Viale di Villa Massimo 57, 00161 Rome, Italy

Key words: derivatives, interest rates, speculative money, monetary base, systemic instability

JEL Classification Numbers: E51, E58, F34

Abstract

The paper deals with the problem of defining money in a system with derivatives. We conclude that derivatives have to be included in the definition of money, and support our conclusions with an econometric test on the New York Stock Exchange (NYSE) and Chicago Board of Trade indexes. We focus on the direct relationship between derivatives' supply and the interest rate, the analytical basis of speculative money demand introduced by Keynes and the foundation of the Fratianni-Savona model to single out the international monetary base. Consequently, monetary aggregates measured by international institutions, such as the Bank for International Settlements, underestimate the actual offshore market size. Derivatives are the primary instruments used by speculators. There is money, mainly in reserve currencies, that is not controlled and that may cause systemic instability (e.g., the recent Asian crisis).

1. An analytic definition of the monetary base

In analyzing the development of the Eurodollar market, Fratianni and Savona (1972) distinguished between the "instrumental" and "functional" definitions of the monetary base, proposed, among others, by Friedman and Schwartz (1963). Use of this instrument of analysis has not only revolutionized statistics, previously centered on the distinction between primary and secondary liquidity, but has opened new paths of knowledge in regard to the theory of money. The "instrumental" definition identifies the monetary base through the instruments by which it is made (e.g., paper money, and, in Italy, postal savings deposits). The "functional" definition specifies that the monetary base is composed of those instruments whose function is that of compulsory reserves at the central bank or excess reserves by banks.[1]

Neither of these definitions allows for an analysis of the mechanisms that regulate international money creation, since it is difficult to distinguish between international monetary base (IMB) and monetary assets. Furthermore, there is no compulsory reserve on bank deposits in foreign currency (the so-called cross-border deposits) for most countries, as there is for domestic money.[2] Generally, such deposits are accepted by other countries, (the "dollar is welcome" principle) and it is not thought necessary to restrain the "global" supply of money. Most active international banks in foreign currency markets maintain excess reserves in the form of deposits or liquid assets located in the countries of the denomination currency: dollars in the United States, marks in Germany, yens in Japan, currencies that act as the monetary base for "international" deposits, i.e., IMB.

Following the old distinction between primary and secondary liquidity, the United States, as creators of international money (IM), felt it necessary to present its balance of payments in a way different than those of other countries. The U.S. balance "on a liquidity basis" had the objective of evaluating precisely the liquidity introduced into the international monetary system, according to the concept in force at that time. Fratianni and Savona (1972, p. 35) quantified the same disequilibria using a functional definition of the monetary base and obtaining a balance on an IMB basis. In this way, the balance of payment of countries creating international money could be considered a proxy of central banks' balance sheets operating in the international monetary system. Countries that provide reserve money have permanent structural balance-of-payments deficits, whereas others have structural surpluses.[3] These two authors (pp. 137–156) identified, and satisfactorily tested, different interest rate reactions to changes in the supplies of each asset considered. Therefore, the "analytical" distinction between monetary base and money was grounded on the liquidity effect: monetary base is composed of all those instruments that when their supply increases the interest rate declines. It should be pointed out that the negative correlation between the interest rate and monetary base holds for unchanged inflation expectations by economic agents; thus, it is an unanticipated increase in the monetary base that affects the nominal and the real interest rate. Without this qualification, the relationship changes. If prevalent expectations are rational, the market will react to a greater creation of monetary base by raising the interest rates in order to incorporate higher inflation expectations.

The final objective of the Fratianni-Savona model was to ascertain whether a multiplier effect was operational in the international money market. The alternative hypotheses were either that this market simply reallocated monetary assets along the lines of the Tobin portfolio approach or that there was accounting duplication through the redepositing of part of the official reserves by countries which were not currency creators.[4] The debate of the 1960s and of the 1970s centered on the appropriateness of regulating the Eurodollar market. The money multiplier hypothesis of the Eurodollar market had the obvious policy implication that some form of regulation of this market was necessary if one wanted to control the growth of international money. The alternative hypotheses were consistent with a hands-off policy. The prevailing American view, which won, was that it would have been a political error to extend domestic money control to international money markets. The Fratianni-Savona hypothesis fell just in the middle of the market-control controversy and its influence on policy did not extend beyond some parts of continental Europe.

We shall finish this brief account of the competing views of the international money market by revisiting two issues, one grounded in history and the other based on evidence. The historical issue is the old clash between the "Banking School" and the "Currency School." The Banking School denied the proposition that a banking system, as opposed to an individual bank, could create money; the Currency School, instead, accepted it. The Currency School won the debate and, in the process, brought about the creation of the modern central bank, an institution that has a monopoly of monetary base creation and operates "best" when it is independent of governments (see Capie, this volume). There is no disagreement on these propositions at the national level. However, at the international level, the "Banking School" has been resurrected as a "Trojan horse" under the rubric of markets' freedom. As to the evidence, an increase in sight deposits (or primary liquidity, using the old terminology) held by nonresidents in the United States correlates negatively with a reduction in international interest rates on dollar assets (and not only on these, given the relevance of this currency in global business). On the contrary, an increase in assets held outside the United States presents an opposite effect.[5] Maccario (1996) has confirmed these effects, using the more recent period 1982–1994.

2. The implications deriving from financial innovations on the analytical definition of money

The use of an "analytical" definition of monetary base and money, focused on different reactions of interest rates to changes in quantities supplied, is bound to create problems when a new instrument, having characteristics similar to monetary base or money, appears on the market. The most efficient way to distinguish between money and monetary base is to test econometrically the reaction of each instrument to the interest rate.

Despite the noted controversy surrounding the working of the Eurodollar market, there is a perception that the sum of national money supplies is less than the quantity of global money, suggesting that something is beyond the control of the national monetary authorities despite their attempt to coordinate policies at the Bank for International Settlements (BIS). Yet, we have seen little action from any of the BIS committees, starting from the Standing Committee on the Eurodollar Market, established in 1972, all the way to the latest Surveillance Committee on Derivatives.

Developments in financial derivatives raise, once again, the question of what is money (von Hagen and Fender, 1998); not only because the Keynesian speculative demand frequently assumes a "derivatives" form, but also because these new instruments affect directly or indirectly interest and exchange rates. Financial innovation is bound to make current definitions of money obsolete. Having moved from the narrow M1 (money + sight deposits) to M2 (M1 + time deposits) and M3 (M2 + other liquifiable assets), we may have to take a further step and land on a money aggregate that includes financial derivatives, say M4. This evolution would be in line with what banks and financial institutions do these days and will usher in the new era where paper money and checks will be replaced by computer registrations, *monetics* or truly *bookkeeper's pen money*.

The stock of money in the world (WM) is the sum of domestic money stocks (DM) and international money (IM):

$$\mathrm{WM} = \sum \mathrm{DM} + \mathrm{IM} \tag{1}$$

IM can be calculated in two different ways. The first way is to sum all deposits in foreign currencies held by residents (D^r_{fc}) plus all deposits in domestic currency held by nonresidents (D^{nr}_{dc}) plus deposits in foreign currency held by nonresidents (D^{nr}_{fc}):

$$\mathrm{IM} = \sum \left(D^r_{fc} + D^{nr}_{dc} + D^{nr}_{fc}\right) \tag{2}$$

The second method is to obtain IM from the IMB and a money multiplier, m:

$$\mathrm{IM} = m(\mathrm{IMB}). \tag{3}$$

The proposed new definition of international money (NIM) includes the total amount of derivatives for international use (IDER):

$$\mathrm{NIM} = \mathrm{IM} + \mathrm{IDER}. \tag{4}$$

The new world money therefore becomes

$$\mathrm{WM} = \sum \mathrm{DM} + \mathrm{DDER} + \mathrm{IM} + \mathrm{IDER}, \tag{5}$$

where DDER denotes the stock of derivatives for domestic uses.

In what follows we offer alternative versions of IMB, IM and NIM and test their impact on interest rates.

3. Quantification of IMB for the period 1982–1995

For Fratianni and Savona (1972, p. 23), IMB is "the complex of activity that can be used by central banks (or institutions with equivalent functions) by commercial banks and by the public to satisfy their requirements in reserve, independent of the nature of such necessity." In the current context of the international monetary system, it is necessary to characterize IMB in terms of total dollar availability, without constraints, and in terms of other currencies only if held by nonresidents, freely.[6]

Creators of IMB are central banks and banking systems of reserve-currency countries; the International Monetary Fund; and nonreserve-currency monetary authorities when they carry out a currency swap involving a reserve currency. IMB is created through the external imbalances of reserve-currency countries, measured on an IMB basis; by IMF decisions that affect international liquidity (e.g., SDR allocations); and by bilateral and multilateral credit agreements of credit, such as currency swaps and standbys. Tables 1 through 4 give an estimate of the total IMB under the current international monetary system. The tables also show the distribution of IMB among large categories of holders. In particular, Table 1 gives the quantifiable sources of IMB, Table 2 the quantifiable uses of IMB, Table 3 the external imbalance of the United States on an IMB basis, and Table 4 the German external imbalance, also on an IMB basis. Japan is the obvious omission; unfortunately, the official statistics of this country do not permit a statistical analysis of this kind.

It can be inferred from Table 1 that, in the period under consideration, 1982–1995, the IMB grew by 192%, a rate that is much faster than the growth of international trade. The abundance of international liquidity in international markets replays the situation of the early nineties, following prolonged U.S. monetary expansion. The Federal Reserve maintained short-term rates close to 3% for about two years. In those circumstances, yields on medium and long-term securities in leading markets declined steadily and substantially until the end of 1993. Those on 10-year U.S. Treasury Bonds fell from 7% at the beginning of 1992 to about 5% in October 1993; and yields on German securities fell from 8% to below 6% at the end of 1993. From February 1994, in connection with the shift in U.S. monetary policy, interest rates rose rapidly everywhere and began to decline gradually after the Mexican crisis in spring 1995 (Fazio, 1998).

Further analysis of Table 1 reveals that the U.S. and German monetary systems have created 87% of the IMB, against 6.8% of the IMF and of the EMS countries. The very rapid growth of the international money supply could be a reason for the success of speculative assaults on currencies such as the Mexican peso in 1994, the Italian lira and other EMS currencies in 1992 and 1993, and the 1997 currency attacks in Asia. This very rapid growth of international money, partly real and partly potential, can be dealt with either through some form of direct control on the international market—for example, compulsory reserves—or by extending the use of international financial instruments like the SDRs to enhance the control of international liquidity. The issue of extending control to the international money markets has been championed recently by the Governor of the Bank of Italy, Antonio Fazio (1998, p. 9): "In the present phase the international economy is exposed to the risk of systemic instability... International portfolio investment flows have been of unprecedented size in the last few years; it is necessary at least to monitor them and to some extent to govern them."

Table 1. Sources of international monetary base (annual changes in billions of US dollars).

Items	1982	1983	1984	1985	1986	1987	1988	1989	1990	1991	1992	1993	1994	1995	Amounts Dec. 1995
1.1 International Monetary Fund: total position in IMB	−0.01	22.45	−1.78	−4.45	−5.65	−4.17	−4.97	5.65	−8.48	6.69	3.71	−8.92	1.93	10.78	92.07
1.1.1 Reserve position	6.09	20.37	3.72	−4.16	−5.05	−5.80	−4.76	−4.16	−2.53	3.12	11.89	−1.64	−1.64	6.29	47.03
1.1.2 SDR	1.93	−4.91	3.12	2.53	1.93	1.04	−0.06	−0.30	−0.15	0.30	−11.45	2.53	1.64	3.73	22.30
1.1.3 Available credit lines	−8.03	6.99	−8.62	−2.82	−2.53	0.59	−0.15	10.11	−5.80	3.27	3.27	−9.81	1.93	0.76	22.74
1.2 Sight liabilities of United States	51.73	57.47	35.37	24.24	73.45	70.61	62.30	22.44	4.00	10.25	16.50	50.23	93.47	47.20	805.82
1.2.1 Deposits of foreign commercial banks at U.S. commercial banks	17.10	9.45	11.89	2.23	15.34	16.64	−0.59	11.15	−2.38	−7.73	9.37	15.01	9.96	−6.60	115.38
1.2.2 U.S. banks short-term liabilities vis-à-vis foreign affiliates	22.59	26.91	5.80	23.64	37.01	39.99	42.37	31.66	2.97	7.73	1.93	−14.87	81.31	0.98	396.54

(*Continued on next page.*)

Table 1. *(Continued).*

1.3 Sight Liabilities of Germany	6.11	0.60	16.50	−1.04	7.73	5.56	12.02	31.81	17.33	5.14	25.27	23.48	40.28	38.57	374.67
1.3.1 Deposits of foreign commercial banks at German banks	2.68	1.04	8.62	0.14	5.35	5.06	8.77	12.78	13.53	12.04	23.64	8.92	42.81	32.17	215.56
1.3.2 German banks short-term liabilities vis-à-vis foreign affiliates	0.30	−0.89	0.59	0.01	0.15	0.06	−0.03	0.01	−0.07	−0.06	1.04	0.74	−3.12	2.07	101.16
1.4 European Monetary System: Total position in IMB	13.08	12.48	0.00	−10.26	1.19	12.34	−2.38	−2.23	−3.57	0.00	5.95	8.77	−0.30	−3.11	84.36
1.4.1 Available credit lines	6.84	6.24	—	—	—	—	—	1.93	—	0.45	—	—	—	—	13.13
1.4.2 ECU created vis-à-vis gold and dollars	6.24	6.24	0.00	−10.26	1.19	12.34	−2.38	−4.16	−3.57	−0.45	5.95	8.77	−0.30	−3.11	71.23
Total (1.1 + 1.2 + 1.3 + 1.4)	70.91	93.00	50.09	8.49	76.72	84.34	66.97	57.67	9.28	22.08	51.43	73.56	135.38	93.44	1356.92

Sources: IMF, "International Financial Statistics"; U.S. Department of Commerce, "Survey of Current Business"; Federal Reserve System, "Federal Reserve Bulletin"; U.S. Treasury Department, "Treasury Bulletin"; Deutsche Bundesbank, "Monthly Report" and "Statistical Supplement to the Monthly Report", 3rd series.
"Balance of Payments Statistics", various issues.

Table 2. Uses of international monetary base (annual changes in billions of US dollars).

Items	1982	1983	1984	1985	1986	1987	1988	1989	1990	1991	1992	1993	1994	1995	Amounts Dec. 1995
2.1 Official agencies holdings of IMB	91.43	116.88	67.78	44.62	127.88	128.63	111.13	102.71	13.44	22.08	56.78	64.93	226.95	90.93	1784.48
2.1.1 Reserve position in the IMF	6.09	20.37	3.72	−4.16	−5.05	−5.80	−4.76	−4.16	−2.53	3.12	11.89	−1.64	−1.64	6.29	47.03
2.1.2 SDR	1.93	−4.91	3.12	2.53	1.93	1.04	−0.06	−0.30	−0.15	0.30	−11.45	2.53	1.64	3.73	22.30
2.1.3 Available credit lines at the IMF	−8.03	6.99	−8.62	−2.82	−2.53	0.59	−0.15	10.11	−5.80	3.27	3.27	−9.81	1.93	0.76	22.74
2.1.4 Sight assets vis-à-vis US monetary system	−6.54	7.43	8.76	−6.24	19.32	16.06	13.53	−25.72	5.94	15.90	12.34	54.25	−2.41	46.89	224.95
2.1.5 Sight assets vis-à-vis German monetary system	2.83	−0.59	2.38	1.34	4.76	−0.15	5.06	16.79	1.34	−8.62	−7.29	8.47	−3.87	1.19	11.16
2.1.6 Available credit lines in the IMF	6.84	6.24	—	—	—	—	—	1.93	—	0.45	—	—	—	—	13.13
2.1.7 ECU created vis-à-vis gold and dollars	6.24	6.24	0.00	−10.26	1.19	12.34	−2.38	−4.16	−3.57	−0.45	5.95	8.77	−0.30	−3.11	71.23

(*Continued on next page.*)

Table 2. (*Continued*).

2.2 Commercial banks holdings of IMF	13.38	11.59	0.59	−10.25	1.34	12.40	−2.41	−2.22	−3.64	−0.06	6.99	9.51	−3.42	−1.04	185.52
2.2.1 Sight and time deposits at U.S. banks	39.69	36.36	17.69	25.87	52.35	56.63	41.78	42.81	0.59	0.00	11.30	0.14	91.27	−5.62	511.92
2.2.2 Sight and time deposits at German banks	2.98	0.15	9.21	0.15	5.50	5.12	8.74	12.79	13.46	11.98	24.68	9.66	39.69	34.24	316.72
2.3 Public holdings of IMB	77.15	99.24	50.09	−1.77	77.91	96.68	64.59	53.51	5.71	21.63	57.38	82.33	135.08	90.33	1428.15
2.3.1 Sight and time deposits at U.S. banks	18.58	13.68	8.92	4.61	1.78	−2.08	6.99	5.35	−2.53	−5.65	−7.14	−4.16	4.61	5.93	68.94
2.3.2 Sight and time deposits at German banks	0.30	1.04	4.91	−2.53	−2.53	0.59	−1.78	2.23	2.53	1.78	7.88	5.35	4.46	3.14	46.80

Sources: IMF, "International Financial Statistics"; U.S. Department of Commerce, "Survey of Current Business"; Federal Reserve System, "Federal Reserve Bulletin"; U.S. Treasury Department, "Treasury Bulletin"; Deutsche Bundesbank, "Monthly Report" and "Statistical Supplement to the Monthly Report", 3rd series.

Table 3. United States balance-of-payments disequilibria on IMB basis (billions of US dollars).

Items	1982	1983	1984	1985	1986	1987	1988	1989	1990	1991	1992	1993	1994	1995
3.1 Net changes in U.S. official reserves (gold, convertible currencies and IMF position)	5.20	1.19	3.27	4.01	−0.30	−9.51	3.72	26.31	2.23	−5.95	−4.01	1.49	−5.50	9.74
3.2 SD (sight liabilities)	51.73	57.47	35.37	24.24	73.45	70.61	62.30	22.44	4.00	10.25	16.50	50.23	93.47	47.20
Of which bank deposits (a + b + e + f + g + h)	59.02	51.82	28.68	32.42	53.83	56.34	45.65	49.35	1.77	−2.68	4.31	0.14	97.48	8.06
3.2.1 Foreign Official Institutions	−6.54	7.43	8.76	−6.24	19.32	16.06	13.53	−25.72	5.94	15.90	12.34	54.25	−2.41	46.89
a) Sight deposits	−0.59	−0.15	−0.01	0.30	0.15	−0.59	0.15	0.30	−0.30	0.74	−1.34	0.30	−0.04	0.54
b) Time deposits	1.34	1.93	2.08	1.64	−0.45	2.38	−3.27	0.89	4.01	2.23	1.49	3.86	1.64	7.21
c) U.S. short-time treasury securities	−5.95	8.03	5.80	−6.99	23.19	13.68	15.46	−27.80	2.53	13.82	12.34	48.31	−12.04	28.78
d) Other obligations, mainly money market paper	−1.34	−2.38	0.89	−1.19	−3.57	0.59	1.19	0.89	−0.30	−0.89	−0.15	1.78	8.03	10.36

(*Continued on next page.*)

Table 3. (Continued).

3.2.2 Nonbank foreigners and international and regional organizations	18.58	13.68	8.92	4.61	1.78	−2.08	6.99	5.35	−2.53	−5.65	−7.14	−4.16	4.61	5.93
e) Sight and time deposits	18.58	13.68	8.92	4.61	1.78	−2.08	6.99	5.35	−2.53	−5.65	−7.14	−4.16	4.61	5.93
3.2.3 Commercial banks, including the foreign branches of US banks	39.69	36.36	17.69	25.87	52.35	56.63	41.78	42.81	0.59	0.00	11.30	0.14	91.27	−5.62
f) Sight deposits	−3.12	0.09	1.93	−0.30	0.03	0.59	−1.04	0.30	−0.30	−1.49	1.64	−0.45	3.42	0.95
g) Time deposits	20.22	9.36	9.96	2.53	15.31	16.05	0.45	10.85	−2.08	−6.24	7.73	15.46	6.54	−7.55
h) Foreign branches short-term assets	22.59	26.91	5.80	23.64	37.01	39.99	42.37	31.66	2.97	7.73	1.93	−14.87	81.31	0.98
Deficit (−) or Surplus (+) of the US balance of payments on IMB basis (3.1–3.2)	−46.53	−56.28	−32.10	−20.23	−73.75	−80.12	−58.58	3.87	−1.77	−16.20	−20.51	−48.74	−98.97	−37.46

Sources: U.S. Department of Commerce, "Survey of Current Business", various years; Federal Reserve System, "Federal Reserve Bulletin," various issues.

Table 4. German balance-of-payments disequilibria on IMB basis (billions of US dollars).

Items	1982	1983	1984	1985	1986	1987	1988	1989	1990	1991	1992	1993	1994	1995
4.1 Net changes in German official reserves (gold, convertible currencies, IMF position and other ECU assets)	1.78	−1.04	−0.59	−0.89	1.78	20.96	−21.41	−14.12	3.86	0.59	41.03	−22.45	5.65	5.37
4.2 SD (sight liabilities)	6.11	0.60	16.50	−1.04	7.73	5.56	12.02	31.81	17.33	5.14	25.27	23.48	40.28	38.57
Of which bank deposits (a + b + e + f + g + h)	3.43	1.49	15.76	−3.12	4.31	7.79	7.41	15.76	16.88	11.68	35.68	14.86	50.39	39.89
4.2.1 Central banks and other official agencies	2.83	−0.59	2.38	1.34	4.76	−0.15	5.06	16.79	1.34	−8.62	−7.29	8.47	−3.87	1.19
a) Sight and time deposits	0.15	0.30	1.64	−0.74	1.34	2.08	0.45	0.74	0.89	−2.08	3.12	−0.15	6.24	2.51
b) German short-term treasury securities	2.68	−0.89	0.74	2.08	3.42	−2.23	4.61	16.05	0.45	−6.54	−10.41	8.62	−10.11	−1.32

(Continued on next page.)

Table 4. (Continued).

4.2.2 Commercial banks, including the foreign branches of German banks	2.98	0.15	9.21	0.15	5.50	5.12	8.74	12.79	13.46	11.98	24.68	9.66	39.69	34.24
c) Sight deposits	1.49	0.89	3.42	0.59	2.82	−0.59	2.23	6.39	9.22	2.82	4.76	9.22	20.51	3.70
d) Time deposits	1.19	0.15	5.20	−0.45	2.53	5.65	6.54	6.39	4.31	9.22	18.88	−0.30	22.30	28.47
e) Foreign branches short-term assets	0.30	−0.89	0.59	0.01	0.15	0.06	−0.03	0.01	−0.07	−0.06	1.04	0.74	−3.12	2.07
4.2.3 Public	0.30	1.04	4.91	−2.53	−2.53	0.59	−1.78	2.23	2.53	1.78	7.88	5.35	4.46	3.14
f) Sight and time deposits	0.30	1.04	4.91	−2.53	−2.53	0.59	−1.78	2.23	2.53	1.78	7.88	5.35	4.46	3.14
Deficit (−) or surplus (+) of the German balance of payments on IMB basis (4.1–4.2)	−46.53	−56.28	−32.10	−20.23	−73.75	−80.12	−58.58	3.87	−1.77	−16.20	−20.51	−48.74	−98.97	−37.46

Sources: Deutsche Bundesbank, "Monthly Report" and "Statistical Supplements to the Monthly Report", 3rd series, "Balance of Payments Statistics," various issues.

Table 3 emphasizes that the United States, even in today's multicurrency system, acts as the world's "banker". Germany is the junior banker. These patterns are consistent with the role of the U.S. dollar and the German mark as dominant currencies (Fratianni et al., 1998). As a case in point, consider the German external imbalance in 1992. In that year the increase in the official Bundesbank reserves is greater than the growth of the German monetary system sight liabilities. This was due to the EMS crisis, which obliged the German central bank to supply large amounts of marks to the central banks of nations whose currencies were under pressure. The effect of these operations was reflected in the large increase in convertible currency reserves at the Bundesbank, underscoring the usefulness of our measure in identifying flows of reserve-currency liquidity in and out of the international monetary system.[7]

4. Empirical findings

Three alternative measures of the dollar IMB will be tested.[8] Table 5 reports 58 quarterly observations, from 1982 to 1996, of six variables:

- CREUUSA = total dollar sight assets of the BIS reporting banks vis-à-vis the U.S. banking system (Source: BIS, "International Banking Activity and Financial Market Developments," various issues);
- LUSB = total dollar sight liabilities of U.S. banks vis-à-vis their branches operating in the off-shore markets (Source: Federal Reserve Bulletin of the Board of Governors of the Federal Reserve System);
- LUSBF = total dollar liabilities of U.S. banks vis-à-vis other reporting banks (Source: Federal Reserve Bulletin of the Board of Governors of the Federal Reserve System);
- IMBP = international monetary base held by the nonbank public (Source: Federal Reserve Bulletin of the Board of Governors of the Federal Reserve System);
- DEU = cross-border deposits, in the form of dollar sight liabilities in dollars, by BIS reporting banks vis-à-vis all sectors (Source: BIS, "International Banking Activity and Financial Market Developments," various issues);
- i_{DEU} = interest rate on three-month Eurodollar deposits (Source: Federal Reserve Bulletin of the Board of Governors of the Federal Reserve System).

We opted for linear relationships between variables. All variables were normalized by DEU and then transformed into natural logarithms. In dealing with statistical series that show problems of stability, the relationships represented in the estimations are characterized by "stochastic trends" as shown by the Durbin-Watson statistic. Therefore, we chose a dynamic error correction model, utilizing the technique of generalized minimum least squares (GLS) which allow for, in the case of co-integrated time series, the separation of the cyclical effect

Table 5. Variables used in the econometric estimations (absolute values).

Period	DEU	CREUUSA	LUSB	LUSBF	i_{DEU}	IMBP
8201	776.70	134.70	108.50	26.20	14.90	24.68
8202	761.60	149.70	117.20	32.50	15.45	31.06
8203	794.80	154.00	119.20	34.80	11.74	34.34
8204	806.30	154.70	118.50	36.20	9.47	37.17
8301	798.90	160.50	124.80	35.70	9.25	40.35
8302	797.00	165.40	120.80	44.60	9.67	42.98
8303	814.10	173.20	129.00	44.20	9.82	46.85
8304	852.60	209.80	144.90	64.90	10.08	48.89
8401	859.90	223.10	146.90	76.20	10.40	52.07
8402	870.40	235.60	157.70	77.90	11.68	56.36
8403	870.00	227.90	148.70	79.20	11.67	58.32
8404	892.70	234.40	150.70	83.70	8.90	59.62
8501	903.50	221.90	154.80	67.10	9.32	61.97
8502	896.80	222.30	155.50	66.80	7.60	61.81
8503	914.20	220.90	157.40	63.50	8.14	63.29
8504	937.10	235.50	173.10	62.40	7.99	63.43
8601	954.10	245.10	175.70	69.40	7.42	64.02
8602	988.30	247.10	177.40	69.70	6.95	64.71
8603	1075.50	269.00	188.20	80.80	5.88	65.68
8604	1161.90	298.60	208.80	89.80	6.23	65.08
8701	1182.80	306.90	204.20	102.70	6.37	61.55
8702	1290.80	327.00	204.20	123.00	7.11	63.19
8703	1329.90	360.80	229.10	131.70	7.51	64.33
8704	1376.10	370.90	247.60	123.30	7.86	63.86
8801	1410.30	348.90	237.00	111.90	6.74	63.65
8802	1420.60	357.50	263.90	93.60	7.61	65.38
8803	1457.10	369.30	267.10	102.20	8.31	67.92
8804	1535.90	384.00	288.20	95.80	9.30	69.57
8901	1615.90	397.90	289.00	108.90	10.18	71.25
8902	1579.00	378.50	275.20	103.30	9.28	74.11
8903	1636.00	404.70	299.70	105.00	8.85	74.53
8904	1675.20	434.30	318.60	115.70	8.39	75.84
9001	1664.90	434.40	307.30	127.10	8.37	77.48
9002	1649.40	443.90	307.70	136.20	8.23	75.91
9003	1710.10	448.40	313.30	135.10	8.07	75.06
9004	1856.60	494.10	320.00	174.10	7.87	73.76

(Continued on next page.)

Table 5. (*Continued*).

9101	1791.40	468.50	314.20	154.30	6.44	72.32
9102	1739.70	451.20	316.70	134.50	6.08	70.62
9103	1732.70	445.70	320.00	125.70	5.50	68.58
9104	1777.80	472.80	327.80	145.00	4.48	66.67
9201	1705.80	475.00	339.70	135.30	4.26	63.65
9202	1700.30	479.40	329.20	150.20	3.87	60.04
9203	1709.00	495.80	337.20	158.60	3.15	60.81
9204	1747.10	510.40	330.20	180.20	3.50	59.43
9301	1631.20	477.40	325.00	152.40	3.11	57.56
9302	1604.30	480.10	316.70	163.40	3.21	55.33
9303	1592.80	485.50	322.50	163.00	3.08	56.54
9304	1623.00	499.80	314.20	185.60	3.26	55.61
9401	1620.00	534.00	337.30	196.70	3.75	56.19
9402	1689.20	546.50	358.90	187.60	4.51	57.24
9403	1732.40	543.90	370.20	173.70	5.01	57.92
9404	1764.40	568.80	393.50	175.30	6.27	58.99
9501	1809.20	574.48	396.90	177.58	6.15	58.96
9502	1816.30	567.80	396.70	171.10	6.03	62.14
9503	1821.70	566.01	386.70	179.31	5.74	63.43
9504	1849.60	587.04	392.50	194.54	5.64	64.36
9601	1898.40	564.21	370.50	193.71	5.28	67.49
9602	1895.70	535.59	365.15	170.44	5.46	68.66

from trend (Favero, 1996, pp. 67–74). The results are:

$$i_{\mathrm{DEU}} = \underset{(2.61)}{0.03}\ \mathrm{DEU} + \underset{(12.40)}{1.54}\ i_{\mathrm{DEU}\text{-}1} - \underset{(5.33)}{0.67}\ i_{\mathrm{DEU}\text{-}2} - \underset{(2.32)}{0.08}\ \mathrm{CREUUSA}_{-1} \tag{6}$$

$$\mathrm{D.W.} = 2.04 \quad \mathrm{Adj.}\ \mathrm{R}^2 = 0.89 \quad \mathrm{S.E.R.} = 10.08 \quad \overline{i_{\mathrm{DEU}^9}} = 7.35$$

$$i_{\mathrm{DEU}} = \underset{(2.26)}{0.03}\ \mathrm{DEU} + \underset{(11.77)}{1.52}\ i_{\mathrm{DEU}\text{-}1} - \underset{(4.93)}{0.63}\ i_{\mathrm{DEU}\text{-}2} - \underset{(1.98)}{0.10}\ \mathrm{LUSB}_{-1} \tag{7}$$

$$\mathrm{D.W.} = 2.04 \quad \mathrm{Adj.}\ \mathrm{R}^2 = 0.88 \quad \mathrm{S.E.R.} = 10.22 \quad \overline{i_{\mathrm{DEU}}} = 7.35$$

$$i_{\mathrm{DEU}} = \underset{(2.26)}{0.02}\ \mathrm{DEU} + \underset{(12.00)}{1.54}\ i_{\mathrm{DEU}\text{-}1} - \underset{(4.98)}{0.66}\ i_{\mathrm{DEU}\text{-}2} - \underset{(2.16)}{0.12}\ \mathrm{LUSBF}_{-1} \tag{8}$$

$$\mathrm{D.W.} = 2.04 \quad \mathrm{Adj.}\ \mathrm{R}^2 = 0.88 \quad \mathrm{S.E.R.} = 10.26 \quad \overline{i_{\mathrm{DEU}}} = 7.35$$

$$i_{\text{DEU}} = 0.02\ \text{DEU} + 1.51\ i_{\text{DEU-1}} - 0.61\ i_{\text{DEU-2}} - 0.38\ \text{IMBP}_{-1} \tag{9}$$
$$(2.26) \qquad (11.38) \qquad (4.65) \qquad (1.98)$$
$$\text{D.W.} = 2.03 \quad \text{R}^2\text{C} = 0.88 \quad \text{S.E.R.} = 10.44 \quad \overline{i_{\text{DEU}}} = 7.35$$

The influence of explanation variables does not seem to be in contrast with the proposed interpretation. In fact, the expectations of a negative relationship between the international monetary base held by European banks (and, overall, by the public) and the yield of sight assets in dollars seem confirmed. The lagged coefficients of CREUUSA, LUSB, LUSBF, and IMBP are all significant up to 95%. In this context it should be noted that we are not dealing with pure money as in Keynes' definition. In the Keynesian scheme, money has a pecuniary rate of return of zero, in contrast to U.S. bank deposits, which, besides performing the typical function of reserve money, function also as international assets for the investing public. Furthermore, the coefficient of U.S. banks sight liabilities vis-à-vis their foreign branches (LUSB) does not refute the hypothesis of the existence of specific instructions on behalf of branch headquarters concerning the need to hold reserves on offshore deposits. This seems, therefore, to respond moderately to the logic we hypothesize. Then, the negative coefficient of the dependent variable lagged two periods is not surprising since an expected increase in the supply of cross-border sight liabilities determines the negative relationship between the dependent variable and the regressor taken into consideration. Based on these results, the objection raised by some scholars (Masera and Savona, 1972) that the international monetary base is endogenous seems to be confirmed. This, in itself, is not an indictment of the multiplier approach. The policy implications, it is true, depend on whether or not IMB is a policy variable. In today's environment IMB is endogenous, but IMB could become a potential policy variable if national central banks wanted to control the growth of the international money market.

The endogenous aspect of the monetary base could determine, therefore, a sort of confidence zone within which the multiplication output would be defined. On the offshore dollar market the multiplier will assume maximum and minimum effective values, according to structural conditions on the markets and on the spread between the offshore and onshore interest rates. The potential maximum value is reachable under the hypothesis that the only losses in the multiplication process occur through reserves held by reporting banks and by the public for transaction motives. The effective minimum values depend on base money losses through the loan process (as in the case of redeposits of the IMB at the creating countries), or, when the redeposit of borrowed funds on the offshore markets is not possible.

5. The multiplier of cross-border deposits

It is useful to present an extremely simplified model of the international monetary market, to quantify and estimate the IM and the multiplier of cross-border deposits. The model, in essence, is an extension of the money supply process applied to cross-border deposits (Fratianni and Savona, 1970).

$\text{IM} = \text{IMBP} + \text{DEU}$	Definition of International money	(10)
$\text{IMBB} = k\text{DEU}$	Reporting banks' behavior	(11)
$k = f(i\text{DEU},...)$	$\delta k/\delta i\text{DEU} < 0; 0 < k < 1$	(12)
$\text{IMBP} = c\text{DEU}$	Public's behavior	(13)
$c = f(i\text{DEU},...)$	$\delta c/\delta i\text{DEU} < 0; 0 < c < 1$	(14)
$\text{IMB} = \text{IMBP} + \text{IMBB} + \text{IMBCB}$	Source and uses of IMB	(15)
$i\text{DEU} = f(\text{DEU}, \text{IMB})$	$\delta i\text{DEU}/\delta\text{DEU} > 0; \delta i\text{DEU}/\delta\text{IMB} < 0$	(16)

where

IMBB = International monetary base held by banks
k = ratio of IMBB to DEU (coefficient of bank reserve)
c = ratio of IMBP to DEU (coefficient of public reserve)
IMBCB = International monetary base held by official authorities
iDEU = Cross-Border deposits rate of return

Using the above equations we can express IM in terms of a multiplier and the IMB net of the holdings by central banks:

$$\text{IM} = m[\text{IMB} - \text{IMBCB}], \tag{17}$$

where m is the cross-border multiplier

$$m = (1 + c)/(k + c). \tag{18}$$

Table 6 presents the quarterly data we have used to quantify IM and the cross-border multiplier. Over the period under consideration "m" lies between 2.84 (March 1994) and 5.03 (March 1982) and displays an erratic path after 1982. The multiplier's substantial drop was due to the high interest rates in the United States, resulting from the restrictive monetary policy carried out by Federal Reserve Chairman Paul Volcker.

There does not seem to be a substantial difference between a bank operating in the offshore dollar market and one operating in the domestic market. The ability of the offshore market to multiply is facilitated by the absence of reserve requirements and by a greater stability in their term structures of assets and liabilities. No multiplication would occur if every dollar passing through the offshore market were sterilized by the onshore market through a full redepositing of it in the U.S. banking system (or in any other reserve country).

Next, we test the existing relationship between IM and the offshore interest rate. Our aim is to verify the existence of an empirical relationship to serve as a basis of the distinction between money and monetary base. Here are the

Table 6. Variables used in the IMB, cross-border deposits multiplier and reserve ratios quantification (absolute values).

Period	DEU	IMBB	IMBP	IM	IMBB + IMBP	MOLT	$K(\%)$	$c(\%)$
8201	776.70	134.70	24.68	801.38	159.38	5.03	17.34	3.18
8202	761.60	149.70	31.06	792.66	180.76	4.39	19.66	4.08
8203	794.80	154.00	34.34	829.14	188.34	4.40	19.38	4.32
8204	806.30	154.70	37.17	843.47	191.87	4.40	19.19	4.61
8301	798.90	160.50	40.35	839.25	200.85	4.18	20.09	5.05
8302	797.00	165.40	42.98	839.98	208.38	4.03	20.75	5.39
8303	814.10	173.20	46.85	860.95	220.05	3.91	21.28	5.75
8304	852.60	209.80	48.89	901.49	258.69	3.48	24.61	5.73
8401	859.90	223.10	52.07	911.97	275.17	3.31	25.94	6.05
8402	870.40	235.60	56.36	926.76	291.96	3.17	27.07	6.47
8403	870.00	227.90	58.32	928.32	286.22	3.24	26.20	6.70
8404	892.70	234.40	59.62	952.32	294.02	3.24	26.26	6.68
8501	903.50	221.90	61.97	965.47	283.87	3.40	24.56	6.86
8502	896.80	222.30	61.81	958.61	284.11	3.37	24.79	6.89
8503	914.20	220.90	63.29	977.49	284.19	3.44	24.16	6.92
8504	937.10	235.50	63.43	1000.53	298.93	3.35	25.13	6.77
8601	954.10	245.10	64.02	1018.12	309.12	3.29	25.69	6.71
8602	988.30	247.10	64.71	1053.01	311.81	3.38	25.00	6.55
8603	1075.50	269.00	65.68	1141.18	334.68	3.41	25.01	6.11
8604	1161.90	298.60	65.08	1226.98	363.68	3.37	25.70	5.60
8701	1182.80	306.90	61.55	1244.35	368.45	3.38	25.95	5.20
8702	1290.80	327.00	63.19	1353.99	390.19	3.47	25.33	4.90
8703	1329.90	360.80	64.33	1394.23	425.13	3.28	27.13	4.84
8704	1376.10	370.90	63.86	1439.96	434.76	3.31	26.95	4.64
8801	1410.30	348.90	63.65	1473.95	412.55	3.57	24.74	4.51
8802	1420.60	357.50	65.38	1485.98	422.88	3.51	25.17	4.60
8803	1457.10	369.30	67.92	1525.02	437.22	3.49	25.34	4.66
8804	1535.90	384.00	69.57	1605.47	453.57	3.54	25.00	4.53
8901	1615.90	397.90	71.25	1687.15	469.15	3.60	24.62	4.41
8902	1579.00	378.50	74.11	1653.11	452.61	3.65	23.97	4.69
8903	1636.00	404.70	74.53	1710.53	479.23	3.57	24.74	4.56
8904	1675.20	434.30	75.84	1751.04	510.14	3.43	25.93	4.53
9001	1664.90	434.40	77.48	1742.38	511.88	3.40	26.09	4.65
9002	1649.40	443.90	75.91	1725.31	519.81	3.32	26.91	4.60
9003	1710.10	448.40	75.06	1785.16	523.46	3.41	26.22	4.39

(Continued on next page.)

Table 6. (Continued).

9004	1856.60	494.10	73.76	1930.36	567.86	3.40	26.61	3.97
9101	1791.40	468.50	72.32	1863.72	540.82	3.45	26.15	4.04
9102	1739.70	451.20	70.62	1810.32	521.82	3.47	25.94	4.06
9103	1732.70	445.70	68.58	1801.28	514.28	3.50	25.72	3.96
9104	1777.80	472.80	66.67	1844.47	539.47	3.42	26.59	3.75
9201	1705.80	475.00	63.65	1769.45	538.65	3.28	27.85	3.73
9202	1700.30	479.40	60.04	1760.34	539.44	3.26	28.20	3.53
9203	1709.00	495.80	60.81	1769.81	556.61	3.18	29.01	3.56
9204	1747.10	510.40	59.43	1806.53	569.83	3.17	29.21	3.40
9301	1631.20	477.40	57.56	1688.76	534.96	3.16	29.27	3.53
9302	1604.30	480.10	55.33	1659.63	535.43	3.10	29.93	3.45
9303	1592.80	485.50	56.54	1649.34	542.04	3.04	30.48	3.55
9304	1623.00	499.80	55.61	1678.61	555.41	3.02	30.79	3.43
9401	1620.00	534.00	56.19	1676.19	590.19	2.84	32.96	3.47
9402	1689.20	546.50	57.24	1746.44	603.74	2.89	32.35	3.39
9403	1732.40	543.90	57.92	1790.32	601.82	2.97	31.40	3.34
9404	1764.40	568.80	58.99	1823.39	627.79	2.90	32.24	3.34
9501	1809.20	574.48	58.96	1868.16	633.44	2.95	31.75	3.26
9502	1816.30	567.80	62.14	1878.44	629.94	2.98	31.26	3.42
9503	1821.70	566.01	63.43	1885.13	629.44	2.99	31.07	3.48
9504	1849.60	587.04	64.36	1913.96	651.40	2.94	31.74	3.48
9601	1898.40	564.21	67.49	1965.89	631.71	3.11	29.72	3.56
9602	1895.70	535.59	68.66	1964.36	604.25	3.25	28.25	3.62

results:

$$i_{\text{DEU}} = \underset{(8.92)}{1.19}\, i_{\text{DEU-1}} - \underset{(2.05)}{0.27}\, i_{\text{DEU-2}} - \underset{(2.01)}{0.01}\, \text{IM}_{-1} \tag{19}$$

$$\text{D.W.} = 2.02 \quad \text{R}^2\text{C} = 0.86 \quad \text{S.E.R.} = 10.99 \quad \overline{i_{\text{DEU}}} = 7.35$$

The estimates were obtained, once more, using generalized minimum list squares with a dynamic error correction model. The critical observation is that the relationship between the offshore interest rates and IM is positive, where the relationship between the same interest rates and IMB is negative.

Next, we verify if the presence of financial innovations, like derivatives, complicates the distinction between money and monetary base.

6. Derivatives

After the Eurodollar market, financial derivatives markets are the most significant financial innovation of the last fifty years. BIS (1996) reports that the total notional amount of derivatives in the over-the-counter markets was $47.5 trillion at the end of 1995, approximately ten times that of 1992. In 1995, derivative exchange markets transacted a notional amount of $8 trillion, compared to $4.6 trillion in 1992.[10] However, the notional principal can be a misleading indicator of market growth. A better measure is the gross market value, defined as the sum of the negative and positive market replacement costs. The gross market value in the over-the-counter markets was $2.2 trillion in March 1995. The gross market value is very sensitive to changes in market volatility and can double or triple in a different environment in a very short time.

The main benefit of derivatives is that they increase market efficiency through hedging, high leverage, and asset substitutability. In fact, the purpose of a derivative contract is to transfer the specific risk of the underlying asset from the buying to the selling agent. Leverage increases the volume transactions and decreases the cost of capital. This, in turn, enhances arbitrage activity across different assets. The redistribution of risk, on the other hand, may cause adverse effects through amplified price movements, systemic risk, and adverse capital flows (Angeloni and Massa, 1994; Folkerts-Landau, 1994; IMF, 1995; Scott, 1991; Von Hagen-Fender, 1998).[11]

In the context of this work, it is useful to consider, first of all, the link between derivatives and the definition of monetary aggregates. Combinations of derivatives can create "synthetic" assets that substitute for existing financial and monetary instruments. For example, a portfolio composed of a long bond position and a short 3-month future on the same bond is equal to a 3-month time deposit. However, since the portfolio, or the synthetic time deposit, can be traded, it is substantially more liquid than a regular time deposit. The problem is that the synthetic time deposit is not included in a broad monetary aggregate like, for example, M3, although the less liquid "normal" time deposit is included. For most of the financial market participants, the synthetic deposit is more attractive, and will be held and negotiated instead of the traditional asset. This will lower the accuracy of the narrower monetary aggregates in estimating money.

So far, research (Throop, 1993; Vrolijk, 1997) has highlighted the significance of derivatives on the stability of money demand functions and on the liquidity degree of the underlying assets, through the bid-ask spread. Apart from some important contributions (Deutsche Bundesbank, 1994; Edwards and Mishkin, 1995; Mishkin, 1996), the impact of derivatives on interest rates and the implications for monetary policy have not been sufficiently investigated. We propose the following research agenda. First of all, one can look at the existing relationship between derivatives and the performance of underlying assets. If such a relationship were significant, monetary aggregates would have to be redefined.

Second, one can look at the relationship between derivatives on financial assets with limited liquidity (stocks and long-term bonds) and the riskless interest rate. If such a relationship were significant, the hypothesis that those derivatives impact on the liquidity degree of the underlying assets, and therefore on interest rates, could not be refuted.

We test these two relationships using OLS on the natural logarithm of the time series. In the first two functional specifications, we compare the 3-month Eurodollar interest rate (i_{DEU}) and the quantity of 3-month Eurodollar futures transacted at the Chicago Board of Trade and at LIFFE in London (EUROCBOT and EUROLIF).[12] There are 55 (Dec. 1982 to June 1996) and 53 (March 1983 to March 1996) quarterly observations obtained from *Datastream* (Table 7). The regression results are:

$$\begin{aligned} i_{\mathrm{DEU}} &= \underset{(2.69)}{0.26\, i_{\mathrm{DEU}\text{-}1}} + \underset{(6.43)}{0.04\ \mathrm{EUROCBOT}} \\ \mathrm{D.W.} &= 2.07 \quad \mathrm{Adj.\ R}^2 = 0.98 \quad \mathrm{S.E.R.} = 6634.96 \quad \overline{i_{\mathrm{DEU}}} = 7.35 \end{aligned} \tag{20}$$

$$\begin{aligned} i_{\mathrm{DEU}} &= \underset{(5.45)}{0.54\, i_{\mathrm{DEU}\text{-}1}} + \underset{(4.49)}{0.03\ \mathrm{EUROLIF}} \\ \mathrm{D.W.} &= 1.10 \quad \mathrm{Adj.\ R}^2 = 0.88 \quad \mathrm{S.E.R.} = 456.00 \quad \overline{i_{\mathrm{DEU}}} = 7.35 \end{aligned} \tag{21}$$

The offshore interest rate is sensitive to changes in traded futures, with coefficients significant at the 99% level. The differences between the two estimates of the Durbin-Watson statistic and the adjusted R^2 are due to the fact that LIFFE Eurodollar futures are, by now, nonexistent, the market having moved to Chicago. The use of the unlagged future is justified by the high speed of reaction in this market.

For our purposes, it appears that derivatives have introduced another mechanism of money creation, justifying in turn a re-examination of existing monetary aggregates. Naturally, we are cautious and much more work needs to be done before we gain an acceptable degree of knowledge of international money creation.

In the following, final two estimates, the relation between the quantity (measured through *open interest*) of two futures on assets with limited liquidity and a riskless rate are reported. The intention here was to verify the impact of derivatives on the degree of liquidity of underlying assets, following a methodology coherent with the monetary analysis developed in this report, while before we wanted to see if the supply of derivatives had the same impact of international money on interest rate. The two futures are those of the stock index of the New York Stock Exchange (NYSE) and the 10-year U.S. Treasury Note. For these two variables, there are 54 and 55 quarterly observations, respectively, (December 1982–March 1996 and September 1982–March 1996). As *proxy* of the riskless interest rate, we used the performance of the 3-month Treasury Bill rate ($i_{\text{t-bill}}$),

Table 7. Variables used in the econometric estimations (absolute values).

Period	EUROLIF	EUROCBOT	TNOTE	NYSE	$i_{t\text{-bill}}$
8201	—	—	—	—	12.90
8202	—	8659	22605	146	12.40
8203	—	13468	17119	22981	9.70
8204	2257	18819	9086	6696	7.90
8301	3176	22232	10885	6592	8.10
8302	4094	22539	8113	9611	8.40
8303	6762	32268	12478	11167	9.20
8304	8104	47231	14881	10893	8.80
8401	11808	54430	24449	9872	9.10
8402	15358	79082	27766	8426	9.80
8403	13223	91027	35918	10400	10.30
8404	11485	91592	35143	10044	9.00
8501	14457	103539	42779	11353	8.20
8502	16936	114588	45003	2124	7.50
8503	15325	129116	65518	9984	7.10
8504	7951	148135	69963	7499	7.10
8601	20399	146643	81345	11399	6.90
8602	20928	167267	67060	14039	6.10
8603	20537	180496	67676	11445	5.50
8604	26424	230128	65791	14169	5.30
8701	31140	266569	56978	13137	5.50
8702	29628	278555	67957	13517	5.70
8703	30970	301459	77036	14920	6.00
8704	38134	336585	74450	10232	6.00
8801	32077	340301	76011	5423	5.80
8802	34060	410622	78262	7505	6.20
8803	37915	477260	95151	7491	7.00
8804	31714	508221	91190	6761	7.70
8901	52467	657515	86392	6557	8.50
8902	61197	744114	89729	8825	8.40
8903	50474	745376	82933	6488	7.80
8904	41974	639295	85880	6812	7.60
9001	39230	652604	87001	5900	7.80
9002	33288	641869	82366	4853	7.80
9003	37090	755326	67273	5930	7.50
9004	44124	722396	72371	5693	7.00

(Continued on next page.)

Table 7. (Continued).

9101	39374	719044	72332	5555	6.00
9102	36535	831277	83753	6087	5.60
9103	30802	868875	89055	5304	5.40
9104	36008	1026332	91885	5919	4.60
9201	41532	1200377	115035	6160	3.90
9202	39362	1332724	101457	4252	3.70
9203	29390	1519587	159985	6928	3.10
9204	27084	1537574	203730	6039	3.10
9301	20058	1557908	203647	5519	3.00
9302	17700	1743110	225089	3798	3.00
9303	13558	1861139	237539	4077	3.00
9304	12317	2143304	284564	4899	3.10
9401	12859	2524950	252399	4807	3.20
9402	9933	2735224	321956	3886	4.00
9403	7007	2693116	266143	3962	4.50
9404	4306	2598890	297239	4065	5.30
9501	2437	2490568	279295	4177	5.80
9502	1184	2536526	282836	3321	5.60
9503	619	2197281	330584	2567	5.40
9504	110	2371461	279036	2791	5.30
9601	0	2645721	302941	4238	4.90
9602	—	2550467	353547	2924	—

which is the most liquid financial asset negotiated in the U.S. market.[13] The results are:

$$i_{t\text{-bill}} = \underset{(4.01)}{0.11}\, i_{t\text{-bill-1}} + \underset{(21.59)}{0.07}\ \text{NYSE} \tag{22}$$

$$\text{D.W.} = 1.36 \quad \text{Adj. R}^2 = 0.95 \quad \text{S.E.R.} = 67.65 \quad \overline{i_{t\text{-bill}}} = 6.55$$

$$i_{t\text{-bill}} = \underset{(13.97)}{0.74}\, i_{t\text{-bill-1}} + \underset{(5.54)}{0.01}\ \text{TNOTE} \tag{23}$$

$$\text{D.W.} = 2.07 \quad \text{Adj. R}^2 = 0.95 \quad \text{S.E.R.} = 959.45 \quad \overline{i_{t\text{-bill}}} = 6.55$$

With the exception of a slight positive autocorrelation of the residuals in the second regression the estimates have been satisfactory and have shown a positive relationship between derivatives and the interest rate, as hypothesized at the beginning of our work. There is strong evidence of the need to broaden the concept of international money in a wide sense. The current method is at risk of being outdated.

Our conclusion is that the less liquid components of money aggregates (M2 or M3) such as time deposits or CDs, should be added to those assets not present in the monetary aggregates, acquiring the same degree of liquidity and creating substitutes for speculative money (i.e., having a relationship with interest rates), when they are covered by derivatives.

We are aware of the fact that, given the impressive development of these markets, and the great number of contracts (especially *over the counter*), it is nearly impossible to completely quantify all derivatives negotiated in financial markets. However, we think the attempt should be made at least to include those *underlying assets* of derivatives for which we find a significant relationship, as we have shown before. All of this would allow for better monetary policy management, domestically and internationally, because the authorities could use more efficient instruments to reach the goal of stabilizing money growth, in order to guide interest rates and exchange rates and to have a degree of control over inflation.

7. Conclusions

Referring to the analytical distinction between monetary base and money, identified in the different reactions of interest rates to changes in stocks, we attempted to understand, theoretically, the impact of financial innovations (most importantly derivatives) on the definition of money. In both national and international markets, one should define monetary base, or money, in view of the existence of financial innovations.

The second part of the research related to the international money market and the determinants of international money. The empirical findings validate the theoretical formulation of the multiplier analysis to understand the offshore currency markets. The offshore interest rate is sensitive to changes in the supply of IMB and IM. The ex-post values of the cross-border deposits' multiplier have declined over the period 1982–1996 but have remained way above one.

Finally, we found a significant relationship between derivatives, riskless interest rates and underlying assets. Two implications stem from this result. First, national and international regulators—such as the central banks that cooperate within the institutional structure of the Bank for International Settlements—have underestimated the actual dimension of the offshore currency markets. Derivatives need to be included in the assets and liabilities of the BIS reporting banks. Second, domestic and international money aggregates need to be redefined to include those assets, at least parts of them, which possess characteristics of speculative money and are "covered" by derivative products. Derivatives are hedging instruments that respond to changes in the yield of the underlying asset. This means that liquidity is a necessary but not a sufficient condition for defining money.

Financial intermediaries react to important new information or to changes in expectations concerning individual economies and shift funds very rapidly from one economy to another (the recent Asian crisis being the latest example) and take positions with very short time horizons in foreign exchange or securities of a size that heavily influences countries with weak financial structures. The primary financial instruments used to carry out these operations are derivatives.

Our broadening of the concept of money does not go so far as to formulate a direct relationship between broad money, inclusive of derivatives, and inflation. Rather, our evidence supports the hypothesis that derivatives have an impact on interest rates, qualitatively similar to the impact of other components of domestic and international money. We leave to others to re-examine the effects of interest rates and broad money on economic growth and inflation.

Notes

1. See Fazio (1968) for an application to Italy of the monetary base.
2. In this multicurrency international monetary system, it is more correct to talk about off-shore currencies markets or cross-border assets and liabilities markets (as defined by the Bank for International Settlements) rather than the Eurodollar market, that was an appropriate definition for the previous system in which the US dollar was the only currency used in international transactions.
3. It was exactly for this reason that Baffi (1965) considered the currencies of reserve countries structurally weak in money markets.
4. A synthesis of the debate over competing hypotheses can be found in Masera and Savona (1972), Friedman (1969), McKinnon (1993) Savona, (1982) and Savona and Sutija (1985).
5. On this subject see chapters 3 and 4 and the Appendix in the above mentioned work by Fratianni and Savona.
6. That is to say, held by people to whom the dollar and other currencies are not a part of the monetary base of the country of residence.
7. Some simplifications were necessary in redefining the statistical series. Here is a summary. We have included in the IMB the entire amount of U.S. Treasury and German short-term bonds, and not simply a portion as one should properly do. In regard to credit lines, we have put only the available parts. These are the only amounts that can be considered central banks' reserves. Although it has always been considered an accepted collateral to obtain liquidity in international markets, we have also excluded gold from the international monetary base because it no longer fulfills the role of an international means of payment, following the Kingston Agreement of 1976. Finally it would seem an error to include in the IMB the entire amount of ECU created through the transfer to the European Cooperation Fund of 20% of gold and dollar reserves. In reality, the IMF subtracts, in its statistics, from the EMS countries and the U.S. reserves the equivalent of the ECU created through this mechanism. Hence, inserting the entire amount of this part of international reserves did not cause a duplication in computation.
8. For simplicity, in the rest of the work we will consider only this part of the IMB (which, however, is the most significant), but the reasoning and the results that will be shown can also be extended to the other components, denominated in other currencies, of the international monetary base.
9. This indicator represents the average of the observations.
10. See also Fazio (1998) on the spectacular growth of financial derivatives.
11. See, for example, the recent cases of some well-known global banks, such as Metalgeschelschaft, Barings, Sumitomo and Orange County, California, that are involved in bankruptcy proceedings caused by the wrong use of derivatives. A broad bibliography on the relation between exchange rate instability and banking crises can be found in Eichngreen (1998).

12. The derivatives proxy is the open interest. The value can be obtained by multiplying the open interest by the notional amount of the contract, which varies from market to market.
13. The sources from which we obtained the time series on variables used in these estimations are the Datastream electronic database, for the futures, and "International Financial Statistics" by the IMF, for the interest rate.

References

Angeloni, I. and M. Massa (1994) "Mercati Derivati e Politica Monetaria," Comunicazione presentata alla *XXXV Riunione Scientifica Annuale della Società Italiana degli Economisti*, Milano.

Baffi, P. (1965) *Studi sulla Moneta*, Giuffré, Milano.

BIS, *Annual Report*, Basle, various issues.

BIS, *International Banking Activity and Financial Market Developments*, Basle, various issues.

BIS (1994) *Macroeconomic and Monetary Policy Issues Raised by the Growth of Derivatives Markets*, Basle.

BIS (1995) *Issues of Measurement Related to Market Size and Macroprudential Risks in Derivatives Markets*, Basle.

BIS (1996) *Central Bank Survey of Foreign Exchange and Derivatives Market Activity*, Basle.

Capie, F. (1998) "Monetary Unions in Historical Perspective: What Future for the Euro in the International Financial Systems." In this volume.

Deutsche Bundesbank (1994) "The Monetary Policy Implications of the Increasing Use of Derivative Financial Instruments," *Deutsche Bundesbank Monthly Report*.

Edwards, F. and F. Mishkin (1995) "The Decline of Traditional Banking: Implications for Financial Stability and Regulatory Policy," *Federal Reserve Bank of New York Economic Policy Review*.

Eichengreen, B. (1998) "Exchange Rate Stability and Financial Stability," in this volume.

Favero, C.A. (1996) *Econometria*, NIS, Roma.

Fazio, A. (1968) "Base monetaria, credito e depositi bancari," Ente per gli Studi monetari, bancari e finanziari Luigi Einaudi, *Quaderno di Ricerche no. 2*, Roma.

Fazio, A. (1998) "Italy and Europe in a World of Global Finance," Address by the Governor of the Bank of Italy, AIOTE, ASSOBAT, ATIC, FOREX, AIAF, Naples.

Folkerts-Landau, D. (1994) *Derivatives: The New Frontier in Finance*, International Monetary Fund, Washington.

Fratianni, M., A. Hauskrecht, and A. Maccario (1998) "Dominant Currencies and the Future of the Euro," in this volume.

Fratianni, M. and P. Savona (1972) *La liquidità internazionale—proposta per la ridefinizione del problema*, Il Mulino, Bologna.

Fratianni, M. and P. Savona (1970) "Una struttura formale per l'analisi della capacità moltiplicativa dell'eurodollaro," *L'Industria*, Bologna.

Friedman, M. (1969) "The Eurodollar Market: Some First Principles," *The Morgan Guaranty Survey*.

Friedman, M. and A. Schwartz (1963) *A Monetary History of the United States 1867–1960*, Princeton: Princeton University Press.

IMF, *Annual Report*, Washington, various issues.

IMF (1993) "International Capital Markets Part II. Systemic Issues in International Finance," *World Economic and Financial Surveys*, Washington.

IMF (1995a) *International Capital Markets. Developments, Prospects and Policy Issues*, Washington.

IMF (1995b) *The Adoption of Indirect Instruments of Monetary Policy*, Washington.

Maccario, A. (1996) "La liquidità internazionale: aspetti teorici, evidenza empirica e futuri scenari," Graduation thesis, Università Luiss, Roma.

Masera, F. and P. Savona (eds.) (1972) "A Debate on the Eurodollar Market," Ente per gli Studi monetari, bancari e finanziari Luigi Einaudi, Quaderno di Ricerche no. 11, Roma.

McKinnon, R.I. (1993) "The Rules of the Game: International Money in an Historical Perspective," *Journal of Economic Perspectives*.

Mishkin, F. (1996) "The Channels of Monetary Transmission: Lessons for Monetary Policy," NBER Working Paper No. 5464.
Savona, P. (1982) *Eurodollars*, Florida International University.
Savona, P. and G. Sutija (eds.) (1985) *Eurodollars and International Banking*, London-Basingstoke: MacMillan Press.
Scott, L. (1991) "The Information Content of Prices in Derivative Security Markets," IMF Working Paper, Washington.
Throop, A. (1993) "International Financial Market Integration and Linkages of National Interest Rates," *Federal Reserve Bank of San Francisco Economic Review*.
Von Hagen, J. and I. Fender (1998) "Central Bank Policy in a More Perfect Financial System," in this volume.
Vrolijk, C. (1997) "Derivatives Effect on Monetary Policy Transmission," IMF Working Paper, Washington.

Open economies review **9:S1** 665–683 (1998)

Central Banks' Management of Foreign Exchange Reserves

ELVIO DAL BOSCO
Economist, Via del Duomo, 8 05018 Orvieto, Italy

Key words: instability, reserve currency, liquidity, exchange rate

JEL Classification Numbers: E58, F31, F33, G11

Abstract

This paper analyzes whether currency instability results from official reserves management, as central banks strive to minimize risk, keep a degree of liquidity degree, minimize risk, and a good return on their portfolio. In recent years the dollar share in official reserves increased, at the expense of the Deutsche mark and yen. The evidence suggests that movements in the exchange rate exert the only influence on reserve currency shares; the long-term interest rate does not have a significant impact on reserves composition. These results confirm the *World Gold Council* thesis, according to which central banks, by investing excess reserves in short-terms assets, are believed to have optimized their portfolio return.

Introduction

Research on management of official foreign exchange reserves has to contend with a dearth of statistics, notably because central banks do not publish figures on the currency composition of their foreign exchange holdings in their annual reports. These data are supplied to the International Monetary Fund (IMF) exclusively for its own use, but IMF publishes them only at a highly aggregated level (Dellas, 1989, p. 6; Fratianni et al., 1998, this volume).[1] In the end this made it necessary to abandon the original plan of research, to focus on the central banks of countries other than the G3 (the United States, Japan and Germany), all the more so, since efforts to obtain data referring to this set of countries from another international financial institution did not meet with success.

IMF began publishing data in 1973, the year the floating exchange rate regime was introduced on a generalized basis. This occurred subsequent to the attempt to revive a modified version of the Bretton Woods system, was suspended upon the declaration of the dollar's inconvertibility into gold in August 1971, and proved to be unrealistic. The time series runs from 1973 to 1996, the latest year for which data are available. It omits 1974, as complete data were not collected that year.

1. Changes in the currency composition

The salient features of the currency composition of reserves held by the monetary authorities in the period considered were the decline in the shares of the U.S. dollar and British pound sterling, and the increase in those of the German mark and the Japanese yen. The importance of other identified currencies was marginal (Fratianni et al., 1998). However, the summary of long-term trends reported in Table 1 shows that the period is divided into two phases. Between 1973 and 1990 the dollar's share in official foreign exchange reserves fell from 78 to 57% and sterling's from 6.5 to 3.4%, while the share of the mark rose from 6 to 19% and that of the yen rose from next to nothing to around 9%. From 1990 to 1996, by contrast, the dollar's share recovered to 64%, those of the DM and yen fell considerably, and that of sterling remained unchanged.

The statistical appendix tables provide more detailed data for all countries (Table A1), industrial countries (Table A2) and developing countries (Table A3). Tables A1 and A2 do not show the European Currency Unit (ECU), but they do include ECU-dollar swaps in the dollar's share. The largest differences in currency composition between industrial countries and developing countries are found in 1973. The dollar's share was much higher for industrial countries (87%) than for developing countries (55%), whereas those of the mark and sterling were much higher for the latter. However, as early as 1975, there was an appreciable rise in the dollar's share and a fall in those of the other two currencies among the developing countries in connection with the large increase in oil-exporting countries' foreign exchange reserves. Subsequently, movements in leading currencies' shares grew less divergent, albeit with some differences in years when troughs were recorded for the dollar and sterling and peaks for the mark and yen. In 1996, industrial countries had higher shares than developing countries for the dollar (64.9% and 62.5% respectively) and the mark (17.5% and 10.6%). Both country groups had equal shares for the yen (6.2%), while

Table 1. The evolution of the currency composition (end-of-year percentages).

	1973	1980	1990	1996
Dollar	63.7	78.4	68.6	57.5
DM	5.5	14.9	18.6	14.0
Yen	—	4.3	8.8	6.2
Sterling	6.5	2.9	3.4	3.5
French franc	0.9	1.7	2.3	1.6
Netherlands guilder	0.3	1.3	1.1	0.4
Swiss franc	1.1	3.2	1.4	0.8
Unspecified currencies	7.3	3.1	6.9	9.8
Total	100.0	100.0	100.0	100.0

Source: IMF, *Annual Report*.

Table 2. Distribution of foreign exchange reserves by country groups.

	1973	1981	1990	1996	1973	1981	1990	1996
	Billions of SDRs				Percentages			
Ind. countries	65.7	159.7	376.5	501.7	64.0	52.4	63.4	48.6
Dev. countries	37.0	145.0	217.3	529.8	36.0	47.6	36.6	51.4
All countries	102.7	304.7	593.8	1031.5	100.0	100.0	100.0	100.0

Source: IMF, *Annual Report.*

the former's was smaller for sterling (2.1% compared to 4.9%) and unspecified other currencies (7.3% against 12.3%).

Tables A4 (all countries) and A5 (industrial countries) report the currency composition including the ECU from 1979, the year of its introduction, to 1996. In 1979 the ECU acquired a 13.9% share in foreign exchange reserves of all countries and a 24% share in those of industrial countries; the dollar's share declined significantly. The following year, the ECU's shares rose to 17% and 29%, respectively, and thereafter they declined almost continuously until 1996, when they reached 5.9% and 11.5%, respectively. The measures taken by the EEC, in attempting to increase the use of official ECU reserves, only succeeded in temporarily reversing the trend in 1986 and 1987.

Table 2 shows the distribution of foreign exchange reserves between the two country groups considered. The distribution recorded ups and downs over the years reported. The industrial countries' share dropped from 64% in 1973 to 52% in 1981 as a result of the sharp rise in the reserves of oil-exporting countries, whose share in the total foreign exchange reserves of developing countries grew from around one-third to one-half over the same period. The industrial countries' share increased to 63% in 1990 and then fell back to less than 50% in 1996. Since the considerable growth in developing countries' reserves between 1990 and 1996, in both absolute and relative terms, was largely attributable to Asia, the currency crisis that struck the countries of Asia in 1997 will unavoidably have adverse repercussions on reserves of developing countries as a whole.

2. An explanation of the central banks' conduct

A broad consensus exists concerning factors explaining central banks' conduct in holding foreign exchange reserves and hence the latter's composition, a view to which the IMF (1984, p. 63) itself subscribes.[2] However, a comparison between movements in currency shares and those in the two variables that should provide an adequate measure of the remuneration of foreign exchange reserves, exchange rates (for capital gains) and long-term interest rates, does not yield clear results. Empirical evidence only vaguely supports a positive correlation between currency shares in reserves and movements in nominal effective exchange rates (figure 1).

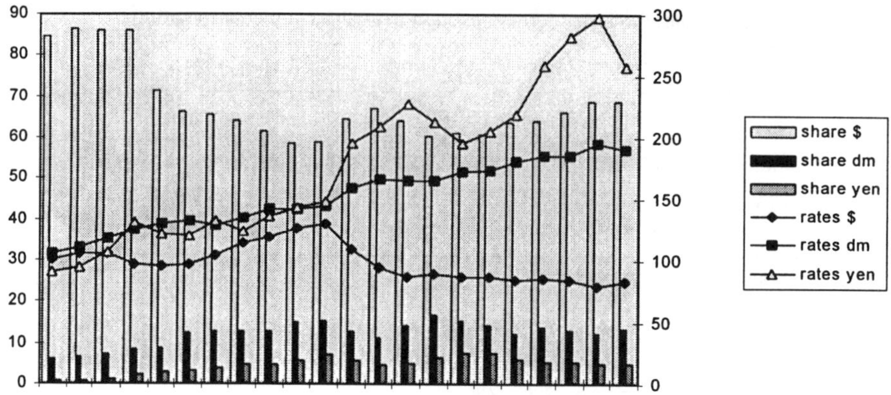

Figure 1. Currency shares (%) and effective exchange rates (indices, 1973 = 100).

At constant exchange rates, the dollar's share steadily declined by a total of around 14 percentage points between 1973 and 1985, excluding the effect of the introduction of the ECU in 1979, whereas its effective exchange rate rose by 29%. Between 1985 and 1996 its share grew by 10 points and its effective exchange rate fell by 35%. The mark's share increased by 10 percentage points in the first period and then declined, with fluctuations, by 2 points in the second, whereas its effective exchange rate rose, nearly without interruption, to 190. The yen's share increased by 7 points, up to 1985, and then fluctuated downwards by 2 points up to 1996. Its effective exchange rate showed wider swings, rising to 281 in 1985 and then falling back to 258 in 1996.

Figures 2, 3 and 4 clearly demonstrate the absence of a positive correlation between shares of the three currencies considered and levels of interest rates in the United States, Germany and Japan.

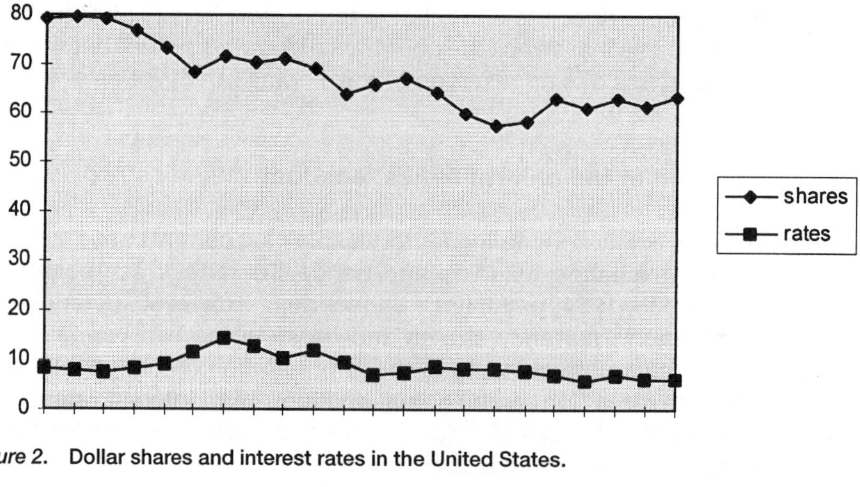

Figure 2. Dollar shares and interest rates in the United States.

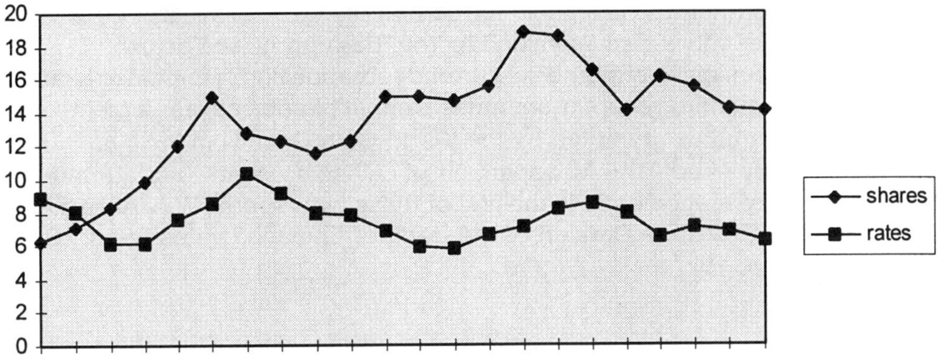

Figure 3. DM shares and interest rates in Germany.

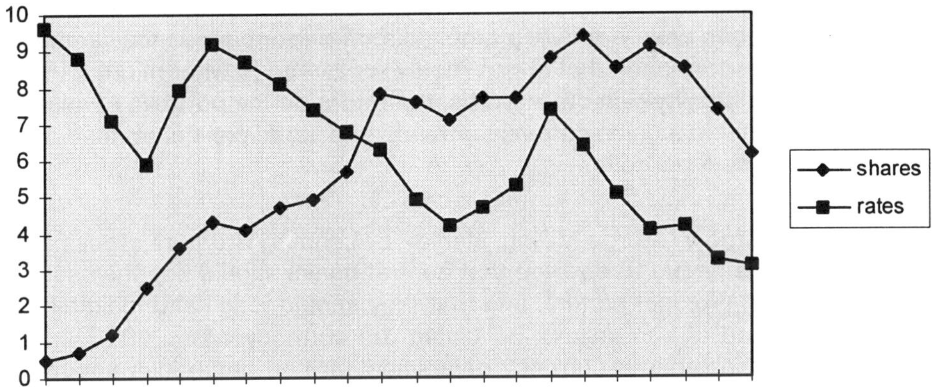

Figure 4. Yen shares and interest rates in Japan.

The standard mean-variance portfolio model, used by Dellas (1989) of the IMF, did not produce brilliant results either, notwithstanding the author's optimistic conclusions.[3] Although the optimal asset shares derived from the model for 1977–84 were roughly in line with those actually recorded for the dollar and sterling for the efficient portfolio, they were about 13 percentage points under for the mark and 14 points over for the yen. In the case of minimum portfolio variance, the optimal asset shares were close to the actual ones for the mark but diverged widely, not only for the yen but also for the dollar and for sterling (20 points under for the former and more than 15 for the latter).

Possible effects on the composition of reserves of central banks' intervention in exchange markets should also be considered. The analytical chronology below draws on the Annual Reports of the Bank for International Settlements (BIS) in order to track official intervention in the period studied but produces ambiguous results, possibly in part because interventions of the opposite sign cancel out over the year. Some authors (Taylor, 1982, pp. 367–368) have asked whether intervention was profitable for central banks' reserve asset management.[4] This question is also examined by the BIS reports (see below).

It appears plausible to attribute the currency composition of foreign exchange reserves for the entire group of countries to multiple objectives, a point confirmed by two studies promoted by the World Gold Council in 1995 and 1996 and significantly titled "The Management of Reserve Assets" and "Trends in Reserve Asset Management". In the first of these two reports, W.A. Allen, head of the Foreign Exchange Division of the Bank of England, writes (World Gold Council, 1995, p. 19):

> The primary responsibility of reserve managers is to ensure that the reserves are readily available for disbursement when they are needed: in other words to ensure the security and liquidity of the reserves. ... For several years now there has been a trend towards increasing sophistication in the management of foreign exchange reserves. ... One of the distinctive features of this development has been a growing emphasis on performance measurement. The kind of performance that is commonly measured is what might loosely be called 'profitability'—in other words, the return on the portfolio of assets, measured either in a given currency or relative to some pre-determined neutral or benchmark portfolio.

In the same study, George Milling Stanley of Lehman Brothers argues that a consensus has begun to develop that central banks should see themselves in the context of a bigger picture, and that they should reach and maintain an appropriate blend of currencies. Following the currency crises of 1992 and 1993, he notes, a broader currency diversification had much less appeal at the end of 1993 than a year and a half earlier. He also observes the growing tendency among central banks to commit funds only to the largest and most viable capital markets, such as those for the U.S. dollar, the yen and the mark. This last consideration could at least partly explain the recovery of the dollar in the past few years.

The contribution by David Williams of the IMF to the World Gold Council (1995, p. 81) study is of particular interest, since it takes derivative instruments into account. Specifically, Williams notes that the currency composition of foreign exchange reserves of industrial countries has become much more volatile than that of developing countries. He suggests that this may be partly due to derivatives trading.

The second study published by the World Gold Council (1996) analyzes reserve management policies of non-G10 central banks and identifies factors contributing to their determination. The currency mix of reserves varies widely among central banks. Excepting the portion of reserves held for day-to-day purposes, choice of currency is constrained by the requirement that reserves should be easily liquidated in case of need, and a very high proportion is held in the three leading reserve currencies, the dollar, mark and yen. There are wide differences among countries as to the extent to which reserves are held in currencies outside these three. Moreover, currency allocation of reserves is strongly influenced by the level and denomination of external indebtedness. In countries without large foreign debts, currency mix is influenced by factors such as the currency denomination of foreign trade, the currency used for intervening in foreign exchange markets, and the reference currency. Some central banks, however, have no such constraints and decide currency allocation and portfolio composition on the basis of prospective rates of return. In this connection, there are large differences among countries in the degree of discretion given to reserve managers in the choice of currency and investment vehicles. Professional investment managers are from time to time entrusted with quite small amounts of reserve assets in order to set a benchmark for in-house management, and provide staff training and other support functions (World Gold Council, 1996).

The evidence presented above points to the conclusion that liquidity and the prevailing utilization of currencies in international markets remain the key determinants of the currency composition of reserves. These two factors account for the dollar's weight in reserve asset management.

3. Analytical chronology

1975. Between 1973 and 1975 shares of the dollar, mark and yen increased at the expense of sterling. The dollar's effective exchange rate remained practically unchanged, the mark's rose by 5% and the yen's fell by 9%. Long-term interest rates rose in the United States and Japan and fell in West Germany. The U.S. interest rate differential, which had been negative in 1973 vis-à-vis both countries, narrowed with Germany and widened with Japan.

According to BIS, the volume of foreign exchange market intervention was limited, even though the band of the European monetary "Snake" reached its maximum width during the year.

1976. Currency shares continued to change in the same direction as in the preceding year, albeit with a very small increase for the dollar. Effective exchange rates rose by around 4 percentage points for the dollar, the mark and the yen. The simultaneous fall in interest rates in all three currencies nearly wiped out the differential between the United States and Germany and reduced that between the United States and Japan.

Although, as the BIS later reported, there was intervention within the framework of the European joint float on a scale without precedent since the Snake's inception in 1972, the overall change in official foreign exchange reserves in 1976 was the same as in 1975, when there had been practically no intervention. BIS (1997, p. 129) offered the following explanation for this paradox:

> The Group of Ten countries, including Switzerland, can be divided into two main categories so far as their intervention policies are concerned, according

to whether they limited themselves to intervention designed merely to smooth out day-to-day market conditions or whether, in addition, they operated in the markets in a way that brought about substantial changes in their net official reserves, including official, or officially inspired, borrowing. In the interpretation of countries' reserve figures it has to be borne in mind that such changes are not always a reliable guide to the size or even, in some cases, the direction of official intervention. For example, reserves can be affected by central-bank transactions with their own governments as customers or by income from the investment of foreign exchange holdings. In addition, changes in reserves are sometimes deliberately manipulated, for instance through the use of swaps or outright forward transactions.

1977. The dollar's share declined slightly, while those of the mark and the yen increased again. The dollar depreciated a little in effective terms and the mark and yen appreciated substantially. The large reduction in interest rates in Germany and Japan, combined with nearly unchanged rates in the United States, gave rise to a positive interest rate differential for the United States of 0.6 percentage points with Japan and 1.5 points with Germany.

The decline in the dollar's share was the accounting result of a proportionately smaller gain in dollar holdings than in total foreign exchange reserves. The increase of almost $30 billion in dollar reserves, calculated in SDR, was in line with the massive intervention reported by the BIS: purchases of around $20 billion by Germany, Britain and Switzerland in the course of the year. According to the BIS, the increase in Japan's foreign exchange reserves was largely due to income from investments of official dollar reserves, a source of change in the reserve holdings mentioned above.

1978. The dollar's share declined considerably, the mark's rose to nearly 10% of total foreign exchange reserves and the yen's doubled. The dollar plunged in effective terms, whereas the mark and, above all, the yen appreciated (the latter by 23%). Interest rates rose in the United States and fell further in Germany and Japan, so that the positive differential for US rates widened to 2.5 percentage points.

The large increase in swap lines between the Federal Reserve System and the central banks of Japan, Germany and Switzerland, used for official intervention in support of the dollar, boosted the reserves of these three banks. The growth in the Bundesbank's reserves was also attributable to intervention within the Snake, which suffered major tensions ahead of its replacement by the European Monetary System (EMS) on 13 March 1979.

1979. The dollar's share declined even more markedly than in 1978; those of the mark and the yen increased considerably. With the launch of the EMS, the ECU was introduced as a reserve asset held by monetary authorities of EMS member countries and acquired a 13.9% share of total foreign exchange reserves, essentially at the expense of the dollar, mark and yen. In effective terms, the dollar depreciated slightly, the mark appreciated strongly and the yen weakened abruptly. Interest rates rose in all three countries, and the positive differential for the dollar remained significant.

For the first time there was an absolute contraction in official dollar reserves (SDR 15 billion). The BIS attributed this to reduction in foreign exchange reserves of G10 countries (excluding the United States), where the dollar component prevailed. Among non-G10 countries, interest in the dollar as a reserve asset appeared to revive owing to the high level of interest rates on dollar-denominated assets and the dollar's appreciation late in the year.

1980. The dollar's share decreased by around 5 percentage points. Those of the mark and yen increased. The effective exchange rates of the dollar and mark improved and that of the yen weakened further. The especially steep rise in interest rates in the United States caused the latter's positive differential to widen substantially.

The reduction in the dollar's share was due to the appreciable growth in reserves held in other currencies, particularly the mark and the ECU, but, in absolute terms, dollar holdings recovered. The *Annual Report* of the BIS underscored the increase in the sum of U.S. liabilities towards foreign official institutions and reported that U.S. official deposits with commercial banks abroad had been larger than other countries' declared foreign exchange reserves. This was probably because statistics on reserves did not include all OPEC countries' official creditor position vis-à-vis banks of other countries. In fact, in 1980, the increase in OPEC countries' foreign exchange reserves corresponded to roughly one-half of their identified deposits with commercial banks outside the United States.

1981. The dollar's share recovered strongly (by around 3 percentage points), whereas those of the mark and yen declined for the first time since 1973. In effective terms, the dollar and yen appreciated (the latter more strongly), and the mark depreciated. The rapid increase in interest rates in the United States widened the latter's positive differential to 4 percentage points with Germany and almost 6 points with Japan.

Dollar reserves accounted for three-quarters of the modest (SDR 8.3 billion) overall growth in foreign exchange reserves. BIS (1992, p. 162) cited three possible reasons:

> In the first place, the geographical distribution of reserve gains and losses may have played a part. It seems likely that those oil-exporting countries which drew down their reserves in 1981 did so to a large extent by reducing their holdings in the Euro-currency market, while Saudi Arabia, which accounted for a substantial part of last year's aggregate OPEC current-account payments surplus, may have invested a significant part of its surplus in the US market. Secondly, the very high interest rates obtainable on longer-term fixed-interest securities in the United States, together with the strength of the dollar in the exchange markets, probably led to a change in some central banks' reserve investment policies, away from both the dollar and non-dollar

> sectors of the Euro-market towards the US capital market.... Thirdly, some central banks may have perceived last year an increased risk in holding their exchange reserves with the international banking system.

1982. The changes in the shares of the three leading currencies were very small in 1982. There was a further rise in the effective exchange rate of the dollar, a 6% upturn in that of the mark (which had fallen by 3% in 1981) and a downturn in that of the yen. The reduction in interest rates in all three countries barely dented the positive differential for US rates. The year was marked by a decrease of around SDR 7.5 billion in foreign exchange reserves, more than half of it due to the dollar, and by intramarginal intervention in support of the French franc.

1983. The three currencies' shares again changed only slightly. Their effective exchange rates rose (by 11% in the case of the yen). Interest rates came down more markedly in the United States than in the other two countries, further narrowing the positive differential for the United States. Foreign exchange reserves turned up and grew by more than SDR 23 billion, around half of which consisted of dollars, despite disposals by the United States, Japan and Germany.

1984. The dollar's share fell by more than 2 percentage points. Those of the mark and yen increased substantially. The effective exchange rate of the dollar and yen rose, and that of the mark fell slightly. Interest rates increased in the United States and decreased in Japan and Germany, widening the positive differential for the United States.

BIS (1985, p. 162) emphasized that most newly acquired reserves had been placed outside the United States, following three years of massive dollar disinvestment, and indicated that there were essentially three reasons for this:

> Firstly, non-OPEC developing countries, out of yield considerations, appear to have invested a major proportion of their 1984 exchange reserve gains in the Euro-market. Secondly, there was a substantial increase in Deutsche Mark reserves held by certain member countries of the European Monetary System. These increases were the product of intra-marginal interventions made by these countries in the framework of the EMS fixed exchange rate mechanism in order to moderate the strength of their currencies against the Deutsche Mark. Thirdly, there was a sizeable build-up of yen deposits, mainly with banks in Japan, which was probably related to the recent Japanese liberalisation measures.

1985. The dollar's share fell by 5 percentage points, almost entirely to the benefit of the mark and yen. There was no movement in the effective exchange rate of the mark, and those of the dollar and yen strengthened slightly. Interest rates moved downwards in all three countries to a varying degree. The resulting convergence narrowed the positive differential for US rates, which nevertheless remained large.

G10 countries carried out sizeable dollar sales (SDR 22 billion). As BIS remarked, there was an apparent contradiction between these disposals and the decrease of around SDR 1 billion in official dollar holdings. The discrepancy may have been due to market investments, for which, according to BIS, only limited statistics were available; for example, investment of official reserves in the Euronote or Eurobond markets, especially in instruments bearing floating rates and with a relatively short residual maturity.

In March 1985, in attempting to promote the international role of the ECU, the EEC central bank governors authorized central banks of EMS countries to trade ECUs for dollars or Community currencies through the European Monetary Co-Operation Fund. At the same time they authorized central banks of non-EEC countries and several international monetary institutions to hold ECUs, fixed the limit on using ECUs in order to extinguish liabilities contracted in the framework of the very-short-term financing facility subject to certain conditions and improved the yield of the ECU by modifying the basis of calculation. These measures had positive effects on the ECU's share in foreign exchange reserves in the two subsequent years.

1986. The dollar's share increased substantially, whereas those of the mark and yen remained unchanged. This happened in spite of the sharp fall in the dollar's effective exchange rate (around 18%) and large increases in those of the yen and mark (almost 30% and 11.5%, respectively), as well as widening interest rate differential.

In both IMF and BIS statistics, the increase in foreign exchange reserves in 1986 was attributed to the "not elsewhere classified" residual after allocating reserves by individual currency. This item probably revealed the growing tendency of monetary authorities to invest reserves in international securities purchased in the market.

1987. Movements in currency shares and effective exchange rates followed the pattern of the previous year but were less pronounced. The rise in rates in the United States and the fall in those in Japan and especially Germany increased the positive differential for the United States.

The dollar accounted for nearly half of the roughly 25% (SDR 91 billion) expansion in foreign exchange reserves. Linking these developments to the record U.S. deficit on current account, BIS (1988, pp. 188–189) wrote:

> It may be estimated that, including the drawing-down of US foreign exchange assets, somewhat over $100 billion, or more than 60%, of the US current-account deficit was directly financed by the official sector last year through the acquisition of assets in the United States, with indirect flows of official funds to the United States via the Euro-markets accounting for about another $20 billion.

1988. The dollar's share fell by 2.5 percentage points; those of the mark and yen rose by three-quarters of a point. Effective exchange rates of the dollar and mark weakened by 7% and 1%, respectively, whereas that of the yen rose by around 11%. The uneven rise in interest rates in the three countries resulted in further widening in the positive differential for United States.

BIS subsequently reported that 1988 had seen a pronounced shift in the currency pattern of the growth of exchange reserves away from the dollar to other currencies, but it was unable to determine the exact magnitude of this shift for reasons mentioned in its two preceding reports and, in particular, the nonidentification of several forms of investment of official funds in the United States. Regarding the large expansion in non-dollar exchange reserves, most notably in mark reserves, BIS (1989, p. 191) remarked:

> The strong growth in official Deutsche Mark reserves was only partly the result of official support purchases by the United States and EMS member countries; it also reflected the efforts of other countries to diversify their exchange reserve holdings.

1989. The dollar's share fell by more than 4 percentage points, largely to the benefit of the mark, which reached its peak for the period considered. The fact that this occurred in a year in which the dollar's effective exchange rate rose by nearly 4% and the mark's fell, with a deterioration of more than 6% precisely opposite the dollar, offers telling evidence of the low correlation between exchange rate trends and currency shares.

The mark accounted for almost half of the growth in foreign exchange reserves. According to BIS, the German currency benefited from some $11 billion of support purchases of marks and yen by the United States as well as from the intervention carried out under the exchange rate mechanism of the EMS. BIS observed:

> Since the United States necessarily holds its exchange reserves in non-dollar form, the growing presence of the United States in the exchange markets automatically entails an enhanced role for other currencies and countries as reserve media and reserve currency centres. A second reason for the fairly strong expansion of official exchange reserves last year was the intervention undertaken by countries participating in the EMS exchange rate mechanism. ... The fact that such exchange market intervention in an ERM context largely takes the form of purchases of currencies other than the dollar, i.e., predominantly other member currencies such as the Deutsche Mark, means that, instead of leading simply to a redistribution of dollar reserves between member countries, it adds to total reserve growth.

1990. The dollar's share decreased again, by almost 3 percentage points, and its effective exchange rate fell by around 4%. The yen's share increased by more than 1 point, although its effective exchange rate weakened by more than

9%, and the mark's share diminished slightly while its effective exchange rate rose by more than 4%. The appreciable increase in interest rates in Germany and Japan substantially narrowed the positive differential for the United States.

The sizeable increase of SDR 49 billion, or 9%; in foreign exchange reserves reflected a growth of nearly one-quarter in holdings denominated in the depreciating yen and less-than-proportionate increases in those in marks and dollars.

1991. The mark's share decreased by around 2 percentage points, the dollar's increased and the yen's reached its peak for the period. The effective exchange rates of the dollar and mark fell and that of the yen rose considerably. Divergent interest rate movements in the United States and Germany caused the differential of US vis-à-vis German rates to turn negative. Its sign was to remain basically negative in subsequent years.

BIS (1992, pp. 100–101) explained the large increase in dollar holdings in both absolute and percentage terms as follows:

> Last year saw signs of a move back towards the reserve investment patterns of earlier decades, with dollar reserves increasing more than those in other currencies and with funds being shifted from bank deposits to Treasury bills and other securities. This expansion in dollar holdings was partly a consequence of the geographical pattern of reserve growth. The developing countries recorded unusually large increases in international liquidity and showed a preference for dollar instruments.

1992. The dollar's share increased by almost 5 percentage points, whereas those of the yen and, more notably, the mark decreased. The dollar depreciated and the other two currencies appreciated in effective terms. The reduction in interest rates in all three countries left the differentials between US rates and those in the other two countries broadly unchanged.

The year was marked by the crises of British pound sterling, Italian lira, Spanish peseta, Portuguese escudo and Swedish krona, and by the massive attack on the French franc, which nevertheless succeeded in maintaining its EMS central rate. Official intervention, mainly in the form of sales of marks amounting to around $180 billion, resulted in an increase in reserves in the form of dollar holdings. BIS (1993, p. 196) commented:

> As to intervention itself, the question necessarily arises as to whether it was, in some sense, insufficient. Or was it simply ineffective in the new globalised financial world? Technology, innovation, free capital mobility and investors' desire for international portfolio diversification have by now all combined to increase vastly the potential for shifting large amounts of financial capital around the world, and across currencies, at great speed.

1993. The dollar's share fell by almost 2 percentage points, whereas those of the Mark and yen grew appreciably. The effective exchange rates of all three currencies rose, above all that of the yen (by around 20%). Interest rates fell across the board, leaving the differential between rates in the United States and the other two countries practically intact.

1994. The dollar's share recouped some of its losses from the previous year, the mark's share declined slightly, as did that of the yen. The mark's effective exchange rate remained unchanged, the dollar's edged downwards and the yen's strengthened sharply. The more rapid rise in US interest rates widened the dollar's positive differential.

BIS reported that around two-thirds of the growth in foreign exchange reserves was attributable to Asia, and not only Japan, in connection with intervention aimed at curbing appreciation of the yen, but also in China, Singapore, India, Taiwan, South Korea and Thailand. It went on to observe (1995, p. 127):

> In view of this concentration of reserve gains in Asia, it is not surprising that the issue of diversification of official holdings away from the dollar and into the yen has attracted greater attention recently. The decline of the dollar against the yen only served to sharpen the issue further, though it was no doubt partly an effect as well as a cause of pressures for diversification.

1995. Shares of all three currencies diminished, to the benefit of those not specified in the IMF data, whose share doubled. The dollar depreciated in effective terms, whereas the mark and yen appreciated. Decline in interest rates in all three countries left the differential between the United States and Japan virtually unchanged.

BIS (1996, pp. 104, 106) provides no relevant information on factors affecting the currency composition of reserves:

> With central banks intervening to brake and subsequently reverse the dollar's decline against the yen and the Deutsche Mark, international reserves grew in 1995 at the fastest pace since 1987. The importance of intervention in the dollar exchanges is evident in both the country and currency composition of reserve growth. ... The stability of the [dollar's] share in the 1990s has surprised many observers, in view of the long list of countries that are thought to have diversified their reserves away from the dollar. The country composition of reserve growth resolves this apparent contradiction: developing countries with currencies closely aligned with the dollar, and with reserves weighted more towards the dollar than the global average, have been gaining reserves at higher-than-average rates. The increasing willingness of industrial country investors to buy into both money markets and equity markets of developing countries suggests that these countries' reserves will continue to enjoy rapid, if not even, growth.

1996. Characteristic up-and-down movements in the dollar's share in the 1990s continued, with the dollar making up ground lost the previous year. The yen's share declined sharply and that of the mark recorded almost no change. The dollar strengthened in effective terms, whereas the mark and, more so, the yen weakened. The situation on the interest rate front remained practically the same as in 1995.

Picking up the line of reasoning it had set out a year earlier, BIS (1997, p. 83) offered the following interpretation of the 1996 developments:

> The United States financed most of its current account deficit in 1996 with official inflows. Although this had also been the case in 1987 and 1995, the underlying process at work differed last year. In 1987 and 1995 the dollar suffered from the unwillingness of private foreign investors to accept the dollars flowing from the US current account deficit at prevailing exchange rates and interest rates; the dollar's weakness against major currencies led Group of Ten authorities to intervene in its support. In 1996, by contrast, the dollar rose against major currencies and a pervasive search for yield in world financial markets led to strong capital flows to emerging markets. Since many of these countries link their currencies to the dollar, the resulting foreign exchange intervention led to increases in reserves, which were generally invested in US Treasury securities and other liquid dollar instruments.

Appendix

Table A1. Currency shares* in total identified official holdings of foreign exchange in all countries (in percent, end of year).

	Dollar	DM	Yen	Sterling	Fr. franc	Neth. guild	Sw. franc	Others
1973	78.4	5.5	—	6.5	0.9	0.3	1.1	7.3
1975	79.4	6.3	0.5	3.9	1.2	0.6	1.6	6.5
1976	79.6	7.0	0.7	2.0	0.9	0.5	1.4	7.9
1977	79.4	8.3	1.2	1.6	1.0	0.4	2.0	6.2
1978	76.9	9.9	2.5	1.5	0.9	0.5	0.9	6.3
1979	73.2	12.0	3.6	1.8	1.3	1.0	2.4	4.8
1980	68.6	14.9	4.3	2.9	1.7	1.3	3.2	3.1
1981	71.5	12.8	4.0	2.1	1.4	1.1	2.2	4.4
1982	70.5	12.3	4.7	2.5	1.2	1.1	2.8	5.0
1983	71.2	11.6	4.9	2.6	1.0	0.8	2.4	5.5
1984	69.4	12.3	5.7	3.0	1.1	0.8	2.1	5.8
1985	64.2	14.9	7.8	3.1	1.3	1.0	2.3	5.4
1986	66.0	14.9	7.6	2.8	1.2	1.1	1.9	4.5
1987	67.1	14.1	7.0	2.6	1.2	1.1	1.6	4.7
1988	64.6	15.5	7.7	2.7	1.0	1.0	1.9	5.5
1989	60.2	18.8	7.7	2.7	1.4	1.1	1.5	6.6
1990	57.5	18.6	8.8	3.4	2.3	1.1	1.4	6.9
1991	58.4	16.5	9.4	3.6	2.8	1.1	1.4	7.0

(Continued on next page.)

Table A1. (*Continued*).

	Dollar	DM	Yen	Sterling	Fr. franc	Neth. guild	Sw. franc	Others
1992	63.2	14.1	8.5	3.3	2.4	1.1	1.3	6.6
1993	61.4	16.1	9.0	3.4	2.2	0.6	1.5	6.8
1994	63.3	15.5	8.5	3.8	2.1	0.5	1.1	5.1
1995	61.5	14.2	7.4	3.5	1.9	0.5	0.9	10.1
1996	63.7	14.0	6.2	3.5	1.6	0.4	0.8	9.8

*ECU-Dollar swaps included with dollars.

Source: IMF, *Annual Report.*

Table A2. Currency shares* in total identified official holdings of foreign exchange of industrial countries (in percent, end of year).

	Dollar	DM	Yen	Sterling	Fr. franc	Neth. guild	Sw. franc	Others
1973	87.3	2.6	—	3.9	—	0.3	0.9	5.3
1975	87.3	4.0	0.2	1.1	0.1	0.3	0.9	6.2
1976	86.9	3.8	0.4	0.7	0.1	0.3	0.9	7.0
1977	89.0	4.0	0.3	0.5	—	0.2	0.7	5.1
1978	86.2	6.6	1.6	0.5	—	0.3	0.4	4.4
1979	83.5	9.4	2.6	0.7	0.6	0.6	1.4	1.2
1980	77.6	14.3	3.3	0.7	0.5	0.7	1.7	1.2
1981	78.7	12.8	3.7	0.7	0.4	0.8	1.7	1.2
1982	77.1	12.2	4.4	0.8	0.3	0.7	1.7	2.8
1983	77.4	12.8	5.1	0.8	0.3	0.5	1.4	1.7
1984	73.6	14.8	6.3	1.6	0.4	0.6	1.4	1.2
1985	65.4	19.4	8.8	2.1	0.5	1.0	1.8	1.1
1986	68.4	17.5	8.2	1.6	0.6	1.1	1.4	1.2
1987	70.6	16.5	6.6	1.5	0.8	1.1	1.1	1.8
1988	67.7	17.3	7.0	1.5	0.7	1.1	1.7	3.0
1989	59.6	22.5	8.1	1.4	1.2	1.2	1.1	4.8
1990	55.9	21.9	9.6	1.9	2.5	1.3	1.1	5.9
1991	55.8	20.0	10.4	2.0	3.2	1.2	0.8	6.5
1992	62.8	16.3	8.0	2.5	2.9	0.5	0.6	6.4
1993	60.7	19.7	8.7	2.7	2.7	0.5	0.6	4.5
1994	62.5	18.3	8.4	2.7	2.5	0.3	0.3	5.0
1995	62.5	16.9	7.4	2.2	2.3	0.2	0.2	8.4
1996	64.9	17.5	6.2	2.1	1.7	0.2	0.1	7.3

*ECU-Dollar swaps included with dollars.

Source: IMF, *Annual Report.*

Table A3. Currency shares in total identified official holdings of foreign exchange of developing countries (in percent, end of year).

	Dollar	DM	Yen	Sterling	Fr. franc	Neth. guild.	Sw. franc	Others
1973	55.2	13.2	0.2	13.4	3.1	0.6	2.0	12.3
1975	70.8	8.8	0.9	6.8	2.4	0.9	2.3	7.1
1976	72.7	10.1	1.1	3.2	1.7	0.7	1.9	8.6
1977	68.6	12.9	2.2	2.8	2.0	0.7	3.4	7.4
1978	62.6	15.0	4.0	3.0	2.2	0.9	2.9	9.3
1979	62.9	14.6	4.5	2.9	1.9	1.3	3.4	8.3
1980	59.8	15.5	5.3	5.0	2.9	1.9	4.7	4.9
1981	64.1	12.8	4.4	3.5	2.3	1.4	3.8	7.7
1982	63.8	12.4	4.9	4.1	2.2	1.6	3.8	7.3
1983	64.7	10.3	4.7	4.4	1.8	1.2	3.4	9.5
1984	64.9	9.7	5.0	4.4	1.7	0.7	2.8	10.6
1985	62.8	9.9	6.7	4.4	2.2	1.0	2.9	10.3
1986	62.0	10.8	6.8	4.6	2.2	1.2	2.8	9.4
1987	59.4	10.9	7.9	5.0	2.0	1.1	2.8	10.9
1988	57.4	11.4	9.2	5.5	1.7	0.9	2.5	11.3
1989	61.3	10.9	6.9	5.5	1.8	0.8	2.2	10.6
1990	60.7	11.6	7.3	6.4	2.0	0.7	2.2	9.1
1991	62.7	10.8	7.6	6.0	2.1	0.8	2.2	7.8
1992	63.2	10.8	9.1	4.5	1.8	0.9	2.4	6.8
1993	62.3	11.4	9.5	4.3	1.6	0.8	2.6	7.5
1994	64.3	12.3	8.6	5.0	1.6	0.7	2.1	5.3
1995	60.5	11.4	7.3	4.9	1.5	0.8	1.8	11.8
1996	62.5	10.6	6.2	4.9	1.5	0.5	1.5	12.3

Source: IMF, *Annual Report.*

Table A4. Currency shares in total identified official holdings of foreign exchange of all countries (in percent, end of year).

	Dollar	DM	Yen	Sterling	Fr. franc	Neth. gui.	Sw. franc	ECU	Others
1979	62.4	10.4	2.6	1.7	0.9	0.7	2.6	13.9	5.4
1980	55.9	11.9	3.3	2.5	1.1	0.8	2.5	17.0	5.0
1981	58.4	11.2	3.6	2.0	1.0	0.9	2.3	15.4	5.0
1982	60.0	10.4	3.5	2.0	1.0	0.7	2.4	14.4	5.6
1983	58.8	10.6	3.8	2.4	1.0	0.7	2.2	13.5	7.0
1984	57.0	11.0	4.8	2.6	1.0	0.7	1.9	11.0	10.1
1985	56.4	14.2	7.0	2.9	1.1	1.0	2.2	10.9	4.3

(Continued on next page.)

Table A4. (*Continued*).

	Dollar	DM	Yen	Sterling	Fr. franc	Neth. gui.	Sw. franc	ECU	Others
1986	55.8	13.6	6.3	2.2	1.2	0.9	1.4	12.2	6.5
1987	56.0	13.4	7.0	2.2	0.8	1.2	1.8	13.6	4.6
1988	55.3	14.5	7.1	2.5	1.0	1.0	1.8	11.7	5.4
1989	51.9	18.0	7.3	2.5	1.4	1.1	1.4	10.8	5.8
1990	50.1	17.3	8.2	3.1	2.3	1.0	1.3	10.1	6.7
1991	50.6	15.9	8.7	3.4	2.8	1.0	1.2	10.6	5.7
1992	54.7	13.7	7.7	3.2	2.5	0.6	1.1	10.1	6.3
1993	56.1	14.2	7.7	3.1	2.2	0.6	1.1	8.6	6.3
1994	55.9	14.3	7.9	3.3	2.1	0.5	0.9	8.1	6.9
1995	56.6	13.7	6.5	3.2	2.0	0.4	0.8	7.0	9.8
1996	58.9	13.6	6.0	3.4	1.6	0.3	0.7	5.9	9.5

Source: IMF, *Annual Report*.

Table A5. Currency shares in total identified official holdings of foreign exchange in industrial countries (in percent, end of year).

	Dollar	DM	Yen	Sterling	Fr. franc	Neth. guil	Sw. franc	ECU	Others
1979	62.2	6.3	1.7	0.5	—	0.4	1.1	24.0	3.8
1980	54.3	9.4	2.1	0.5	—	0.4	1.1	29.0	3.2
1981	55.9	9.2	2.5	0.5	—	0.5	1.2	26.9	3.2
1982	56.6	8.8	3.2	0.6	—	0.7	2.4	24.8	4.3
1983	56.6	10.9	3.8	0.8	0.3	0.4	1.2	25.0	1.0
1984	57.0	12.9	5.3	1.4	0.4	0.6	1.2	20.6	0.8
1985	48.9	16.4	7.3	1.7	0.4	0.9	1.5	20.2	2.7
1986	53.5	15.3	6.6	1.0	0.5	0.8	0.8	20.9	0.6
1987	54.8	14.1	6.3	1.0	0.3	1.1	1.5	19.0	2.0
1988	54.5	15.5	6.4	1.3	0.7	1.0	1.5	16.3	2.8
1989	48.4	20.6	7.5	1.2	1.1	1.1	1.2	15.3	3.5
1990	45.7	19.8	8.8	1.7	2.3	1.1	0.9	14.5	5.2
1991	43.7	18.3	9.7	1.8	3.0	1.1	0.8	16.6	4.9
1992	48.9	15.1	7.6	2.4	2.8	0.4	0.4	16.7	5.7
1993	50.3	16.4	7.9	2.2	2.5	0.4	0.3	15.2	4.8
1994	51.0	16.3	8.3	2.3	2.1	0.2	0.2	14.6	5.0
1995	52.1	16.4	6.7	2.1	2.1	0.2	0.1	13.3	7.1
1996	55.5	16.4	5.9	2.0	1.6	0.2	0.1	11.5	6.8

Source: IMF, *Annual Report*.

Notes

1. Unfortunately, data availability on the currency composition of the official reserves is a major problem. No such data are publicly available for individual countries. The only information on official holdings of foreign exchange pertains to country groups (industrial, developing, world) and is contained in the IMF's *Annual Report*.
2. "Expected rates of return, together with considerations of liquidity and risks, exert an important influence on the allocation of international reserves among assets denominated in different currencies."
3. On page 12, Dellas summarizes his results: "We undertook an empirical investigation of the hypothesis that central banks use the mean variance optimization criterion in forming portfolios of international assets. The examination of the behavior of the industrial and developing country groups offered support to this hypothesis."
4. As Taylor (1982, pp. 367–368) states: "The objective of official intervention should be to promote economic efficiency by reducing deviations from the equilibrium exchange rate. Using this criterion, successful intervention will produce a profit. The record of individual banks varies for each period; however, the central banks, taken as a group, have consistently lost. Some central banks have even tried to maintain an existing exchange rate when its equilibrium level changes. They are able to hold out for a limited period of time, but are eventually forced to allow the adjustment and lose substantial sums in the process."

References

Almekinders, G.J. and Sylvester C.W. Eijfinger (1994) "The Ineffectiveness of Central Bank Intervention." Discussion Paper No. 101, Center for Economic Research, Tillburg University.
Bank for International Settlements, *Annual Report*, Basle, various issues.
Del Giovane, P. and A.F. Pozzolo (1998) "The Behaviour of the Dollar and Exchange Rates in Europe." Temi di Discussione No. 328, Banca d'Italia.
Dellas, H. (1989) "International Reserve Currencies," IMF Working Paper 89/15.
Fratianni, M., A. Hauskrecht, and A. Maccario (1998) "Dominant Currencies and the Future of the Euro." in this volume.
Haldane, A. and S.G. Hall (1991) "Sterling's Relationship with the Dollar and the Deutschemark: 1976–1989." *Economic Journal*, 101.
International Monetary Fund, *Annual Report*, Washington, various issues.
Lucas, R.E., Jr. (1982) "Interest Rates and Currency Prices in a Two-Country World." *Journal of Monetary Economics* 10, 335–360.
Malliaropulos, D. (1994) "Monetary Convergence and the Relationship between European Currencies and the Dollar." *Rivista internazionale di Scienze Economiche e Commerciali*. 41.
Salvatore, D. (1998) "Present International Monetary and Financial Arrangements." in this volume.
Taylor, D. (1982) "Official Intervention in the Foreign Exchange Market." *Journal of Political Economy* 90, 356–368.
World Gold Council (1995) "The Management of Reserve Assets." Research Studies No. 9.
World Gold Council (1996) "Trends in Reserve Asset Management." Research Studies No. 13.

Open economies review **9:S1** 685–687 (1998)

Comments on the Papers by Melitz et al., Eichengreen, Fratianni and Hasukrecht, Savona and Maccario, and Dal Bosco

WILLIAM H. BRANSON wbranson@wws.Princeton.edu
Princeton University, Department of Economics, Princeton, NJ 08544-1021

Let me start with a broad discussion on the general topic of the conference, which is "ideas for the future of the international monetary system," and then come to a more focused discussion of the euro and the European Central Bank (ECB). I will discuss the papers as I go along, drawing on their results to emphasize my points. I would also like occasionally to refer to the Nordic and Asian crises.

I am still a believer in the tripolar world, I think that the recent crisis in Asia basically had part of its genesis in the fact that Asian countries were pegging to the wrong pole. They were pegging to the dollar instead of the yen. With the yen depreciating against the dollar, the Asian countries were appreciating against the yen. Additional flexibility would have been a good idea; at least getting off the dollar peg would have been a very good idea. In that case the crisis would have not been quite as bad as it turned to be. One cannot rule out the possibility of some kind of common currency or pegging to a common basket in the region that could reconstitute a yen zone. There is a real danger that a collapse of Japan would put the entire international monetary system in disarray.

Artis et al. make a nice start on optimum currency areas, uncovering three of them and suggesting a tripolar configuration in the world. One of the difficulties is that their areas tend to link North to South and this may not work out in fact. The paper by Artis et al. could have been a little better connected to the Fratianni-Hauskrecht paper on the bipolar world. Incidentally, I noticed in a very early version of the conference agenda that the Fratianni-Hauskrecht paper was dealing with a tripolar world. Somehow the yen slipped out for reasons I still don't understand. May be the authors were pressured by events unfolding in front of them and were quick to react.

The number "three" carries some pessimism. (Those who brought up three children may know what I am talking about; it is always two ganging up against one in differing combinations.) Tripolarity tends to be unstable; certainly the coordination problem with three is much harder than the coordination problem with two. What are the sources of the instability in the international monetary system? Savona and Maccario point to the growth of derivatives. I was struck by the difference between their numbers—their calculation of international monetary base gives us a world total of about 1.4 trillion dollars—and the estimate of $ 60 trillion in Governor Fazio's paper. Clearly, it is not straightforward computing the amount of derivatives because at some level they are inside money and wash out if one counts both sides of the potential exchanges. Yet, they are a source of instability in the extreme sense that central banks do not know the extent of their banks' liabilities. This actually happened in Thailand where its central bank was surprised by the extent of the banks' implicit outstanding liabilities.

Another source of instability is electronic money, a point on which I slightly disagree with von Hagen and Fender. I think of electronic money as the analogue to the free banking problem where anyone could have issued money. Today, we could reproduce free banking by issuing money through the Internet, an outcome which is not only unstable but for which there is no obvious solution.

Another source of instability was mentioned by Eichengreen: by combining a fixed peg exchange rate and a weak financial systems a banking crisis can become a foreign exchange crisis and a foreign exchange crisis can become a banking crisis. At times it appears as if the Asian crisis emerged as a result of the countries involved falling under their own weight. A slightly better way to think about the crisis is in terms of macroeconomic shocks that activate a process, which is then made worse by the weaknesses of the banking system and the attempt to peg. The fact that Japan has had virtually zero economic growth since 1990 or 1991 and that it attempted to stimulate its economy by easy monetary policy and low interest rate, which generated a depreciation of the yen since around 1995, contributed to capital flows towards the Asian countries. For example, Indonesia's exports to Japan were 10 billion dollars in 1990 and in 1997, while exports to the world have nearly doubled over the same period. There is a macroeconomic shock there.

Another macroeconomic shock affecting the Asian economies is the investment boom, particularly in property. Anyone familiar with the Mundell-Fleming model knows that a domestic investment boom generates a current account deficit and an appreciating currency in real terms until the build up of debt reverses sends the exchange rate in the other direction. In sum, these macroeconomic problems start the crisis, which is greatly exacerbated by the factors mentioned in Eichengreen's paper.

Fratianni and Hauskrecht discuss the coordination problem by trying to peg exchange rates across areas and then advocate that it would be better to adopt common inflation targets. This is a completely sensible idea. With common inflation targets and a successful implementation one can bring about a stable domestic monetary policy in the big areas of the world; the market would probably stabilize exchange rates. A little point that has not been touched on in the paper, which is somewhat popular in the United States now, is to include asset prices in the price index that is being targeted. The Fed seems to be doing that a bit; it seems to be useful, although the idea is just getting started.

Let me come to the euro and the ECB and the papers that discuss some of those topics. First, both Eichengreen and de Grauwe observed that the ECB is not meant to be a lender of last resort and, thus, is very different from a "normal" central bank in that it is not a major player in supervising and regulating the banking systems. Paul Volcker and Jerry Corrigan, in their speeches, used to say that a central bank is a lender of last resort and is responsible for the stability of the domestic banking system. Evidently, the ECB will be neither. This is a problem. Eichengreen writes about the difficulty of the ECB not being a lender of last resort in the face of a banking problem in stage three; de Grauwe points out the difficulties of overlapping supervision and regulation; von Hagen and Fender have a long section on this theme.

The papers, in general, have a long-run view of the euro. My favourite quote from Keynes about the long run is that it is for undergraduates. Keynes and others studied the short run because it is the way to the long run: if one cannot get through the short run one is dead. In this connection, one would think that stage three of EMU would be vulnerable to a form of speculation in which the public decides that one unit of account is better than another; on the basis of that assessment it starts moving funds into banks that are associated with the better unit of account and, thus, instigates the meltdown of the deposit base of the banks in the country of the lesser unit of account. Since the ECB is not a lender of last resort and since national governments are constrained by fiscal restraint, it becomes questionable who is going to help the troubled banking system. This is the potential problem stemming from the fact that the euro starts in 1999 but separate currencies are not eliminated until the middle of 2002.

There is another 2000 problem, one that worry people in the United States, but should worry even more people on the other side of the Atlantic. The slowdown in economic growth, which is expected as a consequence of the necessity to reconfigure computers, could be blamed on the euro and discredit it.

Lastly, the Dal Bosco paper shows nicely the trends in reserve movements. If the euro succeeds in amalgamating the reserves of a large number of countries and in shifting the international demand for reserves away from the dollar, the ensuing dollar weakness could turn out to be disruptive. It could be prevented by some kind of a swap arrangement between the ECB and the Fed, something that would have to be worked out fairly carefully. In sum, the ECB and the national central banks have a task in front of them during the next few years. I wish them well in getting the roof on the house that de Grauwe mentioned before a major storm comes.

Open economies review 9:S1 689–699 (1998)

Ideas for the Future of the International Monetary System: Conclusions and Remarks

MICHELE FRATIANNI
Indiana University, Bloomington

DOMINICK SALVATORE
Fordham University, New York

PAOLO SAVONA
Tor Vergata University, Rome

The Association Guido Carli, charged to research on the working of the international monetary system, selected a Study Group composed of outstanding economists, coming from the six leading countries in the world.[1] The Group met in Rome three times and set out to answer the following questions, sharing the work in accordance with the respective expertise and research interests:

Q1. How does the current international monetary system work?
Q2. How do the authorities regulate the system and react to its unexpected behavior?
Q3. Are the monetary authorities sovereign?

The answers are in the ten papers of this volume. Apart from some qualifications mentioned in the text, the Group answered the questions as follows.

A1.1 The floating exchange rates regime shows great volatility and large misalignments of exchange rates.

A1.2 The international reserve currency nature of the dollar and the leading countries' "internal economic structure" prevent floating exchange rates from leading to equilibrium in the balance of trade and in employment, causing an hysteresis of the European (and *LDCs*) unemployment rate and of foreign accounts—which are structurally negative in the U.S. and positive in Japan and, in a smaller degree, in Germany.

A1.3 In consequence of the high growth in the amounts of *cross-border bank assets & liabilities* (formerly known as *eurodollars*) and *derivatives*, financial assets and markets have become more liquid.

A1.4 Money is progressively losing its medium of exchange function and monetary policy is losing some of its effectiveness because of the abundance of international liquidity and the high degree of liquidity of financial assets;

another effect is the increased volatility in interest rates and exchange rates.

A1.5 The higher substitutability between monetary and financial instruments tends to emasculate the classical distinction between commercial bank activity and investment bank activity, as between monetary and financial risks; for these reasons, the words "monetary" and "financial" can be considered almost synonyms.[2]

A1.6 It is impossible to reconcile the so-called *holy trinity*, i.e., complete liberalization of capital movements, exchange rate stability and monetary policy independence.

A2.1 Increased liquidity of financial markets and increased leverage of financial positions imply that speculators can attack unsustainable fixed exchange rates faster and more powerfully than ever.

A2.2 The smaller importance of central bank money, as the base for monetary multiplication, leads authorities to shift attention from compulsory reserves to capital ratios.

A2.3 Authorities have only the alternative of letting exchange rates fluctuate or joining a monetary union with other countries that have "homogeneous" features.

A2.4 The rapid rate of financial innovation makes it futile to "throw sand in the wheels" through regulation or the introduction of transaction taxes.

A3.1 On the basis of these considerations, it is uncertain whether monetary authorities are still able to fix the amount of money and/or the interest rate or if this power is now in the hands of the markets.

A3.2 The vast array, complexity, and globalization of financial products argue for a market-based approach to bank regulation and supervision.

A3.3 In spite of some theoretical and practical doubts, most of the Study Group members think that monetary authorities are still sovereign, but they are all unanimous in believing that monetary policy is more difficult to carry out, and its effectiveness has been greatly reduced.

The Group[3] considers the current international monetary system (a non-system according to Koichi Hamada) to:

- be more efficient in distributing savings and investments than conceived in the previous Bretton Woods system,
- have reduced transaction and information costs,

but

- have raised financial risks,
- have made monetary policy less effective, and
- have reduced the extent of seignorage revenues.

Having been unable to replace gold (which Keynes himself called a "barbaric relic") with a system as good as gold not based on national currencies, Keynes considered incomplete the international monetary system created by the 1944 Bretton Woods Agreement. Since then, many reform proposals have been put forward, but only one was officially ratified in 1967 at Rio de Janeiro, i.e., the creation of a new International Monetary Fund unit of account—the *SDRs* (Special Drawing Rights).

The reform proposals put forward for reforming the Bretton Woods Agreement can be resumed as follows:

1. to resort to a coordination of monetary policies, referring them to an international monetary base, different from national currencies, and to extend the domestic rules of money control to *cross-border* bank deposits (Fratianni and Savona, 1972);
2. to reintroduce the *gold standard* or another *standard* based on a commodities basket (for a critical assessment see Commission on the Role of Gold, 1982);
3. to enlarge the exchange rates fluctuation band, indicating *target zones* (Williamson, 1986);
4. to match "target zones" with coordination policies (Miller and Williamson, 1987);
5. to indicate "target zones" by fixing exchange rates on the basis of the different currencies' *purchasing power parity* (McKinnon, 1984);
6. to coordinate economic policies by complex performance indexes based on the main real and monetary variables trends (IMF Interim Committee, 1986);
7. to slow down international capital movements by introducing a tax on them, the so-called *Tobin-tax* (Tobin, 1978);
8. to resort to a *dual exchange rate*, one for the trade of goods and one for the capital movements (Dornbusch and Frankel, 1987).[4]

Although the Rio Agreement and the weak policy coordination that took place to face specific problems seemed to be inspired by some of these reform proposals, they never became official. The system has remained basically a floating exchange regime, because of the main countries' belief that they could insulate themselves from external shocks. Salvatore argues that the pure floating regime is just a theoretical hypothesis, because, since 1973, the amount of central bank interventions in foreign exchange markets has been equal to the sum of the interventions undertaken during the Bretton Woods pegged exchange rate regime.

Without any reform, or more precisely, without a monetary world government or, in a wider sense, without a world government (or a major improvement in the functioning of the present international monetary system), countries can only share a monetary union or establish a pure floating regime to face the exchange and interest rates volatility and the loss of effectiveness of monetary policy. Joining a monetary union allows a country to fix the internal exchange rate with other member countries and to manage better those vìs-à-vìs external currencies. This is the choice made on May 2 by the Prime Ministers of the 11

European countries whose currencies will join the euro. Almost all the papers prepared by the Study Group deal with this issue.

Once it is clear that countries face only these two clear-cut options, the choice methods become important. Forrest Capie and Koichi Hamada maintain that the decision on the euro was political, because monetary questions deal with politics and because there is not only one solution for the problem. In fact, the solution does not seem to be clear cut or unique, but diversified according to the different countries' institutional structures and their economic conditions. Joining a monetary union means giving up a great part of national sovereignty in favor of a supranational institution.

Almost all the authors chose to follow economic rationality to provide useful information and avoid uncertainties. Michael Artis, Marion Kohler, and Jacques Mélitz undertake an econometric analysis to search for an "Optimal Currency Area," while Koichi Hamada uses the theory of collective action and of games to the same problem (Artis et al., 1998; Hamada, 1998).

Logical and empirical analyses demonstrate that the authors are not affected by anti-European (EMU) prejudices. They address their criticisms of the way in which the European Monetary Union has been realized and not of the objective pursued. In fact, Artis, Kohler and Mélitz show that the 15 signer countries of the Maastricht Treaty, plus Switzerland and Norway, form the only optimal currency area based on theoretical grounds; the other is that between U.S. and Canada, to be broadened, according to the authors, possibly to Japan. Barry Eichengreen underlines that the EMU, contrary to the U.S. situation, has low labor mobility, coupled with modest internal fiscal transfers. The EMU does not have, according to Capie, the two features necessary to deal with internal shocks in a fixed exchange rates system, and to create a consensus to make the Union survive politically. Moreover, Salvatore underlines the need for a convergence in the European countries institutional characteristics (in Italy, it is called "country-system"); he also thinks that benefits of the euro have been overestimated and costs underestimated. In case of an asymmetric shock, the Stability Pact provides that EMU countries only wait for the effects of the shock to work themselves out, thus paying high growth and employment costs. Many economists, not only the Study Group members, think that this is one of the main unsolved problems of EMU (Dornbusch, 1996; Bayoumi et al., 1997).

As these events have an impact on the working of the domestic banking system, Eichengreen (1998) pays attention to the potential conflict between European fixed exchange rates and the objective of Union financial stability. He maintains that this is an issue neglected by politicians when they have to decide on an exchange rates system.[5]

Apart from these substantial criticisms, the Study Group considers positive the creation of the euro, although with a different emphasis. They recognize that an internally fixed and externally floating exchange rate is a useful way to address both domestic and foreign shocks, in line with handbook explanations. The former, by fixing irreversibly European currency parities and by imposing a monetary and fiscal discipline on member countries. The latter, by introducing floating exchange rates among euro, dollar and yen. Yet, the authors think that other unexpected problems could arise so that theoretical conclusions may have to face a very different reality, difficult to manage by an univocal solution.

Therefore, the influence of the EMU on the welfare of the populations involved is uncertain, both from an economic and political point of view. Using a descriptive method, Hamada examines the historical examples of monetary unions and concludes that they work

- if political integration is reached before the monetary one,
- if there is a leader country,
- if there are few participants,
- if there is real economic integration,
- if monetary base is a metallic,
- if there are simple rules of the game and
- if countries give up economic policies to correct disequilibria and let the market solve them.

It is obvious that when a solution has too many conditions, it is difficult to implement.

Capie (1998) agrees with but insists that political union is the main goal of a monetary union, and this has to be judged on the basis of that objective, instead of by traditional economic theory. He reflects on the weakness of the EMU caused by a "lack of democracy" because there is no Parliament to which the European Central Bank (ECB) has to respond, and because monetary policy transparency does not seem to be guaranteed. Moreover, ECB demands to have the so-called *goal independence* (which allows it to choose objectives, in line with the theoretical *conservative approach*) in addition to the ability to choose instruments (according to the *principal-agent approach*). This is the official position of the former European Monetary Institute President, Emile Lamfalussy.

In a recent interview released to Italian television, the former German Chancellor, Helmut Schmidt, said that these are only ideas advanced by university professors, who do not have the task of pursuing great aims, such as the European Union. The problem is that politicians consider these as simple theoretic principles, without considering people's interests, which are not based only on monetary stability, but also on freedom, democracy, economic development and civilization, as underlined by Tinbergen (1952) when western countries began building welfare system.

Concerning the relationship between central bank independence (CBI), on the one hand, and inflation, real growth and fiscal deficit, on the other hand, the empirical evidence reviewed by Salvatore suggests that in industrialized countries there is a strong negative correlation between CBI and inflation or fiscal deficit, while there is no correlation with growth.

About the relationships between financial assets explosion (whose stock has grown 2.5 times more than GDP, and their daily transactions, which increased ten times in a short period) and monetary sovereignty, the Study Group thesis, mentioned above, is that managing money has become more difficult, but not impossible. That is to say, monetary authorities, especially the Fed, are still sovereign; hence, markets are not so dangerous that they have to be controlled. Facing these instability fears and working failings, the solution is neither control, nor structural reform, but policy coordination to improve the current system. Some authors, however, point out that coordination does not improve very much the welfare of countries that apply it (Frenkel et al., 1991).

Since the prevailing thought is that the increase in financial instability is the cost that we have to pay for improving the distribution of saving among different investments, Eichengreen's analysis focuses on the link between this instability and the exchange rate regime. He specifically refers to commercial banks and the *lender of last resort* function of central banks. Eichengreen also shows an existing relationship between the exchange regime and banking crises, where the liberalization of capital movements increased and where there is not a protection system for bank deposits. He specifies that banking crises may be the result of macroeconomic shocks on bank assets and liabilities. Each kind of crisis needs different policy measures to be solved. Shocks on bank assets may be caused by an economic recession, by a worsening in the terms of trade, by wrong fiscal policies or by speculation. Shocks on bank liabilities can be the result of devaluation expectations and of changes in foreign interest rates. Strict exchange rates fixing methods, such as the *currency board*,[6] cause the loss of the lender of last resort function by central banks, and if markets understand it, banking liabilities crises are more probable.

Eichengreen thinks a deposit owner should exert the first control on banking crises and that, if central banks are engaged in defending exchange stability, the Government should act as lender of last resort without losing control of the budget deficit. This can be done by opening an adequate foreign line of credit. In the recent Asian and Mexican crises, the International Monetary Fund (IMF) did not carry out its institutional task to prevent exchange rates from unexpected changes, but it attempted to stabilize financial markets. But its political line became too deflationary to stabilize agents' expectations.

EMU was born with some uncertainty concerning exchange rates and ordered market conditions. This may be due to institutional experience. It seems to take no interest in banking crises management, leaving it to domestic authorities. In our opinion, it is just an illusion because the ECB pretends to apply to financial intermediaries the same prohibitions regarding public subsidies to industry, ignoring the financial business peculiarity. In addition to defending the internal and external value of the euro, the ECB is responsible for the soundness of the payments system. The ECB will have, by implication, the narrowly defined function of lender of last resort to preserve the integrity of the payment mechanism, but not the broad one that is needed in a financial crisis. Under this structure the ECB can accomplish its goals of price stability and avoid high banking risks

- if it opens foreign lines of credit and
- deposit insurance schemes (they exist but in a limited way);
- if it imposes high base money reserve coefficients on banks (not advised by the EMI) and
- capital ratios (according to the Basle agreement), and
- strict credit standings.

Since all the topics deal with derivatives growth, von Hagen and Fender (1998) try to answer the question if the usual controls on monetary and financial instruments have to be extended to them and, in case of positive answer, in which way, being their market international. Savona and Maccario (1998) try to understand if derivatives can be considered as money and if monetary authorities have to include them in monetary targeting, as an intermediate or final monetary policy objective. Mishkin (1997) does not consider this distinction between intermediate and final objective to be relevant.

Von Hagen's and Fender's idea is that the benefit from derivatives is greater than damages they can cause. These consist in exchange and interest rates instability (meaning loss of monetary base in the multiplication process) and reducing the effectiveness of monetary policy on income and inflation. Concerning the potential instability from derivatives, the arguments are quite similar to those expressed about speculation, with the conclusion that it is impossible to establish a priori if they stabilize markets. There is empirical evidence, which shows that derivatives growth does not increase exchange and interest rate volatility (Board et al., 1995).

About the topic of monetary policy effectiveness, von Hagen-Fender's position is not conclusive. First of all, they recognize that derivatives increase price signals to monetary policy and, as a consequence, its effectiveness. Based on a model à la Poole, they maintain that the intermediate monetary policy target should be the interest rate instead of the quantity of money. In fact, in a scheme à la Hicks, instability should come from LM, i.e., the financial system, instead of IS, i.e., the real sector. They recognize, however, that in the current international market conditions this choice is difficult. Then, in "more perfect" markets, where the prevailing conditions are of a major substitutability among financial assets, thanks also to derivatives, monetary policy loses its effectiveness. This is due to the fact that a monetary target becomes uncertain and links between money and inflation loosen.

In the authors' opinion, central banks could intervene in derivatives markets, balancing speculation, in the same way they operate in financial markets to stabilize exchange and interest rates. It is possible, but they are skeptical about the agents and public opinion reaction. In fact, if a central bank had a profit on these transactions, agents would accuse it of manipulating prices; if it lost, public opinion would charge it with official reserves dissipation. In his paper, Elvio Dal Bosco verifies if central banks are acting in the way hypothesized by von Hagen and Fender, but the research could not be completed because central banks do not provide data on this activity. Data collected in a nonsystematic way show they are operating in derivatives markets to train their personnel.

The work by Dal Bosco (1998) shows that, in recent years, the dollar share in foreign exchange reserves rose against Deutsche mark and yen; moreover, the main central bank purpose in managing its reserves is, generally, liquidity. Only the part considered excessive is managed according to profitability criteria.

Savona and Maccario (1998) find that derivatives have money characteristics, where money is defined as in Fratianni and Savona (1972). Their thesis is reinforced by the conclusions of other research that has dealt on the role of derivatives on asset substitutability.

Michele Fratianni, in two papers (Fratianni et al., 1998; Fratianni and Hauskrecht, 1998) considers possible future scenarios of the international monetary system. In the first of the two papers the international role of the new currency, euro, is analyzed. The central thesis is that the U.S. dollar, despite the inevitable erosion of market share that it will suffer at the hands of the euro, will remain the most important international currency. The reason for this prediction is based on a judgment that EMU financial markets will not be as integrated, and thus as liquid, as the U.S. financial markets for quite some time, thus favoring the use of the dollar as a medium of exchange. Inertia and reputational considerations also favor the dollar.

The future value of the exchange rate dollar-euro will depend on economic fundamentals more than on portfolio shifts. Portfolio shifts argue for an appreciation of the euro; but fundamentals can swamp the effects of portfolio shifts. Should the EMU fundamentals reflect the spirit of the Maastricht Treaty and the Growth and Stability Pact, the chances for an euro appreciation will increase. Fratianni, Hauskrecht, and Maccario—like other Group members—caution that the ECB is a new and untested central bank where consensus for a conservative monetary policy cannot be taken as a foregone conclusion. The fact that the Maastricht Treaty calls for a conservative monetary policy does not automatically translate into actual practice.

Fratianni and Hauskrecht argue that the international monetary system is likely to evolve into a bipolar structure consisting of a dollar area and an euro area, each of which attracting other countries to their gravitational centers. The yen is a big question mark. William Branson, in his comments to the paper, states his preference for a tripolar world, including the yen area. Branson opines that the recent Asian currency crisis would have been less potent had the Asian countries pegged to the yen rather than to the dollar. Yet, the deep and still unresolved financial crisis in Japan works against the enlargement of the yen. Going in the opposite direction, instead, is the expected deregulation of the Japanese financial markets, with would lower costs in yen-denominated transactions. Fratianni and Hauskrecht conclude that the yen area will be much smaller than the dollar and the euro area and, consequently, the two large blocs will shape the international monetary system of the 21st century in a critical way. These two authors also discuss feasible scenarios of interaction between currency blocs. A large EMU works in favor of cooperation because fewer players imply lower decision-making costs in reaching a cooperative solution. The relative closeness of EMU and the United States, on the other hand, works against cooperation and in favor of benign neglect. Exchange-rate agreements are fragile unless supported by strong commitment to economic policy cooperation, and such a commitment may well be premature. The preferred scenario is that both the United States and EMU target common inflation rates and stabilize exchange rates as a by-product, an idea that Keynes proposed back in 1923.

In conclusion:

- analyses on the working of the international monetary system conclude that the role of monetary policy is not crucial in determining income and employment,
- yet, monetary policy has the possibility of contributing to the welfare of populations by guaranteeing ordered conditions in financial markets and by preventing erratic movements or payments system crises that have a negative impact on income, employment and/or inflation.

The Study Group's conclusions are characterized by the common hope, expressed by von Hagen and Fender that a unique authority would rule over the international monetary system. In the awareness of the impossibility of such a solution and to let economic rationality prevail, in the short term the international monetary government second best

- would be to create more effective and efficient coordination mechanisms among the national authorities of the large currency areas; or more simply,
- that large currency areas, such as the euro and the U.S. dollar, pursue common inflation targets rather than targeting exchange rates, thus stabilizing exchange rates as a result of having stabilized inflation rates.

Acknowledgments

The other Study Group members have not examined these Conclusions and Remarks. Therefore, they are on the exclusive responsibility of the authors.

Notes

1. Besides the authors of these *Conclusions and Remarks*, the Study Group original members are Mario Arcelli, Forrest Capie, Elvio Dal Bosco, Marcello De Cecco, Barry Eichengreen, Jürgen von Hagen, Koichi Hamada, Andreas Hauskrecht, Aurelio Maccario, and Jacques Mélitz. During the research progress, Michael Artis, Ingo Fender and Marion Kohler became members of the Study Group.

2. According to the terminology followed by the Study Group members, we will use only the expression "financial" system or market, knowing that the reader will not face interpretation misunderstandings.
3. If not specified, we refer to the authors of the papers produced in the context of the Association's research, and not to those who first expressed the referred concepts. The papers produced by the Study Group include an exhaustive bibliography and explicit references to the literature on single topics.
4. Apart for the synthesis, made necessary by this exposée, the reform proposals analysis is found in the Survey produced by Salvatore (1998).
5. Eichengreen also examines closely the relationships between the international financial system and commercial banks operating in it, and their connections with monetary policies.
6. A currency board involves changes in the monetary base only through changes in official reserves, due to the obligation of defending an exchange parity.

References

Artis, M., M. Kohler, and J. Mélitz (1998) "Trade and the Number of OCA's in the World." in this volume.

Bayoumi, T., B. Eichengreen, and J. Von Hagen (1997) "European Monetary Unification: Implications of Research for Policy, Implications of Policy for Research." *Open Economies Review* 8, 71–97.

Board, J. et al. (1995) "Derivatives Regulation," Financial Market Group Special Paper No. 70, London School of Economics, London.

Brunner, K. and A.H. Meltzer (1976) "An Aggregative Theory for a Closed Economy." In J.L. Stein (ed.), *Monetarism*. Amsterdam: North Holland.

Capie, F. (1998) "Monetary Unions in Historical Perspective: What Future for the Euro in the International Financial System." in this volume.

Commission on the Role of Gold in the Domestic and International Monetary System (1982) Report. Washington, DC: Government Printing Office.

Dal Bosco, E. (1998) "Central Banks' Management of Foreign Exchange Reserves." in this volume.

Dornbusch, R. (1996) "Euro Fantasies." *Foreign Affairs*, Sept.–Oct.

Dornbusch, R. and J. Frankel (1987) "The Flexible Exchange Rate System: Experience and Alternatives," Working Paper No. 2464, National Bureau of Economic Research, Cambridge, MA.

Eichengreen, B. (1998) "Exchange Rate Stability and Financial Stability." in this volume.

Fratianni, M. and A. Hauskrecht (1998) "From the Gold Standard to a Bipolar Monetary System." in this volume.

Fratianni, M., A. Hauskrecht, and A. Maccario (1998) "Dominant Currencies and the Future of the Euro." in this volume.

Fratianni, M. and P. Savona (1972) *La liquidità internazionale-Proposta per la ridefinizione del problema*, Il Mulino, Bologna.

Frenkel, J., M. Goldstein, and P.R. Masson (1991) "Characteristics of a Successful Exchange Rate System," IMF Occasional Paper No. 82, Washington, DC.

Friedman, M. (1953) "The Case for Flexible Exchange Rates." *Essays in Positive Economics*, Chicago: Chicago University Press.

Hamada, K. (1998) "The Choice of International Monetary Regimes in a Context of Repeated Games." in this volume.

IMF (1986) "Interim Commitee Report." Washington, DC.

McKinnon, R.I. (1984) *An International Standard for Monetary Stabilization*. Washington, DC: Institute for International Economics.

McKinnon, R.I. (1988) "Monetary and Exchange Rate Policies for International Financial Stability: A Proposal." *Journal of Economic Perspectives* 8(2).

Miller, M.H. and J. Williamson (1987) *Targets and Indicators: A Blueprint for the International Coordination of Economic Policy*. Washington, DC: Institute for International Economics.

Mishkin, F.S. (1997) “Understanding Financial Crises: A Developing Country Perspective.” *Annual World Bank Conference on Development Economics*, Washington, DC.

Salvatore, D. (1998) “International Monetary and Financial Arrangements: Present and Future.” in this volume.

Savona, P. and A. Maccario (1998) “On the Relation between Money and Derivatives and its Application to the International Monetary Market.” in this volume.

Tinbergen, J. (1952) *On the Theory of Economic Policy*, Amsterdam: North Holland.

Tobin, J. (1978) “A Proposal for International Monetary Reform.” *Eastern Economic Journal*, July–October.

Von Hagen, J. and I. Fender (1998) “Central Bank Policy in a More Perfect Financial System.” in this volume.

Williamson, J. (1986) “Target Zones and the Management of the Dollar,” Brookings Papers on Economic Activity, No. 1.

Open economies review **9:S1** 701–708 (1998)

The International Monetary System

ANTONIO FAZIO
Governor, Banca d'Italia, via Nazionale 91, 00184 Rome, Italy

Key words: external imbalances, currency crises, financial regulation

JEL Classification Numbers: F32, F34, F42, G28

Abstract

This paper outlines the main features of the present international monetary system and the challenges that policy makers face.

Introduction

The present configuration of the international monetary system is the outcome of the spontaneous development of the interactions between different financial systems, in a regime marked by freedom of capital movements. Banking systems' international activity has increased considerably; an even larger expansion has taken place in that of institutional investors, who receive savings and invest on a global scale. New intermediaries and new markets have come into being, new instruments have been developed. Repeated crises have slowed the growth of the international monetary system, but the volume of transactions and intermediated funds has nonetheless grown faster than world output.

It continues to be difficult to reduce the working of the international monetary system to a set of orderly and statistically well-defined flows of funds. It is even more difficult to capture the behaviour of intermediaries, markets and final users of funds in a model. The endogenous forces at work within the system result, from time to time, in exchange rates and interest rates that can become cogent enough to influence the fundamentals and affect the underlying performance even of large economies.

The international monetary system is not governed. It does not have an anchor. It is powerfully influenced by the behaviour of the leading countries and currencies.

1. The international monetary system

Underlying every monetary regime is the search for an equilibrium between two often conflicting requirements: on the one hand, the credibility of the management of the currency, which is vital for maintaining confidence in the value of the monetary yardstick; on the other, the flexibility needed to attenuate the impact on the economy of unexpected shocks, of major events that are independent of the action of the monetary authorities.

The gold standard sacrificed flexibility for credibility. It did not hold up under the pressure generated by the profound economic, social and political changes that began with the First World War and spread in the following decades.

The international monetary order established at Bretton Woods was the last conscious attempt to reconcile credibility and flexibility at the world level. The aim of the agreements was not to reverse the shift towards purely fiduciary money, which had gained momentum in the period between the two world wars. Rather, it was to make the independent conduct of national economic policies compatible with the maintenance of stable international economic conditions. Restricting short-term capital movements was an essential element.

The Bretton Woods system collapsed at the beginning of the seventies when the two conditions that had ensured its success in the preceding decades ceased to obtain: a balanced macroeconomic situation in the country issuing the reserve currency and national financial systems that were essentially closed, in the sense that capital mobility was limited and the monetary authorities exercised effective control.

Subsequent developments led to a credibility deficit, which contributed not a little to the high and persistent inflation of the seventies. Exchange rate flexibility restored the effectiveness of monetary policies in controlling inflation but did not prevent the emergence in the eighties and nineties of severe unemployment, economic stagnation and losses of welfare.

In the last few years determined and successful efforts have been made in the leading countries to restore orderly conditions and return to rigorous fiscal policies. The restrictive monetary policies pursued since the eighties have allowed a lasting reduction in inflation and a curbing of wage pressures. The conviction has grown that the internal and external value of each currency depends on the confidence of investors in the economy's ability to grow and prosper.

It is nonetheless wishful thinking to imagine that each country's "putting its own house in order" is sufficient to ensure stable economic and monetary conditions at the international level. An important part of the international banking system, and more generally of the financial markets, operates outside national borders. The quantity of money and credit created and exchanged is beyond the direct control of any national or international authority.

Uncoordinated national policies find it hard to stem the exuberance of the financial markets, to prevent the fluctuations in the prices of financial assets from imparting destabilizing impulses to the real economy. The high degree of financial and trade integration means that every country can be hit by the shock waves emanating from other regions, including those that are far off or apparently of limited economic significance.

Today's challenges echo the serious problems that the leading countries had to face in the early decades of this century as a result of the deepening of their domestic financial systems. The response to the instability produced by that, often chaotic, growth of banking consisted in the establishment of central banks as we know them today. This solution prevailed, however, only after it came to be generally acknowledged that money and credit were rarely able to reach an equilibrium endogenously.

The solution based on a strong central bank, free from political influence and endowed with considerable discretion is not practicable at the world level, however. The effectiveness and legitimacy of central banks are ultimately rooted in their being part of the state. At the world level the only road open is that of closer cooperation between national institutions and a strengthening and redefinition of the role of those established at Bretton Woods.

2. Imbalances in the world economy and monetary developments

The global market has created new opportunities to achieve welfare and prosperity for countries that lack capital and finance. It frees individual economies from the constraint of having to match saving and investment in each period. It allows intermediaries to hunt out the most profitable investment opportunities throughout the world, thus making for a more efficient allocation of saving. It results in the actions of policy-makers being subject to continuous scrutiny.

However, the risks of instability are enormous. The possibility of financing imbalances may cause their correction to be put off. Sudden switches in investors' expectations lead to rapid shifts in their portfolios, thereby creating disruptive pressures in foreign exchange and securities markets.

The increase in international liquidity engendered by the expansionary stance of monetary policy in one or more of the leading countries normally leads to a fall in interest rates everywhere and stimulates economic activity. But at the same time it fosters the persistence of imbalances.

The ample availability of financial resources fuels a rapid expansion of credit that contributes to a deterioration in loan quality in banking systems that are not adequately regulated and managed; it encourages the taking of speculative market positions, which may lead to prices of financial assets that are inconsistent with economies' fundamentals.

The large and persistent balance-of-payments disequilibria of both industrial and emerging countries are the underlying cause of international capital movements. The external accounts of the United States have been in deficit since 1983. Since 1990 the shortfall on current account has averaged around 1.5% of GDP; this year it is expected to rise to 2.7% of GDP owing to the differential in the rate of growth in domestic demand compared with Europe and Japan and the crisis in Asia. Japan's surplus has averaged around 2.3% of GDP in the nineties; it will rise this year, probably reaching 3% of GDP.

The two leading economies have consequently accumulated very large imbalances in their net external positions. At the end of 1997 America's debtor position, including its gold reserves, amounted to $1 trillion, or more than 12% of GDP; Japan's creditor position was of the same size in absolute terms.

Large deficits developed in the external accounts of some emerging countries and areas in the nineties were one of the underlying causes of the crises that occurred. The deficits of Indonesia, Korea, Mexico and Thailand rose to between 3% and 8% of their respective GDPs; current account deficits have grown to a worrying size in some East European and Latin American countries.

Fueled primarily by private finance, the industrial countries' capital inflows and outflows increased by around 50% in the nineties compared with the previous decade. At the same time the inflows to the non-industrial countries tripled and in 1996 were a shade less than $400 billion.

The proportion of the flows consisting of portfolio investment rose; in 1996 the inflows of this component to the industrial countries amounted to $900 billion, the outflows to $600 billion. The short-term and often speculative nature of such investment means that it is marked by greater variability and reactivity.

The stock of outstanding international bonds exceeded $3.3 trillion at the end of 1997. Encouraged by the fall in long-term interest rates, issues last year rose to a new peak of more than $800 billion, despite the slowdown that occurred following the outbreak of the Asian crisis.

The dollar remains the currency in which the bulk of these securities are denominated, accounting for more than one third of the total in the nineties. The proportion denominated in yen has declined; that in marks has risen to nearly 15%. As the euro becomes established Europe's role in global finance will increase.

For the banks of the countries reporting to the Bank for International Settlements, claims on non-residents grew by 50% compared with 1990, rising to $9 trillion. International loans contribute to the carrying out of major investment projects, support the operations of multinational firms, and assist research and the implementation of more efficient combinations of the factors of production. The financial component nonetheless remains preponderant: more than two thirds of the banks' claims on non-residents had another intermediary as the counterparty.

Interbank activity is a major factor in the multiplication of international liquidity, which, not being subject to direct control by any monetary authority, can expand to the point of creating financial turbulence and inflationary pressures. The cross-border component of overall liquidity, including interbank deposits, is very large, accounting for around one third of the total.

Institutional investors have been the driving force in the development of global finance in recent years. Their aggregate balance sheet has grown by more than 10% a year. The volume of funds they intermediate is estimated at around $28 trillion, the annual output of the world economy.

These intermediaries raise liquidity in the markets where it is abundant and least costly. The composition of their portfolios is decided in the light of the expected risks and returns of a very wide range of investment opportunities, including those offered not only by the leading markets and currencies but also by emerging markets, less widely used currencies and complex financial instruments.

This makes a decisive contribution to unifying the market for finance. It leads to greater uniformity in the movements in financial asset prices across countries and links them more closely to the decisions of a number of leading players.

The trend and fluctuations of interest rates in the key money markets are transmitted worldwide. Japan's growing surplus with the rest of the world is matched by a deficit for the other countries, above all the United States. The *ex post* equality of saving and investment does not determine a particular level of interest rates. It is the *ex ante* shortfall in investment compared with potential saving that is responsible for the current slowdown in economic activity.

Whereas a steady monetary policy stance has prevailed in the United States, Japan's central bank has pursued an aggressively expansionary policy. Money market rates are close to zero but domestic demand is not reviving in Japan. It is a classic liquidity trap, involving a depreciation of the yen, a worldwide reduction in interest rates and a rise in share prices in the United States and Europe.

The weakness of effective demand and the measures taken to consolidate the public finances in all the major countries are preventing the excess of liquidity from translating into inflationary pressure.

Between 1990 and 1997 the notional value of exchange-traded derivative instruments, primarily interest rate futures and options, grew six-fold to exceed \$12 trillion. Even more rapid growth was recorded for over-the-counter instruments, particularly interest rate swaps: between 1990 and 1996 those regularly reported to the Bank for International Settlements increased eight-fold to more than \$25 trillion. The total notional value of derivative finance, that is the amount potentially able to influence the prices of financial assets, can be estimated at around \$60 trillion.

Derivative instruments make it possible to manage complex risk positions, thereby broadening investment opportunities, increasing the scope for portfolio adjustment and enhancing the ability to protect wealth against adverse variations in securities prices and exchange rates.

The complexity of certain financial derivatives can make it hard even for investors to estimate their overall exposure to risk, especially when the size and simultaneity of the movements in financial asset prices are unprecedented. In order to safeguard the soundness of intermediaries, supervisory rules, adopted in part pursuant to international agreements, impose the use of procedures for correctly measuring credit and market risks. Adequate capital is necessary but it is not sufficient; it must be coupled with carefully designed internal controls.

Derivative finance facilitates trading, the working of markets and the pricing of financial assets. Where expectations concerning future movements in asset values converge, it may amplify the fluctuations of exchange rates and securities prices.

3. The recent crises

With an international monetary order lacking an overall system of governance, numerous currency crises have occurred. In particular, the breakdown of the European Monetary System in 1992–93 showed how difficult it is for fixed exchange rate regimes to work in the present context of integrated markets and highly mobile capital. Since 1980 the banking systems of more than 130 countries have been beset by acute difficulties.

The interaction between currency crises and banking crises has become pronounced in recent years. "Twin" crises have occurred in the Nordic countries, Mexico and the Asian countries. In the most serious cases, the entire economic and financial system was shaken. The immediate cause has often been the sudden withdrawal of finance from abroad as a result of international investors losing confidence in firms and banks. The ultimate causes lie in the shortcomings of macroeconomic policies, in the structural weaknesses of financial and banking systems and in inadequate prudential supervision.

The recent Asian crisis is emblematic of how the combination of borrowing abroad and a structurally fragile banking system aggravates the consequences of failure to correct macroeconomic imbalances. The enormous capital inflow made it possible for large current account deficits to be maintained and provided the banking system with the means to finance investments offering low returns, with a consequent deterioration in loan quality. The excessive build-up of debt inevitably brought on the crisis.

4. The challenges ahead

The present configuration of international monetary relationships has no parallel in history. Never before have purely fiduciary currencies coexisted with such a high degree of capital mobility, vast global markets beyond the direct control of the authorities, flexible exchange rates between the major currencies and far-reaching economic integration.

The need to promote adequate forms of international cooperation on institutional structures, economic policy-making and specific measures to safeguard market stability has become urgent in the new context.

In order to restore orderly conditions during the Mexican and Asian crises, the international community made a financial effort of unprecedented proportions. Such an effort would be difficult to repeat.

In the past, the primary concern was that borrowers, often sovereign states, might come to have excessive expectations concerning international protection against the risk of insolvency. The recent crises have reminded us that it is just as important to promote prudent and far-sighted behaviour on the part of creditors.

The creation of an international bankruptcy law or the rapid convergence of national practices and regulations are currently beyond our reach. Nevertheless, there is ample room for improving the existing situation.

We must return and give new vigour to the work begun within the G-10 in the wake of the Mexican crisis on the introduction of contractual clauses to facilitate negotiations between creditors and debtors in crises and the possibility of temporary suspensions of foreign debt servicing in particularly serious situations. Under the vigilant eye of international institutions, such suspensions may prove necessary to allow debtors to formulate a credible adjustment plan and creditors to make a more considered assessment of creditworthiness.

It is important to enhance the soundness of national financial systems, fill the gaps in banking regulations and generally increase the effectiveness of supervision.

There is growing awareness that capital mobility is not a good in itself, an end to pursue without conditions or caution. The main lesson of the Mexican and Asian crises is that when opening up the financial system, it is necessary to ensure a stable domestic environment by strengthening the technical aspects of supervision and prudential controls, with complete independence from political influence. The International Monetary Fund now tends to pursue the more pragmatic objective of ensuring an orderly process of liberalization.

The Basle Committee for Banking Supervision has developed a number of core principles, a set of standards of proper conduct that countries must incorporate in their regulatory systems. The G-10 has proposed their extension to the emerging economies.

The most urgent requirement in dealing with the recurrent risks of endemic or systemic instability is to extend and strengthen action to prevent instability and make effective instruments available.

The first requirement for such action is that information on economies be timely, transparent and reliable. But it is also necessary to interpret, with reference to well-tested models that are also appropriate and sufficiently innovative, the behaviour and prospects of economic systems in which macroeconomic variables, prices, exchange rates, financial variables and structures, and political or administrative measures interact to produce stability and growth or instability and crisis.

Interpreting economic situations may prove too complex for financial intermediaries and investors despite the wealth of data in their possession. They therefore tend to follow leaders, moving in herds and swinging abruptly from pessimism to optimism, both of which are exaggerated and ultimately irrational.

Events in Mexico and the Asian countries are exemplary in this respect. A number of clear signs of macroeconomic imbalance, consisting in repeated large current account deficits and rapidly expanding foreign debt, together with the inefficiency of markets and intermediaries, certainly indicated that conditions were at least conducive to the development of a crisis.

The guarantees that in several cases the political and monetary authorities provided for loans contracted by firms and banks abroad are indicative in such circumstances of a situation of precariousness and in practice to no effect since the entire economic and institutional system is involved in the crisis.

It is important to reinforce the Fund's analytical capabilities and give it a more open and direct advisory role where countries are prone to crises. In other words, the Fund should have a role similar to that performed by national central banks in individual countries. We must address the problem of permanently strengthening the Fund's resources, to be used for "lending of last resort", with penalty rates of interest and stringent conditions attached.

It is being debated whether the Fund's opinions should be made public. Some fear that publication might jeopardize the confidential relationship between the Fund and government authorities or even trigger the crisis. If surveillance and analysis and the assessment of economic policies are carried out systematically, extended to many countries and based on recognized intellectual authority, such concern is unwarranted.

The strengthening of the Fund must be accompanied by the assignment of a larger role to the World Bank in the systematic monitoring of conditions in the banking and financial systems of the developing countries and the economies in transition in order to reinforce them and forestall instability that could originate in these sectors.

The challenges facing us are difficult but not impossible. Earlier in this century financial instability appeared to have gained the upper hand, but an intellectual effort and a reforming drive made it possible to take the necessary counteraction and return to the path of stable growth. Awareness of the enormous economic, political and social costs that endemic financial instability on a global scale inevitably entails must guide us in meeting the challenges.

Open economies review 9:S1 709–712 (1998)

The International Monetary System in a Real Economy

CARLO SCOGNAMIGLIO csaspeit@tin.it
Senator of the Republic of Italy, President, Aspen Institute Italia via Jacopo Peri 1, 00198 ROMA

Key words: real economy, monetary stability, global markets

JEL Classification Numbers: D21, F33

Abstract

The paper offers a brief analysis of the reasons why European Monetary Union receives the support of academics and operators alike as a great step forward in constructing global monetary stability. Cooperation that will lead to a stable international monetary system is recognized as a primary goal for both the real economy and high finance. Technological innovation, increasingly global markets, unlimited access to capital, the disappearance of national sovereignty and, above all, the heightened role of values in the business environment, all contribute to the realization of this goal and to a stronger world economy.

There was general agreement in the analyses and conclusions emerging from the research on "Ideas for the Future of the International Monetary System." This consensus emerged even in consideration of the "real economy", or of that primary category of economic and social agents—the firm.

Explaining the reasons for this consensus requires first providing a premise. Analysis of the nature of the enterprise as far as its functions and objectives are concerned—in its existence as an economic system—has remained on the outskirts of great theoretical economic thought. Distinguishing between theory of enterprise and theory of cost, as part of a more general theory of value, is relatively recent (Coase, 1937). The firm is described as an object that maximizes the profit of its owner, given certain risk conditions, or as an object led by a group of managers who consider profit an instrument to avoid takeovers and therefore something that ensures survival (Machlup, 1967; Marris, 1964).

I will not go into the doubts raised by these definitions here. It is enough to observe that in current thinking, some ethical values as well as strictly economic ones are included in corporate planning, assuming as its objective function the maximization of values, not just of profit. Using this assumption as our starting point, it is possible to judge current trends in the economic system.

Partially external factors have significant influence over the creation of values in the enterprise system, including technological progress and training of human resources, productivity as a function of market extension, competition, stability, and cohesion and consensus. Changes in any of these factors directly affect a corporation's impetus to create value, and therefore its functions. It follows that phenomena in the real economy as well as in finance can be examined in light of the consequences that they have on the factors mentioned above and, therefore, on corporations.

The real economy and high finance have an evolutionary factor in common that originates in technological innovation. The economy seems dominated by the process of globalization, that is by the evolution from markets having a regional or national dimension to markets having planetary dimensions and, simultaneously, by increasingly hegemonic rules of a market economy. At the same time, globalization proceeds at different levels of intensity and speed in the two sectors of economy; consequences also differ.

In the real economy, globalization proceeds more slowly than in financial markets. Only 30% of the world's products have a truly global market, and the number of countries fully involved in it is no more than twenty. Still limited in terms of goods and geography, globalization has generally positive effects on the real economy. Increased competition favors efficient resource allocation; expanding markets favor every kind of scale economy; growth in the volume of production and in consumption of new products rapidly lowers production costs and, by reducing investment-recovery time, diminishes risk.

Globalization in financial markets, on the other hand, is almost complete. From the point of view of the corporations it has both positive and negative consequences. Important positive aspects of finance globalization include a simplified payment system, unlimited access to tools to cover risk, and unlimited access to international capital markets which price investments only on the basis of their risk and return.

Full convertibility of national currencies, together with their unconditional transferability, constitutes an essential factor in the enlargement of markets for goods and services. At the same time, the abundant liquidity in monetary and financial markets allows firms to protect themselves from variations in exchange rates and in interest rates, and allows them to remain neutral with respect to monetary market fluctuations, regardless of the geographic region in which they operate. A direct consequence of this is the exponential growth of derivatives, a phenomenon born from the needs and behavior of the real economy, although amplified by the interests of financial agents. The overriding effect, as has been rightly observed by Fazio (this volume) and Savona and Maccario (this volume), is an exponential increase of market liquidity, difficult governance, and, ultimately, an increase in those risks that derivatives try to insure against.

Unlimited access to the capital market allows corporations to more quickly adapt to the law of decreasing marginal returns, that is to rapidly reach the point of maximum efficiency. This translates into large financial commitments that self-financing could not provide. The worldwide dimension of the capital market and the full mobility of capital provide a powerful stimulus to economic development. Corporations cannot do without it.

On the other hand, the free movement of capital, together with the large existing stocks of financial assets and derivatives, creates serious global risks—see, for example, the recent Asian crisis—and accentuates the instability inherent in the *Holy Trinity*.

The regime of flexible exchange rates highlights instability in the system, and operates in opposition to the goal of creating optimal conditions for economic development. Except for rare cases in which adjustment in exchange rates reflects structural and permanent productivity changes, benefits derived from competitive adjustments in exchange rates make internal prices unstable and, in turn, create negative effects on corporate competitiveness. The exchange rate policies of the 1970s penalized firms through "unjustified" overvaluations of real exchange rates and higher real interest rates, which were instead made necessary to avoid the risk of inflationary spirals.

Instability and crisis best describe the approximately two decades that have followed the end of the Bretton Woods regime. Such a profound crisis finds a precedent only in the Great Depression of 1929–1933. Violent whiplash at the end of the period of stability in international prices led to a recession with a 10% reduction in production (1975) and 13% in international trade.

Economic growth was below average in the period prior to the "golden age" and was interrupted by three recessions: in 1973–75, 1981–83 and 1991–93. There were also serious financial crises (Wall Street, 1987) and currency crises (1992). In Western Europe unemployment went from 1.5% in the 1960s to 11% in 1993. At the same time, in the United States and throughout Europe the gap between the rich and poor grew increasingly wider.

This situation did not end in devastating social disruption (expect in parts of Italy) thanks to a social safety net developed in the prior period of stability. But welfare costs have grown immeasurably, causing taxes to rise accordingly (and, in turn, slowing growth) or, as in Italy and Belgium, leading to State bankruptcy.

Corporations saw their profits fluctuate madly. In Italy instability and loss of confidence led to mass capital export, to which authorities responded by introducing strict exchange rate rules, evocative of the fascist autarchy following the war in Ethiopia.

With the end of the Cold War, and with renewed faith in the dollar as the dominant currency in the international monetary system (thanks to Paul Volcker's monetary policy which led to stability in the US), depression in the West gave way to a new expansive cycle. In any case, the relative stability of the 1990s was based on a precarious equilibrium. The dollar imbeds a contradiction in functions, which in fact led to the crisis of the 1970s: it is simultaneously the principal medium of exchange and the international reserve currency. As an international medium of exchange, it fulfills its role of providing sufficient liquidity, but that implies current-account deficits. As a reserve currency, on the other hand, it can fulfill its role if America's foreign accounts are in good health.

The contradiction does not explode, thanks to the hegemonic vision the rest of the world has of the United States. But the state of the US economy when one looks at the evidence is much like that which preceded the 1971 crisis.

The disappearance of national monetary sovereignty is of critical importance for the real economy. The creation of an international monetary system based on stability must be considered one of the most important goals of cooperation among states. The formation of the European Monetary Union represents a great step toward the construction of global monetary stability. We must hope that it represents—if not a return to the "golden age"—a prelude to the opening of a new phase of development that is "as good as gold."

References

Coase R.H. (1937) "The Nature of the Firm." *Economica*, 386–405.

Machlup F. (1967) "Theories of the Firm: Marginalist, Behavioral, Managerial." *American Economic Review* 57, 1–33.

Marris R.L. (1964) *The Economic Theory of Managerial Capitalism*. New York: Free Press of Glencoe.

Open economies review **9:S1** 713–725 (1998)

Money Markets and Poliarchic Democratic States

ALBERTO PREDIERI cesifin@infogroup.it
Faculty of Law of the University "La Sapienza" of Rome Fondazione Cesifin, Via de' Pucci, 1, 50122, Florence.

Key words: monetary sovereignty, national law, community law, institutions, and negotiation

JEL Classification Number: K33

Abstract

This paper deals with legal and institutional issues that arise from the formation of Economic and Monetary Union. The latter implies a transfer of power from the state to the metastate apparatus of the European Union. Integration in the European Union cannot be completed without a new constitutional structure.

The search for a balance between the objective of price stability—guaranteed by a constitution and assigned to an authority independent of the executive branch and of the parliament—and the legislation on planning first appeared in German law. Article 88 of the German constitution, in fact, makes stability a public good, one of those goods which only the state, not the market, can produce. The example and influence of the German model has led to a major innovation in Western constitutionalism, namely the establishment of a new constitutional goal, stability. Furthermore, it also establishes new policy-framing powers that modify the model of a democratic state. This change hinges on the independent status of the central bank and on the legal prohibition that the central bank may not lend funds to the government, a provision the German government was the first to enforce in 1924, when it put a brake on hyperinflation.

Within the German constitutional model the central bank is declared to be an independent decision-making body pursuing objectives stated in the Constitution and thus different from independent administrative bodies not provided for in the Constitution. In this capacity it makes decisions without being answerable either to the Government or to Parliament, i.e., without being obliged to account for its actions to the electorate or bodies appointed by those elected by the electorate.

Other governments imitated Germany by vesting the responsibility of guaranteeing price stability in a body independent of the government and the parliament. Ensuring price stability is a duty of the central bank. Some experts consider price stability to be in conflict with the full-employment policies pursued by governments and parliaments.

The Maastricht Treaty incorporated the German model of price and monetary stability in its Articles 3A, 102, 104, 105, 107, and 109. The European Central Bank (ECB) as well as the national central banks are not subordinate to any other institution. Both the German and European rules are characterized by a distinctive precision, which stands out in relation to the Italian Constitution where the goal of stability, in general, and price stability, in particular, are nowhere stringently provided. Those concepts have been now introduced into Italian law through the door of European law.

1. Transfer of monetary power to the European union

Many countries of the European Union, including Italy, have decided to adopt a single currency. Devaluations are no longer possible within the Economic and Monetary Union (EMU). Balance-of-payments equilibrium will have to be achieved through price and income changes. The transfer of powers to the EMU implies a loss of national power. There is also a waiver of the right to exercise the power to devalue the currency and to "discriminate" among countries by virtue of exchange rate changes.[1]

Monetary power, understood as the power to issue currency and to regulate liquidity, will no longer exist for the Italian government, or for the other ten members of the EMU, after the adoption of the single currency. The single currency represents a critical step in the integration process. Currency management—that is, setting the exchange rates, the power to decide currency devaluations—also means decisional power as regards the monetary objectives included in the policy statement submitted to the Italian Parliament every year by the Treasury Ministry: the national inflation rate target and the relation between the exchange rate and economic growth.[2] The transfer of monetary sovereignty to a supranational structure or metastate,[3] along with the glory and responsibility for monetary policy (see Herdegen, 1996; de Grauwe, 1995), can have effects of great importance, especially when combined with other policies.[4] It is well known that monetary policy can produce or contribute to recessions, as in the case of German monetary policy following German monetary reunification (Nardozzi, 1997). The German monetary tightness reverberated abroad, for example, with unemployment increases in France and Italy.

EMU implies a transfer of state sovereignty to Community institutions such as the European System of Central Banks (ESCB) and the ECB, which supervises the ESCB. There are obvious differences between a relatively simple system such as that of the national central bank, and a complex system such as the ESCB and the ECB. These differences will have to be interpreted in light of effective actions, as regards both the relationship between the ECB and the ESCB as well as the relationship between the Council and the Board of the ECB. The latter may acquire power as the representative of a technocracy without statehood;

in fact, the six members of the Board are "appointed from among persons of acknowledged caliber and professional experience in the monetary or banking sector, by mutual agreement of the governments of the member countries, at the level of Heads of State or Government, upon the recommendation of the Board after consulting the European Parliament and the Board of Directors" (Roselli, 1998, p. 219). This Board could represent general interests more easily than the Council, which is typically the expression of national interests. There is the risk that the policies of the ECB could become the sum of these interests rather than a true Community institution (Fratianni and von Hagen, 1992, p. 203). It should be borne in mind, however, that the Council is the only institution, in any case, with the right to decide on ultimate and intermediate objectives. This complex system must deal with the articulation of powers defined by the Maastricht Treaty and by the protocol of the ESCB charter.

The ECB and the national central banks, including the Bank of Italy, are independent of Community institutions and, a fortiori, of member states' institutions. The ECB governs the ESCB (Merusi, 1998; Herdegen, 1996; Roselli, 1998; Predieri, 1996). It has a unitary structure and unitary functions, while maintaining a strongly decentralized organization with the articulation of the separate central banks. These are subordinate to the ECB, but act, as "an integral part" of the ESCB, "according to the directives and instructions" imparted by the ECB (Art. 14, third clause of the Charter). Its supremacy extends up to the point that, if "for the functions not regulated by either The Treaty or The Charter, the national central banks maintain their independence." Certainly, the creation of the ECB will drastically limit the discretionary power of national central banks concerning monetary policy. National central banks, however, will retain considerable power on the subject of retention and management of reserves in foreign currency and the payment mechanism (Art. 22 of the Charter).

The European Union appears to take no interest in the problem of bank crises, leaving this to the national authorities. The Commission only enforces regulations that safeguard competition, specifically through the prohibition of government subsidies. The ECB Charter stipulates that the Bank is responsible for the euro payment mechanism, out of which arises the need to assign itself the function of lender of last resort. The commitment to defend the internal and external value of the euro, which is one of the obligations of the ECB, is a potential source of conflict. Some authors (e.g., Eichengreen, 1998) believe that the ECB will be able to do this without losing monetary control and without incurring excessive banking risk, provided the existence of deposit insurance, high reserve and capital requirements, and strict bank supervision.

We had just begun to find a system for organizing this matter, from the constitutional point of view, when the regime changed. The change is peculiar in that the federal-type institutions like the ESCB or ECB take place without a real federation. This is a consequence of a profound change in society that led to financial hegemony, a development that neither Montesquieu, nor the founding fathers of the American constitution, nor the French Jacobeans would have imagined. The state can no longer discharge its obligations, after having transferred its power to the European metastate; it can only negotiate at the highest level, with operations implemented on a case by case basis. It is no longer possible today to speak of a community of stability, or to extend to the entire international community the German concept of *stabilität*. The innovative aspects of this new constitutionalism are the assumption that price stability should be one of the goals of a poliarchic democratic state with an organized poliarchic economy, and devolution to an independent organization with constitutional organs. These powers are significantly increased through the power of primary law making. Equally significant is the completion of the architecture of an innovative jurisdictional structure in present law (La Marca, 1996). Whether a federation of this kind, atypical in history, may actually emerge is another matter. Doubts remain on the imbalance of power that is a feature of an organized poliarchic economy and the base of modern constitutionalism. For example, how can this atypical federation redistribute resources from one country to another in the face of asymmetric shocks?[5]

Soon after the Japanese crisis of June 1998, the governor of the Bank of Italy, Antonio Fazio (see Calderoni, 1998, p. 3) stated that for Japan "it is not enough to restore order to the banking system: if a country does not have a healthy economy, if it does not offer opportunities for productive investment and savings, if it does not reactivate a flow of investments, it can never have a healthy banking and financial system"; the governor then concluded that Japan "will never emerge from the tunnel of the crisis if it does not adopt a coherent policy, such as that outlined by Keynes, based on expansive fiscal measures".

If the assumption of the goal of price stability leads us to consider a Keynesian type of constitution, then we must say that the inclusion of the price stability objective in the Maastricht treaty can be classified as a Keynesian European constitution. Similar considerations hold for the employment objective introduced by the Amsterdam Treaty.

In Community decisions the link with the states is maintained through nomination process and Art. 109 of the Treaty of Maastricht. The text of the article suffers from a compromise between the German position, according to which the fixing of the exchange rates was not a political decision, and the French position, which acknowledged the supremacy of politics.[6] The agreement on a system of exchange rates with non-Community currencies must be stipulated following a unanimous decision of the Council, with a proposal of the ECB or the Commission prior to consulting the ECB, with the intent to arrive at price stability.[7]

It seems that this mechanism introduces an element of tension between the ECB and the Council, institutions which are profoundly different: the first a federal institution with a technical slant, while the second is state-internationalist and has a political orientation. The Council retains its need for unanimity among the member states and thus the maintenance of the state-internationalist model. The mechanism is complicated by the use of terms that differ from those commonly used in community language, creating confusion all the more so on a subject for which uncertainties already exist (Louis, 1998). For example, in the reference to the position of the Community found in Art. 109, fourth item, "consensus" is neither the consensus of the Community law nor the consensus of international law.[8] The term refers not to an act, but to a result (reaching consensus, for which an understanding is foreseen on the mode of negotiation and conclusion of the accords). Some authors, like Dehousse and Ghémar (1994) write that consensus is found between consultation and conforming opinion. Such a formulation does not make sense: an opinion to which one must conform and which is, therefore, binding is not an opinion, but a decision. Consensus on Community law is qualified other times as an act and, as such, constitutes the presupposition of other acts or is referred to by them.[9] One must keep in mind that the formulation of Art. 109 of the Maastricht Treaty, as all those on the ESCB, uses language which is anomalous with respect to the rest of the text and other parts of Community law.

Another example is given by the term "recommendation." It is doubtful that the ECB can request an opinion of the Court of Justice on these accords, as the text does not address it (Chemain, 1996). Tizzano (1997, p. 459) speaks of the "mysterious category of the 'formal agreements' mentioned in Art. 109 of the Maastricht Treaty, which was introduced despite many criticisms at the time of the negotiations, and led to the creation of an annex to the Treaty in the form of an ad hoc declaration to state precisely that these agreements are nothing but common international agreements." This is also valid for the Court of Justice (Di Bucci, 1997). Admitting that the Court is invested with powers does not bring about the legitimization of the ECB. Legitimization is denied in that the Treaty does not address it (Stadler, 1996). Similarly, the reference to guidelines that cannot be binding with respect to the ECB leaves us doubtful regarding what the Bank must do for price stability (Cloos et al., 1993, p. 263). On the issue of the exchange rate regime, Louis (1998, p. 250) starts from the assumption that for their own nature the guidelines do not have any binding effects. Predieri (1997, p. 403) instead introduces the thesis that the guidelines are binding but the ECB could refuse to take them into account because they are in conflict with the objective of price stability. Orientations or guidelines—"Leitlinen" in German, "orientations" in French, and "orientaciones" in Spanish—are atypical acts. Article 109Q of the Treaty of Amsterdam (Art. 121 of the consolidated text) speaks of orientations, and introduces annually deliberated orientations: "Based on the conclusions of the European Council, the Council, deliberating on qualified majority on the proposal of the Commission, prior to consultation with the European Parliament, of the Economic and Social Committee, the Committee on Regions, and the Employment Committee about which Article 109S, annually elaborates on the orientations which the member states must keep in mind in their respective policies on employment." The binding effect for the member states of these orientations or guidelines is explicitly recognized.

Guidelines must be consistent with the economic policies listed in Art. 103 of the Treaty (Art. 99 of the consolidated text), decided by qualified majority and based on the report by the Council in the form of a recommendation: "based on said conclusions, the Council, deliberating in qualified majority, adopts the recommendation that defines the major lines referred to above. The Council informs the European Parliament of this recommendation." The guidelines listed in the Treaty of Amsterdam can now be treated as decisions listed in the same act, Art. K6, second comma, letter b. These follow functionally and structurally the guidelines in the context of the theme "of the legislative and regulatory arrangements of the member states." This statement decrees that "the general policy decisions are binding on the member states in relation to the result to obtain, provided that the duty of the national authorities [is spelled out] with regards to the form and the means. They have no direct effectiveness."[10] It can be added that Community practice confirms that, even if we had to believe the guidelines to be nonbinding, they are binding if explicitly recognized as decisions. In this way, the problem of their effects may be resolved with an explicit attribution.

From Art. 109 three types of possible agreements on exchange rates with non-Community currencies can result. The Council has the right to conclude formal agreements, according to the first comma of the article, or to formulate guidelines, according to the second comma of the article,[11] or it cannot take any initiative. In the last instance the ECB is free to make its own policy, even if the text does not say it explicitly (Partsch, 1998).

The transfer of monetary powers brings about concrete and symbolic changes. International negotiations require not only formal powers, but also institutional efficiency, especially in an area in which credibility is essential. The transfer of power to the European Union will complicate the delegation process for a restructuring of the international monetary system. The euro is a big innovation, permitting EMU to play a strong role in the future shape of the international monetary system.

There are two viewpoints about the significance of the euro. The first is that monetary union is an essential ingredient for political union, a goal that is rooted in history. For example, according to Gaetano Martino, Italian Foreign Minister at the time of the Treaty of Rome, a unified market would have brought us to "a unified monetary system and this, in turn, to a political union," (Cassese and Della Cananea, 1991, p. 901). The transfer of monetary powers implies new negotiations for an expanded integration that cannot be satisfied either by the modern tools of coordination or by agreements.[12] Coordination through the imposition of tough fiscal criteria does not eliminate the risk of divergent macro policies. Sen (1997, p. 15) has remarked that the reduction of employment has not received the same commitment as the reduction of fiscal imbalances. Policy coordination is a difficult task within a country and much more difficult among states with different objectives. As Tietmeyer (1998, p. 15) points out:

> The further development of the European integration process will depend above all on the consequences that monetary union will have on the future. If it will be a success from an economic point of view—in the sense of internal

monetary stability and lack of tensions among the countries—then, it will give, in my opinion, considerable stimuli to political integration and a political role of the European Union in its external relations.

The euro can exert a strong impetus to either a new constitutional structure or to a deep crisis (Dahrendorf, 1998). The former scenario will provide a lasting solution to a long history of enmity and wars in Europe; needless to say, coordination of monetary and fiscal policies is an inadequate tool to achieve this long-run objective.

The second point of view is that, once member states lose national monetary (and fiscal) sovereignty, the integration boundary will be pushed "beyond the macroeconomy, towards a liberalization of the markets, to the search for a better use of the productive resources" (Giavazzi et al., 1998, p. 9). The reorganization of the microeconomy will be made imperative by the convergence of national markets, abolition of barriers to capital movements, privatizations, and deregulation. Just as necessary—even though it may seem less noticeable—is the reorganization of the national public administrations, following the transfer of political and juridical powers to the European Union.[13]

2. Consequences of the single currency

It is a plausible hypothesis that EMU, besides contributing to monetary stability—both internal (price stability) and external (exchange rate stability)—will be a key player in a multipolar world monetary system and, perhaps in the distant future, in a one-currency world. For Bagehot (1869), a great and versatile social scientist, one currency in the world was the logical extension of single world commerce. While the idea of one-world currency appears at the moment utopian, the role of the euro as a great international currency is not. The euro may not be powerful enough to displace the dollar's present role of dominant currency, but it has the potential of being a serious challenger. The euro will reduce the dollar's area of influence and will help stabilize international markets (Scognamiglio, 1998).

According to Fratianni and Hauskrecht (1998), the future international monetary system will be closer to a bipolar than to a tripolar structure. The yen area will be much smaller than the dollar and the euro areas; therefore, these two authors foresee that, in the twenty-first century, the world will primarily aggregate around two currency areas.

The European Union, in the Maastricht Treaty, has reaffirmed the goal of stabilizing international monetary relations. The initial conditions are unfavorable for the European Union, however. In relation to other countries, but in particular the United States, the European Union suffers from several weaknesses: the contrast between monetary union according to a federal model and a yet to be defined political union (Louis, 1997); absence of federal government and parliament (Chemain, 1996); maintenance of residual provisions of international agreements, which deny the establishment of new institutions (Dashwood, 1998); a decision-making process based on unanimity; and a persistent democratic deficit. The absence of a federal type government in the European Union puts an upper limit to the process of European integration and a lower limit to the reduction of transaction costs. Consequently, it puts the European Union at a competitive disadvantage in relation to the United States. The United States, besides being a federal state and having a federal budget, enjoys a higher degree of financial integration than the EMU (Fratianni et al., 1998).

With reference to the differentiated effects of a common monetary policy, consider the probable effects of an increase in the budget deficit. To the extent that interest rates may rise in EMU, the ECB may implement a restrictive policy and spread the consequences onto other members of EMU. The risk for potential conflicts within the ECB is not trivial. The procedure on excessive budget deficits and the Growth and Stability Pact cannot replace political integration; we run the risk of having eleven different points of view (Tietmeyer, 1998, p. 14). There is also the risk, according to Ferrari Bravo and Moavero Milanesi (1995, p. 532), that:

> After having achieved the objectives outlined and set in Maastricht, the margins of action as far as the economy of the individual national governments are concerned, are still rather vast. The Community bonds will serve...essentially to avoid that, through the laws of the various national economic and monetary policies, individual states may introduce disintegrating changes to the free functioning of the single internal market.

An increase in the institutionalization of the Community apparatuses is urgently needed to raise their legitimacy and in turn their credibility.

The growth of the negotiation networks, implied by the emergence of new protagonists in a multipolar world and by increasing interdependencies, makes it necessary to strengthen existing international institutions or create new ones, whether they have decision-making functions or task monitoring.[14] The macroeconomic stability of the entire system depends on the countries' desire and ability to agree and implement converging policies. In the Japanese financial crisis of June 1998, the U.S. and Japanese authorities agreed on a joint intervention in favor of the yen, notifying the G7, but not the European Union. With the advent of EMU the European role in international organizations will rise. Consider the World Trade Organization. This organization has distinctly integrating characteristics, in the sense that it brings countries not only to liberalize, but also to coordinate their national regulations. Such an integration process will require delegation of powers and modifications of procedures. The process will fit well with the European Union, which has evolved from the principle of an international treaty to the institutionalization of common regulations. The International Monetary Fund was created to assist nations with balance-of-payments difficulties. The Fund is a specialized financial institution with laws and goals analogous to those of the EMU central banks and the ECB. It is an "institution able to standardize the data in order to offer all the operators a precise reference point," and analyze data within a framework that aims at avoiding "crises like those of Mexico and Asia which, very often, are preceded by serious external imbalance" (Calderoni, 1998). But the Fund faces a lack of resources in relation to the spatial and temporal intensification of crises and the hostility of a few leading countries.[15]

Poliarchic democracy is connected to an organized economy in which monetary policy guarantees monetary stability, a vital public good. But one has to be mindful that monetary policy's efficacy changes as markets evolve. For example, as Savona and Maccario (1998) emphasize, the traditional concept of monetary base is no longer adequate in light of derivatives, which directly or indirectly influence interest and exchange rates, and, consequently, the prices of goods and services. Globalization imposes the transfer of market functions from the national to the extra-national, but this transfer cannot be made to a nonexistent metastate organization; on the other hand, a "collective leadership of the world economy replacing a declining American leadership" has yet to emerge (Gilpin, 1990, p. 207). Only sustained negotiation can bring about lasting remedies, especially if it tends to a progressive institutionalization of the underlying processes.

3. Conclusions

In a world that tends towards bipolarity or tripolarity, negotiation assures reasonable success for the completion of European integration. While it appears useful at the moment to replace the state with the metastate apparatus of the European Union, this process remains insufficient and incomplete. A new constitutional structure is required to complete the process. EMU is a big innovation on the road towards complete integration. EMU will raise the European Union's bargaining power in the negotiation for a new international monetary system.

Notes

1. For example, in the sentence of May 14, 1998, case N.T 334/94, entitled *Cartoncino*, the Court of Justice states that the fact that the Commission inflicted a fine on the ECU for violation of the rules on competition is not worthy of censure because, although the Commission is not required to determine the amount of the fine, the "risk of currency fluctuation" is "inherent in international trade and monetary exchanges" and is "a nonabolishable element", which has an effect, in any case, on the amount of the fine at the time of payment. Previously, in the sentence of March 9, 1977, combined cases N. 41, 43 and 44/73, *Société anonyme générale Sucrière et al c. Commissione*, in *Racc.*, 1977, No. 2, 445 ff, the Court "has to watch over the effective value of payments made in other currencies to make sure they correspond to that of the amount in national currency fixed in the ruling or sentence. The conversion between the two national currencies in question should therefore be made at the free exchange in effect on the date of payment." The reasoning of the Court cannot be accepted because in using the rates of exchange with the ECU the Commission has implicitly accepted a distortion that penalizes the countries with a weaker currency (Italy and Spain). In fact, exactly during the

most relevant period for evaluating the implications of the Decision (1992–1994), there was a realignment of exchanges combined with a control of the dynamics of internal prices that did not compensate for the depreciation of the exchange rate, and thereby caused a net increase in competitiveness. The criterion adopted by the Commission would therefore further penalize the businesses operating in the more "virtuous" countries, those that had accompanied their realignment of exchange rates with policies of structural adjustment aimed at reducing inflation.

2. The diverging schools of thought on the subject are well known: some claim that devaluation is useful for growth and others that it is harmful. Thus, Bini Smaghi (1998, p. 88) points out: "The convergence of income among the economies of the member countries occurred in a context of stability of rates of exchange and low inflation. Ireland, for example, was one of the poorest countries when it joined the Community in 1974, has achieved high rates of growth since the latter half of the eighties, in a context characterized by stable exchange rates between the Irish pound and the other European currencies, and a low rate of inflation. In just a little over ten years, it has caught up, in terms of per capita income, with the European average. It has been estimated that in 1998 the per capita income in Ireland will exceed that of Italy. The same is true of Spain and Portugal, although convergence took place more slowly, partly because of the delay in the correction of the financial imbalance in those two countries. In Greece, however, where inflation has been steadily higher than in the other European countries, and where the currency has been devaluated repeatedly, the economy has developed more slowly."
3. I shall not dwell on the distinction between transfer of sovereignty and waiver of sovereignty brought about by integration of the Community. The general conclusion is that sovereignty has not been transferred because only the exercise of individual responsibilities has been transferred. On the subject see Donati (1995).
4. The importance of monetary sovereignty can be exemplified by the events of 1992 when Italy left the European Monetary System. The Amato government combined devaluation with an income policy and achieved disinflation, while reducing any adverse effects on output and employment (Fabiani et al., 1998).
5. Bini Smaghi (1998, p. 93) states that "within the European average, the action of the automatic stabilizers included in the public balance compensate for about 25% of the cyclical variations in income. The effect is therefore of dimensions comparable to that connected with the transfer of the American federal balance". Yet, the point remains that there is no institutional structure in the European Union comparable to that of the United States through which resources can be redistributed.
6. For Guigou (1992) the interpretation of Art. 109 leads to the conclusion that the power to determine international monetary policy is the task of the institutional authority of the European Union which gives the political directions, while the ECB will administer the day-to-day transactions. Curti Gialdino (1993, p. 118) notes that: "If, however, the policy of interest rates provokes capital movements which are more or less important, they have effects on the monetary mass and, therefore, on liquidity. It is not difficult, in such a situation, to foresee conflicts between the ECB and the Council of Ministers. In addition, it is debatable that changes in the exchange rate regime, which requires, in order to be efficient, rapidity and reserve, can be realized by the Council of Ministers given its working methods." The French position is approximately consistent with French law no. 93-980, which distinguishes monetary policy from exchange policy, the latter entrusted to the executive branch and therefore considered to be in conformity with Art. 21 of the French Constitution.
7. For the currencies of the Community countries which are not participating in the European Monetary Union, an accord known as EMS II was stipulated. The accord "foresees, for each currency, a core parity in relation to the euro, and wide oscillation margins, presumably 15%, on either side of the established parity. If the exchange rate of the market reached the margin of allowed fluctuation, the ECB and the central bank of the country in question must intervene in the exchange market to avoid the margins being surpassed. If these interventions were to create problems for the achievement of price stability, the ECB and the central bank of the country in question may suspend the interventions in the exchange markets. In case of strong

currency tensions, which render the actual core parities undefendable, these may be modified, by agreement among the ECB, the ministers and the central banks of EMS II countries. All signatories, including the ECB, have the right to start a procedure aimed at reconsidering the core parities" (Bini Smaghi, p. 42). Other European countries may consider a similar procedure.

8. Dehousse and Ghémar (1994) state that the consensus of Art. 109 is somewhere between an advisory opinion and a conforming opinion. The former is an opinion which influences, the latter (notwithstanding its name) is a decision; neither one can be invoked in our case. Similar considerations can be found in Slot (1994).
9. Cf. decision of the Commission of the European Community of 27 November 1991, no. 3855; analogous is the position of Curti Gialdino (1993, p. 120), who, with regards to the use of consensus in Art. 109, says that "consultation rises to a sort of orchestration."
10. General policy decisions are binding only on those mentioned in the decision, and not generally.
11. According to the European Council the general guidelines on exchange policy with non-Community currencies, prescribed by Art. 109, second comma, will be formulated only in exceptional cases.
12. The Growth and Stability Pact was reached in Dublin in December 1996 and reaffirmed by the Council of Amsterdam in June 1997 (cf. regulations N. 1466/97/CE and 1467/97/CE). On the subject read Amtenbrink et al. (1997), Hahn (1998), Lienemeyer (1997) and Häde (1996).
13. This is especially so in Italy. For example, Carli (1993, p. 434 and p. 8) states with satisfaction that "with the Maastricht Treaty, the exercise of this power (of printing paper money) cannot exceed the limits of the defense of price stability. It is a step forward which I did not think I would be able to witness... Once again, we must admit that a structural change came about through the imposition of an 'external restriction'. Once again, as it happened with the Treaty of Rome, in the case of the European Monetary System, a group of Italians actively participated, leaving important traces of their contributions to the elaboration of those treaties which then represented 'external restrictions' for our country. Once again, we had to go around Parliament which is the sovereign authority of the Republic, constructing elsewhere that which we were not able to construct at home."
14. The Peking negotiation, in early July 1998, may seem innovative in this regard. China agreed not to devalue its currency to avoid a financial disaster in Asia, leading President Clinton to state that the situation was less serious than in the 1930s because in those years the "sophisticated understanding of the economy that we have today" was missing (*Il Sole 24 Ore*, 4 July 1998, 7).
15. Camdessus, Director General of the Monetary Fund, in Calderoni (1998) stated very clearly 84% of Fund shareholders favored an expansion of resources, while 16%, including the United States, did not. The United States always, "represents the toughest bone. To find an agreement with them is never easy, especially because of the resistance by Congress; resistance which comes from internal policies, and does not always have noble intentions." The relations between the United States and the Fund have often been quite difficult, because the Fund has been seen as supporting "squandering countries which live above their means. This certainly was the point of view of the Reagan administration which until 1982 did not understand that it needed the International Monetary Fund to save the American banking system, threatened by the world debt crisis."

References

Antenbrink, F., J. De Haan, and O.C.H.M. Sleijpen (1997) "The stability and Growth Pact: Placebo or Panacea." European Business Review, 202–236.

Bagehot, W. (1869) *A Universal Money (A Practical Plan for Assimilating the English and American Money, as a Step Towards a Universal Money)*. London.

Bini Smaghi, L. (1998) *L Euro*, Bologna.

Calderoni, M. (1998) "Coloquio tra Camdessus e Fazio." *Il Sole 24 Ore* 3.

Carli, G. (1993) *Cinquant anni di vita Italiana*. Rome: Laterza.

Cassese, S. and G. Della Cananea (1991) "L'Esecuzione del Diritto Comunitario." *Riv. It. Dir. Pubbl. Comm.* 4.

Chemain, R. (1996) *L Union Économique et Monétaire: Aspects Juridiques et Institutionels.* Paris: Pedone.

Cloos, J., G. Reinesch, D. Vignes, and J. Weyland (1993) *Le Traité de Maastricht: Genèse, Analyse, Commentaires.* Brussels: Brulylant.

Curti Gialdino, C. (1993) *Il Trattato di Maastricht sull Unione Europea: Genesi: Struttura: Contenuto: Processo di Ratifica*, Rome: Istituto Poligrafico and Zecca della Stato.

Dahrendorf, D. (1998) "Désunis par une Monnaie Commune." *Le Débat*; Dashwood, A. (1998) "States in the European Union." *European Law Review* 23, 3.

Dashwood, A. (1998) "States in the European Union." *European Law Review* 23(3), 201–248.

De Grauwe, P. (1995) *The Economics of Monetary Integration.* 2nd ed. Oxford: Oxford University Press.

Dehousse, F. and K. Ghémar (1994) "Le Traité de Maastricht et les Relations Extérieures de la Communauté Européenne." *European Journal of International Law*, 151–156.

Di Bucci, V. (1997) "Advisory Procedures." In R. Plender (ed.), *European Courts Practice and Precedents.* London.

Donati, F. (1995) *Diritto Comunitario e Sindacato di Costituzionalità.* Milan: Giuffrè.

Eichengreen, B. (1998) "Exchange Rate Stability and Financial Stability." this volume.

Fabiani, S., A. Locarno, G. Oneto, and P. Sestito (1998) *Temi di Discussione del Servizio Studi della Banca d Italia.*

Ferrari Bravo, L. and E. Moavero Milanesi (1995) *Lezioni di Diritto Comunitario.* Milan: Editoriale Scientifica.

Fratianni, M. and A. Hauskrecht (1998) "From the Gold Standard to a Bipolar Monetary System." in this volume.

Fratianni, M., A. Hauskrecht, and A. Maccario (1998) "Dominant Currencies and the Future of the Euro." in this volume.

Fratianni, M. and J. von Hagen (1992) *The European Monetary System and European Monetary Union.* Boulder: Westview.

Giavazzi, F., A. Penati, and G. Tabellini (eds.) (1998) *Liberalizzazione dei Mercati e Privatizzazioni.* Bologna.

Gilpin, R. (1990) *Politica ed Economia delle Relaziioni Internazionali.* Bologna.

Guigou, E. (1992) "La Place et le Rôle de l'Autorité Economique dans l'Union Européenne." *ECU* 19.

Häde, U. (1996) "Ein Stabilitätspakt für Europa? Zur Zulässigkeit Völkerrectlicher Verträge Zwischen den Mitgliedstaaten der EU." *Europäische Wirtschafts und Steuerrect.*

Hahn, H.J. (1998) "The Stability Pact for European Monetary Union: Compliance with Deficit Limit as a Constant Legal Duty." *Common Market Law Review* 35, 1.

Herdegen, M. (1996) "Germany's Constitutional Court and Parliament: Factors of Uncertainty for the Monetary Union?" *European Monetary Union Watch* 19, 8.

La Marca, L. (1996) "Il Controllo Giurisdizionale sulla Banca Centrale Europea e sull'Istituto Monetario Europeo." *Il Diritto dell Unione Europea* 3.

Lienemeyer, M. (1997) "Die Sanktionen des Stabilitätspaktes und ihre Vereinnahmung." *Europäische Wirtschafts und Steuerrect.*

Louis, J.V. (1997) "Union Monétaire et Union Politique: Le Rôle du Juge." In *La Tutela Giurisdizionale dei Diritti nel Sistema Communitario, Atti del Congresso di Venezia dell UAE, 30 Maggio-1 Giugno 1996*, Bruxelles.

Louis, J.V. (1998) "A Legal and Institutional Approach for Building a Monetary Union." *Common Market Law Review* 35, 1.

Merusi, F. (1998) "Governo della Moneta e Indipendenza della Banca Centrale." In G. Della Cananea and G. Napolitano (eds.), *Per una Nuova Costituzione Economica.* Bologna.

Nardozzi, G. (1997) "La Disoccupazione Europea e il Capitalismo Tedesco." In P. Ciocca (ed.), *Disoccupazione di Fine Secolo*. Turin: Bringheri.

Predieri, A. (1996) *Il Potere della Banca Centrale: Isola o Modello?* Florence: Passigli.
Predieri, A. (1997) "Gli Orientamenti sulle Reti Transeuropee." *Il Diritto dell Unione Europea* 4.
Roselli, O. (1998) *Governo Valutario, Liberalizzazione ed Unione Monetaria Europea: Profili Istituzionali.* Torino: Giappichelli.
Savona, P. and A. Maccario (1998) "On the Relation between Money and Derivatives and its Application to the International Monetary Market." in this volume.
Scognamiglio, C. (1998) "Il Sistema Monetario Internazionale, l'Economia, la Società." in this volume.
Sen, A. (1997) "L'Occupazione: Le Ragioni di Priorità per la Politica Economica." In P. Ciocca (ed.), *Disoccupazione di Fine Secolo*. Turin: Bringheri.
Slot, P.J. (1994) "The Institutional Provisions of the EMU." In D. Curtin and T. Heukels (eds.), *Institutional Dynamics of European Integration: Essays in Honour of Henry G. Schermes*. vol. 2, Dordrecht, Boston, London.
Stadler, R. (1996) *Der Rechtliche Handlungsspielraum des Europäischen Systems der Zetralbanken.* Baden-Baden.
Tietmeyer, H. (1998) "Politica Monetaria e Integrazione Europea." *Il Diritto dell Economia* 1.
Tizzano, A. (1997) "Qualche Considerazione sull'Union Economica e Monetaria." *Il Diritto dell Unione Europea* 3.